Enterprise
Information Systems
Contemporary Trends and Issues

Enterprise
Information Systems

Contemporary Trends and Issues

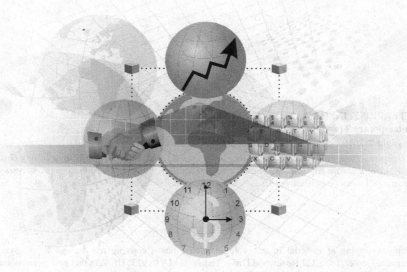

David L Olson
University of Nebraska, USA

Subodh Kesharwani
Indira Gandhi National Open University, India

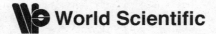 **World Scientific**

NEW JERSEY · LONDON · SINGAPORE · BEIJING · SHANGHAI · HONG KONG · TAIPEI · CHENNAI

Published by

World Scientific Publishing Co. Pte. Ltd.

5 Toh Tuck Link, Singapore 596224

USA office: 27 Warren Street, Suite 401-402, Hackensack, NJ 07601

UK office: 57 Shelton Street, Covent Garden, London WC2H 9HE

British Library Cataloguing-in-Publication Data
A catalogue record for this book is available from the British Library.

ISBN-13 978-981-4273-15-2
ISBN-10 981-4273-15-5

Typeset by Stallion Press
Email: enquiries@stallionpress.com

Printed in Singapore.

PREFACE

The more things change, the more they stay the same! This is a quotation which we all remember, but now the bottleneck is not at the bottom of the bottle but at top of the bottle. The judgment of people who sit at the top of organizations need real-time access to complete information in order to make better decisions. Enterprise Information System (EIS) is a great paradigm shift in the world of information systems, and has revolutionized business in a gigantic manner. In this new and rapidly changing environment it is exceptionally imperative that students should extend their understanding of the impact of these new systems on how organizations operate. Put another way, student researchers must ask themselves the fundamental question: "How can I improve my understanding of information systems?"

Degree programs in information systems vary, but they all have one widespread characteristic: a prerequisite that students embark on at least one substantial individual project or item of course work. This is a typical requirement for an undergraduate degree and for post-graduate students. Over the past two decades the arrival of fully-integrated Enterprise Resource Planning (ERP) systems has shown itself to be a source of significant business value. Many organizations are looking to streamline and gain more from their existing ERP systems. EIS is an integrated solution to the problem of how to control all major business processes with single software architecture in real time. It is a process of planning and managing all resources and their use throughout the organization.

Aim & Objective: One of the aims of this book is to help students develop their overall perspective of the discipline of information systems. Developing such a perspective is of critical importance, for without it the subject will always be in danger of fragmenting into isolated islands of partial insight or empty techniques. We have to recognize that the phrase "information systems" is often used in a loose and fuzzy manner, and that there is still much debate and discussion over what exactly the field encompasses and what its theoretical foundations are. The aim of this book is to provide students with a thorough understanding of Enterprise Information Systems (EIS) which introduces them to Enterprise Resource Planning (ERP) systems and their benefits. The book describes the concepts of EIS, key terms as they relate to EIS, gives a basic EIS model, discusses different EIS maturity levels, the transition from Material Requirements Planning to EIS, states the benefits of EIS and the pitfalls of EIS implementations. This book is meant for corporate executives in steering or project execution committees for EIS implementation, vendors, and consultants. The book will provide the reader an understanding of the architecture and technology of an EIS system and give tools to analyze factors that lead to successful requirements analysis, design, and implementation of an Extended EIS Packages in an enterprise. Even those who are already familiar with some aspects of an EIS system and want to acquire a comprehensive view of EIS would benefit from the book. Students will understand the scope of EIS and corporate motivation for implementing EIS; appreciate the challenges associated with implementing such large-scale systems and the dramatic impact these systems have on key business processes. They will learn how to develop work plans for an EIS implementation, gain an understanding of process integration inherent in EIS, and experience the SAP software system through computer-based training materials and hands-on experience.

Pedagogy of the Book: Case discussions, views and experiences shared by users, vendors and academicians expose readers to EIS software, real life issues, further reading, competency review, etc.

Structure of the Book: This book is well suited as an executive guide for anybody who is considering EIS or evaluating EIS systems. The book is designed for students of technical and management universities where EIS has just been introduced and also senior management and executives because it is focused, hits all of the key points with each chapter treated as a white paper that ends with case studies reinforcing the topic and references. Also, the authors make use of diagrams throughout to demonstrate points.

Unique Selling Proposition: The book could be different from its competitors in the following ways:

a. It uses Indian and American case studies implemented in industry and academia as EIS systems.
b. It explains the utility of EIS systems and make users aware of hidden costs.
c. It covers issues in the form of chapters or subchapters.

The Overall Endeavour of the Book

In the mass-customization of information systems, a need has arisen for high quality analyses. Both the scientific community and professionals will benefit from a book that focuses on this. This book should describe the state-of-the-art, innovative theoretical frameworks, advanced and successful implementations as well as the latest empirical research findings. The main objective is to bridge theory and practice on the one hand and to fill research gaps and answer open questions on the other. It will improve the understanding of the problems that are encountered during the conception of information systems for mass customization. Furthermore, it provides measures to alleviate these problems and simultaneously highlights new directions for future research.

The Target Audience

The target audience consists of professionals and scientists working in the field of computer science and artificial intelligence. In addition, industrial engineers and researchers in business administration with a special focus on information systems and IT Management will find this book an adequate reference that describes current research and presents topics that can be expended in future. Graduate students in the mentioned areas will find practical applications of some theoretical concepts.

Methodology

Most class sessions will involve lecture and extensive discussion of Enterprise Information Systems based on textbooks, readings and cases. Students will be expected to make substantial contributions to the learning process through participation in class discussion and *participation in electronic discussions.*

Teaching and Learning Approach

A mixture of lectures, exercises, laboratories and case studies can be used to deliver the various topics, some of which will be covered in a problem-based format to enhance the learning objectives. Others will be covered through directed study in order to enhance the students' ability of "learning to learn". Some case studies, largely based on consultancy experience, will be used to integrate these topics and thus demonstrate to students how the various techniques are interrelated and how they apply in real life situations.

Technical Acknowledgement

- No part of this publication may be reproduced or transmitted in any form or for any purpose without the express permission of the publisher, World Scientific. The information contained herein may be changed without prior notice.
- Some software products marketed by SAP AG and its distributors contain proprietary software components of other software vendors.
- Microsoft, Windows, Outlook, and PowerPoint are registered trademarks of Microsoft Corporation.
- IBM, DB2, DB2 Universal Database, OS/2, Parallel Sysplex, MVS/ESA, AIX, S/390, AS/400, OS/390, OS/400, iSeries, pSeries, xSeries, zSeries, z/OS, AFP, Intelligent Miner, WebSphere, Netfinity, Tivoli, and Informix are trademarks or registered trademarks of IBM Corporation in the United States and/or other countries.
- Oracle is a registered trademark of Oracle Corporation.

- UNIX, X/Open, OSF/1, and Motif are registered trademarks of the Open Group.
- Citrix, ICA, Program Neighborhood, MetaFrame, WinFrame, VideoFrame, and MultiWin are trademarks or registered trademarks of Citrix Systems, Inc.
- HTML, XML, XHTML, and W3C are trademarks or registered trademarks of W3C®, World Wide Web Consortium, Massachusetts Institute of Technology.
- Java is a registered trademark of Sun Microsystems, Inc.
- JavaScript is a registered trademark of Sun Microsystems, Inc., used under license for technology invented and implemented by Netscape.
- MaxDB is a trademark of MySQL AB, Sweden.

We hope students will be able to use this book some to facilitate their learning.

Prof. David L. Olson
James & H.K. Stuart Professor in MIS,
Department of Management,
   University of Nebraska
Office (402) 472-4521
Email: dolson3@unl.edu

Dr. Subodh Kesharwani
School of Management Studies
Indira Gandhi National Open
   University
New Delhi-110068,India
Mobile: 00-91-9350026685
Email: subodhkesharwani@gmail.com

eis-book@googlegroups.com

CONTENTS

AUTHOR PROFILE

David L Olson

David L. Olson is the James & H.K. Stuart Professor in MIS and Othmer Professor at the University of Nebraska. He received his Ph.D. in Business from the University of Nebraska in 1981.

Professor Olson has published research in over 60 refereed journal articles, primarily on the topic of multiple objective decision-making. He teaches in the management information systems, management science, and operations management areas. He has authored the books *Decision Aids for Selection Problems*, *Introduction to Information Systems Project Management*, and *Managerial Issues of Enterprise Resource Planning Systems* and co-authored the books *Decision Support Models and Expert Systems*; *Introduction to Management Science*; *Introduction to Simulation and Risk Analysis*; *Business Statistics: Quality Information for Decision Analysis*; *Statistics, Decision Analysis, and Decision Modeling*; and *Multiple Criteria Analysis in Strategic Siting Problems*.

Professor Olson has made over 100 presentations at international and national conferences on research topics. He is a member of the Association for Information Systems, the Decision Sciences Institute, the Institute for Operations Research and Management Sciences, and the Multiple Criteria Decision-Making Society. He has been the chair for the Data Mining mini-track at AMCIS 2004 and AMCIS 2005. He has coordinated the Decision Sciences Institute Dissertation Competition, Innovative Education

Competition, chaired the Doctoral Affairs Committee, served as nationally elected vice president three times, and as National Program Chair. He was with Texas A&M University from 1981 through 2001, the last two years as Lowry Mays Professor of Business in the Department of Information and Operations Management. He received a Research Fellow Award from the College of Business and Graduate School of Business at Texas A&M University, and held the Business Analysis Faculty Excellence Fellowship for two years. He is a Fellow of the Decision Sciences Institute.

Subodh Kesharwani

Subodh Kesharwani has a doctorate in ERP Systems. He has done a lot of research on Hidden Cost and Total cost of Ownership [TCO] which is sufficient to sound the death-knell of ERP if it is not properly controlled. He has eight years of experience of teaching and research in computer and management at Indira Gandhi National Open University, IIMT Engineering College and as a research student at Motilal Institute of Research and Business administration [MONIRBA]. He is presently on the faculty of the school of management studies at Indira Gandhi National Open University. He has taught Operation research and Statistics to MBA and B Tech Students. He has developed a training the trainer program in Entrepreneurship in collaboration with Rajiv Gandhi Foundation and Commonwealth of Learning Canada. He is a trainer in ERP and as a key speaker on ERP a conference on Computer Integrated Management System. He has provided exclusive training on CRM and eCRM and how it can be linked with ERP as model. He is presently in New Delhi, India and is planning to develop an ERP-Consortium and educational portal for industry and academia.

Dr. Kesharwani has produced several audio visual aids and one book on ERP. He is a presently flourishing himself as trainer on ERP and EIS related areas that can harmonize the technical and Functional module in a synchronized manner.

CHAPTER 1

ANALYSIS AND FRAMEWORK TO EIS

Quotation

EIS management system model has been proposed to achieve better process integration and data integrity through the entire product development lifecycle in an enterprise.

W. He

Structure

☆ Keywords
☆ FAQ
☆ Terminology Review
☆ Competency Review
☆ Suggested Reading

♣ QUICK LOOK AT CHAPTER THEMES

*The number one benefit of information technology is that it empowers people to do what they want to do, lets people be creative, makes people productive and allows people to learn things which they didn't imagine they could learn before, and so in a sense it is all about potential [**Steve Ballmer**]. EIS is an integrated information system, which is used to endow management with needed information on a regular basis. The information can be used for various purposes such as strategic planning, delivering increased productivity, reducing service cycles, reducing product development cycles, reducing marketing life cycles, increasing the understanding of customers' needs, facilitating business and process reengineering. EIS goes beyond the capabilities of accounting software and other application software. It can help to achieve high operational efficiency, significant cost savings, and thus maximization of profits. It is packed with powerful features, comprehensive in scope, modular and flexible, customizable, totally secure, and incredibly robust. It is often beneficial to organizations to amalgamate applications. The foremost objective is to endow with scalable and reliable data exchange between manifold enterprise applications with functions across compound software packages with elasticity in using software.*

♣ LEARNING OBJECTIVES

EIS has turned out to be the preferred software engine for the development of IT in most recent years. This chapter discusses EIS, its application, and its impact on organizations. This analysis and framework of EIS gives readers a solid introduction to EIS. The primary learning objectives of this chapter are to enable you to:

♣ Identify EIS systems software.
♣ Describe the concept of EIS.
♣ Define key terms as they relate to EIS.
♣ Be acquainted with the enterprise and its systems in general and EIS in particular.
♣ Explain the diverse concepts and applications of EIS.
♣ Discuss operational process support and control of resources with EIS.
♣ Emphasize EIS's integration and its impact on applications & functionality.
♣ Explain the background EIS.
♣ Explain other EIS challenges and capabilities.
♣ Explain the efforts made in creation of these systems.
♣ Identify and discuss their advantages in business applications.
♣ Be informed about widespread range of applications of EIS in business, industry, government & academia.

♣ CASE STUDY

Ericsson's EIS: knowledge to bring people together, automatically with Autonomy[1]

About Ericsson: Ericsson is a world-leading supplier in the telecommunications and data communications industry, offering advanced communications solutions for mobile and fixed networks, and consumer products. Ericsson is the undisputed global leader in mobile systems. Its continuous technology leadership is shaping the future of mobile and broadband.

The Need: To maintain its competitive edge, Ericsson has to stay at the forefront of technological development and that means its 100,000 employees need to know what is happening, both inside and outside the organization, all the time. The challenge was to create a multi-lingual information portal, which Ericsson named Business Intelligence Centre (BIC) that anyone across the entire organization could use to find, and to point users to relevant information, intelligence and points of contact. Ericsson's information management system at the time was not capable of automatically, and effectively managing multiple disparate data sources, like tracking live news feeds, on which the company relies to run its business. While employees needed to monitor and be kept informed of general market shifts to be responsive and provide higher levels of customer satisfaction, the vast amount of available information was not being utilized because employees didn't know it existed or where to find it.

About Autonomy EIS Software: Autonomy's Portal-in-a-Box™ allows all information sources to be available through one interface, and each user can have an automatically personalized splash page, tailored to their area of interest and expertise. The concept is based on the idea that only the end-user should get material relevant to him/her. Ericsson does not believe in "one size fits all" when it comes to information.

---

[1] Autonomy was founded upon a vision to dramatically change the way in which we interact with information and computers, ensuring that computers map our world, rather than the other way round. The company is the second largest pure software company in Europe and has offices worldwide, with a current market cap of $4 billion. Autonomy's position as the market leader is widely recognized by leading industry analysts including Gartner, Forrester Research, IDC and Delphi, with the latter referring to Autonomy as the fastest growing public company in cyber space.

The Benefits: The three big challenges were: Finding new means to exploit internal company-wide knowledge, increasing employee productivity — less day-to-day duplication and fewer interruptions, and saving money — no manual input from employees and an easy-to-maintain system.

Autonomy helped Ericsson achieve all their objectives: As a result, Ericsson found that productivity and quality of work rose because useful information was suddenly easier to get to. In addition, automatic profiling of users improved the exploitation of intellectual capital held around the world. For a company passionate about remaining at the forefront of its field, this is a significant advantage. It also maximizes the company's intellectual assets in helping users create strong project teams by identifying other employees with relevant internal competence. The expertise and knowledge of employees may be one of the organization's most valuable assets but it's also one of the most difficult to exploit. There is huge potential in the intellectual capital throughout the corporation.

In addition, significant amounts of money are likely to be saved by providing a single company-wide portal that can centrally purchase and publish relevant external information. Speedier access to competitive information for employees and greater team working through an appreciation of the expertise available within the organization, will, in turn, deliver improved responsiveness in the marketplace. The outcome was not just cost savings because staff didn't have to interrupt what they were doing to go in search of more information, but also an increase in the quality of that work by supporting end users in their day-to-day tasks. The ability to find second opinion material automatically when they went through their email, to find their way through their own PC, to find relevant internal material throughout the organization and to find the relevant people within their community with whom to interact — all these actually became addictive.

"The benefits of Autonomy are easily measurable: analysts spend less time looking for relevant information; the possibility of identifying relevant competence for collaboration amongst employees is dramatically increased and finally Autonomy facilitates the administration of the system since a lot of the back-end maintenance has been removed." The Business Intelligence Portal is today one of the most visited sites on the Ericsson Intranet.

♣ SKETCH OF EIS

Today a large portion of technology resources is being dedicated to complying with ever changing regulatory requirements from a myriad of sources. At the threshold of the new millennium, there is a marked shift in the business paradigm. An Enterprise Information System is a breed of computing system characteristically offering a high level of service, dealing with massive volumes of data and capable of supporting complex organizations ("an enterprise").

♣ INTRODUCTION

A majority of workers today are knowledge workers who create, distribute, and/or use information. This includes bankers, coordinators, caseworkers, counselors, community organizers, programmers, insurance advisors, consultants, etc.

A critically important question is, "Whether there is a need in our organization for an EIS?" This is a very difficult question to answer which merits a great deal of study. The following points bear this out:

- ♣ About 80 percent of an executive's time is devoted to information receiving, communicating, and use.
- ♣ Information is the starting point for virtually all activities performed in an organization.
- ♣ Key organizational ingredients in organizations include people and information, and it is critical to the organization's success that these ingredients are used efficiently.
- ♣ Effective utilization of information systems in management is important.
- ♣ Productive use of information is also important.
- ♣ Information is a source to augment competence, effectiveness and competitiveness of an enterprise.

Some Examples of EIS

- ♣ Airline reservations (seat, booking, payment, schedules, boarding list, special needs, etc.).
- ♣ Bank operations (deposit, transfer, withdrawal) electronically with payment gateways.
- ♣ Integration of departments with the help of contemporary software like ERP.
- ♣ Logistics management applications to streamline transportation systems.
- ♣ Train reservation with the help of IRCTC.

Per Wikipedia[2]

"Enterprise Information Systems provide a technology platform that enable organizations to integrate and coordinate their business processes. They provide a single system that is central to the organization and ensure that information can be shared across all functional levels and management hierarchies. Enterprise systems are invaluable in eliminating the problem of information fragmentation caused by multiple information systems in an organization, by creating a standard data structure." Figure 1.1 demonstrates this concept of an EIS.

1.1 INFORMATION AND SYSTEMS

Before talking in depth about EIS, we begin with information and systems. Information touches all human activity — it is repeatedly said that we live in the "information age." Information is an important resource to an organization. It represents the organization's tangible and intangible

---

[2] Wikipedia (pronounced /wi-ki-pi-di?/ or /w-k-pi-di?/) is a multilingual, Web-based, free content encyclopedia project. The name Wikipedia is a portmanteau (combination of words and their meanings) of the words wiki (a type of collaborative website) and encyclopedia. Wikipedia's articles provide links to guide the user to related pages with additional information.

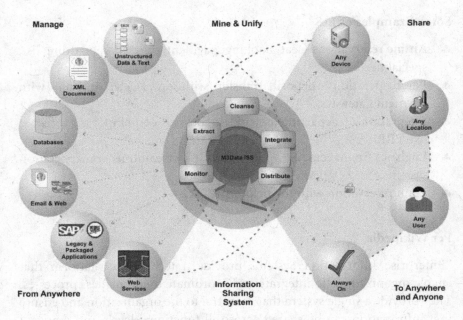

Figure 1.1: Conceptual view of an EIS.

Source: M3Data[3] (2008).

resources and all transactions relating to those resources. Information influences the manner an organization operates. The right information, if it is delivered to the right person, in the right fashion, and at the right time, can lead to progress and make organizational effectiveness and competence more certain. The information system is the mechanism used to deal with and control the information resource. When we talk about Information technology it stands for "Information Technology" (IT). IT refers to anything related to computing technology, such as networking, hardware, software, the Internet, or the people that work with these technologies. Many companies now have IT departments for managing the computers, networks, and other technical areas of their businesses. IT jobs

---

[3] M3Data is an information mining (gathering), processing, profiling, qualifying, distributed application development server built over the existing middleware technologies such as; WebSphere, Jboss, Weblogic, etc. M3Data provides exceptional power to process, store, archive, classify and evaluate information. www.artisnet.com/products.php

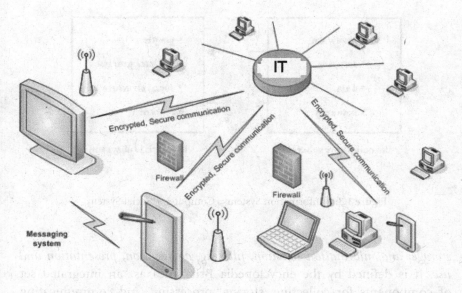

Figure 1.2:   Information Technology within organizations.

include computer programming, network administration, computer engineering, Web development, technical support, and many other related occupations (Tech Terms 2008).[4] There is an another definition given by NDCC 54.59.01, "Information Technology means the use of hardware, software, services, and supporting infrastructure to manage and deliver information using voice, data, and video" as demonstrated in Figure 1.2.

1.1.1 Purpose of Information Systems

There is often misunderstanding between the terms EIS and information system. An *information system is a set of interacting artifacts and human activities that perform one or more functions involving the handling of data and information, including data collection, creation, editing, processing and*

---

[4] The Tech Terms Dictionary is a constantly growing collection of computer and technology terms. Each definition is written in a way that is easy for the reader to understand and serves to explain the term, not just define it. http://www.techterms.com/about.php

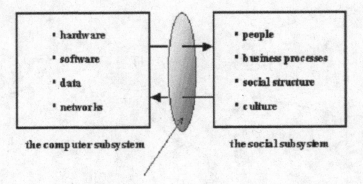

Figure 1.3: Information System = Computer + Social System.

storage; and information selection, filtering, aggregation, presentation and use. It is defined by the encyclopedia Britannica as "an integrated set of components for collecting, storing, processing, and communicating information. Business firms, other organizations, and individuals in contemporary society rely on <u>information systems</u> to manage their operations, compete in the marketplace, supply services, and augment personal lives."

Figure 1.3 shows an information system as the sum of the computer system and the social system. An IS system includes components that are not focused on decision-making. People use information for numerous reasons and in wide-ranging ways. For instance, you almost certainly use information for entertainment and illumination by viewing television, watching movies, browsing the Internet, listening to the radio, and reading newspapers, magazines, and books. In business, however, people and organizations inquire about and utilize information focused on making sound decisions and for solving organizational problems.

1.1.2 Types of Information Systems

New information systems are based on Internet technology, data warehousing concepts (very large databases of operational data), or Web-enabled inter-organizational systems affixed to earlier, more familiar types of systems commonly discussed in the IT literature and found in most organizations. These include transaction processing systems (TPS), management information systems (MIS), decision-support systems (DSS), office automation systems (OAS), and expert systems (ES).

♦ **Transaction processing systems:** Transaction processing systems handle routine information items, more often than not manipulating data in some constructive way as it enters or leaves the firm's databases. An order-entry program is an example of a TPS. Reasons for TP are recording, classification, sorting, calculation, summarization, storage and exhibit of results.

♦ **Management Information systems:** Management Information systems make available a focused vision of information flow as it develops during the course of business activities. This information is constructive in managing the business.

♦ **Decision-support systems:** Decision-support systems are methodical models used to assist managerial or professional decision-making by bringing significant data to a manager's notice. In many cases, these systems use data from management information systems, as well as from external sources, but DSSs purify the data to make it more functional to managers. DSSs support exceptional and non-recurring decisions, which are moderately unstructured.

♦ **Office automation systems:** Office automation systems use electronic mail, word processing, electronic filing, scheduling, calendaring, and other kinds of support for office work. First introduced with personal computers, these "groupware" applications became essential with the extensive use of personal digital assistants. They combine word processing, telecommunications and data processing to computerize office information, draw on stored data as a result of data processing and support handling of correspondence, reports and documents.

♦ **Knowledge work systems (KWS):** Information systems give support to knowledge workers in the creation and integration of new knowledge in the organization. Knowledge work systems (KWS) and office systems provide the information needs at the knowledge level of the organization. Knowledge work systems aid knowledge workers, whereas office systems primarily aid data workers (even though they are also used extensively by knowledge workers).

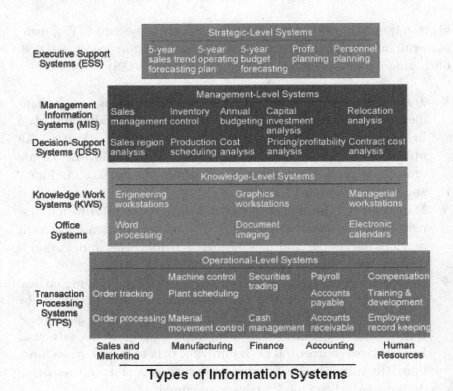

Figure 1.4:   Types of Information Systems.

Source: www.macs.hw.ac.uk/modules/F24SR1/linksis/lec5.htm

♦ **Executive support systems (ESS):** Information systems at the organization's strategic level designed to address non-customized decision-making options through advanced graphics and communications.

Figure 1.4 displays these levels of information systems.

1.2 HOW EIS DIFFERS FROM CONVENTIONAL PACKAGES

Conventional packages are very much restricted. In general terms they are known as legacy systems. A Legacy Information System can be

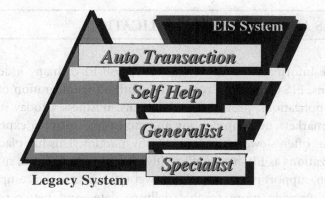

Figure 1.5:   Comparison between Legacy system & EIS system.

defined as "any information system that significantly resists modification and evolution" (Brodie, 1995[5]). Legacy information systems are the main vehicle for consolidating information about its business. It has much less features and less flexible options. EIS packages are radically different. There are back-office & front office concepts. The back-office looks after the raw material, financial issues, logistics and, in brief, internal matters. On the other hand, the front-office interacts directly with the customer. eCRM (electronic Customer Relationship Management) is a recent front-office package. Figure 1.5 shows that while the legacy system is condensed and compressed, the EIS system is auto-transactional and self helping, and would adapt itself as a generalist and a specialist under different conditions.

EIS is critical to organizations today as business practices change and new information technologies provide competitive advantage. EIS evolution becomes more complicated with time as systems are repeatedly modified. This requires modernizing those legacy systems which can accommodate evolving business practices and incorporate modern information technologies.

---

[5] Brodie, M. and Stonebraker, M. (1995). *Migrating Legacy Systems: Gateways, Interfaces and the Incremental Approach.* USA: Morgan Kaufmann Publishers.

1.3 EIS IS AN INTEGRATED APPLICATION

Most large information systems (IS) today consist of many independent applications. EIS generates a robust foundation for integration of heterogeneous applications, protocols and formats. Businesses today must deal with new markets, new competition and increasing customer expectations. Growth has often slowed with lower profit margins. This has placed stress on organizations as EIS has to efficiently synchronize demand, supply and production, support product quality, lower total costs in the complete supply chain, provide more reliable delivery dates and better service to customers, diminish stock to a minimum, condense throughput times, etc.

The EIS Application is a very powerful tool in enterprise perspectives. It takes into consideration logistics, the financial function, supplier, customer on one side with its differentiated approach and on the others, correlates itself with contemporary integrated systems like CRM and ERP. It also facilitates in analysis of business perspectives and help in building databases. All these aspects are very well explained in Figure 1.6.

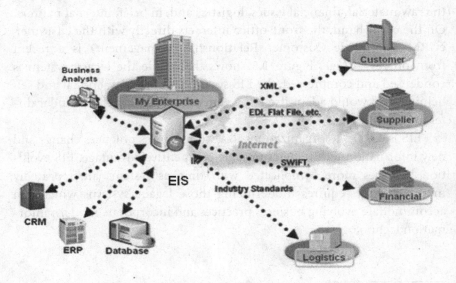

Figure 1.6:   EIS Relationship to Functional Systems.

Source: Artin (2004).

1.4 CONCEPT OF EIS

The EIS concept is not applied merely for the manufacturing environment but for all kinds of enterprises. Early ERP systems focused on manufacturing, although they quickly expanded to support all sorts of organizations. EIS facilitates enterprise-wide integrated information systems covering all functional areas and performs core corporate activities and enlarges customer service. EIS is a business management system that seeks to combine all aspects of the organization. It is capable of taking care of planning, manufacturing, sales and marketing. The concept is to integrate legacy systems within a coordinated integrated system. Typically, an EIS system uses database systems which are integrated with each other.

EIS is not merely reengineering systems; it is reengineering the manner organizations accomplish business tasks. In a recent CIO Magazine case study, Jeri Dunn, CIO for Nestle USA, said it this way, "If you weren't concerned with how the business ran, you could probably (install the EIS software) in 18 to 24 months" (Worthen, 2002). EIS is one of three enterprise-class applications, including Customer Relationship Management (CRM) and Supply Chain Management (SCM) that companies are deploying to automate business processes. EIS includes the internal back office operations and external front office such as financial system, human resources, inventory management, shipping, customer order processing, warehouse etc. Thus Enterprise Information System (EIS) provides resources for EIS-specific functionality to its clients. Examples of an EIS resource include: record or set of records in a database system, business objects in an Enterprise Resource Planning (ERP) system, transaction programs in a transaction processing system, etc. The evolution from a simple information system to a demand-supply chain service provider model is shown in Figure 1.7.

EIS is a development of an enterprise-based management system; it is a consequence of the contemporary enterprise attitude towards how information systems are to be configured to innovative business firms. EIS brings together people who work on shared tasks inside the same enterprise or in their dealings with supplier and customer. Enterprises need a smooth flow of information at all levels and between all parts of their

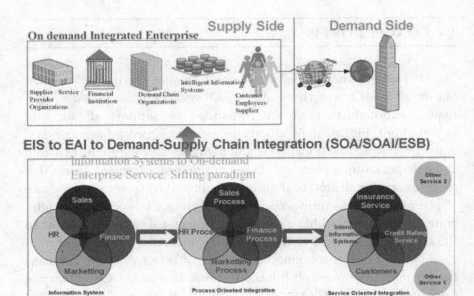

Figure 1.7:   Enterprise Demand-Supply Chain Model.

Source: Software & Support Verlag GmbH. (2008).

enterprise to access up-to-date information flow integrating business processes. EIS is fundamentally an activity that encompasses the entire enterprise, irrespective of its size, number of plants and location. Another implication of EIS is that it does not blindly automate. EIS transcends the classical automation models and is considered to be the subsequent generation of post-automation. Integrated, uniform, relevant, up to date information is imperative for the very existence of an enterprise. It gives authority to the right person to make decisions at the right time. This is only possible when the whole enterprise shares the same information and views it in the same perspective. Lack of integration affects other flows like people, machines and money. EIS is the planning of the 5M's of an enterprise's resources — Man, Money, Material, Method and Machinery — to their best synergistic values. The overall EIS concept reorganizes an enterprise around process and modifies the style of doing business by abandoning the old functional approach and transforming the organization into a process-centric entity.

1.4.1 Common EIS Features

An EIS system is not merely the integration of diverse enterprise processes mentioned above but can also possess key characteristics to meet the requirements. Features often found in an EIS include:

◆ **Best Business Practices:** It seeks a compilation of the best business processes applicable worldwide.
◆ **Beyond The Enterprise:** In supply chain applications, the EIS should not be confined to the enterprise boundaries, but should provide on-line connectivity to the other business entities working with the enterprise.
◆ **Comprehensive:** It should be able to sustain a variety of enterprise functions and must be suitable for a wide range of business enterprises.
◆ **Flexibility:** An EIS system should be flexible to act in response to the changing needs of an enterprise. The client server technology enables EIS to scamper across various database back ends through Open Data Base Connectivity (ODBC).
◆ **Modular & Open:** The EIS system has to have open system architecture. This means that any module can be interfaced or detached whenever required without affecting the other modules. It should hold up multiple hardware platforms for companies with heterogeneous collection of systems. It must also support some third party add-ons.

1.4.2 Customer Expectation of EIS Packages

Customers have to be very cautious and carefully weigh what they expect from the product. They must consider the following factors:

◆ **Number of implementations in the country:** The more experienced EIS vendors are, and the greater their market share, the better after sales service customers are likely to receive. Take the example of Tally or other financial package such as wings, Accpac, etc. Often, these advantages are balanced by higher prices.
◆ **Is the package integrated?** The system should cover all areas from marketing, production, purchase, research and development and many more. Specifically it has to be very exhaustive.

- **Is the package too old or too new?** This includes latest trends, platforms, and compliance with regulations.
- **Is the package localized?** SAP is a German-based company and has a corporate office at that place alone. If an Indian enterprise wants to purchase a package, what strategy is SAP going to follow as far as service and upgrades are concerned?
- **Is implementation of the package easy?** This is a major challenge calling for cooperation from users and vendors.
- **How easy/fast is it to get skills on the package?** This also varies from company to company and also depends on the level of highly skilled specialists employed by the organization.
- **Quality of the consultants hired:** Consultants can be employed to bridge the gap between the vendor and the user. The consultant's job may be to provide training, giving knowledge to both user and vendor about the latest trends, and also guiding them about in-house development of EIS or purchasing from outside.
- **Financial health of the company:** Implementation of EIS can give an organization a new financial status, which may lead to greater profitability, but has led to bankruptcy in the past.
- **How big is the company and is its main focus implementation alone?** EIS's user's total strength and size play a very vital role. The vendor's core benefit is not only implementation, but also the building of long-term relationships for more business i.e. by providing after sales service and more implementation at different places.

1.5 EIS CHARACTERISTICS

There are many reasons to adopt an EIS. They offer an integrated system shared by all users rather than a diverse set of computer applications which rarely can communicate with one another, and with each having its own set of data and files. EIS provides a means to coordinate information system assets and information flows across the organization. The main benefit is the elimination of sub-organizational silos that focus on their own problems rather than serving the interests of the overall organization.

On the downside, EIS systems impose one procedure for the entire organization which requires everyone to conform to the new system. EIS systems are thus less flexible. But the benefits of integration are usually much greater than the costs of conformity.

Data can be entered once, at the most accurate source, so that all users share the same data. This can be very beneficial, because shared data is used more, by more people, which leads to much more complete and accurate data. As errors are encountered, users demand correction. There are limits, as a set of procedures are needed to insure that changes do not introduce new errors. This makes it harder to make corrections, but again, this added inconvenience is usually well worth the gains of data integration.

EIS systems can also provide better ways of doing things. This idea is the essence of best practices, a key SAP system component. The downside to best practices is that they take a great deal of effort in identifying the best way to proceed with specific business functions, and that they often can involve significant change in how organizational members do their work. Further, as with any theory, what is considered best by one is often not considered best by all.

EIS systems are usually adopted with the expectation that they are going to yield lower computing costs in the long run. Ideally, adopting one common way of doing things is simpler and involves less effort to provide computing support to an organization. In practice, savings are often not realized, due to failure to anticipate all of the detailed nuances of user needs, as well as the inevitable changes in the business environment that call for different best practices and computer system relationships. Training needs are typically under-budgeted in EIS projects. Furthermore, these training budgets don't usually include the hidden costs of lost productivity as employees cope with complex new systems. Table 1.1 recaps these pros and cons of EIS systems.

The key rationales for implementing ERP systems are:

♦ Technology — more powerful, integrated computer systems.

  ➤ Greater flexibility.
  ➤ Lower IT cost.

Table 1.1:   EIS Pros and Cons.

Factor	Pro	Con
System Integration	Improved understanding across users.	Less flexibility.
Data Integration	Greater accuracy.	Harder to make corrections.
Best Practices	More efficient methods.	Imposition of how people do their work.
		Less freedom and creativity.
Cost of Computing	More efficient system planned.	Changing needs.
		Under-budgeted training expense.
		Hidden costs of implementation.

♦ Business practices — implementation of better ways of accomplishing tasks.

> ➢ Better operational quality.
> ➢ Greater productivity.

♦ Strategic — cost advantages can be gained through more efficient systems.

> ➢ Improved decision-making.
> ➢ Support business growth.
> ➢ Build external linkages.

♦ Competitive — if an organization's competitors adopt ERP and gain cost efficiencies as well as serve customers better, organizations will be left with declining clientele.

> ➢ Better customer service.

1.6 EIS RESEARCH

The motivations for ERP/EIS adoption were examined by three studies using the same format. Mabert *et al.* (2000) surveyed over 400 Midwestern U.S. manufacturing organizations about ERP adoption. Olhager and

Table 1.2: Reasons for Implementing ERP.

Reason	U.S.	Sweden	Korea
Replace legacy systems	4.06	4.11	3.42
Simplify and standardize systems	3.85	3.67	3.88
Improve interactions w/suppliers & customers	3.55	3.16	3.45
Gain strategic advantage	3.46	3.18	3.63
Link to global activities	3.17	2.85	3.54
Solve the Y2K problem	3.08	2.48	NA
Pressure to keep up with competitors	2.99	2.48	2.94
Ease of upgrading systems	2.91	2.96	3.55
Restructure organization	2.58	2.70	3.33

Source: Mabert et al. (2000), Olhager and Selldin (2003), Katerattanakul et al. (2006).
Rating scale from 1 (not important) to 5 (very important).

Selldin (2003) replicated that study with 190 manufacturing firms in Sweden. Katerattanakul et al. (2006) again replicated the survey, this time in Korea. These studies reported the following ratings with respect to motivation for implementing ERP (see Table 1.2).[6]

Initially, fear of Y2K was a major concern. The Swedish survey was later than the U.S., and that might explain the lower rating for this item in the Swedish study. The later Korean study did not ask about this dated issue. The U.S. response was actually neutral (only slightly higher than 3), but Y2K clearly was a factor in ERP adoption in the mid- to late-1990s. However, more important reasons were always present. In the first two studies, replacing legacy systems received a high positive response. The desire to simplify and standardize systems was the second highest rating in the first two studies, and the highest rating in the later Korean study.

There were two other reasons that received relatively high ratings in the U.S. (a bit lower in Sweden). These were to improve interactions with suppliers and customers, which is one way to gain strategic advantage.

---

[6] Mabert, V. M., Soni, A. and Venkataramanan, M. A. (2000). Enterprise resource planning survey of US manufacturing firms. *Production and Inventory Management Journal*, 41(20), pp. 52–58; Olhager J. and Selldin, E. (2003). Enterprise resource planning survey of Swedish manufacturing firms. *European Journal of Operational Research*, 146, pp. 365–373. Katerattanakul, P., Hong, S. and Lee, J. (2006). Enterprise resource planning survey of Korean manufacturing firms. *Management Research News*, 29(12), pp. 820–837.

The supply chain aspects of ERP have led vendors to modify their products to be more open, although work continues to be needed in this direction (and seems to be proceeding). Linking to global activities was slightly positive in the U.S. survey, more negative in the Swedish study, and relatively higher in the Korean study.

Three other potential reasons received low ratings in both studies. Pressure to keep up with competitors received neutral support in the U.S. study. Ease of upgrading systems is a technical reason that received neutral support both in the U.S. and in Sweden. Restructuring the organization was rated lower.

From these studies, we infer that ERP/EIS systems are an important means to upgrade the quality of information systems. They can provide organizations with coordinated systems that have higher quality data. Once the kinks are worked out, this information may be available in a more responsive way. Not all evidence indicates lower costs, but most evidence does indicate higher quality information systems.

1.7 CONCLUSION

EIS has become the favourite **software engine** for the development of IT in most recent years. This chapter discusses EIS, its application, and experience. This framework of EIS has been explained to give the reader a solid understanding from a number of perspectives.

Integration and consolidation of enterprise systems have proven highly useful to top management and IT divisions. Consequences should be more transparent business processes, better monitoring, faster and more effective response to changes and opportunities. This technology is designated for big companies that are embracing application integration.

To be innovative, in the world of networked markets, one needs not only to think out of the box, but also to think more importantly about contemporary information systems capable of responding to rapid change and linking to those with whom the organization interacts. EIS systems help organizations to maximize their growth & potential.

EIS suites can improve and update corporate resource management, but the training and costs involved can be high-priced. EIS has revolutionized the entire business environment. Thus the contemporary organization is an extremely diverse, decentralized and technologically advanced entity. Large volumes of information must be stored and processed at immense speeds with an elevated degree of accuracy and reliability. Paper flow systems which were widespread a few years ago cannot deal with the requirements of today's businesses, governments, universities, churches, charitable societies, etc.

☆ KEYWORDS

☆ **Client:** A software program that is used to contact and obtain data from a server software program on another computer, often across a great distance. Each client program is designed to work with one or more specific kinds of server programs, and each server requires a specific kind of client. A Web browser is a specific kind of client.

☆ **Module:** A segment of a program that carries out a specific function and may be used alone or combined with other modules of the identical program.

☆ **MRP (Materials Resource Planning):** Manages the same or similar process as an ERP, with an orientation to manufacturing.

☆ **Oracle:** Oracle claims to be the world's leading supplier of software for information management and ERP too, but it is best known for its sophisticated relational database products, Oracle 8 and Oracle 8i, which are used in Fortune 1000 corporations and by many of the largest Web sites.

☆ **Resource:** A resource could be labour hours, dollars or other resource factors. This could be used for Rough Cut Capacity Planning.

☆ **SAP:** A pioneer developer of ERP systems, and still the leading vendor of ERP/EIS systems.

☆ **Site:** Organization or facility where a host is located.

☆ **URL:** This stands for Universal Resource Locator. It facilitates in identifying an exact location on the Internet.

☆ TERMINOLOGY REVIEW

1. What are the strategies used for successful implementation of EIS application?
2. How have EIS systems changed the work of IT organization?
3. What do you mean by resource and what is its relationship with EIS?
4. Where has EIS originated from and what are the concepts behind its beginning?
5. Can CRM be EIS?
6. What are three major reasons to undertake EIS?
7. What do you mean by components of EIS?
8. Write in brief the technologies required for EIS.
9. How does EIS enhance the company's business performance?
10. Define Moore's Law and explain why it is significant in the development of EIS.
11. What are the main characteristics of an EIS system? List the benefits and disadvantages of implementing an EIS system.

☆ COMPETENCY REVIEW

1. Enterprise systems are all concerned with the enterprise and not the systems. Their success to a great extent depends on the responsibility of top management and energetic participation of the HR people. Implementation of an EIS is not a technology decision. In actual fact, it is a decision that ideally should be based on business needs and benefits.
2. "The idea behind EIS is to have a single enterprise of the customer for the purpose of cultivating these high-quality relationships that lead to improved loyalty & profits." Explain.
3. "EIS solution contributes greater user adoption, an enhanced user experience and real-time intelligence for your enterprise to make smarter decisions." Justify the statement.
4. Explain and elaborate on the above statements in the light of EIS systems.

5. What are the objectives of implementing EIS? Explain distinctive ways of implementing an EIS. In short, throw some light on the guidelines for EIS implementation and the practicalities faced during implementation.

6. Today business managers try to think in terms of business processes that integrate the functional areas, thus promoting efficiency and competitiveness. An important aspect of this is the need to share information between functions and functional areas. EIS software provides this capability by using a single common database.

☆ CHECK YOUR PROGRESS

1. Briefly comment on the following statements

   a. Information can be identified by effective parameters.

   ....

   ....

   b. Computers and communications have produced a technological revolution.

   ....

   ....

   c. Information technology refers to both the hardware and software that are used to store, retrieve, and manipulate information.

   ....

   ....

   d. Information can be identified by effective parameters.

   ....

   ....

2. Fill in the blanks

   a. EIS is _____ transaction processing software that supports an organization value chain.

   b. _____ is the creation of entirely new & more business process, with regard to what has gone before.

3. True & False

   a. EIS application modules are integrated interactively.

   b. EIS software are stand-alone modules that handle the transactions processing requirements of individual business units.

   c. Any EIS module is the same as an any EIS application server.

☆ SUGGESTED READING

Books

Brady, J., Monk, E. and Wagner, B. (2001). *Concepts in Enterprise Resource Planning*. Thomson Learning.

Curran, T. A. and Ladd, A. (2000). *SAP R/3 Blueprint*. Prentice Hall.

Turban, E., Rainer, R. K. and Potter, R. E. (2003). *Introduction to Information Technology*. New York: John Wiley & Sons.

Journal Articles

Joseph, G. and George, A. (2002). ERP, learning communities, and curriculum integration. *Journal of Information Systems Education*, 13(1), 51–58.

Lee, A. and Lee, J. (2000). An ERP implementation case study from a knowledge-transfer perspective. *Journal of Information Technology*, 15(4), 281–288.

Soh, C., Kien, S. S. and Tay-Yap, J. (2000). Cultural Fits and Misfits: Is ERP a Universal Solution? *Communications of the ACM*, 43(4), 47–51.

Van Hillegersberg, J. and Kumar, K. (2000). ERP Experience and Evolution. *Communications of the ACM*, 43(4), 23–26.

White Papers and Conference Papers

Jones, M. C. (2001). Organizational Knowledge Sharing and ERP: An Exploratory Assessment. In *Proceedings of the Seventh Americas Conference on Information Systems*, Strong, D. M., Straub, D. and DeGross, I. I. (eds.), 1030–1032.

Pan, S. L., Newell, S., Huang, J. C. and Cheung, A. W. K. (2001). Knowledge Integration as a Key Problem in an ERP Implementation. In *Proceedings of the Twenty-Second International Conference on Information Systems*.

Parr, A. and Shanks G. (2000). Taxonomy of ERP Implementation Approaches. *33rd Hawaii International Conference on System Sciences* (*HICSS*).

Online Resources

Davenport, T. H. (2000). Does ERP Build A Better Business? http://www.cio.com/archive/021500_excerpt.html (Accessed on 20.08.01).

Emily (2004). Integrating ABC & ERP system. www.focusmag.com/back_issues/issue_02/pages/bci.htm (Accessed 13-09-2004).

Koch, C. (2002). The ABCs of ERP. CIO Magazine. http://www.cio.com/research/erp/edit/erpbasics.html (November).

Worthen, B. (2002). Nestle's ERP Odyssey. CIO Magazine. http://www.cio.com/archive/051502/nestle.html (December).

Extreme ERP Makeover. CIO. (November 15, 2003).

The Information Cannot Speak for itself. IntelligentEnterprise.com (July 10, 2004).

CHAPTER 2

ENTERPRISE SYSTEM DEVELOPMENT AND DEPLOYMENT

Quotation

Enterprise Systems include applications and associated information and have as a fundamental premise a structure that permits the integration of data held in any enterprise system with that held in other enterprise systems through the use of appropriate common identifiers.

Structure

- ♣ *Quick look at chapter themes*
- ♣ *Learning objectives*
- ♣ *Case study:* **The State of South Carolina EIS**
- ♣ *Sketch of EIS development*
- ♣ *Introduction*
- 2.1 The Manufacturing Roots of ERP
- 2.2 Stages
- 2.3 Historical Background
- 2.4 Evolution of ERP
- 2.5 Material Requirements Planning (MRP-I)
- 2.6 Manufacturing Resource Planning (MRP-II)
- 2.7 ERP and ERP Modules
  - 2.7.1 Relative Module Use
  - 2.7.2 Customization Issues
- 2.8 Comparative Coverage Between MRP, ERP, EIS
- 2.9 EIS as per the Gartner View

♣ QUICK LOOK AT CHAPTER THEMES

Although most people have a dissimilar outlook about 'the new economy' everyone seems to agree about at least one thing, i.e. the Internet which is going to radically transform how companies do business. But the million dollar questions are: how is this expansion in reality going to take place? Will the economy as we are acquainted with it change? Manufacturing software options used to be much simpler than the choices that confront manufacturers today. In the old days quality and price were the primary concerns of the buyer. As additional products became available, convenience was added to the mix. If a local manufacturer had good quality and a reasonable price, that company could get the sale over some distant company who might have a better price. Enterprise system provides a tightly integrated solution to an organization's information system needs for both manufacturing and service organizations. In the last decade, nomenclature has evolved from material requirements planning to manufacturing resource planning to enterprise resource planning [ERP] and now enterprise information system, as added functionality has been added.

♣ LEARNING OBJECTIVES

In highly competitive business, firms repeatedly have to review their business objectives to accomplish their organizational purposes. EIS technologies provide the means to incorporate strategic business solutions within and across the component parts of organizational information system infrastructures. The learning objective of this chapter is to introduce you to the world of enterprise systems and enable you to:

- ♣ Understand manufacturing operating systems which determine how you make your product, maintain quality, supervise operations, purchase components and materials, and handle customer orders and complaints, and other activities.
- ♣ Guesstimate the costs and benefits obtained from MRP-I and MRP-II implementation.
- ♣ Understand the set-up of manufacturing systems including processes, quality assurance, production control, purchasing and customer service.
- ♣ Understand how manufacturing management systems have developed as part of MRP (material requirement planning).
- ♣ Desire to standardize and improve business processes.
- ♣ Aim to assimilate the organization's existing information systems.
- ♣ Understand the need for enhanced and timelier information.
- ♣ Review development of Enterprise systems.
- ♣ Present the concept of Enterprise systems, specially the ERP modules.
- ♣ View relative use and modification of modules.

♣ CASE STUDY

The State of South Carolina EIS

The State of South Carolina has undertaken a statewide effort to transform the way state government operates. The state is putting into place enterprise systems to support efforts to better gauge the price of government. South Carolina has implemented a pilot project and a business case study for their current effort to deliver an enterprise solution that will among other things: 1. Reduce the time and cost to provide quality customer service. 2. Provide tools for monitoring and measuring cost savings and process improvements estimated at $100M per year. 3. Deliver enabling technology to allow for use by persons with disabilities. South Carolina's goal is to use this enterprise information system to automatically collect information on programs and activities, determine the actual cost of doing business, align resources, and establish consistent business processes and to better serve their constituents.

APPLICATION

Pilot Implementation

The objective of this large pilot project included a sweeping reengineering of out-of-date processes as well as improving information available to management and others. Processes had become burdensome and costly. For example, on average the State spends more than $22 to process a single vendor invoice for payment. Yet, the benchmark for best practice is $10 apiece — and some organizations have cut this cost to less than $5 per invoice. The Comptroller General's Office and the pilot agency also wanted an opportunity to gain valuable experience with the software and its implementation, with a view toward implementation as a State enterprise system. These objectives necessitated a fully integrated system that would provide access to current information; eliminate unnecessary paperwork, reviews, approvals, and duplication of efforts; adopt best practices; significantly reduce manual processes; implement document management for electronic routing and approvals of documents; and interface new systems with the Comptroller General's legacy systems.

Business Case Study

To fully evaluate the merits of the project, the State chose to invest in a return-on-investment (ROI) analysis and prepared a formal business case study to document the expected costs and savings from an enterprise implementation. The team conducted an extensive assessment of the State's cost of doing business today, to provide an accurate baseline for comparison. The team then determined the potential savings and benefits available to the State by implementing the solution beyond the pilot agency. The business case study identified potential annual savings of more than $120 million annually by adopting best practices and reengineering its business processes accordingly. These potential savings were centered on 4 major areas: 1. Finance and General Accounting. 2. Procurement and Inventory Management. 3. Human Resources and Payroll. 4. Document Management. When compared to the costs of implementation, if only 10 percent–20 percent of these potential savings are realized, the project pays for itself in 5–7 years.

BENEFITS

Pilot Implementation

By taking an enterprise approach to running government, the State will improve government's bottom line — service delivery. This is not an idealistic dream, but a pragmatic reality. The agency is now using enterprise-wide systems to automatically collect information on programs and activities, determine the actual cost of doing business, align resources and results, establish consistent business processes, and better serve its customers. Actual annual process savings of approximately $600,000 have been documented by our pilot agency. This was despite the fact that the pilot agency continues to have to work within the limits of the State's current inefficient business processes. With this experience, the State now has a basis and the tools to expand on this success.

Business Case Study

The business case study first gives the State objective information on which to base the feasibility of implementing the project. In addition it will also give the state a yardstick by which to measure the ultimate success of an enterprise solution.

IMPORTANCE

Information technology plays a key-enabling role for the State to reengineer its currently inefficient business processes. Without rock solid technology provided by the SAP software, any effort to implement an enterprise solution would fail.

ORIGINALITY

While ERP technology is not ground breaking, governments have been slow to adopt it. As such, enterprise implementation is somewhat leading edge for state governments. That is certainly the case in South Carolina. Additionally, the use of a business case study to justify and move a project forward while not ground-breaking, has not been done to this level before.

SUCCESS

Pilot Implementation

The pilot project was a success in many ways. First it was completed on time and within budget. It resulted in documented savings. To illustrate, prior to implementation, the central procurement function of the agency averaged a backlog of approximately 1 week. After implementation, this backlog was eliminated. In fact central buyers can now concentrate on being true buyers, rather that paper shuffling clerks. In addition the pilot project allowed us a real world example from which to learn valuable lessons on how to approach the enterprise implementation. These lessons learned will be invaluable to the project team as we move forward through the enterprise implementation.

DIFFICULTY

The technology involved, while complex, is certainly not the largest challenge for the project. The cultural aspects of the business process reengineering represent the highest hurdle to clear. People who have been following what are essentially the same business practices for over 20 years are sometimes very slow to accept change. The change management piece of this cannot be under-estimated. This includes accurate and consistent communications along with training and risk management.

Source: http://www.cwhonors.org/laureates/government/20055400.pdf

♣ SKETCH OF EIS DEVELOPMENT

EIS software ideally covers all areas in an organization cutting across functional boundaries and business procedures. An EIS covers a broad array of automated tasks such as SCM (Supply Chain Management), Inventory Replenishment, CRM (Customer Relationship Management), MRP-I (Material Requirement Planning), and MRP-II (Manufacturing Resource Planning). What were stand-alone applications like inventory sales and receivables, financial etc. are integrated in an EIS. An EIS covers all business dimensions of the company such as people, method, structures and technology. Thus, the unique nature of EIS is that it covers all mutually dependent functions in day-to-day operations of an organization. An expert in the field of information system has been quoted as saying that, "It is important that companies know exactly what ERP can do; it is the building blocks on which you add other elements that give you competitive advantage." Thus ERP/EIS is about connecting business systems with computer systems including human beings. Moreover, an ERP/EIS system can be used as a tool to improve the performance level of a supply chain network by helping to reduce cycle times.[1]

♣ INTRODUCTION

Enterprise information systems can be traced back to inventory control packages, material requirements planning (MRP-I), and manufacturing resource planning (MRP II). An inventory control system was software performing conventional inventory processes. It was one of the early

---

[1] Gardiner, S. C., Hanna, J. B. and LaTour, M. S. (2002). ERP and the re-engineering of industrial marketing processes: A prescriptive overview for the new-age marketing manager. *Industrial Marketing Management*, 31, 357–365.

business applications, which was not integrated with finance and accounting. ERP systems evolved from 1970s-era systems that helped manufacturers identify component and material requirements and availability, leading to a comprehensive and integrated set of functionalities. Now, they have become the organization's information keystone integrating a wide variety of functions including sales and distribution, planning, purchasing, production, cost accounting and finance. Some systems also include engineering management, finite scheduling, production control, and enterprise information system capabilities. The power and benefit of ERP/EIS systems lie in their ability to "mirror" or "model," in electronic form, the company's core and supportive business processes. They provide a global view of an organization, help better manage and utilize company resources, while minimizing duplication and potential for errors. EIS accomplish this objective by modeling business processes. For example, an EIS provides the capability to track a sales order from the order desk, to production planning, purchasing, production, warehousing, shipping and accounts receivable (referred to as "Order to Payment" process). An EIS will also help identify the impact of the order on other departments, for example, purchasing and production, to determine additional material and capacity requirements to fulfill orders.

In today's competitive business environment, companies try to provide customers with goods and services faster and cheaper than their competition. How do they do that? Often, the key is to have efficient, integrated information systems. Increasing the efficiency of information systems results in more efficient management of business processes. When companies have efficient business processes, they can be more competitive in the marketplace.

2.1 THE MANUFACTURING ROOTS OF ERP

The term "MRP" is used as a general term to include all MRP versions, namely, MRP I (i.e. material requirements planning), Closed-loop MRP (i.e. MRP I with capacity planning and shop floor), and MRP II (i.e. Closed-loop MRP integrated with the other functions such as finance and marketing).[2,3] The concept of an integrated information system took shape on the factory floor. Manufacturing software developed during the 1960s and 1970s, evolving from simple inventory tracking systems to material requirements planning (MRP) software. MRP at its core is a time-phased order release system that schedules and releases manufacturing work orders and purchase orders, so that subassemblies and components arrive at the assembly station just as they are required. Some of the benefits of MRP are reduction of inventories, improved customer service, enhanced efficiency and effectiveness.[4] MRP software allowed a plant manager to plan production and raw materials requirements by working backwards from the sales forecast, the prediction of future sales. Thus, the manager first looked at Marketing and Sales' forecast of demand (what the customer wants); looked at the Production schedule needed to meet that demand; calculated the raw materials needed to meet production; and finally projected raw materials purchase orders to suppliers. For a company with many products, raw materials, and shared production resources, this kind of projection was impossible without a computer to keep track of various inputs.

The basic functions of MRP could be handled by mainframe computers using sequential file processing. Electronic data Interchange (EDI), the direct computer-to-computer exchange of standard business documents, allowed companies to handle the purchasing process electronically, avoiding the cost and delays resulting from paper purchase order and invoice systems. The functional area now known

---

[2] Duchessi, P., Schaninger, C., Hobbs, D. and Pentak, L. (1988). Determinants of success in implementing material requirements planning (MRP). *Manufacturing and Operations Management*, 1, 263–304.

[3] Sum, C., Yang, K., Ang, J. and Quek, S. (1995). An analysis of material requirements planning (MRP) benefits using alternating conditional expectation (ACE). *Operations Management*, 13, 35–58.

[4] Siriginidi, S. R. (2000). Enterprise resource planning in re-engineering business. *Business Process Management Journal*, 6(5), 376–391.

as Supply Chain Management (SCM) began with the sharing of long-range production schedules between manufacturers and their suppliers.

2.2 STAGES

Companies realized that the management and flow of information was just as important as materials and inventory management. ERP systems are rooted in Material Requirements Planning (MRP) and its Manufacturing Resource Planning (MRP-II) System.[5] ERP has also evolved considerably with computer and technology advances.

There are various stages to ERP (Figure 2.1), which can be explained as follows:

◆ **MRP-I:** Material requirements planning which was the historical background of ERP; its purpose being to tap inventory i.e. raw materials planning etc.

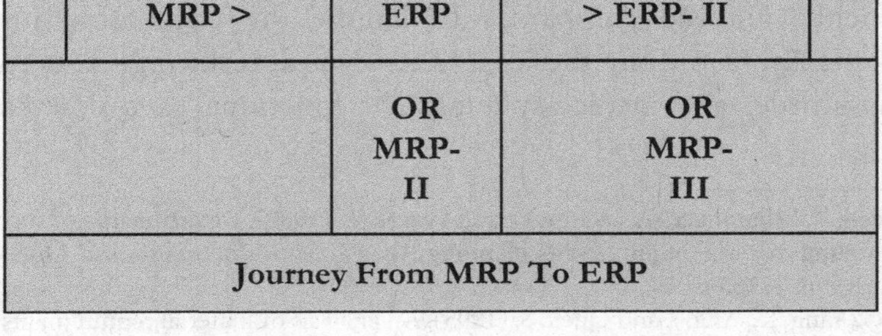

Stage – 1 → Stage – 2 → Stage – 2			
MRP >	ERP	> ERP- II	
	OR MRP- II	OR MRP- III	
Journey From MRP To ERP			

Figure 2.1: Stages of Enterprise Systems.

---

[5] Hong, K. K. and Kim, Y.-G. (2002). The critical success factors for ERP implementation: An organizational fit perspective. *Information & Management*, 40(1), 25–40.

♦ **MRP-II:** Manufacturing resource planning which looks after production-related activities. The concept of MRP-II evolved to look after the shop floor and distribution management activities.

♦ **ERP:** Enterprise resource planning has a broader role and is not confined to one department but has an elaborate purview.

♦ **ERP-II or MRP-III:** Money resource planning or ERP-II emphasises more on planning of capital or managing the situation when surplus money arises.

➢ **1960s** The focus of manufacturing systems in this era was on Inventory Control. Software packages were designed to handle inventory based on traditional inventory concepts.

➢ **1970s** MRP (Material Requirements Planning) systems emerged in this era. This system translated the Master Schedule built for the end items into time-phased net requirements for the sub-assemblies, components, and raw materials planning and procurement.

➢ **1980s** The concept of MRP I evolved to extend MRP to the shop floor and distribution management activities.

➢ **1990s** The term MRP I was extended in to a new form known as ERP which covers areas like engineering, finance, human resources, and project management as a whole. Enterprise resource planning is a technological approach for EIS.

➢ **2000s** ERP-II or MRP III (Money Resource Planning) originated with the motive to emphasize on the planning of money in a optimal manner.

➢ **2005s** The term EIS was formed with the objective of providing a contemporary version which included web enabled features, full integration, multi-enabled (Figure 2.2).

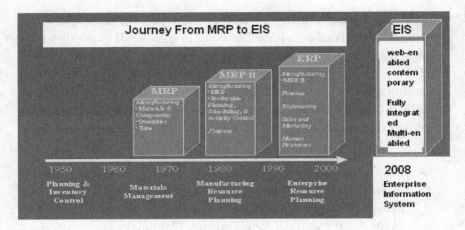

Figure 2.2:   EIS Development.

2.3 HISTORICAL BACKGROUND

ERP continues to be one of the largest, fastest-growing and most influential players in the application software industry.[6] ERP (Enterprise Resource Planning) is an industry term for the broad set of activities supported by multi-module application software that helps an organization in the important parts of its business, including product planning, parts purchasing, maintaining inventories, interacting with suppliers, customer service, and tracking orders. ERP can also include application modules for the finance and human resources aspects of a business. Characteristically, an ERP system uses or is integrated with a relational database system. The deployment of an ERP system can involve considerable business process analysis, employee retraining, and new work procedures.

Information available shows that 70 percent of Fortune 1000 firms have or will soon install ERP systems, which will boost the global ERP market from $15 billion already installed as of now to $50 billion over the

---

[6] Adam, F. and O'Doherty, P. (2000). Lessons from enterprise resource-planning implementations in Ireland: Towards smaller and shorter ERP projects. *Journal of Information Technology*, 15, 305–316.

next five years. ERP applications make up the largest segment of Information Technology budgets. Thirty-nine percent of large companies and 60 percent of smaller companies are deploying ERP systems. The expected annual growth rate for the ERP market over the next five years is 37 percent. With the power ERP exercises over business, it is imperative to see who the key vendors of ERP software are.

ERP integrates the old isolated computer systems in Finance, Human Resource, Manufacturing and Warehousing, and replaces them with a single unified software program organized into software modules. Finance, Manufacturing and Inventory all still get their own software, except that now the software is linked together so that someone in finance can look into the warehouse software to see if an order has been shipped. Most vendors' ERP software is flexible enough so that you can install some modules without buying the whole package. Many companies, for example, will immediately install an ERP finance or HR module and leave the rest of the system for later.

Enterprise resource planning systems arose from a variety of origins. SAP developed their product around supporting the function of manufacturing and integrating that with financial and accounting functions. Other vendors developed their products from other sources. For instance, PeopleSoft began by developing a respected human resources software product, which they expanded to include a slate of other modules. Prior to entry into the ERP market directly, Oracle was the leading database software vendor.

Development of ERP

In the early 1970s, business computing relied upon centralized mainframe computer systems. These systems proved their value by providing a systematic way to measure what businesses did financially. The reports these systems delivered could be used for analysis of variance with budgets and plans, and served as a place to archive business data. Computing provided a way to keep records much more accurately, and on a massively larger scale than was possible through manual means. But from our perspective at the beginning of the 21st century, that level of computer support was primitive.

Business computing systems were initially applied to those functions that were easiest to automate, and that called for the greatest levels of consistency and accuracy. Payroll and accounting functions were an obvious initial application. Computers can be programmed to generate accurate paychecks, considering tax and overtime regulations of any degree of complexity. They also can implement accounting systems for tax, cost, and other purposes; because these functional applications tend to have precise rules that cover almost every case, computers can be entrusted to automatically and rapidly take care of everything related to these functions.

Prior to 2000, ERP systems catered to very large firms which could afford the rather high costs of purchasing ERP systems. Even focusing on a selected few modules would typically cost firms $5 million and up for software. After 2000, demand dropped, in part because firms were often concerned with Y2K issues prior to 2000 which motivated many ERP system acquisitions. Demand noticeably dropped off after 2000 came and went. Vendors reacted in a number of ways. First, the market consolidated, with Oracle purchasing PeopleSoft (which had earlier acquired JD Edwards). Microsoft acquired a number of smaller ERP software products, consolidating them into Microsoft Dynamics which caters to a smaller priced market, thus serving a needed gap in ERP coverage for small businesses. Notably, SAP advertises that they can serve small business too. But it appears that they are more valuable in the large-scale enterprise market. There are also many other systems to include open sourced systems (at least for acquisition) like Compiere in France. Many countries, such as China, India, and others have thriving markets for ERP systems designed specifically for local conditions, although SAP and Oracle have customers all over the globe.

2.4 EVOLUTION OF ERP

In an ever-growing business environment the following demands are placed on organizations:

- Emphasis on customers rather than other factors like market share, brand image etc.
- Aggressive cost control initiatives.

- Need to analyze costs/revenues by product or customer.
- Flexibility to respond to changing business requirements.
- More informed management decision-making.
- Changes in ways of doing business.

Difficulties in getting accurate data, timely information and improper interfaces across business functions have been identified as hurdles in the growth of any business. Depending upon the velocity of the growing business needs, various applications and planning systems have been introduced into the business world for overcoming these obstacles and to achieve required growth. They include:

- Management Information Systems (MIS).
- Integrated Information Systems (IIS).
- Artificial Intelligence (AI).
- Corporate Information Systems (CIS).
- Knowledge Management (KM).
- Enterprise Wide Systems (EWS).
- Business Intelligence System (BIS).
- Material Requirement Planning (MRP).
- Manufacturing Resource Planning (MRP-II).
- Money Resource Planning (MRP-III).

The latest planning tool added to the above list is Enterprise Resource Planning. Any ERP implementation is a special event since it involves the entire organization with long-term impact. It brings together different functionalities, people, procedures and philosophies, and brings sweeping changes throughout the enterprise. ERP implementation is one of the top growing segments in the information technology industry today. To take advantage of emerging technologies and business practices and meet the evolving business requirements of a thriving industry, companies like People Soft, SAP-AG, BaaN, QaD, IFS, Siebel, Oracle, JD-Edward, Makess, Ramco, etc. have launched their products in this field. Shrinking geographical borders, integration of currencies, ever decreasing product life cycles, condensed profit margins and the need to raise productivity can all be addressed by ERP solutions.

2.5 MATERIAL REQUIREMENTS PLANNING (MRP-I)

The MRP system begins with three documents. A forecast for end-items being assembled is needed by time period. A bill of materials (BOM) describes the components that go into an assembled product. It lists each part in a hierarchical tree, by quantities required for each subassembly, all the way up to the final end-item. Finally, inventory records describing quantities of each component on hand is needed, as well as ordering policies with vendors and lead times. Relationships of these and other MRP documents are given in Figure 2.3.

The material requirements planning document should **provide four basic items of information**, when to place the order, how much to order, who to order from and when the items need to be on hand.[7] Material requirements planning systems are used to acquire or fabricate component quantities on time both for internal purposes and/or sales and distribution. MRP is a planning instrument that is geared exclusively to assembly

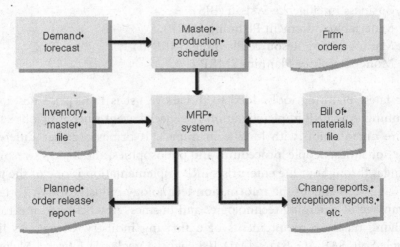

Figure 2.3:   MRP Documents.

Source: John Wiley & Sons, Inc, 2006.

---

[7] www.invatol.com, 2008.

operations. Each manufacturing unit informs its suppliers what parts it needs and when it requires them. The main aim for evolving MRP was to tackle the problem of "dependent demand"; determining how several of a particular component is required to produce the number of finished products.

MRP-I features include:

- Focus on time delivery.
- Incorporate in-house and vendor lead times.
- The date the order is required can be used as the starting date from which to develop the schedule.
- Lead times are known, or can be estimated, in advance.
- MRP calculates procurement quantities and dates as well as plans the corresponding procurement elements.
- MRP calculations are time-phased, i.e. material should be in stock following the JIT philosophy, not earlier, not later, so it is extremely important to get accurate lead times.
- Reduce inventory levels.
- Requirements sorted by vendor.
- Specifying the type, quantity, and time of requirements, in addition to calculating when and for what quantity an order has to be created.
- Time-phased orders.
- Value-projected inventory.
- Valued-projected inventory balance report.

Figure 2.3 shows the hierarchy of relationships of these systems.

Most manufacturing problems would be a lot easier if you could merely perceive them coming. Materials planning entails managing sales forecasts, creating master schedules, and running MRP. In layman's terms, this is equalizing future supply and demand. MRP enables one to plan for the future. Thus MRP involves the monitoring of stocks and, in particular, the mechanical formation of procurement proposals for purchasing and production. SAP's view of MRP is given in Figure 2.4, while Table 2.1 displays input and output information.

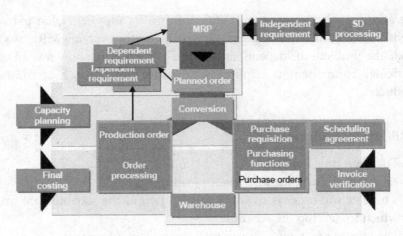

Figure 2.4:   SAP View of MRP Documents.

Source: SAP AG Germany, 2008.

Table 2.1:   Information Needed and Obtained in MRP-I.

Information needed for MRP-I	Information obtained from MRP-I
♣ Demand for all products. ♣ Lead times for all finished goods, components, parts and raw materials. ♣ Lot-sizing policies for all parts. ♣ Opening inventory levels. ♣ Safety stock requirements. ♣ Any orders previously placed but not arrived yet.	♣ Planned orders: replenishment orders to be released at a future time. ♣ Order release notice: notices to release planned orders. ♣ Action notices: notices to expedite, de-expedite, or cancel orders, or to change order quantities or due dates. ♣ Priority reports: information regarding which orders should be given priority. ♣ Inventory status information. ♣ Performance reports such as inactive items, actual lead times, late orders, etc.

Source: http://www.uoguelph.ca/~dsparlin/mrp.htm, 2008.

Module MM covers the functions of MRP. MRP began as an inventory re-ordering tool in operations involving dependent demand (the demand for materials depends upon the demand for end-items in which the materials are used). The capability of MRP systems evolved to support planning of all company resources, and currently can support business planning, production planning, purchasing, inventory control, shop floor control, cost management, capacity planning, and logistics management. The use of MRP resulted in better inventory and raw materials control, reduced need for clerical support, and reduced lead times in obtaining materials. Improved communication and better integration of planning were also gained.

2.6 MANUFACTURING RESOURCE PLANNING (MRP-II)

Like MRP-I, MRP-II focuses on the manufacturing process. The next stage of MRP-II evolution was just-in-time (JIT) methodology in the late 1980s. **MRP-II (manufacturing resource planning)** is a method to plan all resources for a manufacturer. A variety of business functions are tied into MRP-II systems to include order processing as in MRP, business planning, sales and operations planning, production plans, master production scheduling, capacity requirements planning, and capacity planning. MRP-II systems are integrated with accounting and finance subsystems to produce reports including business plans, shipping budgets, inventory projections, and purchase plans. A major purpose of MRP-II is to integrate primary functions (i.e. production, marketing and finance) and other functions such as personnel, engineering and purchasing into the planning process to improve the efficiency of the manufacturing enterprise.[8,9]

There is a tendency within the operations management field to consider ERP as a natural extension of MRP-II. Manetti (2001)[10] gave the

---

[8] Chung, S. H. and Snyder, C. A. (2000). ERP adoption: A technological evolution approach. *International Journal of Agile Management Systems*, 2(1), 24–32.

[9] Mabert, V. A., Soni, A. and Venkataramanan, M. A. (2001). Enterprise resource planning: Common myths versus evolving reality. *Business Horizons*, 69–76.

[10] Manetti, J. (2001). How technology is transforming manufacturing. *Production and Inventory Management Journal*, 54–64.

APICS definition for ERP as a method for effective planning and control of all resources needed to take, make, ship, and account for customer orders. There is some truth to this view, but ERP systems are even more comprehensive than simply extensions of manufacturing operations. ERP systems are found in practically all types of large organizations, to include chemical facilities and even universities. MRP-II functions are covered by the PP modules as well as other modules. Figure 2.5 displays the systems typically linked by an MRP system.

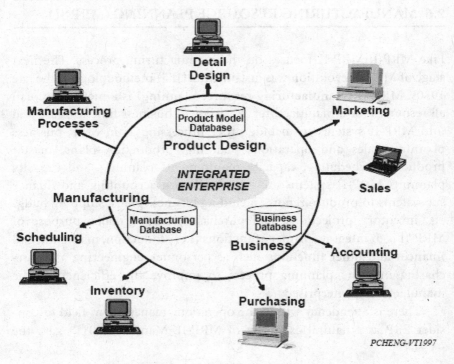

Figure 2.5:   MRP System Links.

Source: Adapted from the thesis "Effective Use of MRP-Type Computer Systems to Support Manufacturing," W. Cheng,[11] Virginia Polytechnic Institute and State University.

---

[11] Adapted from the thesis "Effective Use of MRP-Type Computer Systems to Support Manufacturing," by W. Cheng, Virginia Polytechnic Institute and State University.

2.7 ERP AND ERP MODULES

The launch of ERP systems have spawned a multi-billion dollar global supplier and consulting industry.[12,13] As more and more established organizations realize that they need to form alliances with their customers, partners and suppliers over the internet, ERP systems become a critical global issue.[14] Enterprise Resource Planning is derived from Material Resource Planning.[15] ERP systems are similar to management information systems that incorporate and automate many of the business practices associated with the operations or production aspects of a company. The term ERP was used originally to illustrate a new kind of manufacturing system that has material resource planning, human resource, finance and many other modules on a single database.[16] These typically comprise manufacturing, logistics, distribution, inventory, shipping, invoicing, and accounting. ERP software can lend a hand in the control of many business activities, like sales, delivery, billing, and production; inventory management, and human resource management systems. ERP systems are information systems that "integrate information and information-based processes within and across functional areas in an organization."[17]

They are repeatedly called back office systems indicating that customers and the general public are not directly involved. This is contrasted

---

[12] Gosain, S. (2004). Enterprise information systems as objects and carriers of institutional forces: The new iron cage? *Journal of the Association for Information Systems*, 5(4), 151–182.

[13] Umble, E. J., Haft, R. R. and Umble, M. M. (2003). Enterprise resource planning; implementation procedures and critical success factors. *European Journal of Operational Research*, 146, 241–257.

[14] Markus, M. L. C. and Tanis, C. (2000). Multisite ERP implementations. *Communications of the ACM*, 43(40), 42–46.

[15] Kesharwani, S. (2005). *ERP System Application Experience and Upsurge*. India, Pragai Prakashan.

[16] Miller, B. D. (2003). What is ERP? www2.cio.com/analyst/report2003.html

[17] Kumar, K. and Van Hillegersberg, J. (2000). ERP experiences and evolution. *Communications of the ACM*, 43(4), 23–26.

with front office systems like customer relationship management systems that deal directly with the customer. ERP systems are "commercial software packages that facilitate the integration of transaction-oriented data and business processes throughout an organization."[18] Thus their intention is to endow with a single integrated data model for several core business functions such as sales, distribution, human resources, accounting and inventory.[19]

So all functional departments that are involved in the operations or in the process of production are integrated in one system. In addition to manufacturing, warehousing, and shipping, this would embrace accounting, human resources, marketing, and strategic management. In the early days of business computing, companies used to write their own software to organize their business processes. This is an expensive approach. Since many of these processes are common across various types of businesses, common reusable software may provide cost-effective alternatives to custom software. Thus ERP software caters to a wide range of industries from service sectors like software vendors and hospitals to manufacturing industries and even to government departments. ERP systems provide cross-organization integration through embedded business processes and are generally composed of several modules including human resources, sales, finance, etc.[20] The greatest benefit that an ERP system delivers to an enterprise is its integration of many of the information systems into one enterprise-wide system.[21] Thus ERP-type systems emphasize a seamless integration

---

[18] Markus, M. L., Axline, S. *et al.* (2001). *Learning From Adopters' Experiences with ERP: Problems Encountered and Success Achieved. Enterprise systems: ERP implementation and effectiveness.*

[19] Al-Mashari, M. and Zairi, M. (2000). The effective application of SAP/R3: A proposed model of best practice. *Logistics Information Management,* 13(3), 1–10.

[20] Esteves, J. and Pastor, J. (2001). *Enterprise Resource Planning Systems Research: An Annotated Bibliography. Communications of the association for information systems.*

[21] Emily (2004). Integrating ABC & ERP system. www.focusmag.com/back_issues/issue_02/pages/bci.htm.

of data throughout an organization.[22] An enterprise resource planning (ERP) system is a business management system that comprises integrated sets of comprehensive software, which can be used, when successfully implemented, to manage and integrate all the business functions within an organisation. These sets usually include a set of mature business applications and tools for financial and cost accounting, sales and distribution, materials management, human resource, production planning and computer integrated manufacturing, supply chain, and customer information.[23,24]

ERP systems conceptually cover all computing for an organization. The idea is to centralize data and computation, so that data can be entered once in a clean form, and then be used by everyone in the organization (even by supply chain partners outside the organization) with confidence that the data are correct. However, in practice, ERP vendors sell their software in modules. Table 2.2 gives a list of SAP modules in July 2009. This information was extracted from www.oracle.com and www.microsoft.com. As with any Web site, content is subject to change.

SAP has moved away from focusing on modules, using the term **solutions** that relate to function. These solutions were last seen as:

♦ Financials.
♦ Human resources.
♦ Customer relationship management (CRM).
♦ Supplier relationship management.
♦ Product lifecycle management.
♦ Supply chain management.
♦ Business intelligence.

---

[22] Fan, M. Stallaert, J. and Whinston, A. (2000). The adoption and design methodologies of component-based enterprise systems. *European Journal of Information Systems*, 9, 25–35.

[23] Chan, R. (2001). Knowledge management in implementing ERP for SMEs. www.fit.qut.edu.au/student/?n2227169/paper.html.

[24] Yen, D. C., Chou, D. C. and Chang, J. (2002). A synergic analysis for Web-based enterprise resources-planning systems. *Computer Standards & Interfaces*, 24(4), 337–346.

Table 2.2: SAP Modules.

SAP	Description	Oracle
FI	Financial Accounting: general ledger account transaction, generates financial statements.	AP–Oracle payables. AR–Oracle receivables. AX–Global accounting engine. CE–Oracle cash management. FV–Oracle Federal financials. GL–Oracle general ledger.
CO	Controlling: internal management, cost analysis by cost center.	XTR–Oracle treasury.
AM	Asset Management: fixed-asset purchase & depreciation.	CSP–Oracle spares management. EAM–Oracle enterprise asset management.
PS	Project System: manage projects.	PA–Oracle projects.
HR	Human Resources: recruiting, hiring, training, payroll, benefits.	BEN–Oracle advanced benefits. GHR–Oracle Federal HR. HXC–Oracle Time and Labor. PER–Oracle human resources.
PM	Plant Maintenance: preventive maintenance, resource management.	OFA–Oracle assets.
MM	Materials Management: purchasing & raw materials inventory, WIP, finished goods.	BOM–Oracle bills of material. FLM–Oracle flow manufacturing. GMx–Oracle Process Manufacturing. MRP–Oracle master scheduling/MRP.
QM	Quality Management: product inspections, material certifications, quality control.	QA–Oracle quality.
PP	Production Planning: production planning & scheduling, actual production.	CHV–Oracle supplier scheduling.
SD	Sales and Distribution: records sales orders & scheduled deliveries, customer information.	AS–Oracle sales. ASO–Oracle order capture. AST–TeleSales.
CA	Cross application: workflow, business information warehouse, e-mail, industry solutions, CRM, SRM, others.	ASG–Oracle CRM gateway. BIC–Customer intelligence. SIL–Sales intelligence. BIM–Marketing intelligence. BIX–Call center intelligence. CLN–Supply chain trading.

Source: Vendor Web sites.

Only selected Oracle application modules are given here from well over 100 that they offer. Microsoft Dynamics represents the new focus which is part of the evolution in SAP and Oracle systems. CRM, supply chain management, and business intelligence used to be major add-on applications, tapping external software vendors such as Siebel Systems for CRM and SAS, IBM, or SPSS for data mining (business intelligence), and linked to ERP systems through middleware. Oracle purchased Siebel Systems and made their CRM product a module in their system. SAP responded by developing their own CRM. Both vendors provide internal modules for what had been external add-on (bolt-on) products. This demonstrates the continuing evolution of ERP/EIS systems.

2.7.1 Relative Module Use

The degree of module use is reported in Table 2.3 while Figure 2.6 presents information extracted from the three studies of ERP use that we have been monitoring.

The most popular module in the U.S. was financial and accounting, which is the most obvious application needed by an organization. The Swedish study indicated that materials management, production planning, order entry, and purchasing modules were just as popular. In the Korean study, all modules had relatively high usage, but the first five listed were very high at over 90 percent. This might indicate a trend for manufacturing organizations to use more modules, but it might also be specific to Korea. Other modules, given at the bottom of Table 4 and each with adoption rates of less than 50 percent, are either not considered as critical or involve less specificity in best practices. These are similar for both studies, although human resources modules were slightly more popular in Sweden. There have been noted differences in the ease with which different modules are implemented. All financial modules tend to be relatively easy to implement. Those modules relating to manufacturing and human resources also have been implemented with noted success. On the other hand, modules supporting less structured activities, such as sales and marketing, have encountered notable implementation difficulty. Therefore, one reason to implement

Table 2.3: Relative ERP Module Use.

Module	Use — Midwestern U.S. (%)	Use — Sweden (%)	Use — Korea (%)
Financial & Accounting	91.5	87.3	92.5
Materials Management	89.2	91.8	94.1
Production Planning	88.5	90.5	91.5
Order Entry	87.7	92.4	90.5
Purchasing	86.9	93.0	93.1
Financial Control	81.5	82.3	85.0
Distribution/Logistics	75.4	84.8	85.9
Asset Management	57.7	63.3	81.4
Quality Management	44.6	47.5	77.6
Personnel/Human Resources	44.6	57.6	78.4
Maintenance	40.8	44.3	72.2
R&D Management	30.8	34.2	69.5

Source: Mabert *et al.* (2000), Olhager and Selldin (2003), Katerattanakul *et al.* (2006).

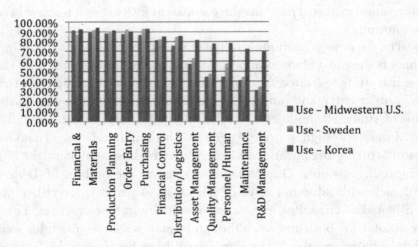

Figure 2.6: Display of Relative ERP Module Use.

ERP in modules is because of the relative need for components of the overall system.

Another (and probably the compelling) reason is cost. Full ERP systems cost a reported $5 million for very small versions to over $100 million for very large implementations. The fewer modules implemented, the lower the cost. Additionally, it sometimes makes sense to implement the system in bits (phased implementation) rather than try to bring the entire massive system on-line at one time (big-bang implementation). Thus, rolling out an ERP by module sometimes makes sense as well. For a number of reasons, ERP in practice is usually implemented by module.

Often firms will apply the concept of "**best-of-breed**," mixing modules from different vendors. The Mabert *et al.* study found that a single ERP package was utilized as designed by the vendor in only 40 percent (56 percent in Sweden) of the over 400 respondents to their survey. The most common strategic approach in the U.S. (50 percent, as opposed to 30 percent in Sweden) was to supplement a single ERP package. In fewer cases, the idea of best-of-breed was applied (4 percent in both studies). As might be expected by the enormity of the undertaking, few of the surveyed implementations were entirely constructed in-house (less than 1 percent in the U.S., 2 percent in Sweden).

The idea of best-of-breed approaches is to take advantages of what is perceived as specific vendor-relative advantage in particular areas of application. One vendor's human resource module might be used in conjunction with another vendor's financial and accounting system, and yet a third vendor's materials management modules. Stevens reported one instance of best-of-breed integration triggered by merger.[25] In 1999, Honeywell and AlliedSignal were merged, and the best approaches of each firm's existing ERP systems were examined, with those components judged to be superior retained in the merged firm. Quite often third-party software designed to integrate software applications from several vendors (**middleware** — see Chapter 10) is needed.[26] The role of middleware products is to enable cross-platform operating system communications. This means that software applications such as e-commerce, data warehouses, customer relationship management, supply chain software, and other enhancements can be added to ERP systems.

---

[25] Stevens, T. (2001). All's fair in integration. *Industry Week*, 24–29.
[26] Bingi, P., Sharma, M. K. and Godla, J. K. (1999). Critical issues affecting an ERP implementation. *Information Systems Management*, 7–14.

Middleware also allows connection of best-of-breed modules to the ERP backbone.

If a firm chooses to utilize their own methods within an ERP, Davenport (1998) gave choices of rewriting the code internally, or using the existing system with interfaces.[27] Both approaches add time and cost to implementation, and thus would dilute the integration benefits of the ERP. The more customization of an ERP, the less ability to communicate seamlessly within system components and across supplier and customer systems.

A related concept is the idea of **federalization**. Davenport (1998) used this term to describe the process of rolling out different versions of an ERP system in each regional unit, tailoring each location's system to accommodate local operating practices.[28] Hewlett-Packard, Monsanto, and Nestle have all used this approach, establishing a common core of ERP modules shared by all units, but allowing other modules to be operated and controlled locally.

2.7.2 Customization Issues

Organizations adopting ERP systems face the problem of what degree of customization to adopt. The best fit with organizational needs would involve intensive reengineering, and development of ERP software by internal staff. But this method is unrealistically slow and expensive. It is much faster and less troublesome to adopt a vendor's software directly. However, in practice, almost every organization adopting an ERP must modify vendor software to at least some degree. Customization is a major issue in ERP design.

2.8 COMPARATIVE COVERAGE BETWEEN MRP, ERP, EIS

Table 2.4 compares characteristics of the three broad periods of software evolution, from MRP through ERP and on to EIS.

---

[27] Davenport, T. H. (1998). Putting the enterprise into the enterprise system. *Harvard Business Review*, 121–131.
[28] *Ibid.*

Table 2.4: Comparison of three periods of software evolution.

Particular	MRP	ERP	Extended ERP or EIS
Year	1960–70 MRP-I 1980 MRP-II	1990	2000s
1. Features	MRP-II extends MRP systems to share information with other functional areas. Key component of MRP-II is storing operational information centrally. Just-in-time (JIT) is a Japanese concept which has transformed manufacturing management. It has reduced product cost, and enhanced productivity, product quality and delivery time by as much as 80 percent in some companies. Manufacturers are anxious to implement this system but it needs a high level of co-operation and support from the vendors.	ERP systems seek to integrate all business activities and processes throughout the organization. Goal is to provide real-time information to all employees that need it.	An EIS is a particular category of DSS designed to maintain decision-making at the pinnacle of an organization.

(Continued)

Table 2.4: (*Continued*)

Particular	MRP	ERP	Extended ERP or EIS
2. Diagram			
	Source: ScmEdge, 2008.	*Source:* John Wiley, 2006.	*Source:* EIS Directory service.
3. No parameter for Implementation	Big-Bang Implementation.	Phased implementation, Big-Bang, vanilla Approach.	The Big-Bang approach: organizations implement the new ERP system all at once and scrap their existing legacy systems. The "United Federation" approach: business units/divisions are free to implement independent systems but common processes such as financial reporting are linked across the enterprise. The "Test the Waters" approach: focus is on a few key processes.

(*Continued*)

Table 2.4: (Continued)

Particular	MRP	ERP	Extended ERP or EIS
4. Vendors	Conventional Tailor-made Legacy System developed In-house.	SAP-AG, BaaN, Oracle.	Microsoft Dynamics.
5. Time and Cost	Much Less-cost and Less time-consuming	Costs of implementing an ERP are driven by a number of factors including; Number of employees, number of modules that will be implemented, organization's processes must be modified to conform with the ERP system, amount of consulting.	Cost is very high as there is often Web linkage. But in the long-term there is a great potential for cost reduction.
6. Components	Manufacturing and Production related modules.	Includes all the functions of management planning, coordination, decision making, staffing, etc.	Early EIS products were developed for use on high-powered computers, but current products target the client/server platform. These more flexible platforms can adapt to changes in the organization and in technology. Use of real-time data leads to faster, more informed decisions.

Table 2.5: Gartner View of Evolution.

	1980s	1990s	2000s
Competitive focus	Manufacturing	Enterprise	Supply Chain
Enterprise strategy	Inventory reduction	Business process efficiency	Revenue enhancement
Technology focus	Automation	Integration	Inter-operability
Process focus	Departmental alignment	Enterprise-wide closed loop	Customer differentiating
Organizational focus	Department	Business process	Product/Market channel

Note: The term EIS was first coined at MIT in the 1970s. The first EISs were developed by huge firms willing to take risks to increase competitive advantage. By the mid-1980s several vendors had urbanized wide customer bases and EIS technology continues to be shored up today.

2.9 EIS AS PER THE GARTNER VIEW

An EIS is a particular category of DSS designed to maintain decision-making at the top of an organization. An EIS may facilitate a top-level management function i.e. the Managing Director gets an accurate macro-picture of operations, and a synopsis of what competitors are doing. These systems are by and large trouble-free in effortlessly accessing information in ways that can be rapidly absorbed via graphs, charts, etc. Table 2.5 gives this comparison.

2.10 CONCLUSION

Enterprise Resource Planning (ERP systems) has been adopted by many businesses in the past decade. These systems have revolutionized ways of doing business by integrating an organization's business processes, sharing common data and practices across the entire enterprise, producing and accessing information in a real-time environment. Organizations have realized important tangible and intangible benefits from ERP/EIS including general and administrative, expense reduction, margin enhancement, revenue growth, improved customer satisfaction, personnel and information technology (IT). Despite these benefits, many companies have had serious problems implementing ERP/EIS systems. These problems have caused many companies to abandon their ERP/EIS initiative or implement the system in a limited capacity. Companies have misled ERP/EIS implementation when they see ERP/EIS as a magic way to become competitive, and not as a tool that depends on the way the company uses it. The tool can help companies to become competitive, or it can also take them out of business. A loss of control can occur for many reasons when an ERP/EIS system is implemented; inadequate project definition, planning and implementation is one of the most significant causes for loss of control.

The core idea of ERP/EIS is the complete integration of an organization's computing system. Despite obvious advantages to vendors of each adopting organization installing the entire suite of modules offered, only about half of the implementations seem to be of this nature. Organizations select common modules because not every organization needs every module vendors develop. In fact, vendors seem to recognize this through their recent emphasis on products tailored to specific industries.

There are also other important reasons for implementation of ERP/EIS products different from vendors' original design. A very important one is that full system implementation is very expensive. By selecting particular modules, organizations can cut initial implementation costs significantly. While vendors might argue that in the long run this might be ineffective than full implementation at the beginning, in practice information systems projects rarely go as planned, nor do they tend to stay within originally planned budgets. Thus there is a great reduction in risk to organizations by trying particular modules first, often seeing how the new system is digested by the organization before taking on additional modules.

There is also a difference in the difficulty of implementing different modules. Financial and accounting modules are typically installed first, as they involve the most structured application. This makes it easier to implement, and easier for the organization to digest. Other modules such as materials management and planning also tend to work well. Conversely, support to less structured environments, such as sales and marketing, tend to be more problematic.

Related to the idea of implementing ERPs in modules are the concepts of best-of-breed, middleware, customization, and federalization. Best-of-breed implementation is idealistic, seeking the best module across vendors and combining whatever mix is viewed as best for the particular organization. This approach is not widely adopted, probably because it involves obvious risks of coordination. It also tends to be more expensive. Middleware is an important type of software making it possible to add on specialty software products. Customization is an approach to implement a vendor's ERP/EIS system tailored to organizational needs. Customization is done internally, as opposed to middleware, which is usually accomplished with third party vendor software. Federalization allows different parts of the organization to utilize different modules, or possibly different levels of customization.

☆ KEYWORDS

- ☆ **By-product:** A by-product is an additional product resulting from the normal processing of the primary item but whose input is not planned; often found in the process industry.
- ☆ **Co-product:** A co-product is an additional product resulting from the process whose input and output is planned.
- ☆ **FIFO stock rotation:** Items may be sequenced for put away using the First In First Out principle.
- ☆ **LIFO storage:** Items may be sequenced for put away using the Last in First Out principle.
- ☆ **Manufactured:** Those items that are designed and fabricated in-house.
- ☆ **Maximum quantity:** The largest quantity that should be planned for any discrete order.
- ☆ **Minimum quantity:** Specifies the smallest order quantity that will be planned by the system.

☆ **MRP control code:** This field specifies whether or not the part is under MRP control when planning replenishment orders.

☆ **MRP planning policy code:** Specifies how MRP will plan orders for replenishment of material. Planning methods such as order point, lot for lot, period order point, etc. are usually included.

☆ **Multiple quantity:** Specifies that material will be ordered in increments e.g., multiple-pack sizes.

☆ **Purchased:** Those items that are bought from outside sources.

☆ TERMINOLOGY REVIEW

a. What is meant by material requirements planning [MRP-1]?
b. Define manufacturing resource planning [MRP-II].
c. Explain the different stages of an integrated system.
d. Elaborate how the material requirements planning (MRP) system uses a database approach to manage the large amount of information involved in the material-requirements estimation process.

☆ COMPETENCY REVIEW

1. **Pragmatic Questions**

   a. How do enterprise-wide information systems facilitate in motivating organizations to enlarge or adopt systems?
   b. How do the various functions of manufacturing management accommodate integrated software?
   c. To design an efficient and effective inventory control system for the manufactured housing (MH) industry, it is necessary to accelerate the flow of information and products across the supply chain with the help of an integrated system. Explain.
   d. Comment on this statement! *"To achieve this goal, the system needs three ingredients: generators of quick information flow, generators of*

> *quick material flow, and facilitators of both information flow and material flow."*

2. **Briefly comment on:**

    a. The alternative perspectives on data to be included in an enterprise-wide area.

    b. The MRP system can be used to develop better planning strategies and to respond quickly to unexpected changes in demand for the organization.

    c. The roles Enterprise Resource Planning Systems (ERPs) play in an organization and the challenging task of implementing and managing the IS function.

    d. The ERP system investigates the interaction among different business processes.

☆ SUGGESTED READING

Books

Brady, J., Monk, E. and Wagner, B. (2001). *Concepts in Enterprise Resource Planning.* Course Technology.

Curran, T. A. and Ladd, A. (2000). *SAP R/3, Business Blueprint*, 2nd Ed. Prentice Hall.

Hopp, W. J. and Spearman, M. L. (2001). *Factory Physics: Foundations of Manufacturing Management.* Irwin.

Sheikh, K. (2003). *Manufacturing Resource Planning (MRP II): With an Introduction to ERP, SCM, and CRM.* New York: McGraw-Hill Professional.

Wallace, T. F. and Kremzar, M. H. (2001). *ERP: Making it Happen — The Implementers' Guide to Success with Enterprise Resource Planning.* John Wiley & Sons.

Journal Articles

Agrawal, A., Minis, I. and Nagi, R. (2000). Cycle time reduction by improved MRP-based production planning. *International Journal of Production Research*, 38(18), 4823–4841.

Ho, C. J., Kim, S. C. and Koo, M. (2001). MRP system performance under lumpy demand environments. *Production Planning & Control*, 12(4), 316–325.

Koh, S. C. L., Saad, S. M. and Jones, M. H. (2002). Uncertainty under MRP-planned manufacture: Review and categorization. *International Journal of Production Research*, 40(10), 2399–2421.

Kumar, K. and van Hillegersberg, J. (2000). ERP Experiences and Evolution. *Communications of the ACM*, 43(4), 23–26.

Manetti, J. (2001). How technology is transforming manufacturing. *Production and Inventory Management Journal*, 54–64.

Nagendra, P. B. and Das, S. K. (2001). Finite capacity scheduling method for MRP with lot-size restrictions. *International Journal of Production Research*, 39(8), 1603–1623.

Palaniswamy, R. and T. Frank (2000). Enhancing manufacturing performance with ERP systems. *Information Management Journal*.

Stevens, T. (2001). All's fair in integration. *Industry Week*, 24–29.

White Papers

Komiega, K. (2001). The ABC's of ERP. www.search390.techtarget.corrVtip/1,289483,sid10_gci760533,00.html

Mohan, R. (2003). Will Your ERP/MRP address all direct materials needs? IT toolbox ERP. www. erp.ittoolbox.com (accessed on January 2005).

SAP (2004). Manufacturing Strategy: An Adaptive Perspective, Flexible, Fast, Adaptive Processes — The Key to Competitive Manufacturing. www.thespot4sap.com/Atricles/SAP_Modules.asp.

CHAPTER 3

IMPLEMENTATION LIFE CYCLE

Quotation

Implementation cycle is characterized by complexity, uncertainy and a long time-scale. It is about people and issues that affect the business — it is a multi-disciplinary effort.

Structure

- ♣ *Quick look at chapter themes*
- ♣ *Learning objectives*
- ♣ *Case study:* Logistics Modernization: Lessons learned from the army's largest ERP implementation
- ♣ *Sketch of EIS implementation life cycle*
- ♣ *Introduction*
- 3.1 Impact of EIS Projects
- 3.2 Guidelines for EIS Implementation
- 3.3 Implementation Strategies
    - 3.3.1 Implementation Issues
    - 3.3.2 Understanding EIS
    - 3.3.3 Implementation Methodologies
    - 3.3.4 Post-Implementation Depression
- 3.4 Advantages and Disadvantages of Alternative EIS Development Methods
- 3.5 EIS Proposal Evaluation
- 3.6 Managing Risk on EIS Projects

♣ **QUICK LOOK AT CHAPTER THEMES**

Enterprise Information Systems, or EIS, take a major share of most large firm's IT budget. These systems form the backbone of a firm's business processes and link the firm's key information assets. In today's IT-enabled business atmosphere, where service is a top priority, almost all employees have to interact with EIS systems. EIS implementations markedly improve delivery, increase inventory turns, and result in faster financial closings for the companies that implement them. The promise these systems provide catch the attention of most enterprise executives. In combination with best practices, enterprises report that EISs reduce IT budgets up to 25 percent. So, it is not surprising that more than 60 percent of the Fortune 1000 companies have installed or implementing EIS packaged software solutions. But companies pay for the results. EIS systems have price tags up to billions of dollars.

♣ LEARNING OBJECTIVES

This chapter reviews the usage of Enterprise Information Systems (EIS) and presents an EIS development life cycle that will improve system development and usage. They are the software tools used to manage all the data of the organization and to provide information to those who need it when they need it.[1] Consideration of the EIS development life cycle enables identification of critical issues. This chapter covers managerial issues related to implementing and customizing enterprise systems, with the objective of broadening student understanding of how leveraging enterprise systems can gain tactical advantages for a firm. Successful EIS implementations require the buy-in and coordination of many internal and external parties. Implementation of the developed system is an important phase where the old or manual system is replaced fully or partially by a new system. This chapter explains the details of how implementation is accomplished and the important points to be considered while doing so:

♣ Avoidance of pitfalls, remuneration, internal and external factors, and training are important issues.
♣ Actual implementation is done in various phases.
♣ Range of relevant topics include EIS market-place development, and vendor selection.
♣ Range of issues which an implementer should be aware of.

---

[1] Ragowsky, A. and Somers, T. M. (2002). Special section: Enterprise resource planning. *Journal of Management Information Systems*, 19(1), 11–16.

♣ CASE STUDY

Logistics Modernization: Lessons learned from the army's largest ERP implementation

The Logistics Modernization Program (LMP) is one of the largest and most comprehensive business transformation and technological modernization efforts in existence and forms the cornerstone of the Army's full-scale logistics transformation effort, the Single Army Logistics Enterprise (SALE). Since deploying 4,000 users in July 2003, the LMP has delivered impressive results. LMP manages $4.5 billion in inventory, processes transactions with 50,000 vendors, and integrates with more than 80 Department of Defense systems. Compliant with the Clinger–Cohen Act and certified by the DoD Information Technology Security Certification and Accreditation Process, LMP has achieved these accomplishments while sustaining two large legacy systems simultaneously and concurrently with enterprise resource planning (ERP) development and deployment. On March 8, 2006, under the direction of Kevin Carroll, the Army's Program Executive Office Enterprise Information Systems (PEO EIS) assumed operational control of LMP to offer its expertise managing large-scale systems implementations. LMP hasn't made such strides without challenges. In reviewing what the program has done right and wrong, there is significant value in communicating lessons learned to other program managers, many of whom may be embarking on their first information technology-related programs. Project Managers can take the lessons learned and leverage the good decisions while avoiding those that were less than advantageous. In doing so, we ensure America's war fighters get the products and services they need at the best price without entangling taxpayer dollars in bureaucratic red tape — an approach that is crucial in wartime.

Communications: Critical to Manage User, Stakeholder Expectations ERP implementation is about business transformation, not technology. Business transformation cannot occur without well-planned and executed communications activities to deliver the context in which people need to understand the goals of the project. This is particularly critical to the success of long-term projects affecting thousands of users and contributing to national security objectives. In fact, communications in such circumstances are crucial when you take into account the natural resistance users feel on being asked to give up a homegrown system to learn new processes required by an ERP. In most cases, soldier-users have been employing the legacy systems for years to accomplish their daily work. They thoroughly understand the old systems, and even as they curse old systems' shortcomings, many users have come to judge themselves as experts in their use. And there is a certain level of comfort, confidence, and pride inherent in that attained expertise. The implementation of an ERP solution will upset this apple cart. This is where an active change management, communications, and outreach program becomes necessary.

Today, Army G4, Army Materiel Command, and PEO EIS engage in frequent communications with LMP's current and potential customers as well as stakeholders in the Army and DoD. LMP has made it a priority to make the community more aware of the success as well as the challenges of LMP. This outreach involves keeping everyone informed of the program's progress and ensuring the new PM office, G4, Army Materiel Command, and the customers all have a clear line of common factual knowledge and understanding among them. Communications and outreach to all interested stakeholders, but especially to the users, play a pivotal role in ensuring the system deployment exceeds all positive expectations. A lack of effective communications contributed to a falloff in support for LMP from executive-level and middle management staff. Specifically, LMP failed to set realistic expectations about initial productivity. It is a fact in any systems implementation that productivity levels decline temporarily during the initial period after deployment. Because of the huge productivity improvements that are available with ERP, failing to adequately communicate expectations led to a distorted perception about what the system could immediately achieve. The effects have persisted until today, even though the system consistently exhibits superior performance according to all metrics. These lessons haven't been lost on the Communications-Electronics Life-Cycle Management Command, one of the first LMP deployment sites. C-E LCMC commanders have advised senior leadership to get users involved early on in the process and to explain the importance of the program and how it fits into the bigger picture. While bracing team leaders to expect a dip in productivity to go along with the learning curve, LMP has learned that good communications up front will be instrumental in making that learning curve shallower and shorter. Another key lesson learned by LMP: Any approved changes to processes and procedures need to be effectively communicated through a series of planned notifications. In addition, Army and other government management structures need to be thoroughly briefed and educated on any aspects of the project that affect all the organizations collecting, owning, and using the logistics data contained within the system.

These communications activities enable more effective and structured management reviews and greater understanding of any course corrections required during the project. In any large ERP implementation, improved communications activities have pervasive effects throughout the project, even impacting the technical performance of the system. For example, during early phases of the project, it is important to communicate how all key processes and transactions are mapped to user roles within the organization. In doing so, the project team can more easily work with users to restrict roles to functional levels, and more readily configure the solution to meet higher-level business requirements (as opposed to aligning the system to meet specific job responsibilities, which nevertheless must be modified to realize the goal of delivering standardized data). As a result, the system has fewer variables to manage and maintain; managers and end-users get a more simplified view of the new environment; the system has a cleaner data feed into security systems; and training and technical support activities are simplified.

Training: The User Glue One of the important factors LMP had to address regarding training was an initial failure to have the new business processes fully documented before going into training. In addition, the team found that some of the hesitancy related to implementing the system had to do with a subset of end-users who needed a more in-depth explanation of the new processes — an explanation that went beyond what was needed to operate the system. For example, in supply and demand planning exercises, some individuals readily gravitated to the new operations, while others needed a complete picture of the underlying reasoning behind why the processes were changing. Training must ensure that users understand the value LMP brings to the war fighter. Logistics transformation allows soldiers on the front lines to have insight immediately into the supplies they need. When applied to LMP, an effective training approach ultimately allows soldiers to get supplies faster at a time when having supplies means the difference in mission success. Moreover, users are more interested in a new system and new business processes when they can provide input on how to improve them. This mutual exchange of information within training and other site-readiness activities creates a more knowledgeable workforce and lowers anxiety levels. In addition, the project staff needs to assure site personnel that they are equal contributors within a single team, together managing the training resources and the training content. To achieve this total-team approach, LMP leaders recommend including site-training coordinators, operational experts, functional experts, and managers who contribute to defining training requirements in the training mix. Training coordinators and instructors need to work with project personnel to plan for available training facilities and equipment, review and refine the description of new roles and responsibilities, and conduct overview training on the new software's capabilities. In addition, Army subject matter experts need to participate in quality-assurance and dry-run activities to ensure that new system requirements are adequately addressed in course material.

Comprehensive Data Cleansing: A Must-Do Eager to meet the urgent needs of wartime logistics, LMP and C-E LCMC jumped to convert legacy systems over to LMP in July 2003. The lesson for both the program office and the deployed sites was clear: Doing what one can to understand the data in one's legacy systems, and very carefully following the procedures to prepare the data will pay off. It is not so easy to go back and fix data once the conversion has taken place. Whenever any organization undergoes a transition from using a large number of systems to a single-system environment, conflicting sets of data must be reconciled to provide an accurate view of reality. LMP learned that Army subject matter experts could have simplified much of the complexity underlying the data cleansing efforts. Much of the data interaction between systems is a government customer function, and the Army understands these data. The appropriate role of contractors in data migration should be to guide the Army in understanding the end-state data requirements, which reflect the much more disciplined approach inherent in an ERP system. LMP found that factors such as a lack of serial numbers and invalid inventory locations compounded the transfer of data between legacy systems and the new environment. Before the staff could perform any data migration to the new environment, item names, units of measure, unit price, and obsolete items to be deleted all had to be precisely identified. For example, if the bill of material of any acquisition is inaccurate, personnel at the receiving end are often confronted with a situation where a shipment lacks a simple part to complete the installation or configuration of a needed solution. Thorough data cleansing activities are critical to achieving the total asset visibility enabled by LMP. In addition, the system reduces the time spent on activities that would otherwise require follow-up work stemming from discrepancies among numerous systems. For example, legacy systems often contain multiple versions of a single business transaction, which makes logistics and finance information difficult to reconcile.

System Support: Helping the Customer the Smart Way Lessons learned during the initial LMP deployment resulted in the team implementing several improvements to system support activities. Support personnel now use a root-cause-analysis procedure to establish the source of all problems and identify the appropriate fixes. LMP leaders have worked to ensure that support procedures take advantage of the knowledge of end users, functional experts, and other subject matter experts — people who are already familiar with the new environment — to develop scripts for support personnel responding to user requests. In addition, by establishing rules for properly categorizing all help desk calls, support personnel now serve as a feedback loop, contributing to information the project team uses to improve the system. LMP found that automated help desk tools, processes, and procedures complemented a strong site-support staff. Problem tickets are documented using the Advanced Help Desk Tool, which assigns tickets to workflow coordinators and improves response time; and support staff document repeat conditions in the system for use by other personnel. The key lesson learned is that developing and implementing a support strategy make a significant difference in system availability and customer satisfaction. As a result, LMP has achieved a sustained 99.998 percent level of system availability, beating the industry-accepted standard of 99.5 percent.

LMP: Poised to Deliver the Full Benefits of ERP LMP is operational, proven, and has been supporting the requirements of soldiers around the world, including those on the frontlines in Iraq and Afghanistan, on a daily basis since 2003. As LMP worked through quality issues and strengthened project-management controls, the system's performance markedly improved and is well positioned to achieve its ultimate, intended benefits: delivering real-time situational awareness, vastly improved decision-making capabilities in logistics and finance, significantly reduced costs, and major productivity improvements. LMP requires Army logistics professionals to adopt new business processes, policies, and procedures to fully realize the benefits of the system. All organizations have an inherent resistance to change, so making the transition from multiple systems and localized processes to a unified logistics information environment requires a commitment to change. The transition often involves sacrificing previously established methods for new, standardized processes, but the benefits are enormous. These new processes result in the delivery of data applicable to all organizations across the Army, rather than a system marked by isolated islands of information difficult to reconcile, and errors that make the entire organization less efficient and flexible.

When fully deployed with 17,000 users, LMP will deliver total situational awareness of Army assets within five seconds of submitting a request, enabling more rapid decision-making capabilities and improving soldier readiness. Inventories will be significantly reduced because LMP allows logisticians to better plan and allocate resources, which will also dramatically reduce theater footprint. In addition, by delivering the capability to improve planning for maintenance and supply activities, LMP will have a direct effect on weapon systems' operational availability and will positively impact operational readiness.

Source: Coker (2006).[2]

♣ SKETCH OF EIS IMPLEMENTATION LIFE CYCLE

Developing and deploying enterprise information systems means dealing with multifaceted and cross-disciplinary enterprise integration issues. EIS is one step ahead of ERP systems, as shown in Figure 3.1.

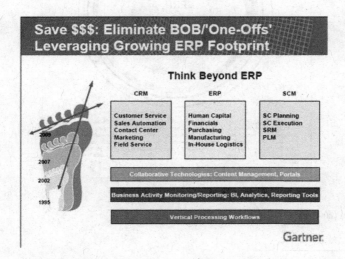

Figure 3.1: Relationship of EIS Components.

Source: http://blogs.zdnet.com/BTL/images/erp.png

---

[2] This case study was adapted from Defense AT&L (2006). http://www.dau.mil/pubs/dam/11_12_2006/11_12_2006_cok_nd06.pdf

The rationale of any information system is to sustain the activities of an organization. EIS provides a means to compete on a global basis. It is something which can better integrate all departments. The best way to go into the depth about the EIS implementation lifecycle is to build on the ERP System implementation life cycle as shown in Figure 3.2.

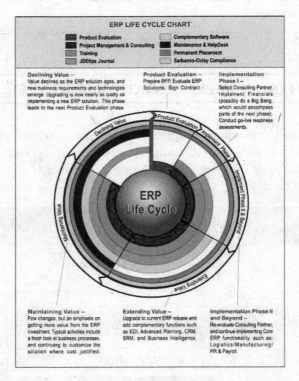

Figure 3.2: ERP Life Cycle.

Source: Klee (2000).[3]

---

[3] Adapted from the article written by Klee, A. The ERP Life Cycle: From Birth to Death and Birth Again. Andy Klee is the President of Klee Associates, Inc. established in 1998, after his decade-long career with JD Edwards, Klee Associates publishes the JDEtips and SAPtips Journals, read by thousands of IT staff and key business users at over 750 JDE and SAP clients. Klee also runs successful consulting, training, permanent placement, and helpdesk services. www.erptips.com/ERPLifeCycleArticle.asp

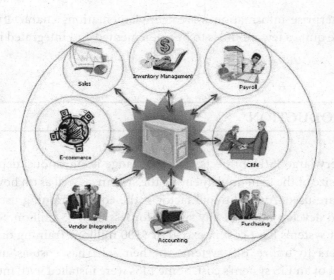

Figure 3.3: Internet-connected EIS Components.
Source: www.erpsoftwarebusiness.com[4]

EIS Application is a name for formerly developed ERP systems which take account of all parts of a business, using normal Internet browsers as their clients (Figure 3.3).

The implementation of an enterprise system requires a set of process changes. Effectual communication will lead to the development of conviction and exchange of information needed for these process changes and ultimately the acceptance of the technology. Finally, there are several "unknowns" in an enterprise system implementation environment and enhanced communication which can lead to more acceptances of these unknowns and the reduction of needless anxiety. There is a growing need to understand challenges, issues, and solutions associated with the design, implementation and management of EIS. The current development of equipment planning tools has combined traditional planning and management functions with the other business functions to generate an EIS.

---

[4] ERP Software Business is a website which facilitates in providing knowledge on ERP-related areas. http://www.erpsoftwarebusiness.com

These enterprise information system implementations characteristically necessitate quite a few modules to be implemented and integrated into the business.

♣ INTRODUCTION

EIS are very large IS/IT projects. The cost range is enormous, depending upon the size of the firm implementing the system, as well as on how many modules are used. An additional factor is the cost of training users. It is difficult to develop much of any system for less than $5 million. Some of the largest systems have cost in excess of $100 million. Training organizational users to utilize EIS systems in their jobs has cost as much as 20 percent of an EIS system's cost. Some EISs were installed with much less training, but this usually proves to be a major mistake. All IS/IT projects begin with a project proposal, generated by users or management. Because of their large size and their pervasive impact on an organization, the first step for an EIS proposal is a thorough analysis of the proposal as an investment. Once EIS projects are adopted, their cost and progress should be carefully monitored to keep track and control the project's progress. A properly implemented EIS system can dramatically enhance the organization's ability to lower costs, run leaner, and improve customer service.

EIS implementations vary with what has worked well with ERP implementation. Many organizations today, particularly EIS customers, have an EIS platform in position. Systems such as eCRM/SCM/Product Life Cycle Management entail an elevated level of integration with existing applications. In a conventional EIS implementation, the ERP application, typically SAP R/3, is the natural focus of IT (see Figure 3.4). Integration becomes a question of how to connect other applications to the EIS application. Now integration itself can be the focus of the implementation.

The process of EIS implementation is referred to as "ERP Implementation Life Cycle". Figure 3.5 shows the steps involved in completing the lifecycle.

EIS implementation projects characteristically progress through five major phases of the development lifecycle, as shown in Table 3.1.

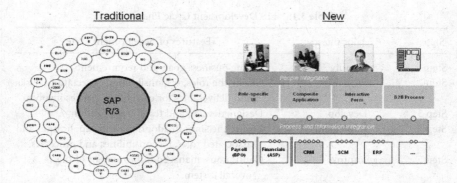

Figure 3.4: Comparison between Traditional ERP and Contemporary EIS.

Source: SAP AG (2005).[5]

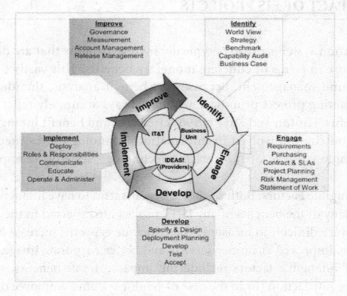

Figure 3.5: ERP Implementation Life Cycle.

Source: http://www.ideas.com.au[6]

---

[5] With more than 47,800 customers, it's no wonder SAP is the recognized leader in collaborative business software. For more details, see the vendor chapter of this book which will exclusively discuss distinguished vendors.

[6] IDEAS! is a national organization that has evolved its services and product offering through steady, profitable growth and investment. With offices in Melbourne, Brisbane and Canberra, IDEAS! has the ability to share resources and knowledge nationally to better service clients within given geographic regions.

Table 3.1:   EIS Development Cycle Phases.

Steps	Major phases	Features of development cycle
Step 1	Identify	Define business goals and requirements.
Step 2	Engage	Clarify the roles, responsibilities, expectations, risks and deliverables for each of the parties involved.
Step 3	Develop	Design, develop and test the application.
Step 4	Implement	Ensure the smooth adoption of the application and associated roles, responsibilities and processes.
Step 5	Improve	Continuous, managed improvement of the overall system.

3.1 IMPACT OF EIS PROJECTS

Information systems projects typically involve benefits that are difficult to measure in terms of concrete monetary benefits. This vastly complicates sound management, because cost-benefit analysis, the ideal tool for evaluating project proposals, will not always accurately reflect project benefits. Hinton and Kaye (1996) cited cost and benefit intangibility, hidden outcomes involved in information technology investment, and the changing nature of information technology systems as important issues.[7]

Intangible Factors: Both costs and benefits tend to have intangible features. Many of the benefits of any IS/IT project are expected in the future, and are very difficult to measure. These include expected increase in market share, improved customer service, and better corporate image. Other types of intangible factors include the impact of soft benefits, such as employee satisfaction (or in the case of vendor systems, employee dissatisfaction), supply chain integration, and the ability to support e-business operations. These intangible benefits often lead to real competitive advantage, although the precise economic impact is often difficult to accurately estimate.

---

[7] Hinton, M. and Kay, R. (1996). Investing in information technology: A lottery? *Management Accounting*, 74(10), p. 52.

Hidden Outcomes: Other aspects of EIS projects often involve complex results. EIS may change organizational power. Specific groups may have held power in the older system, and a new EIS system can have negative impact on the teamwork of the organization. EIS systems include components of the organization's communications network. Experienced employees may have established power bases because they were efficient at accessing key information. An EIS system can be viewed as a threat, in a positive sense, by making more information more readily available to those who need it. On the other hand, an EIS system is complex, and those who are involved in its implementation may at least temporarily gain a power base because they know how to access information from the EIS while others are still learning its intricate workings. Figure 3.6 shows a view of these hidden costs.

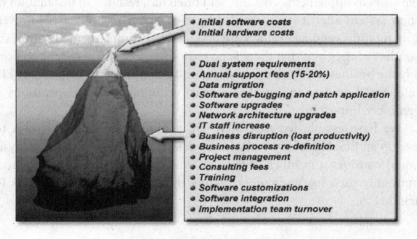

Figure 3.6: Hidden Software Project Costs.
Source: Enlightening Solutions (2008).[8]

---

[8] *Casey Lawrence* "The hidden costs behind ERP software", *Enterprise Software Specialist* Enlightening Solutions has over 25 years of experience in the selection, implementation and integration of technology into business processes in over 100 companies worldwide. Our professionals have a strong working knowledge of the best practices in finance, distribution, manufacturing, Logistics, CRM, WMS, SCP, PLM and POS. http://www.enlightening-solutions.com/about.html

There is also the behavioral factor of working with more automated systems. Computers can make work more productive and more attractive. But they can also change work roles to emphasize skills in which specific employees have no training, making them feel less productive.

Failure to identify the impact of projects often is not noticed until project implementation. At that stage, the problems created are more difficult to deal with. It is important to consider the systems aspects of projects, and try to predict how the project will change how people do their jobs. Thorough user-involvement can make project impact more obvious, as well as make it easier to reconcile and convince users of the project's benefits.

The Changing Nature of Information Technology: There are many excellent applications of computer technology to aid businesses. But a major problem is that technology is highly dynamic. Some EIS projects take years to implement. This can, and often has, resulted in installation of a new system after it is superseded by even newer technology. However, more recently, vendor products are designed to be implemented within six months or less, given that there is no customization of the system, so possibly the business rule still applies. If long-term projects to implement EIS are adopted, understanding their impact on organizational operations is even more important.

We have established that there are a number of optional ways to develop an EIS. Hopefully we have also established that a rational analysis should consider a number of factors. Now we review some of the most commonly used methods of evaluating information systems projects to include EIS.

3.2 GUIDELINES FOR EIS IMPLEMENTATION

The implementation process of an information system is highly risky. Repeated research has reported that one-half to two-thirds of implementation projects fail. First you have to formulate your strategy; without it, it's like kicking a ball around with no goal and no goalkeeper in place. A fast implementation can take as few as six months; a slow one can take up to five years or more.[9] A few of the guidelines related to EIS implementation are mentioned below.

- **Understand your corporate needs and culture:** An EIS implementation will bring about a change in the roles of different departments and their responsibilities; in short, it will result in a change in the existing power structure.
- **Complete business process change:** EIS can change the whole outlook of business by fully reengineering it and giving it a new shape and direction which could be unimaginable.
- **Provide strong leadership:** Leaders plays a vital role in influencing the destiny of the followers. So while selecting a team leader/project leader, this point has to be kept in mind.
- **Choose a balanced team:** The system environment of today's EIS solutions is complex: RDBMS, servers, networking, LAN, WAN, etc. There will be no longer a lot of documentation to specify the requirements. These will be on-line as an integral part of the package. So the team should be balanced in order to rectify the error.
- **Select a good implementation methodology:** It will be advisable for the project leaders to set out clear and measurable objectives in the very beginning and review the progress after certain intervals, so as to ensure its successful implementation.
- **Train every one:** Since the EIS package is not confined to specific people but beneficial for the whole enterprise, training will be given to all and not restricted to a few who are in the implementation process. This is because it is indirectly going to benefit the enterprise as a whole, because EIS software comprise gigantic packages tapping the entire enterprise.
- **Commitment to adapt and change:** An EIS implementation should not be looked upon as a short-distance run. It's an ongoing process. It has wide implications, and will impact the future of the potential of the entire enterprise for many years to come.

---

[9] Davenport, T. (2000). *Mission Critical: Realizing the Promise of Enterprise Systems.* Boston: Harvard Business School Press.

3.3 IMPLEMENTATION STRATEGIES

EIS has become recognized as a very powerful system providing great benefit to organizations. But there are a few caveats that come with EIS. This is well explained from the architecture displayed in Figure 3.7.

Implementation process

There are three broad approaches to the timing and location of EIS implementation: Pilot, Big-Bang and Phased.

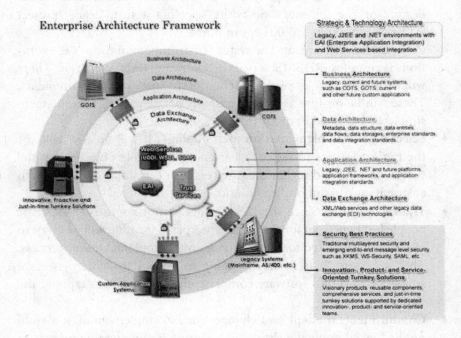

Figure 3.7:   Enterprise Architecture Framework.

Source: www.enfotech.com[10]

---

[10] Enfotech has been providing environmental systems and environmental consulting services to State water utilities, municipalities, and the pharmaceutical industry since 1994. Environmental compliance information management systems for industrial waste pretreatment, safe drinking water, and air emissions are being refined continuously and evolve with the development of new technologies.

- **Pilot implementation approach:** This approach starts with a small-scale version applied to a small division or with one specific module, such as finance and accounting, with the intent of seeing how that initial effort works before committing the rest of the organization. The aim is to prioritize the functional areas and to bring into operation that area offering the greatest advantage first. This requires an enormous amount of interface programming to preserve the data flows between the legacy system and the new module being implemented. It is also the lowest-risk alternative but also takes the most time as each module is rolled out.

- **Big-Bang implementation approach:** This requires simultaneous implementation of multiple modules of an EIS packages at one time. Why is it called Big-Bang? An organization prepares, tests, trains, and does everything else needed to get ready, and then over a weekend or a few days the data in the old system is migrated to the new one. One morning everyone in the company starts using the new system and the old one is simultaneously turned off. This is the most risky alternative. There will always be unforeseen and unexpected events. Several famous companies have been caught in this trap. Usually high technology companies that thought it could not happen to them found that it could. A variant of the Big-Bang approach is to combine it with a phased approach. This entails a series of "mini-bangs" that affect a logical segment of the business. One example uses a division-by-division approach where each one uses a Big-Bang to migrate to the new ERP system. A second example might use a functional approach which requires interfaces with both systems running their parts of the company, i.e. finance goes first with the new system implemented in all divisions at one time, followed by manufacturing and customer support.

- **Phased implementation approach:** This consists of designing, developing, testing & installing different modules of the EIS over time, or rolled over different elements of the organization at different times.

Implementation will usually take one to three months each for the sub-stages and thus, a project based on the above approach, and employing solutions from a simple package should take at the most 16–18 months.

However, depending on the business and nature of operations of the company, the time frame may change. Sometimes this may of the order of years. The first area of investigation and reconciliation is cost, both in terms of money and time. A solution from SAP-R/3 will cost a minimum of $400,000 to implement and may take as much as three years. Therefore, the size of the business and the return on the capitalized investment become factors of prime interest. According to V. Ramanathan, Divisional Manager of Ramco, "Buying an EIS package should not be done on the basis of 'feature-rich' offerings. It is pragmatic to have 80 percent of the product becoming productive in three to four months. Every software package requires implementation. "Implementation" means installing the package at the user's location and giving proper training in its use to the fullest extent so that the user is able to gain advantage of that particular package. Successful EIS requires proper implementation, in light of the following issues."

3.3.1 Implementation Issues

EIS solutions ultimately help in ensuring that data is transparently available across the enterprise. The advantages of implementing a good EIS system are manifold. With its integrated applications, an EIS system optimizes the core processes of an organization, accelerates transactions with its business workflow, and makes strategic management information available in a transparent form at all levels of the company, within the framework of its information warehouse concept. An EIS system guarantees strategic freedom in designing an organization's information management communication. This enables uniformity in storage and restricted exchange of business data between two physically divided application systems. Ready-to-wear solutions for more than a few hundred business processes are available in an EIS solution that can be promptly constructed using modeling tools to optimize the processes of an organization. With its business-oriented functions, an EIS solution opens up new opportunities for improving an organization's market and customer orientation through data-mining techniques. EIS systems provide a high level of flexibility and enables the flexibility to respond to a continually changing market situation.

Technologies: An EIS package facilitates a virtually unrestricted distribution of applications and databases, as well as extraordinary integration of in-house and external software components. An EIS system brings into play:

♦ Cost-efficient implementation on a centralized or two-tier client/ server system that is often a very good fit for small- and mid-sized installations.
♦ Mid-sized and huge installations are better served by a three-tier client/ server implementation.
♦ Extremely large installations involve a very high level of system availability. The use of corresponding database servers in three-tier client/ server architecture is considered to be best.
♦ Group-wide and worldwide installations have the greatest requirement for performance and ease of use.

Hence, an EIS's infrastructure technology meets the diverse real-world needs with different options for distributing applications.

Avoiding Pitfalls: Senior management's commitment to modify management processes and piloting the EIS implementation becomes absolutely necessary for successful implementation. Over a period of time, the additional functionalities that are available in the EIS can be implemented. Implementation strategy is context-dependent so what is successful in one company may not yield similar results in another organization. As a result, the policy and approach to execution is a key enabler for successful implementation.

Executing EIS: The accomplishment of an EIS solution depends on how rapid the benefits can be reaped from it. This dictates rapid implementations which lead to shortened ROI periods. The traditional approach to implementation has been to carry out a Business Process Reengineering (BPR) exercise and define a 'TO BE' model before the EIS system implementation. This shows possible mismatches between the anticipated model and the EIS functionality, the consequences of which were customizations, higher costs and loss of user confidence.

Defining a successful EIS implementation: We have to keep in mind the following questions:

➢ How do you discriminate between a successful EIS implementation and an unsuccessful one?
➢ How does one identify success of an EIS (or for that matter any emerging technology) project?

◆ **Organization vision/mission and success factors**

Nearly every one of us has a vision, but how many associations have the success factors defined, analyzed and documented after wide-ranging top-down/bottom-up brainstorming sessions? This is a top management responsibility that is not to be delegated to subordinates. The vision is an apparent, easy-to-understand picture of the future organization. EIS or for that matter any up-and-coming technology might be just one of the many tools that are being anticipated to meet the business objectives. Restructuring might be another; identifying and cutting down fat might be the next.

◆ **How does the EIS fit into the larger picture of our vision and business?**

One major issue that we need to concentrate on is how and how much are we going to alter the way we do business. Are we going to overhaul our business processes? In an old organization if we try to place new technology without ironing out the business processes then the result is an expensive old organization! As Peter Drucker has said, "There is nothing more useless than to do efficiently, things that are not supposed to be done at all."

◆ **Predictable Payback Period**

If top financial people in the organization have been involved from day one (which is normally the case), this activity should be the easiest to finish. The payback period for EIS or any technology project is ideally not more than two to three years, because that is the rate at which core technology is varying.

♦ **Who is the project titleholder?**

In most organizations, initial work is done by the IT department since they are in close contact with technology developments. Here the problem is: Who is to champion the cause? Ask your IT team colleagues to think over "Why EIS?" and you will perpetually get all the possible technical answers in return. This includes: Hardware has become outdated, we do not have the latest in communication, client server technology is what we need to graduate to, etc. Ask your business heads and they would say that the competition already has it Is this sufficient? Obviously not. So who should be the titleholder? The hard-hitting answer — any person high in the chain of command who understands this project's fit into the business (not the department) of the future. He might or might not understand technology. The challenge is to identify and pick that individual. The easy alternative is a person who is relatively free and available. One does not have to be a management guru to tell which of the substitutes is better. The champion then selects a dedicated team to organize a case that aligns the project with the long-term strategy.

3.3.2 Understanding EIS

EIS not only changes the culture of the organization, but also impacts the larger environment in which an organization flourishes. Most people have questions about:

➢ Do I need an EIS?
➢ Where am I standing with respect to my business rivals?
➢ Where do I want to be?
➢ And in order to get there, what is the best enabler?

Old ways of doing business simply don't work any more. Unexpectedly and abruptly, the world is a diverse place. The "here and now" calamity of competitiveness that conglomerates face today is not the consequence of a temporary economic recession or of a low point in the business cycle. In today's environment, nothing is constant or predictable and the one thing that remains constant in this world is change. We can no longer calculate on a unsurprising market growth, customer demand, product life-cycle, and rate of technological change.

Operate long-term

The long-term approach should be adopted. "If we were re-creating this company today, given what we know and given the current state of technology, what would it look like?" It means looking at innovative choices. It entails going back to the basics and inventing a better way of doing things. The procedure of undergoing such prototype shifts might fluctuate from organization to organization. Depending on the willingness to absorb modification and experiment with substitute business processes, the approach can be anything between fundamental and incremental. What remains constant is the necessity of an appropriate IT infrastructure that uses technology to do necessary things in a more efficient manner.

Inductive thinking

Applying information technology in recasting business demands inductive thinking. Simply throwing computers at a business problem does not cause it to be resolved. In fact, it can reinforce old ways of doing things. To be able to compete, thrive and stay ahead, organizations, almost without exception, are being driven to:

- ➢ Cut down throughput times.
- ➢ Condense stock to the lowest amount.
- ➢ Enlarge the range of products and customize to order.
- ➢ Improve product quality.
- ➢ Schedule flexibly to deliver at varying quantities and lead-times.
- ➢ Efficiently synchronize global demand, production supply and replacement.
- ➢ Stay alert and be agile to change continuously with ever-changing business dynamics.
- ➢ Have foresight in predicting new customer needs and seize market opportunities as they arise.

Disperse borders

Operations are being decentralized and multi-location operations are more popular. Risks are being extended over manifold products and an assortment of classes of manufacturing — discrete, process and make/engineer-to-order — coexist. End products for some are raw materials for others and manufacturing is blending with distribution in extended supply chains. Organization boundaries themselves are disappearing, as more and more stakeholders are forming synergistic and harmonious business ecosystems, each entity delivering value to the other. What is needed is an infrastructure that primarily provides flexibility and speed to act in response and readjust, on the one hand, and make certain tight control checks and balances work across all enterprise resources, functions and processes, on the other hand.

Open and modular

Organizational systems should have a structural design that allows components or modules which can be used separately and flexibly to meet the specific requirements of the business, as well as industry-specific functionalities. Systems should merge smoothly with in-house/third-party applications, solutions and services including the Web.

Integrated

Functions like sales and materials planning, production planning, warehouse management, risk-management, financial accounting, and human resource management should be integrated and incorporated into a workflow of business events and procedures across departments and functional areas, facilitating knowledge-workers to receive the right information and documents at the right time at their desktops across organizational and geographical boundaries.

Most excellent business practice

The software should facilitate integration of all business operations which encompasses planning, controlling and monitoring. It should also propose a choice of multiple ready-made business processes including best business practices that replicate the experiences, suggestions and requirements of leading companies across industries.

EIS system's future

The Internet symbolizes the next major technology enabler, which allows rapid supply chain management between multiple operations and trading partners. Most EIS systems are enhancing their products to become "Internet Enabled" so that customers worldwide can have direct interaction with the supplier's EIS system. EIS systems are building in Workflow Management functionality which provides a mechanism to manage and control the flow of work by monitoring logistic aspects like workload, capacity, throughout times, work queue lengths and processing times. Recognizing the need to go beyond the MRP-II, EIS vendors are busy adding to their product portfolio. BaaN for example, has already introduced concepts like IRP (Intelligence Resource Planning), MRP-III (Money Resources Planning) and has acquired companies for strategic technologies like Visual Product Configuration, Product Data Management and Finite Scheduling.

3.3.3 Implementation Methodologies

Bigger, better and more nimble. That's what the EIS systems promise to deliver to the organizations of the new millennium. In many cases, this happens; in some cases though, it doesn't. Why? There are a variety of reasons; one of the more critical among them being the choice of a suitable implementation methodology. The CEO and top team must understand that enterprise packages can be tailored (customized), but only within limits. The EIS application already has a gamut of best practices incorporated by design. They also assume standardization of business processes across the enterprise.

There are two extremes as to how an EIS can be built:

➢ **Vanilla implementation approach:** This refers to minimal customization of EIS packages.

➢ **Customization:** Here the vendor software is modified to fit the practices of the user organization.

Customization is a major issue. Vendors and IT systems personnel will shun customization like the plague, arguing that customization should always be resisted, no matter how strong the temptation to make the package work exactly the way your legacy system used to. This is a very self-centered view, and should be over-ridden by the need to make the software do what the organization needs. Some things the legacy systems did were inferior, and should be replaced by the vendor software's approach. That is why SAP does all of its best practices research. However, SAP can't be expected to identify what is best for each and every organization. Those things that the organization does better than their competitors may be competitive advantages, and sacrificing these competitive advantages to do things the vendor's way would be a very bad decision.

If the old IT system for the company was bad, inferior, and in need of replacement, it is far better to use the vendor's best practices and avoid customization. This avoids problems when the vendor decides to discontinue service on its old version and switches to a new "improved" version. Most EIS vendors, such as SAP, often withdraw their product warranty if their source code is customized. But not customizing also locks the user organization into the same practices that every other organization has access to, eliminating any competitive advantage it may have developed.

In order to respond to growing customer demand for shorter implementation life-cycle, many methodologies have tried to shorten the time-frame by prioritizing activities and by incorporating greater degree of parallelism. For instance, SAP's ASAP framework is called the roadmap. Such methodologies are usually shorter versions of their predecessors, and are applicable with certain ingrained assumptions.

➢ **First and foremost** among these is that the organization will accept the standard package functionality in totality; i.e. no "as-is" analysis of business processes.
➢ **Secondly,** there will be little or no custom development, i.e. no client-specific requirements will be met outside the functionality provided by the package.

While this approach will work for most small-to-medium enterprises, larger organizations will find it difficult to do away with their past totally. A methodology creates a "safety net" by giving you a comprehensive list of all activities that you need to carry out from "kick-off" to "go-live" and beyond. It also gives you a recommended way of executing such tasks. The quality of the project deliverables that you produce by executing these tasks depends on how successfully you follow such recommendations. There are a lot of EIS projects which start off by professing to follow a methodology and end up compromising the quality of delivery because of short cuts that were adopted mid-stream. It helps to remember that today's smart and convenient "quick-fix" solution may be tomorrow's "show stopper" in an EIS implementation framework.

3.3.4 Post-Implementation Depression

Post-implementation blues are a reality. It could be kept to the minimum by taking preventive measures, starting with communicating the message throughout the organization, cutting across functions and hierarchy. It is very well recognized that technological advances of any nature bring change. Enterprise Resource Planning is no different. The introduction of EIS systems has created a minor revolution in the functioning of industries. Like problems faced with any new technology, EIS implementation and usage has its own set of unknowns to be tackled. These have to be proactively handled to derive maximum benefits. Surely, there are mechanisms for putting in place a continuous improvement program.

Expectations, fears, reality

To start with, many post-implementation problems can be traced to wrong expectations and fears. The expectations that corporate managements have while choosing an EIS is summed up rather succinctly by a popular Indian business magazine by referring to it as "the new corporate Viagra." Of course, some of the blame for this has to be laid at the doorstep of the EIS vendors and their pre-implementation sales hype.

(i) **Expectation** A few of the popular expectations are:

➢ An improvement in processes.
➢ Increased productivity on all fronts.
➢ Total automation and disbanding of all manual processes.
➢ Improvement of all key performance indicators.
➢ Elimination of all manual record-keeping.
➢ Real-time information systems available to people concerned on a need-basis.
➢ Total integration of all operations.

(ii) **Fears** EIS implementation also engenders a host of fears like:

➢ Job redundancy.
➢ Loss of importance as information is no longer an individual prerogative.
➢ Change in job profile.
➢ An organizational fear of loss of proper controls and authorization.
➢ Increased stress caused by greater transparency.
➢ Individual fear of loss of authority.

Balancing the expectation and fears is a very necessary part of the implementation process.

(iii) **Reality** A few of the realities that any organization must keep in mind are:

➢ Changing the organization involves three levers — strategic, business process and organization change, usually with fewer but more empowered employees.
➢ Changing the organization requires a mindset change. Without a willingness to change, it would be a classic case of an old organization plus new technology leading to an expensive old organization. In most companies in India, many process-related key performance indicators have not been measured till now — either because the company did not find it necessary or it lacked the tools to do so. Measuring such indicators brings in a new culture.

> ➤ The generic nature of the EIS packages is such that there would be processes peculiar to some sectors and organizations, which may have to be kept out of the process.
> ➤ Some of the processes are better done manually.

Finally, a successful EIS implementation is not the end of the road as far as change is concerned, and continuous improvements are required to reap the benefits. One of the most obvious ways to balance the expectations, fears and reality underly the process of implementation.

3.4 ADVANTAGES AND DISADVANTAGES OF ALTERNATIVE EIS DEVELOPMENT METHODS

There are a number of approaches that can be used to design an EIS. Table 3.2 compares advantages and disadvantages of some representative points on a continuum.

The simplest is to adopt a vendor's product completely. This is the option that vendors will suggest. This option has some strong advantages, especially with respect to relative time and cost. The opposite extreme is to develop an EIS totally with in-house assets. This approach offers the greatest opportunity to gain competitive advantage. However, the in-house approach is a very difficult information systems project, probably the most difficult imaginable. The ideal way to do this is to combine it with extensive business process reengineering (see Chapter 5), identifying the best way to do everything, and then building the computer system to accomplish this. This is a very slow and expensive way to obtain an EIS, with the primary relative advantage of being the most flexible and responsive to organizational needs.

As with many other aspects of life, there are compromises available within these extremes. As discussed in Chapter 2, most firms adopt only a few modules of vendor software. This is a partial form of EIS, which has the relative advantage of minimizing organizational risk and expenditure in the short run, and minimizing the trauma of incorporating the EIS into organizational operations. The disadvantage is that the full functionality of the vendor system is not obtained, and users still must

Table 3.2: Advantages and Disadvantages of Alternative EIS Development Methods.

Method	Advantages	Disadvantages
Develop in-house.	Best fit with organizational needs.	Most difficult to develop. Most expensive. Slowest.
In-house system with vendor supplements.	Gain commercial advantages combined with organizational fit.	Difficult to develop. Expensive. Slow.
Best-of-breed.	Theoretically gain best of all systems.	Difficult to link modules. Slow. Potentially inefficient.
Customized vendor system.	Retain flexibility while keeping vendor expertise.	Slower. Usually more expensive.
Selected vendor modules.	Less risk. Relatively fast. Least expensive.	If expand, long run-time & higher cost.
Full vendor system.	Fast. Less expensive. Efficient.	Inflexible.
Application service provider.	Least risk. Least cost. Fastest. Least subject to vendor change.	At the mercy of ASP provider. No control. Subject to price increases.

conform to the procedures that the vendor has programmed into the system.

Many companies adopt another hybrid approach, customizing a vendor software product. This gains flexibility over simply adopting the vendor system, but risks loss of the efficiencies built into the system through best practices. A form of this hybrid approach is best-of-breed (discussed in Chapter 2). In the best-of-breed approach, modules considered to be competitively strong are selected from multiple vendors. Using the best-of-breed approach, custom interfaces can be developed using in-house information system development assets.

The final approach is to, in effect, rent an EIS through an application service provider (ASP). This is a form of outsourcing. The benefit of an ASP is that the user organization doesn't have to worry about system development, nor about being at the mercy of vendors when they make changes to their software. However, the risk is simply transferred, because the user is now subject to the mercy of the ASP. The decision is very similar to that of deciding to buy or rent housing. In the long run, you are usually better off buying a house. However, the cash flow impact and risk avoidance of renting is much better than buying.

3.5 EIS PROPOSAL EVALUATION

The three studies we have been tracking[11] asked subjects about expected installation time (Table 3.3) and expected installation cost (Table 3.4). These firms for the most part anticipated that the adopted system would serve their organizations over seven years. The time that they expected their EIS installation projects to last is reported in Table 3.3.

The reported times are very similar. Obviously, the scope of the EIS project would be a major factor in this time expectation. Projects implemented in less than one year would have to be relatively small in scope (implementation of one or only a few modules, for instance). But a general

Table 3.3:   Expected EIS Project Installation Time Requirements.

Installation time	U.S. (%)	Sweden (%)	Korea (%)
12 months or less	34	38	49
13 to 24 months	45	49	40
25 to 36 months	11	8	7
37 to 48 months	6	4	2
Over 48 months	2	1	3

Source: Mabert *et al.* (2000), Olhager and Selldin (2003), Katerattanakul *et al.* (2006).

---

[11] Mabert, V. M., Soni, A. and Venkataramanan, M. A. (2000). Enterprise resource planning survey of US manufacturing firms. *Production and Inventory Management Journal,* 41(20), 52–58; Olhager, J. and Selldin, E. (2003). Enterprise resource planning survey of Swedish manufacturing firms. *European Journal of Operational Research,* 146, 365–373; Katerattanakul, P., Hong, S. and Lee, J. (2006). Enterprise resource planning survey of Korean manufacturing firms. *Management Research News,* 29(12), 820–837.

Table 3.4: EIS Installation Project Cost Proportions.

Installation cost proportion	U.S. (%)	Sweden (%)
Software	30	24
Consulting	24	30
Hardware	18	19
Implementation team	14	12
Training	11	14
Other	3	1

Source: Mabert *et al.* (2000), Olhager and Selldin (2003).

Table 3.5: Expected ROI from EIS Projects.

Expected ROI	U.S. (%)	Sweden (%)	Korea (%)
<15%	30.5	54.4	59.6
16% to 25%	36.4	30.4	15.8
>25%	29.2	15.2	24.6

Source: Mabert et al. (2000), Olhager and Selldin (2003), Katerattanakul *et al.* (2006).

trend is indicated, given the different times of the surveys. There clearly is a shift to shorter implementation times.

Gartner Group consistently reports that IS/IT projects significantly exceed their time (and cost) estimates. Thus, while almost half of the surveyed firms reported expected implementation expense to be less than $5 million, we consider that figure to remain representative of the minimum scope required. However, recent trends on the part of vendors to reduce implementation time probably have reduced EIS installation cost. Mabert *et al.* also investigated the proportion of total costs by EIS component, with results given in Table 3.4.

In the U.S., vendors seem to take the biggest chunk of the average implementation. Consultants also take a big portion. These proportions are reversed in Sweden. The internal implementation team accounts for an additional 14 percent (12 percent in Sweden). These proportions are roughly reversed in Sweden with training.

The expectations of return on their investment varied widely (as must be expected) as given in Table 3.5.

From these numbers, it appears that manufacturers in Sweden expect a bit less return than did those in the U.S. (much of which might be explained by economic timing). Korean expectations are much more variable. Since the motivation for adopting EIS in some cases was either competitive or viewed as forced for other reasons, some firms expect low payoff from their EIS systems. However, roughly as many adopters expect clearly significant returns on their investment.

Van Everdingen *et al.* conducted a survey of European firms in mid-1998 with the intent of measuring EIS penetration by market. The survey included questions about the criteria considered for information systems selection, as well as criteria for supplier selection. The criteria reportedly used are given in Table 3.6 in order of ranking.

Fit with business procedures was selected among the three most important criteria by about one-half of the respondents, and was listed as the single most important criterion by over one-third. While EIS vendors have devoted a great deal of effort to making their packages match existing business processes, the importance of this criterion is based upon the high cost and bother of configuring and implementing

Table 3.6: Criteria Considered for IT and EIS Supplier Selection.

Information systems selection criteria ($n = 2401$)	EIS supplier selection criteria ($n = 2623$)
1. Fit with business procedures	1. Product functionality
2. Flexibility	2. Product quality
3. Cost	3. Implementation speed
4. User friendliness	4. Interface with other systems
5. Scalability	5. Price
6. Support	6. Market leadership
	7. Corporate image
	8. International orientation

Source: Van Everdingen *et al.* (2000).[12]

---

[12] van Everdingen, Y., van Hellegersberg, J. and Waarts, E. (2000). EIS adoption by European midsize companies. *Communications of the ACM*, 43(4), 27–31.

EIS systems. Selection of a vendor involved less variance among criteria. Product functionality and quality were the criteria most often reported to be important.

3.6 MANAGING RISK ON EIS PROJECTS

Managing risk on an EIS project is crucial to its success. What is risk? Simply defined, a risk is a potential failure point. There are thousands, maybe even millions of potential failure points on an EIS project, in the form of untested technology (and untested staffl), political landmines, and even nature's fury. (Tornados during the weekend when an EIS goes live? Yes, it's happened.) So, how do you keep the failures at bay? While various risk management books and methodologies offer variations on a theme, there are generally five steps to managing risk.

Five steps to managing risk:

1. Find potential failure points or risks.
2. Analyze the potential failure points to determine the damage they might do.
3. Assess the probability of the failure occurring.
4. Based on the first three factors, prioritize the risks.
5. Mitigate the risks through whatever action is necessary.

Project team members must rely on their experience and advice from others to find potential failure points or risks, track all the way through the entire project plan and look for areas of ambiguity.

Step 1: One of the easiest and most effective ways to find potential failure points is to talk to other organizations that have implemented the same projects. Cost estimates are probably the most common potential project failure point. Other potential failure points include lack of an executive sponsor, an under-qualified project manager, and no clear objectives for the project.

Step 2: The next step is to determine the severity of the potential failure on the budget, project timeline, or the users' requirements.

Step 3: Assessing the likely impact and the probability of the failure occurring is more art than science, requiring in-depth knowledge of both the EIS package and the business. A risk management team should be built that brings together those individuals that have the knowledge and experience to know what might happen. This team must have experience in implementing the specific EIS package for an organization approximately the same size and in the same industry as yours.

Step 4: Based on the first two factors, prioritize the risks. Decide which risks should be eliminated completely, because of potential for heavy impact on critical business processes. Set up a monitoring plan for risks that should have regular management attention. Make the entire team aware of those risks which are sufficiently minor to avoid detailed management attention, but which the team should watch for potential problems.

Step 5: You mitigate risks by reducing either the probability or the impact. The probability can be reduced by action up front to ensure that a particular risk is reduced. The project risk plan should include a set of steps for recovery from each risk, should failure occur. The team must know the person accountable for recovery from each specific risk, and the action to be taken to resolve it. The team must know the symptoms of the impending failure, and act to prevent it from occurring, if possible. An example is to test a particular operating system or hardware component to prove that it works prior to going live. Doing a pilot implementation or prototyping the first set of EIS interfaces are both examples of risk mitigation.

Precautions taken to control implementation failures

➢ Always select a full-time project manager for EIS implementation as it is a continuing process.
➢ Give emphasis to documentation of implementation procedures/ selection i.e., things should be crystal clear and in black & white.

➢ Maintain internal communication with the top executives regarding project implications, so that they are able to see the progress and not create any obstacles in releasing the funds.
➢ Try to generate vendor support and teamwork: Proper synchronization and cooperation are required for a system to be streamlined and smooth.
➢ Stress on reengineering effort and adherence to current practices.

We should first analyze the system, then proceed in accordance with the plan developed from this analysis.

3.7 CONCLUSION

Implementing an EIS is not an inconsequential effort. Considerable attention should be given to the preliminary stages of planning. User requirements and selected functionality should be communicated to all involved in the project. Critical success factors need to be considered to carefully coordinate the efforts of the many people involved which include consultants and managers. Gaining employee commitment to the EIS project is very important. Because the EIS integrates diverse company elements and data from many departments, the effects of delays ripple with dramatic impact. Therefore, control of the EIS implementation project is paramount.

Deciding to implement an EIS solution will probably be one of the top five business decisions an organization will make. The way the industry is moving, if you don't do it now, you will do it later. EIS packages can store, retrieve, and process transactions of all business functions of an organization in an integrated fashion. Implemented on a computer network, using client/server or Web technology, an EIS package accomplishes its tasks through enterprise — wide shareable databases. The expectations generated by these packages in the corporate sector are phenomenally high. If properly implemented, an EIS system can provide significant competitive benefit to the user. Yet, the reported experiences in using this technology are a mixture of successes and failures. The enthusiasm with which an EIS project is initiated is rarely matched by the resources and effort committed to its implementation. The time required for an ER implementation project is usually underestimated. In some cases, the performance of the system after implementation do not match the expectations raised at the time of its selection. It is, therefore, vital for the prospective users of this technology to be clear on the factors that contribute to the success of an EIS implementation and to fully realize the implications of adopting an EIS solution.

☆ KEYWORDS

☆ **Customer Relationship Management:** Sales and Marketing, Commissions, Service, Customer Contact and Call Center support and various Self-Service interfaces for Customers, Suppliers, and Employees.

☆ **EIS:** EIS is one of the vital solutions that are required for any businesses. EIS helps improve customer services, optimize inventory, reduce expenses, increase revenue and profits, improves efficiency. Some of the important modules of the EIS solutions are Production Management, Supply Chain Management, Inventory Management, Sales Management, Customer Relationship, Project Management, Finance Management and Business Intelligence.

☆ **Enterprise Resource Planning:** ERP systems integrate (or attempt to integrate) all data and processes of an organization into a unified system. A typical ERP system will use multiple components of computer software and hardware to achieve the integration. A key ingredient of most ERP systems is the use of a unified database to store data for the various system modules.

☆ **Financials:** General Ledger, Cash Management, Accounts Payable, Accounts Receivable, Fixed Assets.

☆ **Human Resources:** Human Resources, Payroll, Training, Time & Attendance, Benefits.

☆ **Manufacturing:** Engineering, Bills of Material, Scheduling, Capacity, Workflow Management, Quality Control, Cost Management, Manufacturing Process, Manufacturing Projects, Manufacturing Flow.

☆ **Product life cycle:** Product life cycle includes management from beginning to obsolescence, including product revisions and upgrades. The primary repository is called the product data management system. It is the beginning and end of the data needed for the supply chain. In this process the part numbers, product structures, options, warranty period, and initial suppliers are identified. This information is used for purchasing, manufacturing, and sales to do forecasting and budgeting in all areas impacted by new products. At the end of the product life cycle, product structures and components are made obsolete.

☆ **Projects:** Costing, Billing, Time and Expense, Activity Management.

☆ **Supply Chain Management:** Inventory, Order Entry, Purchasing, Product configuration, Supply Chain Planning, Supplier Scheduling, Inspection of goods, Claim Processing, Commission Calculation.

☆ **To-Be:** In creating the To-Be process, the first thing that must be done is to evaluate what processes are critical to the business (Zhang, 2002).[13]

☆ **As-Is:** The As-Is process model can be developed in a number of ways. The fastest way to do this is with a multiple-step process. This time limit will force the issue of how deep to go into the layers of the As-Is process and cause you to focus on the most important or largest areas of concern (Ridgman, 1996).[14]

☆ TERMINOLOGY REVIEW

Review Questions

1. Explain the nine stages of the EIS Implementation life-cycle with the help of a diagram.
2. What are the objectives of implementation?
3. How are the different stages of implementation evaluated?

---

[13] Zhang, Q.C. (2002). Business process re-engineering for flexibility and innovation in manufacturing. *Industrial Management & Data Systems*, 102(3), 146–152.
[14] Ridgman, T. (1996). Windows of opportunity: Timing and entry strategies. *Industrial Management & Data Systems*, 96(5), 26–31.

4. What are the phases for EIS implementation? Explain briefly.
5. What are the implementation issues for defining a successful EIS implementation?
6. What is mean by "understanding EIS"?
7. What is implementation methodology?
8. How can EIS be implemented?
9. What is post-implementation and how will you manage "life after implementation."
10. What do you understand by PERT & CPM and where are these techniques used?
11. What is an elastic EIS project?
12. What strategies are used for successful implementation of EIS application?
13. How has the EIS system changed the work of IT organizations?
14. What is meant by risk? What are the five steps of Managing Risk?
15. What are the guidelines for EIS implementation?
16. Much has been written about EIS, both in the popular press and on the Internet. Using library resources or the Internet, report on (1) one company's positive experience with implementing EIS, and (2) one company's disappointing experience.
17. Visit the online magazine, CIO.com/EIS. Choose an example of an EIS implementation and write a memo to your instructor describing the procedure. Make comments as to areas the company could have improved on its implementation.
18. Explain briefly the knowledge needed for planning a successful EIS System implementation.
19. Describe some of the intangible costs and benefits typically found in EIS proposals.
20. Why do students need to understand the context of Information Systems within enterprises?
21. Describe the relative advantages of an EIS system developed in-house versus a full vendor EIS system.
22. Describe the hidden outcomes of adopting an EIS.

☆ COMPETENCY REVIEW

1. Pragmatic Questions

   a. The last of the three implementation approaches is the Big-Bang. Why is it called this? Explain.

   b. Some of the important modules of the EIS solutions are Production Management, Supply Chain Management, Inventory Management, Sales Management, Customer Relationship, Project Management, Finance Management and Business Intelligence. How do you justify your answer?

2. What do we have to do differently from our previous ERP implementation? Why does the old methodology not work this time?

3. What skills do we need while implementing EIS? Who from our organization needs to be involved in implementation?

4. When do we do what? How do we align all activities? Do we have to finish all the architecture work before we start our "real" project implementaion?

5. Briefly comment on the following:

   a. A variation on the Big Bang approach is to combine it with a phased approach.

   ....

   ....

   b. EIS is one of the vital solutions that are required for any businesses.

   ....

   ....

c. EIS helps to improve customer services, optimize inventory, reduce expenses, increase revenue and profits, improve efficiency.

....

....

d. Business opportunities drive ad-hoc solutions.

....

....

e. Original IT department structure and architecture is overwhelmed.

....

....

f. Many of these hidden costs become surprises along the implementation path.

....

....

☆ SUGGESTED READING

Books

Bendoly, E. and Jacobs, F. R. (2005). *Strategic ERP Extension and Use.* California: Stanford Business Books.

Jacobs, F. R. and Whybark, D. C. (2003). *Why ERP? A Primer on SAP Implementation.* New York: McGraw Hill.

O'Leary, D. E. (2000). *Enterprise Resource Planning Systems: Systems, Life Cycles, Electronic Commerce, and Risk.* New York: Cambridge University Press.

Olson, D. L. (2004). *Managerial Issues in Enterprise Resource Planning Systems.* Boston: McGraw-Hill/Irwin.

Shields, M. G. (2002). *E-Business and ERP: Rapid Implementation and Project Planning.* Canada: John Wiley & Sons.

Wallace, T. F., Kremzar, M. H. and Kremzar, M. (2001). *ERP: Making It Happen: The Implementers' Guide to Success with Enterprise Resource Planning.* Canada: John Wiley & Sons.

Journal Articles

Aladwani, A. M. (2001). Change management strategies for successful ERP implementation. *Business Process Management Journal,* 7(3), 266–275.

Caldas, M. P. and Wood, T. J. (2001). Reductionism and complex thinking during ERP implementations. *Business Process Management Journal,* 7(5), 387–393.

Gunasekaran, A., Madan, M., Mirchandani, D. and Motwani, J. (2002). Successful implementation of ERP projects: Evidence from two case studies. *International Journal of Production Economics,* 75(1–2), 83–96.

Hong, K.-K. and Kim, Y.-G. (2002). The critical success factors for ERP implementation: An organizational fit perspective. *Information & Management,* 40, 5–40.

Parr, A. and Shanks, G. (2000). A model of ERP project implementation. *Journal of Information Technology,* 14(4), 2289–2304.

Umble, E. J. (2002). Avoiding ERP Implementation failure. *Industrial Management.*

Willis, T. H., Willis-Brown, A. H. and McMillan, A. (2001). Cost containment strategies for ERP system implementations. *Production & Inventory Management Journal,* 36–42.

White Papers and Conference Papers

Bonner, M. (2000). Roadmap to ERP Success. http://www.194.242.155.146:2468/subEnterprise_resource_planning.htm (accessed on 2 October 2001).

Chang, S. L., Gable, G., Smythe, E. and Timbrell, G. (2001). A Delphi Examination of Public Sector ERP Implementation Issues. In *Proceedings of the 21st International Conference on Information Systems,* Brisbane, Australia, pp. 494–500.

Chatfield, C. (2000). Organisational Influences on the successful Implementation of an ERP system. Honours Dissertation, Brisbane, Australia, Griffith University, Faculty of Engineering and Information Technology.

Nielsen, J. L. (2002). Implementation of an Enterprise Resource Planning System and its affects on the Knowledge Perspective (Tacit and Explicit focus). Paper for *conference*, UKAIS, p. 15.

Sarker, S. and Lee, A. S. (2000). Using a case study to test the role of three key social enablers in ERP implementation. In *Proceedings of the 21st International Conference on Information Systems*, Brisbane, Australia, pp. 414–425.

CHAPTER 4

ENTERPRISE SYSTEM SELECTION AND PROJECT PLANNING

Quotation

To stay at the forefront of an industry, many companies have to integrate various and different business application together with their existing information systems, in order to create a successful business and enhance productivity.

Structure

- ♣ *Quick look at chapter themes*
- ♣ *Learning objectives*
- ♣ *Case study*: Wm. Bolthouse Farms
- ♣ *Sketch of EIS budgeting*
- ♣ Introduction
  - 4.1 EIS Project Management
  - 4.2 EIS/ERP Proposal Evaluation
  - 4.3 Project Evaluation Techniques
    - 4.3.1 Cost-Benefit Example
    - 4.3.2 Net Present Value Calculation
    - 4.3.3 Return on Investment
    - 4.3.4 Payback
    - 4.3.5 Other Factors
  - 4.4 EIS ROI Issues
  - 4.5 Total Cost of Ownership
  - 4.6 Alternative Evaluation
    - 4.6.1 Value Analysis

♣ QUICK LOOK AT CHAPTER THEMES

Recently, in an ERP/EIS seminar, a General Manager for Materials, described the ERP/EIS system thus: "It is a rabbit during evaluation, transforms into an elephant during implementation, and at last a dinosaur at a final stage." Clearly, this organization did not adequately gain the benefits of the ERP/EIS system. Is this the rule rather than the exception? An implementation should include a formal review, with an accurate estimate of the cost and a list of realistic benefits. Companies, which fail to do this often find their ERP/EIS implementation not succeeding. That company who did not go through the above process paid dearly for it. Unfortunately, such mistakes get amplified and lead to wrong conclusions about ERP/EIS systems.

♣ LEARNING OBJECTIVES

Enterprises more often than not make use of dissimilar technologies and architectures, and constantly update their infrastructure. This makes system integration attractive. Enterprise systems (ERP/EIS) are very large IS/IT projects. The cost range is enormous, depending upon the size of the firm implementing the system, as well as on how many modules are used. An additional factor is the cost of training users. It is difficult to develop much of any system for less than $5 million. Some of the largest systems have cost in excess of $1 billion. This chapter will address the problem of system selection, and will show how the most commonly used selection methods work. Analytic methods support this selection process in two ways. First, they provide decision-makers with an analysis of expected outcomes from adopting specific projects. Second, they provide a basis for communication, so that the reasoning behind a selection can be explained to others. This chapter will discuss:

- ♣ Factors that add cost to the overall ERP/EIS project implementation and maintenance.
- ♣ Effective strategies for selecting a successful project team and building an effective project plan.
- ♣ Budgeting concepts and ERP control systems.
- ♣ The different costs involved in the overall ERP/EIS process.
- ♣ Developing a skill set profile of the "ideal" project manager.
- ♣ IS/IT financial project evaluation methods.
- ♣ Keeping the project on track and within budget.
- ♣ Knowing the difference between the role of the vendor's project management staff and the role of your organization's project manager.
- ♣ Multiple objective analysis as a basis for decisions.
- ♣ Problematic areas: Planning and management, Training, Testing, Integration, Dirty data, Documentation, Data Conversion, Data Analysis, Consultants.
- ♣ Understanding the complex role of the project manager throughout the implementation.
- ♣ Value analysis as a basis for decisions.
- ♣ Apart from normal cost of development and implementation other associated costs are: Training cost, Warehousing cost, Additional software for old report copying.

♣ CASE STUDY

Wm. Bolthouse Farms

ORGANIZATION PROFILE

Wm. Bolthouse Farms is located at Bakersfield, California. Bolthouse Farms is one of the world's largest producers of carrots, including pre-peeled and pre-packaged baby carrots and carrot juice. Bolthouse produces carrots for consumers and the food service industry, and has recently expanded its product line to produce and distribute blended juices from their brand-new beverage processing facility to stores around the United States.

Solution Profile: Modules Implemented	Environment
Oracle's JD Edwards EnterpriseOne Financials, Distribution and Manufacturing. CIBER's Grower Management Solution.	Hardware: IBM iSeries (AS/400). Database: IBM iSeries. Operating System: OS/400.

Bolthouse Farms has grown significantly over the years, from its beginnings as a seasonal producer of carrots, onions and other vegetables in Michigan, to the world's first year-round producer of carrots and one of the largest produce growers and distributors. Today, Bolthouse ships more than 35,000 tons of carrot products each month. That's one pound each month for every family in the United States! Bolthouse's enterprise systems did not meet the needs of such a major producer and innovator of agricultural products. Bolthouse was using a heavily customized legacy system that was able to meet Bolthouse's business process needs, as long as they did not change. However, Bolthouse is an innovator and change was becoming a constant in the organization. Massive modification was going to be necessary to support some of the new business processes that had already been discussed, let alone future innovations. Bolthouse needed a stable, integrated solution for their enterprise that would allow them to quickly and easily make configuration changes to support new business processes as their organization grows.

THE SOLUTION

CIBER[1] became involved with the project prior to the selection of Oracle's JD Edwards EnterpriseOne, when the need to upgrade systems was still in the early planning stages. CIBER had already completed a number of projects with other agricultural producers and processors, and so had a strong understanding of Bolthouse's needs before walking in the door. In addition, CIBER was the only consulting firm to offer a complete solution for Grower Management. CIBER worked with Bolthouse through the software vendor selection process, and was selected as their primary implementation partner and hardware supplier. CIBER provided project management, application, and technical expertise that helped the project team implement a new business solution and make dramatic changes to their business processes.

Bolthouse selected JD Edwards EnterpriseOne to handle its Financials, Distribution and Manufacturing processes, along with CIBER's Grower Management Solution, which integrates the needs of growers and processors, from initial contracts and harvest forecasts to settlement and payment. This solution would provide a foundation upon which Bolthouse could easily grow and expand its business.

As part of the implementation, Bolthouse reviewed and standardized many of its business processes to streamline their operations and take advantage of functionality in the software that was not available with their legacy system. They also restructured their Chart of Accounts during this project. Resource constraints posed a challenge to the project. Bolthouse assigned several key individuals to the project, but because Bolthouse runs a lean enterprise, they often could not be spared from their day to day tasks to assist on the project. To help overcome this problem, CIBER provided additional consulting support and monitored resource commitment to the

[1] CIBER, Inc. (NYSE: CBR) is a pureplay international system integration consultancy with superior value-priced services for both private and government sector clients. CIBER's global delivery services are offered on a project or strategic staffing basis, in both custom and enterprise resource planning (ERP) package environments, and across all technology platforms, operating systems and administrations founded in 1974 and headquartered in Greenwood Village, Colo., the company now serves client businesses from 60 US offices, 20 European offices and 4 offices in Asia. Operating in 18 countries, with 8,000 employees and annual revenue of nearly $1 billion, CIBER and its IT specialists continuously build and upgrade clients' systems to "competitive advantage status." CIBER is included in the Russell 2000 Index and the S&P Small Cap 600 Index. www.ciber.com. CIBER, Inc. 2006.

project, escalating issues to the executive steering committee as necessary when project timelines needed to be extended to accommodate these resource constraints. Technical development was also challenging. The legacy system was heavily customized to meet Bolthouse's business requirements, and the company was not willing to accept loss of functionality in many areas.

The amount of technical development required to maintain this functionality was more than their internal resources could handle within the original project timeline. To assist, CIBER technical experts were brought in to complete a large portion of the work. In addition, temporary interfaces to legacy systems were needed to handle some business processes until additional JD Edwards' functionality could be added. These business process interfaces included incoming carrots, Maintenance Work Orders, HR/Payroll and Scale interfaces in Production. CIBER also assisted with customizations related to its Grower Management Solution, which provided functionality not available in JD Edwards EnterpriseOne. CIBER's agribusiness industry expertise allowed the team to creatively configure and enhance the software to meet Bolthouse's business requirements.

THE BENEFITS

Bolthouse has now implemented JD Edwards EnterpriseOne solutions in Finance, Purchasing, and Inventory. These applications are the foundation of a fully integrated system that will provide visibility into Bolthouse's entire operation — from contract to harvest, to payment and reconciliation, to distribution and beyond. The solution's configurable setup and robust functionality will allow them to flexibly respond to changing business requirements without having to modify the software. CIBER is currently assisting Bolthouse with the implementation of JD Edwards EnterpriseOne Human Resources, Payroll, Plant and Equipment Maintenance, Job Cost, Fixed Assets and Expense Management applications, as well as the extension of Distribution and Manufacturing to additional product lines. Other specific benefits of the JD Edward EnterpriseOne and CIBER Grower Management solutions include:

- ♣ Replacement of the existing system, which was becoming obsolete.
- ♣ More system functionality and access to information to better manage Bolthouse's business, increasing profitability and strategic growth.

♣   Documentation of all new business processes.

♣   Common operating practices within and across Bolthouse facilities.

♣   Support for new and planned segments of the business, including retail beverage.

♣   "Best Practices" are being followed through all business processes.

♣   Reduction of period-end closing times after Phase 2 is complete.

HOW CIBER ADDED VALUE

CIBER's understanding of the Agribusiness industry, combined with its software expertise, provided a unique offering to help Bolthouse meet their industry-specific requirements with a software solution. Its project management expertise kept a balance between the budget/timeline/scope so that changes were handled efficiently, with constant communication to the client's project manager and executive steering committee. CIBER also provided application, technical and CNC expertise that allowed Bolthouse to improve processes, minimize customizations and modifications, and gain sufficient understanding of the complexities of a new technology to keep their systems operating efficiently.

Source: Ciber (2005).

♣ SKETCH OF EIS BUDGETING

Many EIS/ERP implementations fail. According to Drury (2000)[2] the budget is not something that originates "from nothing" each year; it is developed within the context of ongoing business, and is ruled by previous decisions that have been taken within the long-term planning process. Today when financial performance is undergoing microscopic scrutiny, careful attention to the budget is becoming more of a necessity than ever.[3] In today's globalised economy, each organization must appraise their strategies in order to survive. Budgeting is often regarded as the foundation

[2] Drury, C. (2000). Management & Cost Accounting.
[3] Cohn, M. (2000). Budget Tools Boost Bottom Line. Internet World.

of business planning. A budget is a control mechanism.[4] An EIS is a strategic tool for business process automation. It integrates or consolidates numerous data sources and technology processes of an organization into a single computer system that standardizes many day-to-day processes. These processes include purchasing and procurement, cash management, fixed assets and inventory, human resource management and employee benefits, training, recruiting and accounting. A typical EIS will use modular components of computer software and hardware to achieve the integration. A key ingredient of most EIS is the use of a unified database to store data for the various system modules. Thus we can say that "a budget is a financial projection for the future and therefore is a valuable managerial planning aid."[5]

♣ INTRODUCTION

Introducing a new or improved information system into an organization is a change process.[6] IT organizations are being asked to reduce operational expenses while, at the same time, the competitive pressures facing enterprises require an infrastructure that supports new applications to stimulate new initiatives. As enterprises extend back-office applications to customers and supply-chain partners, ensuring complete system availability becomes paramount. New technologies such as Web services continue to add to the complexity and the cost of interconnected systems. The business impact associated with failing to productively administer the interdependence between information and telecommunications technologies is staggering. Breaks at any point in an extended value chain process will result in lost revenue, diminish customer service, and augment costs. Hundreds of examples bear this out.

---

[4] Byrne, S. (2003). *Budgeting and ERP Control Systems in Third Level Educational Institutions: Some Evidence from the Republic of Ireland and the United Kingdom.* Dublin City University.
[5] Moscove, S. A., Simkin, M. G. and Bagranoff, N. A. (2002). *Core Concepts of Accounting Information Systems*, 8th edition. Hoboken, NJ: Wiley.
[6] Hoffer, J. A, George, J. F. and Valacich, J. S. (2002). *Modern Systems Analysis & Design*. Third Edition.

ERP/EIS packages are versatile by nature and IT departments often tailor the software to fit the company's specific requirements and business processes. Installing an ERP/EIS system is an enormous undertaking. Even after the preliminary operation, an ERP/EIS system must be continually personalized to reproduce changes in the business and software upgrades and extensions. ERP/EIS projects are expensive. Before adopting an ERP/EIS project, it's important to appreciate the project's TCO (Total Cost of Ownership), which involves far more than the price of the ERP/EIS software. In a survey of 63 companies, Meta Group found that the average TCO was $15 million for ERP/EIS when real project costs such as software, staff time, consulting, and hardware were incorporated. Those who have implemented ERP/EIS packages report that that many costs are more commonly overlooked or underestimated. If you want to avoid out-of-control costs and project failure, it's essential to identify an ERP/EIS system's hidden costs and the principal issues involved with implementing a project.

4.1 EIS PROJECT MANAGEMENT

Normal IS/IT projects have an implicit tradeoff among time, cost, and function. In ERP systems, the importance of the project does not allow for sacrifices in time or in functionality. Therefore, cost becomes the primary variable to deal with project contingencies. As discussed in Chapter 1, the cost of this training component is typically underestimated a great deal. This means that adequate budget must be allocated to training, and also that the many interrelated activities involved in training as well as in implementing the ERP system need to be carefully coordinated.

ERP systems involve a large collection of complex hardware and software. There are many organizational, employee, and political issues that further add to implementation project complexity.[7] Successful ERP project management has been found to benefit most from clear definition of objectives, development of a work plan and a resource plan, and careful

---

[7] Somers, T. M. and Nelson, K. G. (2003). The impact of strategy and integration mechanisms on enterprise system value: Empirical evidence from manufacturing firms. *European Journal of Operational Research*, 146, 315–338.

tracking of progress.[8] These are features that critical path tools are designed to support.

Project plans need to be aggressive, because ERP systems are very critical to organizational efficiency. It is difficult to reliably estimate durations of any information systems projects. Due to the need to balance realism with urgency, schedules should be aggressive but achievable. Clear definition of project aims can reduce the risk of scope creep, the tendency for information systems projects to be changed during implementation. Scope creep arises because the need for change (modification) is identified while the project is under way. Obviously, prior careful planning would reduce such changes.

The type of ERP system adopted will impact the need for changes. Adoption of a single vendor package without modifications will reduce the need for customization, and thus will reduce project complexity, which fosters better schedule performance. However, the primary objective is to develop the right system for the organization. Implementing the ERP on time and on budget is important, but it is more important to implement the right ERP system.

A project management steering committee is very important to ERP implementation project success.[9] This committee should include senior management representing affected corporate functions, as well as representative end users. This committee usually is involved in system selection, as well as monitoring project progress and management of external consultants. Consultants provide experience missing from the organization, and can be invaluable. However, consultants should be screened to avoid those with financial ties to software vendors, and lack of experience in the specific system being implemented.

Perhaps the single most decisive element of EIS/ERP success or failure is the knowledge, skills, abilities, and experience of the project manager. An EIS/ERP project manager must understand both the business and the technology.[10] Private and public-sector organizations are

---

[8] Umble, E. L., Haft, R. R. and Umble, M. M. (2003). Enterprise resource planning: Implementation procedures and critical success factors. *European Journal of Operational Research*, 146, 241–257.

[9] Somers and Nelson (2003), op cit.

[10] PeopleSoft-Planet.com is a FIVE Pillar member site.

increasing their use of EIS systems which make available integrated financial and human resources solutions that facilitate public-sector business processes. While procuring the right EIS system is an important factor, the genuine challenge lies in implementing these systems which can be tremendously complex. Today's EIS project managers are faced with overwhelming challenges. As government and private system users' budgets have become leaner, project managers have to achieve more with less in tighter time frames. This chapter addresses the explicit needs of the private/public-sector EIS project manager, with wide-ranging know-how in private/public-sector project management. There are in general three stages of project management with relevance to EIS/ERP as shown in Figure 4.1.

1.1 System project planning is needed to consider the installation of an EIS/ERP as a project. Sound project management practices are needed to offer any hope of system installation success.

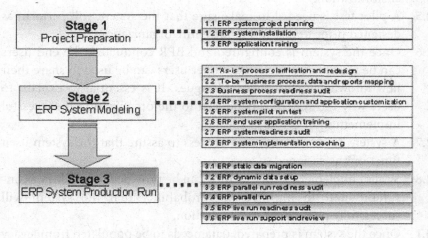

Figure 4.1: EIS/ERP Project Elements.

Source: Hong Kong Productivity Council (2005).[11]

---

[11] HKPC offers "Total ERP Solution for Productivity Enhancement". The mission of the ERP Centre is to transfer state-of-the-art ERP and e-supply chain technologies and management practices to Hong Kong manufacturers and related industries to increase their competitiveness.

1.2   Installing the EIS/ERP itself is a computer system matter, and works best as a cooperative effort between organizational IS/IT staff, vendor staff, and consultant staff, along with the participation of system users.

1.3   Initial training is often focused on a set of selected super users from each organizational division. These super users can gain in-depth understanding of how to use the system, which they can pass on to their divisional colleagues after the system is installed.

2.1   ERP system modeling begins with understanding the current legacy system.

2.2   After an understanding of the existing system is attained, the system design team focuses on an ideal system.

2.3   Business process reengineering provides a means to attain the "to-be" vision of what the EIS/ERP should do for the organization.

2.4   Once system designers know what the system is to do (from BPR), they can configure the vendor system, along with required customization.

2.5   A pilot test is needed to make sure that the system will perform as designed prior to disrupting the entire organization.

2.6   Once the system is configured and BPR conducted, the end users can be trained in system use. Super users can be used to share their new knowledge with their colleagues. It is essential to explain to users why the system is beneficial to the organization if successful implementation is to be expected.

2.7   A system readiness audit is a process to assure that the system itself functions as designed.

2.8   System implementation coaching can be provided by vendor or consultant staff to improve the probability that the system will successfully be brought into operation.

3.1   Once the system is prepared, data needs to be populated from legacy systems.

3.2   Data will continuously be generated by organizational operations, and the system needs to accurately accept it in real time.

3.3   It is usually wise to implement systems in parallel with legacy systems until assurance is gained that the new system performs as designed. An audit by technical personnel can make this step easier to accomplish.

3.4 The new system is brought on-line (whether the parallel, pilot, or big-bang approach is used).

3.5 A live-run readiness audit is a final check prior to bringing the system on-line.

3.6 Once the system is implemented and operating, an audit should be conducted to record lessons learned.

4.2 EIS/ERP PROPOSAL EVALUATION

Mabert *et al.* surveyed a large number of Midwestern US manufacturing firms which had implemented ERP systems. Olhager and Selldin replicated the study in Sweden, and Katerattanakul *et al.* did the same in Korea.[12] These surveys yielded the proportions of analysis applied to ERP decisions adopted as shown in Table 4.1.

Note that payback use reported in the U.S. was much lower than the Swedish percentage. Korean reported techniques were very close to those

Table 4.1:   ERP Proposal Evaluation Technique used.

Financial method	Reported use U.S. (%)	Reported use Sweden (%)	Reported use Korea (%)
ROI	53	30	37
Payback	35	67	36
Expected NPV/value added	15	12	15
Other	11	20	16

Source: Mabert *et al.* (2000), Olhager and Selldin (2003), Katerattanakul *et al.* (2006).

---

[12] Mabert, V. M., Soni, A. and Venkataramanan, M. A. (2000). Enterprise resource planning survey of US manufacturing firms. *Production and Inventory Management Journal*, 41(20), 52–58; Olhager, J. and Selldin, E. (2003). Enterprise resource planning survey of Swedish manufacturing firms. *European Journal of Operational Research*, 146, 365–373. Katerattanakul, P., Hong, S., and Lee, J. (2006). Enterprise Resource Planning Survey of Korean Manufacturing Firms. *Management Research News*, 29(12), pp. 820–837.

in the US. As it is, it seems counterintuitive that not all firms implementing ERP applied formal ROI analysis, although the argument still holds that detailed analysis of imprecise estimated figures is often a waste of time. In this study, some firms used multiple evaluation methods. These firms for the most part anticipated that the adopted system would serve their organizations over seven years. The time that they expected their ERP installation projects to last is reported in Table 4.2.

The reported times show a clear trend to faster installation. This reflects the economic realities that most organizations cannot afford to wait for years to get their systems in place. Furthermore, there is a notable trend towards vendors upgrading their software (and discontinuing support to older versions) on an accelerated schedule. Obviously, the scope of the ERP/EIS project would be a major factor in this time expectation. Projects implemented in less than one year would have to be relatively small in scope (implementation of one or only a few modules, for instance). ERP system cost expectations are given in Table 4.3.

Table 4.2: Expected ERP Project Installation Time Requirements.

Installation time	U.S. (%)	Sweden (%)	Korea (%)
12 months or less	34	38	49
13 to 24 months	45	49	40
25 to 36 months	11	8	7
37 to 48 months	6	4	2
Over 48 months	2	1	3

Source: Mabert *et al.* (2000), Olhager and Selldin (2003), Katerattanakul *et al.* (2006).

Table 4.3: ERP Estimated Installation Project Cost.

Installation cost	U.S. (%)	Sweden	Korea
Less than $5 million	42	94%	93%
$5 million to $25 million	33	6%	7%
$26 million to $50 million	10	(in prior category)	(in prior category)
$51 million to $100 million	7	(in prior category	(in prior category)
Over $100 million	7	(in prior category)	(in prior category)

Source: Mabert *et al.* (2000), Olhager and Selldin (2003), Katerattanakul *et al.* (2006).

The Swedish and Korean results indicate a magnitude of investment much lower in scale than in the US. This could reflect the opportunity to utilize less expensive vendors. The most commonly used Swedish vendor was Intentia. SAP was used by about 30 percent of the Korean firms, and Oracle by another 19 percent, but over 40 percent reported using Bizentro, a local vendor, which could establish a lower market price. The expense of a system as a proportion of organizational revenue was found to be directly related to the firm's scope of revenue. For smaller firms, with revenues of less than $50 million per year, anticipated enterprise system installation costs were solidly in the less than $5 million range, with an associated implementation cost of about 14 percent of revenues. Firms with annual revenues above $250 million obviously had larger implementation budgets, but their implementation cost as a percent of revenue was only three percent or less.

Gartner Group consistently reports that IS/IT projects significantly exceed their time (and cost) estimates. Thus, while almost half of the surveyed firms reported expected implementation expense to be less than $5 million, we still consider that figure to be representative of the minimum scope required. However, recent trends on the part of vendors to reduce implementation time probably have reduced ERP/EIS installation cost. Mabert *et al.* also investigated the proportion of total costs by ERP/EIS component, with results given in Table 4.4.

In the U.S., vendors seem to take the biggest chunk of the average implementation. Consultants also take a big portion. These proportions are reversed in Sweden The internal implementation team accounts for an

Table 4.4: ERP Installation Project Cost Proportions.

Installation cost proportion	U.S. (%)	Sweden (%)
Software	30	24
Consulting	24	30
Hardware	18	19
Implementation team	14	12
Training	11	14
Other	3	1

Source: Mabert *et al.* (2000), Olhager and Selldin (2003).

Table 4.5: Expected ROI from ERP Projects.

Expected ROI	U.S. (%)	Sweden (%)	Korea
Less than 5%	14	17	(in below)
5% to 15%	18	38	60%
16% to 25%	36	30	16%
26% to 50%	18	11	25%
Over 50%	13	4	(in above)

Source: Mabert *et al.* (2000), Olhager and Selldin (2003), Katerattanakul *et al.* (2006).

additional 14 percent (12 percent in Sweden). These proportions are roughly reversed in Sweden with training. (The Korean survey didn't report this detail.)

The expectations of return on their investment varied widely (as must be expected) as given in Table 4.5.

From these numbers, it appears that manufacturers in Sweden expect a bit less return than did those in the U.S. (much of which might be explained by economic timing). Korean firms were more diverse in expectations. Since the motivation for adopting an enterprise system in some cases was either competitive or viewed as forced for other reasons, some firms expect low payoff from their systems. However, roughly as many adopters expect clearly significant returns on their investment.

4.3 PROJECT EVALUATION TECHNIQUES

EIS selection does not happen overnight and it can take almost a year.[13] This section will demonstrate some of the most widely used methods

---

[13] Rebecca Gill is serving as vice president at Technology Group International (www.tgiltd.com). TGI is a leading provider of Enterprise 21 (ERP software solution) and related enterprise business solutions for manufacturers and distributors. TGI's primary business focus, and where the majority of our ERP software customers exist, is the small to medium size business (SMB) market, with annual business revenue up to $500 million and user counts up to 700 concurrent users. She is an author of TGI's Software Selection Took Kit, as well as a number of articles in both technical and industry-specific publications.

mentioned above, and show how other methods can be used to consider other factors describing expected project performance. Cost-benefit analysis seeks to identify accurate measures of benefits and costs in monetary terms, and uses the ratio benefits/costs (the term benefit-cost ratio seems more appropriate, and is sometimes used, but most people refer to cost-benefit analysis). Because enterprise systems involve long time frames (for benefits, if not for costs as well), considering the net present value of benefits and costs is important.

4.3.1 Cost-Benefit Example

Consider a proposed EIS implementation involving an implementation study in year 1 conducted by a small team of company personnel, aided by a hired consultant. This is a fairly small implementation, and at this stage of the analysis, typically expected costs are underestimated. It has numbers that are relatively small compared to average EIS implementation projects, but could well represent ballpark costs for a small firm implementing one or a few modules. This analysis in year 1 includes some business process reengineering study, and the formation of a training team. This cost analysis assumes purchase of a $6 million software system from a reputable vendor, with maintenance costs for patches and upgrades of $1 million a year thereafter. The internal team is expected to double in payroll cost during year 2, and consulting expertise will double as well. The second year will also see investment in extra hardware to support the proposed system. Finally, in year 3, the internal implementation team, assisted by consultants, will finish implementation. An extra budget of $500,000 is allowed for additional hardware. The training team will grow after the first year. The firm wants to treat all expenses in the first three years as investment.

There will be costs for a team to operate the system. This budget is expected to be $2 million in year 4, growing at a rate of 10 percent per year thereafter. There will be a continued need for training personnel during years 4 and 5, but at lower rates than during system development and implementation.

The firm's cost of capital is 10 percent. There is some disagreement among the board concerning the expected rate of growth of benefits. The dominant group on the board expects benefits from the EIS to be

Table 4.6: Cost-Benefit Analysis Input Data — Example of a Proposal.

Year	Internal team	Consultants	Software	Hardware	Training	High benefit
1	500,000	500,000			200,000	
2	1,000,000	1,000,000	6,000,000	2,000,000	500,000	
3	1,500,000	1,000,000	1,000,000	500,000	2,000,000	6,000,000
4	2,000,000		1,000,000		1,000,000	7,800,000
5	2,200,000		1,000,000		300,000	10,140,000
6	2,420,000		1,000,000			13,182,000
7	2,662,000		1,000,000			17,136,600

$6 million per year in year 3, and to last for 7 years, growing at 30 percent per year. A vocal minority thinks that this expectation is far too high, and benefits will be $4 million in year 3. This data is summarized in Table 4.6.

These numbers reflect the expectations of the majority of the board.

4.3.2 Net Present Value Calculation

We will first demonstrate calculation of net present value of the project proposal, using both expected rates of benefit growth as shown in Table 4.7. First, we use the 30 percent benefit growth rate assumed by the majority of the board, and a cost of capital of 10 percent per year.

The net present value for the majority board opinion shows that adopting the project is equivalent in worth to a gain of $9.3 million. This takes some faith, as most of the outflow of cash is at the beginning, while expected benefits are late. Furthermore, in seven years' time technology will undoubtedly have changed significantly, making the value of the current system dubious. That is a good reason to cut off the analysis at 10 years. The problem is that the expected benefits peak at that distant time horizon.

The more conservative group on the board would view the proposal as equivalent to throwing away $1.4 million today. This would be the basis for a strong argument against the proposal. There is a possible mitigation, in that competitive pressures or other reasons may compel adoption of more modern computer systems.

Table 4.7: Net Present Value Calculation.

Year	Expenses	High benefits	High NPV	Low benefits	Low NPV
1	1,200,000		−1,090,909		−1,090,909
2	10,500,000		−8,677,686		−8,677,686
3	6,000,000	6,000,000	0	4,000,000	−1,502,630
4	4,000,000	7,800,000	2,595,451	5,200,000	819,616
5	3,500,000	10,140,000	4,122,918	6,760,000	2,024,204
6	3,420,000	13,182,000	5,510,395	8,788,000	3,030,096
7	3,662,000	17,136,600	6,914,600	11,424,400	3,983,339
NPV			9,374,769		−1,413,970

4.3.3 Return on Investment

Companies adopting ERP certainly acquire benefits such as an increase in suppliers' and customers' satisfaction and an increase in productivity but the level of the return on investment (ROI) is rather low.[14] The internal rate of return (IRR) on investment of a proposal is simply the discount rate (10 percent per year was used in Table 4.7) that would yield a zero net present value. This can be identified easily on a spreadsheet by placing the discount rate used in net present value calculations in a particular cell, and entering data until the net present value is closest to zero. In the example, assuming a 30 percent rate of benefit growth per year would yield an internal rate of return of 30.7 percent per year. For the conservative group on the board, the corresponding IRR would have 6.4 percent per year.

4.3.4 Payback

One of the most common reasons for company failure in the U.S. is lack of cash flow. Webb has examined the tradeoff between cash flow and net present value in economic analysis.[15] In this case, if the firm has cash-flow

---

[14] Themistocleous, M, Irani, Z. and O'Keefe, R. M. (2001). ERP and applications integration: Exploratory survey. *Business Process Management Journal*, 7, 195–204.

[15] Webb, D. C. (1993). The tradeoff between cash flow and net present value. *Scandinavian Journal of Economics*, 95(1), 65–75.

difficulties, the investment would be less attractive than if they had adequate cash reserves.

Another measure of value is to identify the time for an investment to be repaid. A time-related factor is the need for cash flow. One alternative may be superior to another on the net present value of the total life cycle of the project. However, cost-benefit analysis does not consider the impact of negative cash flow.

Payback is usually a simplified form of analysis. Its calculation is very simple in cases where investment is heavy up front, and benefits are later in the time horizon. That is usually the case with ERP proposals; although care must be taken that possible negative cash flows in later periods don't mess up the calculations. The operation is to identify cumulative net cash flow, and identify how long it will be before it turns positive, as shown in Table 4.8.

Here the payback period is over five years, using undiscounted values. (Either discounted or non-discounted values could be used.) The calculation using the more conservative rate of growth in benefits is given in Table 4.9, showing payback delayed until late in year 7 (about 6.5 years).

Payback analysis converts the analysis from currency into time. In this case, the firm would have to wait six to seven years (based upon some rather heroic assumptions) to get their investment back. Negative cash flow would be expected to reach almost $14 million up front.

Table 4.8: Payback Calculation Assuming High Benefits.

Year	Costs	High benefits	Net	Cumulative
1	1,200,000		−1,200,000	−1,200,000
2	10,500,000		−10,500,000	−11,700,000
3	6,000,000	6,000,000	0	−11,700,000
4	4,000,000	7,800,000	3,800,000	−7,900,000
5	3,500,000	10,140,000	6,640,000	−1,260,000
6	3,420,000	13,182,000	9,762,000	**8,502,000**
7	3,662,000	17,136,600	13,474,600	21,976,600

Table 4.9: Payback Calculation Assuming Low Benefits.

Year	Costs	Low benefits	Net	Cumulative
1	1,200,000		−1,200,000	−1,200,000
2	10,500,000		−10,500,000	−11,700,000
3	6,000,000	4,000,000	−2,000,000	−13,700,000
4	4,000,000	5,200,000	1,200,000	−12,500,000
5	3,500,000	6,760,000	3,260,000	−9,240,000
6	3,420,000	8,788,000	5,368,000	−3,872,000
7	3,662,000	11,424,400	7,762,400	**3,890,400**

4.3.5 Other Factors

There are a number of complications that can be brought into the calculation of cost-benefit ratios. One of the most obvious limitations of the method is that benefits, and even costs, can involve high levels of uncertainty. The element of chance can be included in cost-benefit calculations by using expected values. The Appendix to this chapter demonstrates two methods that provide ways to quantify the analysis of enterprise system investment problems in ways that consider more than simply estimates of cash flow.

4.4 EIS ROI ISSUES

EIS can be very effective tools in managing large organizations. Unfortunately, more than 90 percent of the companies that have implemented ERP/EIS have not had a truly successful implementation the first time around. Despite common reports of the limited returns from ERP/EIS, however, the ROI potential is there. The warning is:

➢ ERP/EIS must be motivated by accurate strategic and tactical process improvement objectives, with documented assumptions and valid ROI expectations and metrics.

➤ ERP/EIS must be implemented appropriately and in a timely manner to attain ROI expectations.

These two points may seem obvious, but ERP/EIS and supply chain management are hardly ever initially approached in this manner. As a result, many problems come to pass during and after implementation. This often requires a re-implementation effort or at least a major tune-up. ROI comes from process improvements ERP/EIS supports, not from new ERP/EIS software. What's the difference? ERP/EIS software alone, no matter how good it is, has little impact on improving business performance. If you continue to use pre-ERP/EIS business processes after implementation, you can anticipate identical or possibly worse performance. ERP/EIS software can, on the other hand, enable many new processes.

4.5 TOTAL COST OF OWNERSHIP

There are different types of distinct costs involved in an EIS application. Some of these are mentioned below.

1) **Awareness Cost** — most understandable is the cost of the software itself.

2) **Cost of Custom Software Maintenance** — this is probably the single major factor in determining the long-term cost of a system. For example, let's say a small company buys an inventory control and accounting system but they desire the system be interfaced with their CRM system and also to their shipping system in the warehouse. Let's also imagine that the company needs some modifications to the central part order entry system, which interacts with customer and shipping data. Interfaces and customization are costly, as they involve more time.

3) **Cost of Implementation** — this is the cost of getting the system live in the first place. Implementation costs vary widely based on the application. Components of this cost are data movement services,

systems integration, training, consulting, process engineering and project management.

4) **Cost of System Integration** — While companies would characteristically prefer a single turnkey solution that meets all of their needs, it is infrequently practical, if available at all.

5) **Expenses of Customization** — Of the thousands and thousands of business software implementations the company has performed, only a handful have gone into production without some form of customization. As technology has advanced, the cost of customization has come down; however this continues to be a major cost with EIS software.

6) **Obligatory Platform** — Software requires a computer platform. The older the computer platform, the higher the likelihood that a more powerful platform will be required to adequately support a new EIS.

7) **Safeguarding Costs** — There is an ongoing annual cost of maintenance to sustain the system. Companies often charge 17–20 percent of the purchase price per year for this cost category.

Total Cost of Ownership (TCO) has long been recognized as a significant factor in ERP strategies and decisions. Yet while both end users and EIS/ERP solution providers tend to talk about lower TCO, and many vendors claim it as a point of differentiation, seldom do they speak in terms of specific metrics.[16] Figure 4.2 shows one opinion about Cost of Ownership and Maintenance by an EIS/ERP vendor.

Optimizing total cost of ownership requires looking beyond the price per unit. To actually achieve optimization, management of a product's full life cycle is vital. Rough estimates of typical relative costs by category are shown in Figure 4.3.

---

[16] Aberdeen Group is the leading provider of fact-based research focused on the global technology-driven value chain. Founded in 1988, Aberdeen has established the market-leading position as the "voice that matters" when it comes to understanding the measurable results being delivered by technology in business.

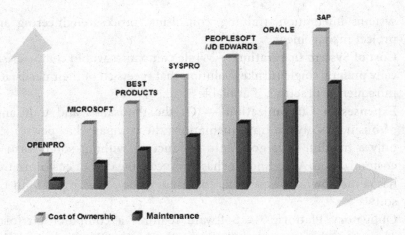

Figure 4.2: Relative Total Cost of Ownership by Vendor.

Source: OpenPro.[17]

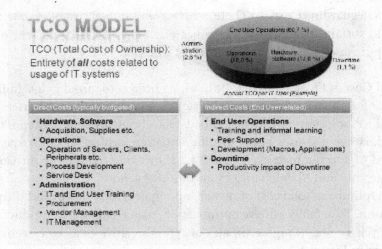

Figure 4.3: Relative Total Cost of Ownership by Category.

Source: Microsoft.[18]

---

[17] OpenPro is the first company to build a complete Web-Based SQL Server ERP system. It created three versions: Easy ERP for the smaller manufacturer with basic needs, OpenPro ERP for companies with over 10 user seats and Enterprise ERP for the larger Organizations.

[18] https://www.microsoft.com.nsatc.net/asia/partnersolutionmarketplace/india/CaseStudy Detail.aspx?casestudyid=4000000605

4.6 ALTERNATIVE EVALUATION

Peter Keen (1981) proposed value analysis as an alternative to cost-benefit analysis in the evaluation of proposed information system projects. These projects, clearly attractive to business firms, suffer in that their benefits are often heavily intangible. For instance, decision support systems are meant to provide decision makers with more complete information for decision-making. But what is the exact dollar value of improved decision-making? We all expect the success of firms to be closely tied to effective decision-making, but there is no rational, accurate measure of making better decisions.[19]

4.6.1 Value Analysis

Value analysis was presented as a way to separate the benefits measured in intangible terms from costs, which are expected to be more accurately measurable. Those tangible benefits as well as costs can be dealt with in net present terms, which would provide a price tag for proposed projects. The value of the benefits would be descriptive, with the intent of showing the decision-makers' accurate descriptions of what they were getting, along with the net present price. The decision would then be converted to a purchasing choice. Many of us buy automobiles, despite the fact that the net present cost of owning an automobile is negative. Automobiles provide many intangible benefits, such as making the driver look very sporty, letting the driver speed over the countryside, and letting the driver transport those they would like to impress. The dollar value of these intangible benefits is a matter of willingness to pay, which can be identified in monetary terms by observing the purchasing behavior of individuals. This measurement requires some effort, and is different for each individual.

Assume a firm is considering four different ways to implement some or all of an ERP system (also including an alternative of doing nothing). The options, with estimated investments and benefits, are given in Table 4.10.

---

[19] Keen, P. G. W. (1981). Value analysis: Justifying decision support systems. *MIS Quarterly* 5(1), 1–16; www.peterkeen.com.

Table 4.10: Alternative System Implementation Options for an EIS Example.

Alternative	Investment	Benefits (NPV)
A. Full vendor implementation, all modules	$15 million	$21 million
B. Vendor, only FA and MM modules	$11 million	$17 million
C. Vendor, only FA module	$8 million	$12 million
D. In-house development	$25 million	$27 million
E. Open-sourced system	$5 million	$8 million
F. Current situation	0	0

Value analysis would consist of presenting the decision-maker with the intangible comparisons in performance, and placing the decision in the context of whether or not the decision-maker thought the improvements provided by the new machine were worth their price tag. This requires an analysis of expected benefits from each system. The reasons this particular management team is interested in an EIS project are:

➢ To update current business processes (through business process reengineering).
➢ To standardize procedures within the organization.
➢ To make possible interaction with suppliers and customers over Web technology.
➢ To gain strategic advantage.
➢ To keep up with competitors.
➢ To minimize system disruption.
➢ To maximize positive net financial impact.

The expected performance of each alternative on the six qualitative factors is given in Table 4.11.

In this approach, the expected benefits are understood to be highly variable, and are treated as a rough estimate. Costs are assumed to be a bit more reliable. Thus, the options, in descending order of price, are:

A. Full implementation of vendor product: expected cost $15 million.

Complete BPR analysis and standardization.
Top-of-the-line Internet access for suppliers and customers.

Table 4.11: Qualitative Features of ERP Options in Example.

Alternative	BPR	Standardize	Internet	Advantage	Keep up	Disruption
A. Full	Complete	Complete	Best	Equal	Best	5 years
B. FA, MM	Partial	Partial	Best	Less than A	Less than A	4 years
C. FA	Minimal	Partial	Best	Less than B	Less than B	1 year
D. In-house	Complete	Complete	Problematic	Best	Mediocre	7 years
E. Open source	Minimal	Partial	Best	Moderate	Moderate	2 years
F. Nothing	Nothing	Nothing	Worst	Worst	Worst	0

State-of-the-art ERP system, which competitors also have access to.
Serious disruption of operations through installation in 5 years.
Expected benefit NPV: $21 million, for net gain of $6 million.

B. Partial implementation of vendor product: expected cost $11 million.

Partial BPR analysis and standardization.
Top-of-the-line Internet access for suppliers and customers.
State-of-the-art EIS, which competitors also have access to.
Serious disruption of operations through installation in 4 years.
Expected benefit NPV: $17 million, for net gain of $6 million.

C. Minimal implementation of vendor product: expected cost $8 million.

Minimal BPR analysis, partial standardization.
Top-of-the-line Internet access for suppliers and customers.
State-of-the-art EIS, which competitors also have access to.
Serious disruption of operations through installation in 1 year.
Expected benefit NPV: $12 million, for net gain of $4 million.

D. In-house implementation: expected cost $25 million.

Complete BPR analysis and standardization.
Suspect Internet access for suppliers and customers.
Custom-designed system with features competitors don't have, but no best practices.
Serious disruption of operations through installation in seven years.
Expected benefit NPV: $27 million, for net gain of $2 million.

E. Open-sourced system: expected cost $5 million.

Minimal BPR analysis and standardization.
Strong Internet access for suppliers and customers.
Proven EIS, but with less functionality than others.
Minimal disruption of operations.
Expected benefit NPV: $8 million, for net gain of $3 million.

F. Do nothing: expected cost $0.

No BPR analysis and standardization.
Primitive Internet access for suppliers and customers.
No ERP system in market where competitors do.
No disruption of operations.
Expected benefit NPV: $0, for net gain of $0 million.

Management can now view each option as a market basket of benefits, each with its own price tag. In this case, the key difference is building the system in-house, adopting a variant of the vendor system, or doing nothing. Building the system in-house clearly has many risks, and involves the most out-of-pocket investment. Management might well discard that option unless they are very confident in their ability to develop complex software projects. The open-sourced option has attractive features, but involves more uncertainties, and doesn't provide the best BPR options. Among the vendor options, Alternative A has the best features on reengineering, standardization, and Internet connectivity. But it would involve 5 years of disruption, and call for a $15 million investment. Option B would save $4 million in investment with the same Internet access at only 4 years of disruption, but sacrifice a bit on BPR factors, standardization, relative competitive advantage, and keeping up with competitors. Management might feel that the gains in disruption are worth the sacrifices in BPR, standardization, competitive advantage, and competitiveness. For only $8 million investment, Option C would involve sacrifice of even more BPR, strategic advantage, and competitiveness, but would save 3 additional years of disruption. However, it may be paramount to obtain higher degrees of methods improvement through business process reengineering and standardization of business functions across the organization. By focusing on the important features involved, management may be able to conclude that option A or B is preferable to the other options available.

Taking value analysis one more step, to quantify these intangible benefits in terms of value (not in terms of dollars) takes us to multiple criteria analysis.

4.6.2 Multiple Objectives

Profit has long been viewed as the determining objective of a business. However, as society becomes more complex, and as the competitive environment develops, businesses are finding that they need to consider multiple objectives. While short-run profit remains important, long-run factors such as market maintenance, product quality, and development of productive capacity often conflict with measurable short-run profit.

Conflicts are inherent in most interesting decisions. In business, **Profit** is a valuable concentration point for many decision-makers because it has the apparent advantage of providing a measure of worth. Minimizing **risk** becomes a second dimension for decision-making. There are cash flow needs which become important in some circumstances. Businesses need **developed markets** to survive. The impact of advertising expenditure is often very difficult to forecast. Yet decision-makers must consider advertising impact. **Capital replenishment** is another decision factor which requires consideration of tradeoffs. The greatest short-run profit will normally be obtained by delaying reinvestment in capital equipment. Many U.S. companies have been known to cut back on capital investment in order to appear reasonably profitable to investors. **Labor** policies can also have impact upon long-range profit. In the short run, profit will generally be improved by holding the line on wage rates, and risking a high labor turnover. There are costs which are not obvious, however, in such a policy. First, there is training expense involved with a high turnover environment. The experience of the members of an organization can be one of its most valuable assets. Second, it is difficult for employees to maintain a positive attitude when their experience is that short-run profit is always placed ahead of employee welfare. And innovative ideas are probably best found from those people who are involved with the grass roots of an organization — the work-force.

This variety of objectives presents decision-makers with the need to balance conflicting objectives in ERP option selection. We will present the simple multi-attribute rating technique (SMART), an easy-to-use method to aid selection decisions with multiple objectives.

4.6.3 Multiple Criteria Analysis

Multiple criteria analysis considers benefits on a variety of scales without directly converting them to some common scale such as dollars. The method (there are many variants of multiple criteria analysis) is not at all perfect. But it does provide a way to demonstrate to decision-makers the relative positive and negative features of alternatives, and gives a way to quantify the preferences of decision-makers.[20]

Fit with business procedures was selected among the three most important criteria by about one-half of the respondents, and was listed as the single most important criterion by over one-third. While EIS vendors have devoted a great deal of effort to making their packages match existing business processes, the importance of this criterion is based upon the high cost and bother of configuring and implementing EIS systems. Selection of a vendor involved less variance among criteria. Product functionality and quality were the criteria most often reported to be important.

Perhaps the easiest application of multiple criteria analysis is the simple multi-attribute rating theory (SMART), which identifies the relative importance of criteria in terms of weights, and measures the relative performance of each alternative for each criterion in terms of scores.[21] We will first explain scores.

Scores: Scores in SMART can be used to convert performances (subjective or objective) to a zero-one scale, where zero represents the worst acceptable performance level in the mind of the decision-maker, and one represents the ideal, or possibly the best performance desired. Note that these ratings are subjective, a function of individual

---

[20] For description of methods, see Olson, D. L. (1996). *Decision Aids for Selection Problems*, New York: Springer.

[21] Edwards, W. (1977). How to use multi-attribute utility measurement for social decision-making. *IEEE Transactions on Systems, Man, and Cybernetics*, 7(5), 326–340.

preference. Scores for the criteria given in the value analysis example are seen in Table 4.12.

Weights: The next phase of the analysis ties these ratings together into an overall value by obtaining the relative weight of each criterion. In order to give the decision-maker a reference about what exactly is being compared, the relative range between best and worst on each scale for each criterion should be explained.[22] There are many methods to determine these weights. In SMART, the process begins with rank-ordering the four criteria. A possible ranking for a specific decision-maker might be as given in Table 4.13.

Table 4.12: Scores by Criteria for each Option in EIS Example.

Option	BPR	Standard	Internet	Advantage	Competition	Disruption	Financial
A	1.0	1.0	1.0	0.7	1.0	0.1	0.85
B	0.9	0.7	1.0	0.5	0.8	0.3	0.95
C	0.6	0.7	1.0	0.2	0.6	0.9	0.90
D	1.0	1.0	0.6	1.0	0.1	0.0	0.2
E	0.6	0.7	1.0	0.6	0.4	0.8	1.0
F	0.0	0.0	0.0	0.0	0.0	1.0	0.0

Table 4.13: Worst and Best Measures by Criteria.

Criteria	Worst measure	Best measure
Update systems (BPR)	Nothing	Complete
Standardize business processes	Nothing	Complete
Internet connectivity to suppliers & customers	None	Modern
Gain strategic advantage	Do nothing	Develop unique system
Keep up with competition	Do nothing	State-of-the-art vendor
Minimize disruption	7-year installation	Current system
Financial implications	Risk $25 mill, gain $2 mill	Risk $5 mill, gain $3 mill

---

[22] Hobbs, B. F. and Horn, G. T. F. (1997). Building public confidence in energy planning: A multi-method MCDM approach to demand-side planning at BC Gas. *Energy Policy*, 25(3), 356–375.

To obtain relative criterion weights, the first step is to rank-order criteria by importance. Two estimates of weights can be obtained. The first assigns the least important criterion 10 points, and assesses the relative importance of each of the other criteria on that basis. This process (including rank-ordering and assigning relative values based upon moving from worst measure to best measure according to most important criterion) is demonstrated in Table 4.14(a).

The total of the assigned values is 283. One estimate of relative weights is obtained by dividing each assigned value by 283. Before we do that, we obtain a second estimate from the perspective of the least important criterion, which is assigned a value of 10 as in Table 4.14(b).

These add up to 345. The two weight estimates are now as shown in Table 4.15.

The last criterion can be used to make sure that the sum of compromise weights adds up to 1.00.

Value Score: The next step of the SMART method is to obtain value scores for each alternative by multiplying each score on each criterion for an alternative by that criterion's weight, and adding these products by alternative. Table 4.16 shows this calculation.

This value score (shown in the totals row) provides a relative score that can be used to select (take the alternative with the highest value score), or

Table 4.14(a): Weight Estimation from Perspective of Most Important Criterion.

Criteria	Worst measure	Best measure	Assigned value
1. Gain strategic advantage	Do nothing	Develop unique system	100
2. Keep up with competition	Do nothing	Use state-of-the-art vendor	70
3. Internet connectivity	None	Modern	50
4. Update systems (BPR)	Nothing	Complete	30
5. Minimize disruption	7-year installation	Current system	20
6. Financial implications	Risk $25 mill, gain $2 mill	Risk $17 mill, gain $6 mill	10
7. Standardize business processes	Nothing	Complete	3

Table 4.14(b):   Weight Estimation from Perspective of Least Important Criterion.

Criteria	Worst measure	Best measure	Assigned value
7. Standardize business processes	Nothing	Complete	10
6. Financial implications	Risk $25 mill, gain $2 mill	Risk $17 mill, gain $6 mill	25
5. Minimize disruption	7-year installation	Current system	30
4. Update systems (BPR)	Nothing	Complete	50
3. Internet connectivity	None	Modern	60
2. Keep up with competition	Do nothing	Use state-of-the-art vendor	70
1. Gain strategic advantage	Do nothing	Develop unique system	100

Table 4.15:   Criterion Weight Development.

Criteria	Based on best		Based on worst		Compromise
1. Gain strategic advantage	100/283	0.35	100/345	0.29	0.33
2. Keep up with competition	70/283	0.25	70/345	0.20	0.23
3. Internet connectivity	50/283	0.18	60/345	0.17	0.17
4. Update systems (BPR)	30/283	0.11	50/345	0.14	0.12
5. Minimize disruption	20/283	0.07	30/345	0.09	0.08
6. Financial implications	10/283	0.04	25/345	0.07	0.05
7. Standardize business processes	3/283	0.01	10/345	0.03	0.02

to rank-order (by value score). In this case, the SMART analysis indicates a preference for Option A, the full version of the vendor ERP system. This is followed relatively closely by Option B, which is to reduce functionality to finance & accounting and materials management modules. Building Other options have lower ratings, while doing nothing is practically off the chart in a negative way.

Other Multiple Criteria Methods: Note that there are many other approaches implementing roughly the same idea. The best known is multi-attribute utility theory, which uses more sophisticated (but not

Table 4.16: Value Score Calculation.

Criteria	Weight	Option A	Option B	Option C	Option D	Option E	Option F
Strategic advantage	0.33	× 0.7 = 0.231	× 0.5 = 0.165	× 0.2 = 0.066	× 1.0 = 0.330	× 0.6 = 0.198	× 0.0 = 0.000
Competition	0.23	× 1.0 = 0.230	× 0.8 = 0.184	× 0.6 = 0.138	× 0.1 = 0.023	× 0.4 = 0.092	× 0.0 = 0.000
Internet	0.17	× 1.0 = 0.170	× 1.0 = 0.170	× 1.0 = 0.170	× 0.6 = 0.102	× 1.0 = 0.170	× 0.0 = 0.000
Update (BPR)	0.12	× 1.0 = 0.120	× 0.9 = 0.108	× 0.6 = 0.072	× 1.0 = 0.120	× 0.6 = 0.072	× 0.0 = 0.000
Minimize disruption	0.08	× 0.1 = 0.008	× 0.3 = 0.024	× 0.9 = 0.072	× 0.0 = 0.000	× 0.8 = 0.064	× 1.0 = 0.080
Financial	0.05	× 0.85 = 0.043	× 0.95 = 0.048	× 0.9 = 0.045	× 0.2 = 0.010	× 1.0 = 0.050	× 0.0 = 0.000
Standardize	0.02	× 1.0 = 0.020	× 0.7 = 0.014	× 0.7 = 0.014	× 1.0 = 0.020	× 0.7 = 0.014	× 0.0 = 0.000
Totals	1.00	0.822	0.713	0.577	0.605	0.660	0.080

necessarily more accurate) methods to obtain both scores and weights.[23] The analytic hierarchy process is another well-known approach.[24]

4.7 CONCLUSION

We have reviewed some of the primary methods used to evaluate ERP/EIS proposals. Screening provides a way to simplify the decision by focusing on those projects that are acceptable on all measures. Profiles provide information that displays tradeoffs on different measures of importance. Cost-benefit analysis (with net present value used if the time dimension is present) is the ideal approach from the theoretical perspective, but has a number of limitations. It is very difficult to measure benefits, and also difficult to measure some aspects of costs accurately. One view of dealing with this problem is to measure more accurately. Economists have developed ways to estimate the value of a life, and the value of scenic beauty. However, these measures are difficult to sell to everybody.

A more common view is that it is wasted effort to spend inordinate time seeking a highly unstable and inaccurate dollar estimate for many intangible factors. Value analysis is one such alternative method. Value analysis isolates intangible benefits from those benefits and costs that are more accurately measurable in monetary terms, and relies upon the decision-maker's judgment to come to a more informed decision. The SMART method, one of a family of multiple criteria decision analysis techniques, provides a way to quantify these intangible factors to allow decision-makers to tradeoff values.

Cost-benefit provides an ideal way to proceed if there are no intangible factors (or at least no important intangible factors). However, usually such factors are present. Intermediate approaches, such as payback analysis and

---

[23] Keeney, R. L. and Raiffa, H. (1976). *Decisions with Multiple Objectives: Preferences and Value Tradeoffs*. New York: John Wiley & Sons.
[24] Saaty, T. L. (1977). A scaling method for priorities in hierarchical structures. *Journal of Mathematical Psychology*, 15, 234–281.

value analysis, exist to deal with some cases. More complex cases are better supported by multiple criteria analysis.

Proper planning and management is very important in EIS/ERP implementation. Project management in the implementation of EIS/ERP includes requirements to accomplish the following:

a. Software and hardware selection.
b. Business process reengineering to gain effective advantage from the new system.
c. Assess the ERP readiness of the organization and plan change management to make the new system effective.
d. Proper project management to include selection of an effective project management team.

☆ KEYWORDS

☆ **Cost-Benefit Analysis:** Generically, the set of financial analyses that consider return on investment. Specifically, the ratio of gains to expenses for a project.

☆ **Development Criteria:** Estimates of system impact on technical system operations.

☆ **Hidden Costs:** Unanticipated expenses incurred when implementing a complex system.

☆ **Intangible Factors:** Factors involved in estimating costs and benefits that include subjective elements that are difficult to quantify.

☆ **Internal Rate of Return (IRR):** Discount rate that returns a net present value of 0 for a given stream of cash flow.

☆ **Management Criteria:** Estimates of impact of a system on non-financial business measures.

☆ **Multiple Criteria Analysis:** Quantification of subjective elements in terms of preference value functions of various kinds.

☆ **Net Present Value (NPV):** Current worth of a stream of cash flow given a stated discount rate.

☆ **Payback:** Estimated amount of time required to regain an investment.

☆ **Project Management Programs:** Programs used in Project Management Systems as apparatus for project management.

☆ **Project Management System:** Organization system facilitating the running of essential tasks to arrive at an objective, according to the operative plan, as well as customary checks and co-ordination of allocated resources.

☆ **ROI:** Stands for Return on Investment. Statement reporting predictable returns aligned with a given investment. ROI is a measure of investment profitability, not a measure of investment size. While compound interest and dividend reinvestment can increase the size of the investment (thus potentially yielding a higher dollar return to the investor), Return on Investment is a percentage return based on capital invested.

☆ **Value Analysis:** View of information system projects considering costs as in cost-benefit analysis, but gains in subjective terms.

Faq

FAQ: How much money will EIS certification cost me?

ANSWER: The total cost incurred depends largely on your study approach. Many people have earned their ERP/EIS certification for less than $325 using self-study methods. Other approaches can cost moderately up to a thousand dollars.

☆ TERMINOLOGY REVIEW

A. Review Questions

1. ERP/EIS software is expensive to purchase, time-consuming to implement, and requires significant employee training, but the payoffs can be spectacular. For some companies, however, the ROI may not be immediate or even calculable.

2. Describe some of the intangible costs and benefits typically found in EIS proposals.

3. Describe the relative advantages in the extremes of an EIS system developed in-house versus a full vendor EIS system.

4. Describe hidden outcomes of adopting EIS systems.

5. Why are EIS systems usually treated as capital expenditures rather than required business expenses?

6. Discuss the financial criteria typically used to analyze information system technology proposals.

7. Discuss the management criteria sometimes used for analyzing information system technology proposals.

8. Discuss the development criteria sometimes used for analyzing information system technology proposals.

9. Discuss the relative costs involved in EIS installation projects.

10. Given the following data for an EIS proposal, estimate payback, net present value, and cost-benefit ratio. Use a discount rate of 10 percent per year.

Time	Outflow	Inflow
Begin year 1	$5,000,000	0
End year 1	$10,000,000	$1,000,000
End year 2	$5,000,000	$9,000,000
End year 3	$3,000,000	$10,000,000
End year 4	$3,300,000	$11,000,000
End year 5	$3,700,000	$12,000,000

11. Estimate net present value for the data in Question 10 using a discount rate of 25 percent per year.

12. Use a spreadsheet to calculate internal rate of return for the data in the question above.

13. Discuss the difference between value analysis and cost-benefit analysis.

14. Why are other objectives besides profit important in business?

15. Apply SMART analysis to the following data. Develop your own weights of relative importance for NPV, market share, and technical

learning, as well as scores for each of these measures with respect to each project.

Option	NPV	Market share	Technical learning
Vendor	$80 million	Little impact	Minor gain
Vendor-custom	$90 million	Significant	Minor gain
In-house	$110 million	Very significant	Major gain
ASP	$150 million	Average	Minor gain

16. Develop weights of attribute importance using your own judgment. Then use your own judgment to score each option on each of the three criteria. Finally, apply SMART analysis to rank the three options. In Question 15, apply managerially imposed weights of: NPV 0.7, Market share 0.2, Technical learning 0.1. Use the same scores for NPV, market share, and technical learning for the four projects that you developed in Question 15.

17. What additional software packages are people using to efficiently navigate the budget planning cycle?

18. How does EIS help us to improve customer satisfaction? How much and where?

19. How does EIS contribute to increasing our market share? How much and where?

20. How does EIS decrease our operating expenses? How much and where?

21. How does EIS help to increase revenue? How much and where?

22. How does EIS decrease our inventory investment? How much and where?

23. How does EIS shorten our order-to delivery cycle time? How much and where?

24. How does EIS help us keep pace with or surpass our competitors? How much and where?

25. How does EIS shorten our time-to market? How much and where?

26. How will we be able to reduce our material costs through improved supply base management? How much and where?

27. How can we appropriately define responsibility and accountability for these business performance improvements?

28. What are the metrics for measuring performance improvement in both tactical and strategic areas?
29. Management did not answer the question, "How do we want to run our business and why?" and therefore, maximizing performance through significant business process improvement did not occur.
30. With the implementation success rate so low and positive ROI often nonexistent, many now think that EIS are expensive, wasteful exercises.
31. Enterprise Strategies report will not only quantify TCO but also present side by side comparison of these metrics from five of the top ERP vendors.
32. With an intense focus on ROI and Total Cost of Ownership (TCO), EIS software offers a new approach to "value," geared to the reality of present-day IT budgets. Elaborate.
33. Why is the total cost of ownership (TCO) approach a solution for communication technology? Explain.

☆ CHECK YOUR PROGRESS

Briefly comment on the following:

a. The goal is to find software that will best mirror the organization's business processes.

....

....

b. The responsibility for financial control often fails to match management responsibility.

....

....

c. The existence of restrictive, complicated and confusing financial procedures.

....

....

d. Financial information is often poorly presented and out of date.

....

....

e. Financial expertise is too remote.

....

....

f. EIS implementations have been plagued by a long list of other afflictions.

....

....

g. EIS software was installed to mirror a set of existing, inadequate business processes.

....

....

h. Organizations were painfully ill-prepared to conform to best practice process templates chosen by the EIS integrator.

....

....

i. Most new ERP system implementations have been disappointing, and have needed significant cleaning up to achieve positive ROI.

....

....

j. EIS became a software replacement project, and after expenditure approval, management often stepped aside and let information technology and systems integrators take over the installation of software.

....

....

k. ROI comes from process improvements ERP supports, not from new ERP software.

....

....

☆ COMPETENCY REVIEW

1. Your organization has decided to implement an EIS system. Whether the driver for change is that the current Legacy system is out-of-date, cannot handle the volume or is causing customer service issues, it is imperative that your organization not fall into the trap that has plagued hundreds of early EIS adopters.
2. Create an Implementation Team composed of 10–15 people in the organization that are identified as the best people in each area. Factor in the costs involved.
3. Identify and advocate a set of principles to which the operation of the internal audit function and structures and other financial controls and procedures in the organization should adhere.

☆ SUGGESTED READING

Books

Bodie, Z., Kane, A. and Marcus, A.J. (2004). *Essentials of Investments*, 5th Ed. New York: McGraw-Hill/Irwin.

Brealey, R. A., Myers, S. C. and Allen, F. (2006). *Principles of Corporate Finance*, 8th Ed. McGraw-Hill/Irwin.

Meigs, W. B. and Meigs, R. F. (1970). *Financial Accounting*, 4th Ed. New York: McGraw-Hill.

White Papers and Internet Sites

Curtis, D. *et al.* (2001). Enterprise Management and IT Cost Reduction in 2002. Gartner Group Research Note (SPA-14-8161).

Donovan, M. (2000). Why the Controversy Over the ROI from ERP? www.rmdonovan.com.

Hall, L. and Mieritz, L. (2000). How Technology-Related Factors Influence Indirect TCO. Gartner Group Research Note (COM-10-6344).

Hurley, D. (2002). Managing ERP Modifications in Higher Education. Gartner Group Research NOTE (DF-14-5000).

Kaludis, G. and Stine, G. (2001). Strategic Management for Information Technology. *Educause Review*, 48–56.

Kinare, S., Tatkare, V. and Dixit, A. (2005). Getting Maximum Business Value out of ERP. http://www.patni.com/resource-center/collateral/manufacturing/tp_MFG_EAS_ERP_Getting-Maximum-Business-Value.html.

Lembke, R. and Rudy, J. (2001). Top Campus IT Challenges for 2001. *Educause Quarterly*, 4–19.

Mein, J. and Gammage, B. (2002). Cost Control through Asset Management: Easy Pickings. Gartner Group Research Note (HARD-WW-DP-0184).

Mieritz, L. and Hall, L. (2000). How People and Process Factors Influence Indirect TCO. Gartner Group Research Note (COM-10-6124).

Micromation Consulting Group (Asset Life-Cycle). available at www.micro-mation.com

Oberst, D. (2001). Enterprise Systems Management. *Educause Review*, 58–59.

What is business process management? www.gartner.com.

Pereira, B. (2000). Making ROI on ERP Happen. www.networkmagazineindia.com.

Pitney, R. and Paust, M. (2003). Increasing the ROI in ERP through Business Process Optimization. http://www.crm2day.com/library/EpylZFkAVkTMbRhMNQ.php.

Zrimsek, B. *et al.* (2001). Estimating the Time and Cost of ERP and ERP II Projects: A 10-Step Process. Gartner Group Research (R-14-5140).

——— (2005). Cost of ERP — What does ERP really cost? http://www.sysoptima.com/erp/cost_of_erp.php.

——— (2005). ERP Implementation Methodologies. http://www.sysoptima.com/erp/implementation_methodologies.php.

——— (2005). History and Evolution of ERP. http://www.sysoptima.com/erp/history_of_erp.php.

CHAPTER 5

BUSINESS PROCESS REENGINEERING
AND BEST PRACTICES

Quotation

"Business is increasingly digital business." In the future, even more than today, most business will be either digital or depend critically on aspects that are digital. Business thus depends crucially on IT.

Benjamin Grosof

Structure

- ♣ *Quick look at chapter themes*
- ♣ *Learning objectives*
- ♣ *Case study:* Northwards Housing — Business Process Re-engineering
- ♣ *Sketch of BPR*
- ♣ *Introduction*
- 5.1 All about the Business and its Processes
  - 5.1.1 Business Processes
  - 5.1.2 Typical Business Processes
  - 5.1.3 Reengineering
  - 5.1.4 Business Process Reengineering
  - 5.1.5 Business Process Management
  - 5.1.6 BPR with Respect to EIS
- 5.2 Best Practices In EISs
- 5.3 Reengineering Options
  - 5.3.1 Clean Slate Reengineering
  - 5.3.2 Technology-Enabled Reengineering

♣ QUICK LOOK AT CHAPTER THEMES

The previous decade has seen an explosion in projects that pertain to Enterprise Information Systems (EIS). Many types of organization are involved — governments, academia, small- to medium-sized enterprises, large corporations, inter-governmental organizations, and non-profit and non-governmental enterprises. In spite of the massive effort and resources behind these projects, it has been difficult to accomplish these EIS installations on time, within budget, and according to their intended aims. Enterprise information technology provides value to organizations primarily through appropriate business process re-engineering (BPR) — improvement of the current business processes — to ensure that all the business processes and functions are clearly defined, concise and effective.

♣ LEARNING OBJECTIVES

This chapter examines the design of an organization's structure and business processes. It principally focuses on the application of information technologies to renovate organizations. Methods of introducing and implementing information technologies to enable organizational change are examined. It explores the principles and assumptions behind reengineering, examines a case study, and presents alternatives to "classical" reengineering theory. In conclusion, some specific recommendations regarding reengineering are given. In summary, the chapter will:

- ♣ Describe business processes.
- ♣ Present a discussion of how BPR was used in a real case.
- ♣ Pay particular attention to the role of BPR in Enterprise Information Systems.
- ♣ Assess business processes through their key operational characteristics; e.g., efficiency, intended service quality, process flexibility and costs associated with delays, material volume and level of service or product customization.
- ♣ Observe process diagnosis and formulation of improvements including estimating the effects of these improvements in terms of the above process metrics.
- ♣ Model simple business processes in terms of the people and activity sequences involved, the data and materials flowing through those sequences and the dependencies between business information and operational activities.
- ♣ Compare clean slate and technology-enabled business process reengineering.

♣ CASE STUDY

Northwards Housing[1] — Business Process Re-engineering

BACKGROUND

Northwards Housing is an Arms Length Management Organization (ALMO) which was established in December 2005 to manage approximately 12,500 council homes on behalf of Manchester City Council. Following an Audit Commission inspection in autumn 2006, Northwards was judged as a good, two-star organization with excellent prospects for improvement. However, one area that was highlighted as needing significant improvement was that of re-letting of empty properties. In January 2007, Northwards commissioned Enterprise to undertake a root and branch analysis of the voids management process including a detailed review of existing practices, an assessment of how performance was being measured, and the status of partnership arrangements.

INITIAL SITUATION

The focus for Northwards Housing following the Audit Commissions report was the management of their voids properties. The current situation had been highlighted through existing poor performance levels in the related Best Value Performance Indicators. In 2006, the average number of days to re-let a property (i.e. BV212) was between 70 and 75 days, compared with 28 days for top quartile ALMOs whilst rent loss also underperformed at around three percent of total rent roll, compared with 1.21 percent for the top quartile.

KEY CUSTOMER REQUIREMENT

The key deliverable from the project was to identify inefficiencies in the current process and to present a prioritized list of recommendations for future improvement.

OUR RESPONSE

The Enterprise team commenced the Voids Review in March 2006 — the project was scheduled to be completed in an intensive, five-week period and

---

[1] Enterprise plc Lancaster House Centurion Way Leyland Lancashire www.enterprise.plc.uk

in accordance with PRINCE2 methodology. The approach involved collection of qualitative data through a series of workshops, interviews, attendance at meetings, extensive process mapping, and analysis of quantitative data. The review also involved benchmarking activities, including visits to other housing organizations to share best practice and find new solutions to common problems. The project was far-reaching and involved all stakeholders, including tenant representatives, staff at all levels of Northwards Housing, the City Council, and the repairs & maintenance Joint Venture partner, Manchester Working. The Northwards Project Sponsor was kept informed at all times of progress and major findings, and worked closely with the team to ensure the necessary resources were available.

IMPROVEMENTS ACHIEVED

At the end of the Review, Enterprise presented its findings and conclusions to the Northwards Executive Board, together with a series of prioritized recommendations. The final report included both 'As Is' and 'To Be' process maps, detailed recommendations together with impact/resource analysis, an outline Project Plan for implementation of the improvement project, and proposed stepped targets for BV212 together with identification of achievable, cashable efficiency gains. In addition, the Review highlighted a number of relationship and managerial issues that were having an indirect adverse impact on voids performance.

CONCLUSION

Northwards Housing accepted all of the findings and has been fully committed to implementing the improvement project that involves radical change in order to achieve improvement in the voids process. Staff at all levels is now involved in the project that is being championed by both the Chief Executive of Northwards Housing and the Chief Executive of Manchester Working.

♣ SKETCH OF BPR

Reengineering is the deep-seated rethinking and radical redesign of business processes to accomplish dramatic enhancement in significant measures of performance, such as cost, quality, service and speed.[2] BPR is usually the primary driver in EIS implementation. BPR is frequently used by companies in financial trouble to cut costs and return to productivity. The risk is that the company may jeopardize future growth. "Business processes are methods, steps and activities we perform to do our jobs. For example, in most companies, filling a customer order involves several business processes from processing the order to shipping the product. Some companies have strong business process cultures; others have varying degrees of business process discipline."[3]

♣ INTRODUCTION

Michael Hammer invented the term BPR in 1990 in an article for the *Harvard Business Review* where he challenged managers to obliterate non-value adding work rather than automating it via technology. The article was followed in 1993 with the book *Reengineering the Corporation: A Manifesto for Business Revolution*, written in cooperation with James Champy. The concept of "Business Process Reengineering" traces its origins back to management theories developed as early as the 19th century. The purpose of reengineering is to "make all your processes the best-in-class." Frederick Taylor suggested in the 1880's that managers use process reengineering methods to discover the best processes for performing work, and that these processes be reengineered to optimize productivity. BPR echoes the classical belief that there is one best way to conduct tasks. Accomplishing this goal depends on maximizing the effectiveness of policy development and program delivery, planning and budgetary

---

[2] Michael Hammer and James Champy are two of the most famous pioneers in the area of business process reengineering, and their 1993 best-selling book, *Reengineering the Corporation: A Manifesto for Business Revolution*, provides the definition of BPR used in this research (p. 32).

[3] Interfacing Technologies Corporation develops award-winning business process management (BPM) software that helps clients map, model and manage business processes and knowledge. Our mission is to empower clients to optimize overall performance and meet compliance regulations by documenting, standardizing, improving and setting clear ownership of their processes, policies and procedures.

arrangements, decision-making processes, organizational structures, workplace relations and people management. Significant gains in performance have been attained through BPR. Increasingly, information and communications technology (EIS) plays a vital role in determining the quality and accessibility of services. Expansion in EIS has opened the door for even greater efficiencies and enhanced service delivery through integrated processes. There are opportunities for even greater gains as public and private sector enterprises transform their existing processes by the strategic application of EIS. For individual enterprises and government agencies, the most noteworthy gains are achieved when EIS decisions are business-driven. Shared arrangements in the private sector have demonstrated considerable benefits — for example, the banking sector's credit card arrangements and the travel industry's booking facilities. Shared arrangements also recommend significant opportunities to improve efficiency and service delivery in the public sector. The strategic use of EIS enables departments and agencies to improve existing program models and introduce new ways of delivering government information and services.

5.1 ALL ABOUT THE BUSINESS AND ITS PROCESSES

Business process reengineering (often referred to by the acronym BPR) is the main way in which organizations become more efficient and modernize. Business process reengineering transforms an organization in ways that directly affect performance.[4] Figure 5.1 shows the evolution of multi-enterprise processes.

5.1.1 Business Processes

A **process** is a logical set of related activities taking inputs, adding value through doing things, and creating an output.[5] In business, there are many

---

[4] Peter Carter is Managing Director of Corporate Information Systems Ltd, a UK firm providing consultancy and training services in business process reengineering and associated areas.

[5] Harrington, H. J., Essing, E. K. C. and van Nimwegen, H. (1997). *Business Process Improvement Workbook: Documentation, Analysis, Design, and Management of Business Process Improvement.* New York: McGraw-Hill. p. 1.

History of Multi-Enterprise Processes

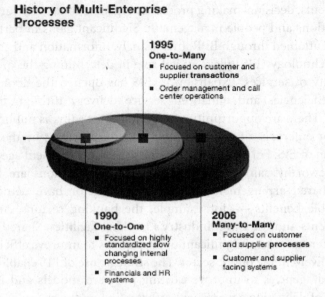

**1995
One-to-Many**
- Focused on customer and supplier **transactions**
- Order management and call center operations

**1990
One-to-One**
- Focused on highly standardized slow changing internal processes
- Financials and HR systems

**2006
Many-to-Many**
- Focused on customer and supplier **processes**
- Customer and supplier facing systems

Figure 5.1:   Multi-Enterprise Processes.

Source: One Network (2008).[6]

different ways to get work done. Information systems play a key role in providing a means to collect data, store it efficiently, generate reports to let management know what the organization is doing, and archive data for future reference as needed. Figure 5.2 gives a picture of the process of placing an order, showing the many systems involved in such a typical process.

There are, in general, two kinds of processes. Operational processes have to do with accomplishing typical business functions, including product development, order management, and customer support. Infrastructure processes are more administrative, such as establishing and implementing strategy, and managing many aspects of the organization including human

---

[6] One Network was founded in 2002 with a clear vision: pioneer the use of next-generation technology to enable precision execution of collaborative, multi-enterprise operational processes. Virtual business models have an impact on operations that is matched only by the challenge of managing processes that span so many organizational and IT system silos.

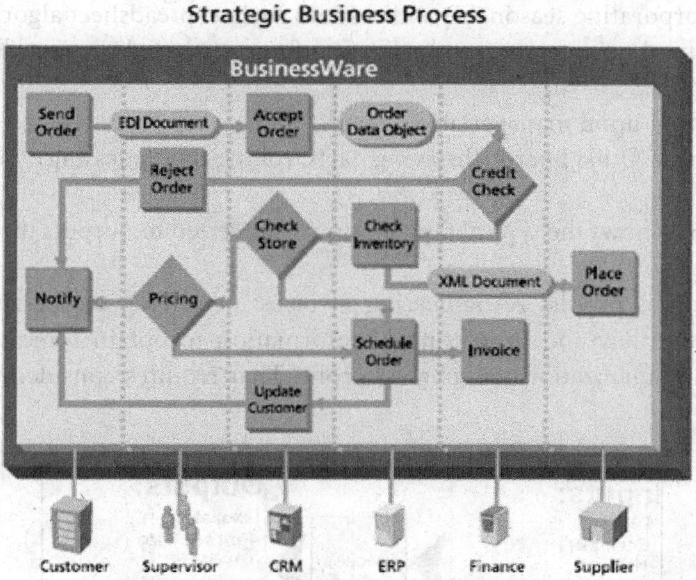

Strategic Business Process

Figure 5.2: Example of a High-Level Business Rrocess.
Source: Vitria (2008).[7]

resources, physical assets, and information systems. Each of these generic processes, whether operational or relating to infrastructure, involves sets of tasks needed to accomplish work. For example, in the operational process of order management, it is necessary to forecast the volume of demand expected for the products produced by an organization. The function of forecasting can be accomplished in many ways:

♦ Using last month's demand as a prediction for this month.
♦ Using the monthly demand from a year ago as the prediction for this month.
♦ Applying a spreadsheet algorithm such as exponential smoothing over available monthly data.

---

[7] Established in 1994, Vitria combines technology leadership with industry expertise in telecommunications, healthcare and insurance, manufacturing and supply chain, and financial services to dramatically improve strategic business processes across systems, people, and trading partners. www.vitria.com

◆ Incorporating seasonality indices into such a spreadsheet algorithm.
◆ Taking known orders and adjusting forecasts based on past demand records.
◆ Relying upon managerial judgment.
◆ Using a Ouija board (throwing darts; rolling dice; guessing).

Figure 5.3 shows the typical flow of inputs converted to outputs through a process.

Business process reengineering involves identifying the best way to design the flow and processing of information to obtain forecasts that yield the organization the greatest profit. That requires consideration of

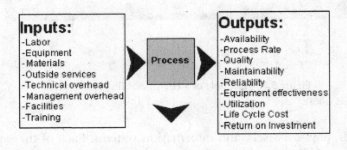

Figure 5.3:   Input/Output Diagram of Process.

Source: www.skf.com[8]

---

[8] SKF @ptitude Exchange is a Web site that provides information to professionals from maintenance technicians to top-level decision-makers, enabling efficient and effective decision-making for improved reliability results. Through SKF @ptitude Exchange, customers gain access not only to SKF's extensive knowledge and experience in rotating equipment, but to a wealth of essential information from SKF's alliance partners as well. These include a range of machinery, component, software, instrumentation manufacturers, and more.

accuracy in avoiding the most damaging kinds of forecast error, and giving the organization the greatest flexibility to respond to risk.

5.1.2 Typical Business Processes

Table 5.1 shows some of the many processes involved in accomplishing operational functions within an organization.

Table 5.2, in turn, lists some infrastructure processes.

Table 5.1: Operational process examples.

Operational	
Function	Process
Develop new products/services	Plan & manage the development process.
	Research and analyze need.
	Define customer requirements.
	Develop & design new product/service concepts.
	Refine existing product/service concepts.
	Conduct prototype and market tests.
	Plan, release, and roll out new products/services.
	Plan, release, and roll out changes to existing products/services.
Market & sell products/services	Develop & execute market plans.
	Conduct market & consumer research.
	Develop competitor intelligence.
	Manage product/service pricing.
	Identify and qualify target customers.
	Develop/maintain customer relationships.
	Define customer's buying requirements.
	Develop and propose a solution to the customer.
	Estimate solution cost and price.
	Influence customer buying process.
	Negotiate and close the sale.
Order management	Forecast order volumes.
	Enter & process orders.
	Manage customer credit exposure.
	Plan production/service delivery.
	Bill and collect revenue.

(Continued)

Table 5.1: (*Continued*)

Operational	
Function	Process
Manufacture products and/or provide services	Manage overall production/service requirements & capacity. Plan production/service delivery. Design & engineer customer solution. Produce products and/or provide service. Manage change orders. Plan & manage subcontract services. Control production/service schedule.
Manage logistics	Define logistics strategy. Establish & maintain supplier relationships. Measure & certify supplier performance. Procure materials/services. Manage inventory storage & movement. Manage packing & packaging. Manage outbound logistics.
Provide customer support	Provide customer training. Provide customer interface to the organization. Receive & respond to customer inquiries. Receive & respond to internal inquiries. Dispatch & provide field service/support. Manage return/warranty activities.

Table 5.2: Examples of infrastructure processes.

Infrastructure	
Function	Process
Plan & manage performance	Formulate business strategy & vision. Establish & prioritize goals & objectives. Develop financial/operational performance. Measure & monitor financial/operational performance. Manage business performance. Plan & manage quality & service levels. Design & improve business processes.

(*Continued*)

Table 5.2: (*Continued*)

Function	Process
	Infrastructure
	Design & improve organizational structures & job roles.
	Manage change.
	Establish policies & procedures.
Manage finances & accounting	Manage accounts receivable.
	Manage accounts payable.
	Manage payroll.
	Manage the general ledger.
	Plan & manage taxes.
	Plan & manage cash.
	Plan & manage budgets.
	Plan & manage capital expenditures.
	Plan & manage risk to corporate assets.
	Plan & manage loans & equity.
	Report financial performance.
	Perform financial analysis & cost accounting.
	Maintain financial records.
	Ensure financial control.
Manage human resources	Define human resource needs & skill requirements.
	Manage the acquisition & termination of human resources.
	Educate, train & develop employees.
	Ensure employee communication.
	Establish reward & recognition systems.
	Manage compensation & benefits.
	Provide employee services.
Manage information resources	Define & plan for information resource needs.
	Develop & enhance data architecture.
	Develop & enhance communications infrastructure.
	Develop & enhance software applications.
	Manage information systems operations.
	Provide information user support.
	Archive & dispose of information.
Manage physical assets	Acquire production/service equipment & technology.
	Maintain production/service equipment & technology.
	Acquire facilities.

(*Continued*)

Table 5.2: (*Continued*)

Infrastructure	
Function	Process
	Manage & maintain facilities.
	Manage other fixed assets.
Manage support	Manage public/external relations.
services	Perform the legal function.
	Manage administrative services.
	Plan & manage environmental programs.

5.1.3 Reengineering

Reengineering traces its origins back to management theories developed as early as the 19th century. The underlying principle of reengineering is to "formulate all the course of action that is the best-in-class." Frederick Taylor recommended in the 1880's that administrators use procedure reengineering methods to find out the paramount developments for performing work, and that these processes be reengineered to optimize efficiency. BPR stands for the fundamental rethinking[9] and radical[10] redesign of business processes[11] to bring about dramatic improvements in performance.

An illustration will help to explain this.

A typical business process would key in the details into the computer once an order has been received before checking on the customer's credit. Subsequent steps would include taking the goods, from the warehouse, packing and arranging for mode of delivery. None of these, however, is of any value or interest to the customer who is only concerned with the end result of these tasks i.e., delivery of the goods.

What is reengineering? It is not:

♦ downsizing.
♦ getting rid of, only unnecessary work jobs.
♦ merely "restructuring".

---

[9] Total rethinking begin with the proverbial clean slate and reinvents how you would do your work.
[10] To be radical is to go to the root of things and not about improving what already exists.
[11] Business processes refer to a group of related tasks that together create value for the customer.

- ◆ mechanization.
- ◆ reengineering an organization or a department in an organization.

The driving force behind reengineering is the 3 C's:

- ◆ CUSTOMER
- ◆ COMPETITION
- ◆ CHANGE

Central to the success of reengineering is the coordination of EIS all the way through the organization. Fundamentally, EIS characterizes the central system of information flow. When organizations improve the central IT processes, such as gathering data only once, integrating cross-functional systems or getting information quickly to customers, radical business process change is achievable. Nevertheless, for IT to be an enabler of reengineering or organizational transformation, it is very important that managers are acquainted with a choice of methods by which EIS can facilitate progress through procedural change. At the same time, administration needs to be conscious of the risks in changing EIS processes.

Reengineering is concerned with questioning the fundamentals of what you do and the services you distribute. Figure 5.4 shows how risk increases with the scope of work involved.

Reengineering works best under the following conditions:

- ◆ Case teams should include both managers and those who will do the work.
- ◆ Consider reengineering of fragmented processes to reduce obstacles to improving customer service.
- ◆ The EIS group should be an essential part of the reengineering team from the beginning.
- ◆ BPR should be "owned" throughout the organization, not driven by a group of exterior consultants.
- ◆ Top management support is required.
- ◆ BPR should be associated with tactical planning, leveraging EIS as a competitive tool.
- ◆ A project timetable, preferably between three to six months, reduces the probability of project failure.

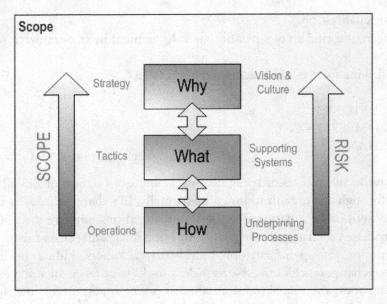

Figure 5.4: Scope of Work and Risk.

Source: JISC (2008).[12]

♦ Organizational culture should be considered and the BPR process supported by constant communication.

5.1.4 Business Process Reengineering

Contemporary organizations are under great pressure to improve their efficiency while continuing to reduce their costs. The question is not whether to revolutionize, but how to change. BPR is a step in this journey. Hammer[13] and Champy[14] define BPR as "*the fundamental rethinking and radical redesign of business processes to achieve dramatic improvements in critical contemporary*

---

[12] JISC infoNet aims to be the UK's leading advisory service for managers in the post-compulsory education sector promoting the effective strategic planning, implementation and management of information and learning technology. The mission of the Joint Information Systems Committee (JISC) is to provide world-class leadership in the innovative use of ICT to support education and research, by funding a national services portfolio and a range of programmes and projects. www.jiscinfonet.ac.uk

measures of performance, such as cost, quality, service, and speed." Business process re-engineering (BPR) is being attempted by many firms that are looking for radical gains from the successful redesign of their processes. BPR is a high risk, time-consuming activity, with no guarantee of success, and yet many businesses claim to be re-engineering their processes.[15] Figure 5.5 displays different levels of BPR attainment with respect to process quality design.

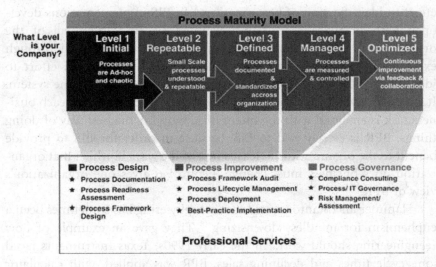

Figure 5.5: Process Quality Design Levels.

Source: APQC (2008).[16]

---

[13] Dr. Michael Hammer is the leading exponent of the concept of reengineering. He was named by *BusinessWeek* as one of the four preeminent management gurus of the 1990s and by Time as one of America's 25 Most Influential Individuals. He lives in Massachusetts.

[14] James Champy is chairman of Perot Systems consulting practice. He is a leading authority on organizational change and development and business strategy. He lives in Massachusetts.

[15] Named the "Best Online Reference Service" by the CODiE Awards, HighBeam is a premiere online library where you can find research, facts, and articles. It collects millions of articles from newspapers like *The Washington Post* and *The Boston Globe*, magazines like *The Economist* and *Newsweek*, and journals like *JOPERD* and *Journal of Research in Childhood Education* which are all delivered in a single research Web site.

[16] APQC's Process Classification Framework SM (PCF) is a taxonomy of cross-functional business processes intended to allow objective comparison of organizational performance within and among organizations. http://www.apqc.org.

Once an organization decides what form of EIS system they want to adopt, they will next need to specify how the EIS system will be designed. In conventional IS/IT projects, requirements analysis involves a lot of effort to identify what it is that the users of the project need. EIS projects vary highly in the amount of effort needed to identify system requirements. In vendor EIS projects, functionality is given based on vendor research into best practices. (SAP in particular has devoted significant effort to identification of best practices.) In EIS implementations developed with in-house assets, an integrated system serving all of the organization's information system needs must be developed through extensive business process reengineering (BPR).[17] BPR is an effort to identify the best way to do each business task supported by the system. It is an activity in which the way an organization accomplishes each business task is analyzed with the intent of identifying the best way of doing things. BPR is closely tied to EIS, because in order for EIS to provide benefit to the organization, at least some of the ways in which that organization does business must change. Figure 5.6 gives one organization's view of BPR.

Hammer and Stanton noted that reengineering has sometimes been a euphemism for mindless downsizing.[18] They gave an example of how reengineering should work. In the early 1990s, Texas Instruments faced long cycle times and declining sales. BPR was applied, with calculator development accomplished by cross-disciplinary teams from engineering, marketing, and other departments. These teams were to be in control of every aspect of product development from design to marketing. The first pilot teams failed, sabotaged by the existing organization which felt threatened. Functional departments were unwilling to give up good people, space, or responsibility. Power continued to lie in the old functional departments. Texas Instruments responded by changing the way it was organized. Development teams became the primary organizational units. Functional departments focused on redefined missions supporting the product teams. Budget was accomplished by process instead of by

---

[17] An article on BPR by its most vocal academic proponent is Hammer, M. and Stanton, S. (1999). How process enterprises really work. *Harvard Business Review,* 108–118.
[18] Hammer, M. and Stanton, S. (1999), op. cit.

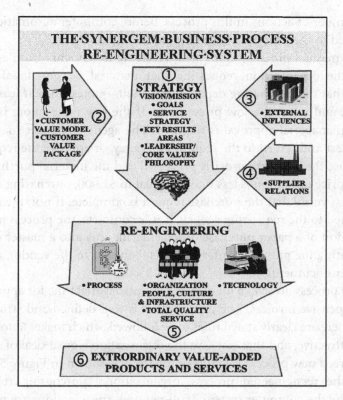

Figure 5.6: An Example BPR System.

Source: Synergem (2008).[19]

department. Office space was reallocated. After the new system became established, new product launching time was cut by as much as one-half, and profitability was enhanced, with return on investment multiplied fourfold.

A business process is what the organization does to get its work done. For instance, almost every organization deals with paying invoices. There

[19] Synergem Management Inc. offers highly experienced & senior management consulting services to private and public sector organizations world wide. Synergem's innovative structure is designed to foster the creativity, responsiveness, quality, breadth, management, accountability, synergy and the administration capabilities required to meet the changes in the modern organizational environment.

are a number of actions in this process. Before computer automation, this amounted to the process given in Figure 5.7.

The manual process begins with receiving documents from agencies within the organization requesting that material be purchased. Rules require that the purchasing department obtain quotes from at least three vendors, and select the low price quote. If the low price quote is above $1,000, managerial approval is required. The agency manager may reject the request and return to the requesting agency, or approve the request in which case the purchase order is processed and the material purchased. If the low price quotation is less than or equal to $1,000, purchasing department staff verify that the purchase request is complete. If not, the request is returned to the requesting agency. If it is complete, the process involves preparation of a paper purchase order, entering this into a master records file, printing the purchase order which is then sent to the vendor, and filing paper documents.

This process involves a lot of expensive managerial time for approval of more expensive invoices. The process itself is well-defined and structured, in that there are clearly stated rules to be followed, which makes automation highly attractive, and that can save the organization a great deal of money. Therefore, a new process might take the from as shown in Figure 5.8.

In the reengineered process, organizational purchasing rules are applied by the computer system. If all required specifications are met, the purchase order is automatically processed, much faster than the old system and with far less people involved, at much lower cost. If all required specifications are not met, the request is returned to the requesting agency in a much faster manner.

This is only one of many ways to perform this business process. Business process reengineering would analyze how a particular operation is performed, and seek better ways to do it, either through more automation, or by adding people to do specific tasks to relieve bottlenecks in the process.

Business process reengineering predates the popular phase of EIS. Most reengineering efforts in the 1980s, which sought more efficient ways to do business, degenerated into wholesale layoffs.[20] The old ways of doing business sometimes remained, but with fewer people to do them.

---

[20] Hammer, M. (2000). Reengineering redux, *CIO*, 13(10), 143–156.

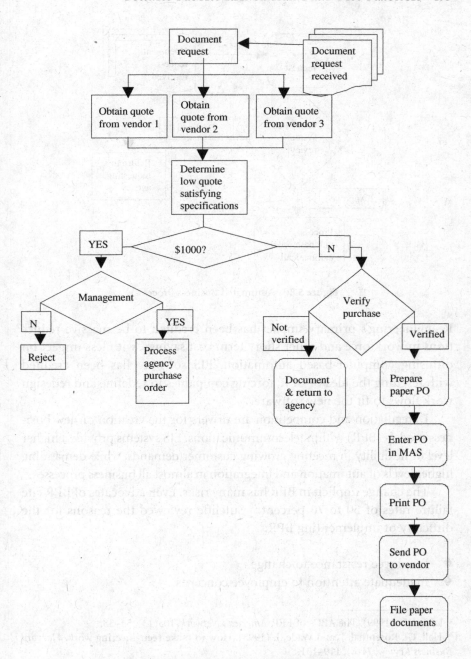

Figure 5.7: Manual Business Process.

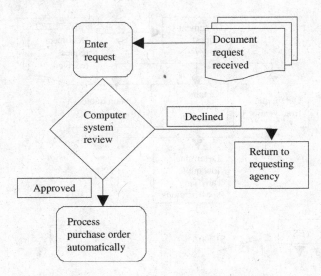

Figure 5.8: Automated Business Process.

Reengineering's primary impact has been credited to be massive reductions in workforce and other short-term cost savings, with less impact on diffusing computer-based automation. EIS software has been credited with rescuing the idea of BPR, forcing companies to redefine and redesign work flows to fit the new software.

Deregulation and competition are drivers for the creation of new business models (BPR) within telecommunications. EIS systems provide a higher level of flexibility in meeting growing customer demands, while demanding higher levels of automation and integration in almost all business processes.[21]

The change implicit in BPR has many risks. Even advocates of BPR cite failure rates of 50 to 70 percent.[22] Sutcliffe reviewed the reasons for the difficulty of implementing BPR:[23]

◆ Employee resistance to change.
◆ Inadequate attention to employee concerns.

---

[21] Levine, S. (1999). The ABCs of ERP. *America's Network*, 103(13), 54–58.
[22] Hall, G., Rosenthal, J. and Wade, J. (1993). How to make reengineering work. *Harvard Business Review*, 71(6), 119–131.
[23] Sutcliffe, N. (1999). Leadership behavior and business process reengineering (BPR) outcomes: An empirical analysis of 30 BPR projects. *Information & Management*, 36(5), 273–286.

◆ Inadequate and inappropriate staffing.
◆ Inadequate developer and user tools.
◆ Mismatch of strategies used and goals.
◆ Lack of oversight.
◆ Failure in leadership commitment.

Blanket adoption of an EIS product will discard processes in which the organization has developed a competitive advantage.[24] Instead of changing those processes, the EIS system should be modified. Other activities will be better done following the EIS system's best practices. Even here, a transition period can be expected where employees will have to radically change what they do. Productivity degradation will occur while users learn to adapt to the new system. In the long run the new system is most often better. Those who refuse to adapt to it usually have to learn new skills with their next employer.

The following example demonstrates business process reengineering in an EIS system applied to an academic institution.[25] Babson College implemented a three-year project to transform its business processes. The primary objective was to improve the quality of service delivery to students for admission, records, registration, advising, financial aid, career services, and field-based learning. The college also sought to reduce administrative costs, to redirect these funds to teaching and academic support. Change management teams were formed to reengineer each of the operational areas supported by the system. Critical performance measures were established for each application. The focus was on easy-to-use and effective information systems that students could access themselves. The pre-existing system was a mainframe system with dial-up network and text-based applications. The new system was a multi-tiered client/server infrastructure with 6,000 nodes, over 50 servers, and 1,500 workstations. Data warehousing was used. The system reduced operating costs about 20 percent, half of the planned 40 percent, because some vendor systems were late. One of the problems faced by the information technology team

---

[24] Schultz, J. D. (2000). Hunt for best practices. *Traffic World*, 41–42.
[25] Kesner, R. M. (1998). Building an Internet commerce capability: A case study. *Information Strategy*, 27–36.

was how to organize access to the system for customers or service providers. Initially it was decided that a graphical electronic mail system front end would be used, with applications written as executables within mail system file folders. But this design was not approved by end users because the mail system was not robust or fast enough for the transaction volumes experienced. The Internet proved to be the solution by providing widespread access. The platform was not as reliable as it needed to be, but it was expected to improve with time.

In an additional example of how best practices can be implemented, Nestle obtained a very large mySAP.com system from SAP for over $200 million in 2000.[26] This system impacted the way in which all 230,000 Nestle employees in 80 countries did their work, because each Nestle employee would have a customized browser-based start page relating to his or her job function to guide the employee to the selected best practice.

Yet another example is Sunoco Products Co., which implemented an e-procurement software allowing the company to reduce purchasing costs for operating resources.[27] The software aided the company in monitoring and enforcing business process changes as part of the EIS implementation. Sunoco was able to reduce its supplier base by 5 percent to 10 percent. They had a goal of a 10 percent reduction in spending on operating resources, which, if attained, would more than pay back their investment.

On the negative side, lack of up-front business process changes has been blamed for installation problems at Farmland Industries Inc.[28] Without BPR, finance and order-entry operations were unable to get the savings they anticipated. This led to the company having to redo BPR and to revise their system implementation.

Within the manufacturing arena, a concept related to BPR is **lean manufacturing**. We will look more at lean manufacturing in Chapter 9. Lean manufacturing is an effort to cut out waste by avoiding activities that don't add value. Throughout a supply chain, manufacturing can often

---

[26] Konicki, S. (2000). Nestle taps SAP for e-business. *Informationweek*, 792, p. 185.
[27] Shaw, M. (2000). ERP and e-procurement software assist strategic purchasing focus at Sunoco. *Pulp & Paper*, 74(2), 45–51.
[28] Stedman, C. (1999). ERP flops point to users' plans. *Computerworld*, 33(46), 273–286.

involve continuous flows of material without bottlenecks, only producing what the customer has ordered. This reflects a system of demand pull rather than supply push. In the personal computer market, for instance, Dell has a demand-pull system. Some of their competitors had a supply-push system, where product was made in the most efficient way from the perspective of manufacturing. Finished goods would be inventoried in a supply-push system. It appears that Dell's demand-pull approach is out-performing the supply-push approach.

5.1.5 Business Process Management

In today's rapidly changing world, communication service providers are facing a variety of challenges from high capital investments, increasing customer turnover and consolidation of new technologies. These challenges are compelling service providers to focus on processes and their implementation through computerization. New services are being rolled out to customers through new business models and processes to satisfy changing customer requirements, competition and technology advances. This makes the wide-ranging definition of business processes and their effectual management through automation necessary for service providers. **The aim of the BPM** is to facilitate clients in the areas of business strategy realization, refocusing diverging activities through better coordination, communication and collaboration and finally allocating organizational resources to tackle challenges in a coordinated and efficient manner. Figure 5.9 shows one view of how this might happen.

5.1.6 BPR with Respect to EIS

Proficient business process management (BPM) can facilitate new returns opportunities, trim down operational costs, distribute products and services faster, facilitate customer service, and control operational staff, management, customers, and partners. As more systems and organizations are involved, more process automation gaps materialize, intermingled manual processes are more complex to coordinate, and delays and mistakes become more numerous. Tracking the real-time transactions is very difficult when this information is scattered across different locations.

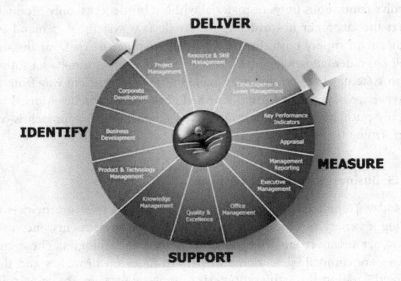

Figure 5.9: Business Process Management.

Source: Pernec (2008).[29]

5.2 BEST PRACTICES IN EIS

One of the primary features of the SAP EIS product has been **best practices**. Business process reengineering is an activity designed to identify a best practice. Once a best practice is identified that would seem applicable to most organizations, it can be incorporated into an EIS system. SAP spends considerable research efforts to identify the best way of doing conventional EIS tasks. They have 800 to 1,000 best practices included in their R/3 software.[30] Consultants often develop further specialized expertise that

---

[29] Pernec Corporation Berhad (PERNEC) is a Malaysian joint-venture company between Amanah Raya Berhad (Skim Amanah Saham Bumiputra), NEC Corporation (Japan) and Permodalan Nasional Berhad. Its main business activity is to provide Information and Communication Technology (ICT) solutions to customers in Malaysia and abroad. http://www.pernec.com.

[30] Scott, J. E. and Kaindle, L. (2000). Enhancing functionality in an enterprise software package. *Information & Management*, 37(2), 111–122; Dean, C. (2002). ERP Best Practices Checklist. www.deansystem.com.

firms can purchase. A best practice is a method that has been judged to be superior to other methods. This implies the most efficient way to perform a task.

A related concept is **benchmarking**. Benchmarking is comparing an organization's methods with peer groups, with the purpose of identifying the best practices that lead to superior performance. Best practices are usually identified through the benchmarking phase of a business process reengineering activity. Best practices thus often change the organizational climate, and attempt to bring about dramatic improvements in performance.

Vendors attempt to be comprehensive and to be all things to all people. Yet Scott and Kaindle (2000) state that at least 20 percent of the functionality needed by EIS users is missing from vendor packages.[31] There are also many reports of missed deadlines, excessive costs, and employee frustrations in the implementation of EIS. A more participative design approach could help in implementing EIS. If a client implements the entire suite of SAP modules, as well as their tools for system implementation, SAP can ensure timely implementation within budget. However, this approach disregards the human factors of the client business culture.

While business process reengineering was designed to consider human values and business purposes, Taylor states that these factors are clearly neglected in EIS application, and outlines a process emphasizing human factors in EIS implementation. The human factor costs of training and obtaining cooperative participation are key to the successful implementation of EIS.

5.3 REENGINEERING OPTIONS

O'Leary gives two basic ways to implement reengineering: clean slate vs. technology-enabled BPR.[32] While these are not the only choices (they are

---

[31] Scott and Kaindle (2000), op. cit.

[32] O'Leary, D. E. (2000). *Enterprise Resource Planning Systems: Systems, Life Cycle, Electronic Commerce, and Risk*. Cambridge: Cambridge University Press.

the extremes of a spectrum of reengineering implementation possibilities), they are good concepts to explain the choices available in accomplishing reengineering.

5.3.1 Clean Slate Reengineering

In clean slate reengineering, everything is designed from scratch. In essence, clean slate reengineering involves reengineering followed by selection of the software that best supports the new system design. Processes are reengineered based on identified needs and requirements of the organization. As its name implies, clean slate reengineering has no predefined constraints. This theoretically enables design of the optimal system for the organization. This approach is more expensive than technology-enabled reengineering, but clean slate reengineering is more responsive to organizational needs.

Clean slate reengineering is slower and harder to apply than the technology-enabled approach to implementation. However, clean slate reengineering offers a way to retain competitive advantages that the organization has developed. Ideally, this approach can develop the optimal system for the organization. Clean slate reengineering can also involve significant changes in the way that the organization does business. However, the adjustment in how organization members do their business often retains the features that were found to work well in the past. Thus, while training is required, the impact is probably less than in the technology-enabled approach.

5.3.2 Technology-Enabled Reengineering

In technology-enabled reengineering, first the system is selected and then reengineering is conducted. O'Leary refers to this approach as constrained reengineering. The reengineering process is thus constrained by the selected system. This approach is faster and cheaper than clean slate reengineering, because the software does not have to be changed (it is the basis of the design). Cap Gemini refers to technology-enabled reengineering as concurrent transformation.

The technology-enabled approach designs the organizational system around the abilities of the vendor software. SAP's best practices, for instance, are designed to do things right in the first place. If SAP's research came up with ways to do everything you do better than you used to do them, this would be the best option. It is the easiest to implement, is usually much faster to implement, and thus costs less to implement. On the negative side, it also usually involves the most change in organizational practice, and thus the most complications for training. In practice, therefore, while the EIS installation project looks great from time, budget, and functionality perspectives, the actual benefits to the organization are often disappointing.

O'Leary considered the technology-enabled approach as the most dominant in practice. He cited a survey of SAP R/3 implementers that found that only 16 percent had planned reengineering before they obtained SAP. Of this set of implementers, 33 percent felt that no BPR was needed before implementation, although only 10 percent felt that way after implementation. The most common approach was to undertake BPR simultaneously with implementation of R/3. After the fact, 35 percent thought that reengineering should have come first (the clean slate approach). Table 5.3 compares advantages and disadvantages of both extremes.

O'Leary's advice is that clean slate reengineering should be used by large firms with ample reserve funds. Such firms would have the resources needed and would be more likely to use processes as a basis of strategic advantage. Technology-enabled reengineering should be used by firms that are constrained by budgets or with urgent time requirements. The more standard the processes used by an organization, the more attractive technology-enabled reengineering is. Whichever approach is used, business process reengineering is considered a necessity for firms adopting EIS.

As to practice, O'Leary cited industry surveys of SAP R/3 implementers. The technology-enabled strategy dominated within this group. Firms were surveyed before and after their EIS implementation. Prior to their experience, only 16 percent of those firms surveyed thought BPR should be applied prior to installation of the SAP system. This statistic jumped to 35 percent after the experience. Prior to implementation, 33 percent of

Table 5.3: Comparison of Clean Slate and Technology-Enabled Reengineering.

Clean slate advantages	Technology enabled advantages
Not constrained by tool limitations.	Focus on EIS best practices.
Not limited by completeness of best practice database.	Tools help structure & focus reengineering.
Company may have unique features where vendor best practices aren't appropriate.	Process-bound and thus easier.
Not subject to vendor software changes.	Know that design is feasible.
May be only way to embed processes like Web, bar coding into new technology.	Experience of others ensures design will work.
Maintain competitive advantage.	Greater likelihood of cost, time achievement.
	Software available (already developed).

Clean slate disadvantages	Technology enabled disadvantages
No pre-existing structure to design.	Reengineering limited by tool.
Greater likelihood of infeasibility.	System evolution possibly limited by technology.
May involve more consultants.	
May be more costly, slower.	No relative advantage (others can purchase same system).
May not work with selected EIS.	All best practices may not be available.

Source: O'Leary (2000).

those surveyed thought that BPR was unnecessary. After their experience, only 10 percent felt the same. Thus, even if the technology-enabled strategy is adopted, it seems clear that BPR is needed.

Many organizations find it difficult to switch from old legacy systems to EIS. These legacy systems included distribution, financial, and customer service systems developed in-house over the years.

5.4 GENERAL BENEFITS FROM USING EIS

EIS/ERPs have become the driving force for a new business and economic paradigm with far reaching effects for all types of industries and for the competitiveness of countries. The application of information and communication technology is expected to affect profitability, productivity and employment levels. International comparisons are becoming increasingly significant as the employment of ERP is commonly considered to be a critical factor contributing to national performance on both micro- and macro-economic levels. Benefits can include:

♦ Enhanced communication through quicker and easier reporting.
♦ Superior management through electronic data transfer.
♦ Better networking opportunities, including greater social contact and support.
♦ Higher quality and accuracy of records.
♦ Greater access to information.
♦ Superior efficiency throughout the enterprise.
♦ Better flexibility for when and where tasks are carried out.
♦ Facilitates sharing of resources, expertise and advice.
♦ Less paperwork, with associated reductions in tasks such as filing and photocopying.
♦ Using templates, pro-forma and shared teaching resources reduces duplication of effort.

The significant benefits while using an ERP Systems can be itemized.

1. Appreciably enhanced service to customers (i.e., individuals, companies and staff) all the way through:

   ➢ The development of customer-centric systems.
   ➢ Amplified provision of self-service capabilities.
   ➢ Redesigned processes leading to enhanced efficiency and competency within the enterprise.

2. Improved policy and decision-making through:

   ➢ Well-timed and precise information.
   ➢ Mechanisms to monitor and deal with the system.
   ➢ Aptitude to allocating information and making decisions on preceding skill.

3. Enhanced deliverance of ERP services and projects via:

   ➢ Formal planning and prioritization of processes in place.
   ➢ Amplified focus of IT resources on core competencies and requirements.
   ➢ Outsourcing non-core activities (e.g., helpdesk, network support, etc.).
   ➢ Reassignment of staff.

4. Long-term gains in competence within IT through:

   ➢ Reduced support requirements for new applications.
   ➢ Standardized desktops, hardware and software.

5.5 PR/BPM SOFTWARE

Business Process Management (BPM) or BPR software is a fast-growing segment of the enterprise software market, due to its support of communal re-engineering. Using BPM software tools, business people can document workflow and processes in their enterprises, to identify bottlenecks and other impediments to effectiveness, and recommend alternative and improved business processes. The purpose of BPM software is to shore up the documentation, analysis, monitoring, and re-design of the business processes in an enterprise. Although tools cannot offer any magic "reengineering button," **business process reengineering and management software/tools** offer essential features, e.g.,

◆ Documentation of any category of system objects.
◆ Cross-referencing of information and material related to business processes and tasks.
◆ Automatic cost aggregation to the superior level.
◆ Method-driven interface between business process modeling and data modeling.
◆ Reusage of all identified components for future business processes.

Casewise[33] is a globally recognized leader in Business Process Analysis, Enterprise Architecture, Service-Oriented Architecture and IT Governance & Compliance.

5.6 CONCLUSION

BPR is an important philosophy. It aims to achieve improvements in performance by redesigning the processes which an organization operates, maximizing their value-added content. This approach can be applied at an individual process level or to the whole organization. Business process reengineering is often a major component of an EIS installation. This implies massive changes in the way in which organizations do their business. This has great potential payoff, but also implies a great deal of change in people's work lives, which requires a lot of attention to demonstrating benefits, as well as a great deal of retraining.

Requirements analysis is important in identifying what a proposed system is to do. In EIS projects, requirements analysis takes the form of business process reengineering, to identify the best way (best practice) for each business process supported by the system. There are two extremes in the many ways in which business process reengineering can be accomplished. Clean slate BPR starts from scratch, and is the ideal approach. Technology-enabled BPR begins with the software selected. This is faster and less expensive, as many of the processes are selected from the system. In practice, neither extreme is necessarily best. Hammer and Stanton credited reengineering as doing a great deal of good, despite being a euphemism for mindless downsizing by some.[34] BPR has enabled companies to operate faster and more efficiently, and to use information technology more productively. Employees often obtain more authority

---

[33] Casewise is a market leader in the provision of software and consultancy solutions to over 3,000 major global organizations for Business Process Modeling, Enterprise Architecture, Service-Oriented Architecture and IT Governance & Compliance solutions.

[34] Hammer and Stanton (1999), op. cit.

and a better understanding of the role their work plays for the organization as a whole. Customers get higher-quality products and more responsive service. Shareholders obtain larger dividends and higher stock value because BPR reduces cost and increases revenues. Executives no longer see their organizations as separate entities, but instead see them as related elements in larger systems linked through information flows across the business, reaching customers and suppliers.

The aim of Business Process engineering within EIS is to

- improve service levels.
- reduce operational cost.
- enhance operational flexibility and efficiency.
- expand customer satisfaction resulting in higher customer retention.
- decrease the cost of customer retention.
- reduce cost of development and maintenance.
- retain revenues.
- reduce 'Time-to-Market,' resulting in faster rollout of new services and features.
- reduce response times, resulting in faster reactions to competitive moves.
- enhance process agility.
- gain improved scalability of processes/systems.
- easier mergers and acquisitions.

To be successful, BPR projects should be top down, cover the entire organization, and include end to end processes. BPR projecs should be supported by tools that make processes easier to follow and study.

We can say that BPR is about fundamentally changing the way firms conduct business. Integrated technology can be a key enabler in this change, but should not be the primary focus of BPR projects.

The following are the vital principles underlying these recommendations:

- **Accessibility:** Ensuring quality information is accessible when required to all staff within the enterprise and external users of the management information.
- **Allocation and collaboration:** Providing information sharing and collaboration and ensuring information is only provided to relevant parties.

♦ **Amalgamation:** Providing information sourced from multiple systems in an integrated manner across business units and to exterior parties.

♦ **Competency:** Eliminating information duplication and "re-inventions of the wheel," allowing staff to learn from previous experiences within the enterprise.

♦ **Ownership:** Development of a culture of information and data ownership to assure improved quality and sharing of information.

♦ **Relevancy:** Increasing the fit between requirements and information presented by focusing on user requirements and key performance indicators.

♦ **Unity:** Using common tools and processes for recording, storing and distributing information.

☆ KEYWORDS

☆ **Activity:** A process, rationale or assignment that occurs over time and has identifiable results. Activities combine to shape business processes.

☆ **AS-IS Model:** A model that corresponds to the contemporary stage of the organization modeled, without any specific improvements included.

☆ **Benchmarking:** Comparison of organizational procedures with those of peer organizations.

☆ **Best practices:** The set of best ways to accomplish business processes.

☆ **Business Process Management (BPM):** An extension of the work flow management movement of the 1990s to include the Business Process Reengineering (BPR) concept of process improvement.

☆ **Business Process Reengineering (BPR):** Analysis of the set of tasks making up a business process with the intent of identifying best way of accomplishing it.

☆ **Clean slate reengineering:** BPR conducted from scratch.

☆ **Conceptual design:** Process of developing a model of what the system should do.

☆ **Concurrent transformation:** Synonym for technology-enabled reengineering.

☆ **Formal specification:** Output of requirements analysis.

☆ **Lean manufacturing:** BPR applied to cut waste in supply chains by eliminating non-value-adding activities.

☆ **Process:** Logical set of related activities taking input, adding value through doing things, and creating an output.

☆ **Redesign:** The transformation of a business process to achieve significant levels of improvement in one or more performance measures relating to fitness for purpose, quality, cycle times, and cost by using the techniques of streamlining and removing non-value added activities and costs. Redesign projects typically take about six months to complete.

☆ **System:** From the Latin and Greek, the term "system" means to mingle, to set up, and to place together. A system is a collection of interrelated elements comprising an amalgamation in totality. A system typically consists of components (or elements), which are connected together in order to facilitate the flow of information (en.wikipedia.org).

☆ **Technology-enabled reengineering:** BPR conducted after system is adopted, so that BPR is constrained by system features.

☆ **To-be-model:** Models that are the outcome of applying expansion opportunities to the current (AS-IS) business environment.

☆ **Validation:** Process to ensure that a valid set of requirements have been developed.

☆ TERMINOLOGY REVIEW

Review Questions

1. Describe business processes.
2. Define business process reengineering.
3. Search the library and/or Internet for business process reengineering practice.
4. Identify risks involved in adopting BPR.

5. Identify a specific business process, and analyze it with the intent of improvement through the use of information technology.
6. Describe the concept of best practices.
7. Search the library and/or Internet for best practices in EIS.
8. Describe benchmarking, and its relationship to EIS.
9 Search the library and/or Internet for benchmarking practice in EIS.
10. Contrast clean slate reengineering with technology-enabled reengineering.
11. Search the library and/or Internet for use of business process reengineering, especially associated with EIS.
12. Understand what and how business processes can be radically improved, dramatically reducing process cycle time and cost, improving the quality of the process products or outcomes.
13. Emphasize challenges and opportunities for BPE/BPR across the process life cycle using Electronic Commerce and Intranet and Extranet technologies.
14. Understand and apply knowledge-based concepts, techniques, and tools for BPE/BPR centered on Electronic Commerce and network information system applications.
15. Was the ROI analysis believable or not? Why? What should be included in the analysis?
16. Can you identify one or more potential business redesign heuristics in the case?
17. What are the basic skills for analyzing and improving business methods, procedures and systems so that they are able to take part in a business re-engineering project in a company for the purpose of productivity improvement?
18. How a working knowledge of the business re-engineering tools and methodologies in the business organizations in terms of business automation, value, processes and risks.
19. What are the abilities needed to select the essential elements and practices needed to develop and implement the business reengineering projects?

20. What are the abilities needed for the analysis and evaluation of the best practices of the business reengineering projects?
21. How do you understand the methods used to changing processes and the impact it has on company culture, people and the integration with other information systems?
22. Develop a strategic plan of IS/IT to support a business strategy aimed at providing an organization with competitive advantage.
23. How do you manage information as a resource and have an understanding of systems development lifecycle?
24. How do you implement, evaluate and analyze strategic business change processes?
25. What can the learning organization strategy bring to knowledge-based organizations?
26. Explain how specific departments and units of functions could be involved in the process of order fulfillment for either a product or service order.
27. Explain with two examples why customer problems could result from lack of integration among functional activities in order processing.
28. Explain how the following technologies must be integrated to provide effective supply chain management and e-business: TPS, databases, LANS and telecom.
29. Explain the steps in planning: an integrated database; a business process re-engineering project; and the technology needed to perform B2B effectively.
30. Explain with two examples each, the legal and ethical issues related to use of IT.
31. How does BPR with the help of EIS facilitate relationships with suppliers and customers. Who are the suppliers of your process? How do products get to customers?
32. Why do BPR efforts rarely produce positive results?
33. When the company demands particular EIS software they have to make compromises on the budget because reworking modules and supplying an EIS Software would be expensive. This is because of the complications involved in doing the same. What is

☆ COMPETENCY REVIEW

1. A functional area is served by an information system. Information systems capture, process, and store data to provide information needed for decision-making.
2. When an ERP system is installed, various configuration decisions are made. These decisions reflect management's view of how transactions should be recorded and later used for decision-making. For example, the system can be configured to limit selling price discounts, thus avoiding unprofitable pricing. Justify your answer.
3. What are the compelling reasons to do this? Is it a "qualifier" in certain industries? Are the efficiencies real? Explain all these point with relevance to ERP and organization.
4. How much are we willing to change the organization? Are these practices really better than what we are currently doing? Do we lose or gain a strategic advantage? If everyone is doing this, how can we gain an advantage? Justify your answers.
5. Provide examples of typical business functions, their related units and activities within those units.
6. Furnish specific examples of how IT has changed: business practices, employee roles, and consumer expectations of business.
7. Give examples of principal and supporting processes. Describe a sub-process and its related procedures and tasks for specified processes.
8. "The BPR exercise throws open an opportunity to give a fresh, radical and global outlook on the entire business process. The organization should try to cash in on this opportunity and come out with a new power packed engine that could propel it into the new millennium." Explain this statement.
9. Why are so many companies still eager to experiment with reengineering, even when they have experienced previous failures themselves?

☆ CHECK YOUR PROGRESS

---

1. Briefly comment on the following:

    a. BPR has unfortunately been associated with "downsizing" or "rightsizing," both of which mean laying off workers.

        ....

        ....

    b. Business Process Reengineering is approached by examining the strings of processes or cycles.

        ....

        ....

    c. BPR is an excellent tool to use in helping to make work processes faster.

        ....

        ....

    d. The importance of technology as a driver for organizational change.

        ....

        ....

    e. Business Process Reengineering is a significant exercise because it takes the whole business into consideration and relates everything back to delivering value to the customer.

        ....

        ....

f. An EIS implementation is NOT an IT Project, it is a business rejuvenation project.

....

....

g. The BPR exercise throws open an opportunity to give a fresh, radical and global outlook on the entire business process.

....

....

☆ SUGGESTED READING

Books

Hammer, M. and Champy, J. (2003). *Reengineering the Corporation: A Manifesto for Business Revolution*. Collins Business.

Harmon, P. (2007). *Business Process Change: A Guide for Business Managers and BPM and Six Sigma Professionals*, 2nd Ed. Morgan Kaufmann.

Kalakota, R. and Robinson, M. (2001). *E-Business 2.0*. Addison-Wesley.

Metters, King-Metters, Pullman, Walton (2007). *Business Process Management*. Thomson Southwestern.

Tan, A. (2007). *Business Process Reengineering in Asia: A Practical Approach*, 2nd Ed. Prentice Hall.

Journal Articles

Arora, S. and Kumar, S. (2000). Reengineering: A focus on enterprise integration. *Interfaces*, 30(5), 54–71.

Chang, S.L. (2000). Information technology in business processes. *Business Process Management Journal*, 6(3), 224–237.

Chenn, J. (2001). Planning for ERP systems: Analysis and future trend. *Business Process Management Journal*, 7(5), 374–386.

Davenport, T. (2005). The coming commoditization of processes. *Harvard Business Review*.

Davison, R. and Martinsons, M. G. (2002). Empowerment or enslavement? A case of process-based organizational change in Hong Kong. *Information Technology & People*, 15, 42–59.

Gallivan, M. J. (2001). Meaning to change: How diverse stakeholders interpret organizational communication about change initiatives. *IEEE Transactions on Professional Communication*, 44(4), 243–266.

Grant, D. (2002). A wider view of business process reengineering. *Communications of the ACM*, 45(2), 85–90.

Koch, C. (2001). BPR and ERP: Realising a vision of process with IT. *Business Process Management Journal*, 7(3), 258–265.

Kovacic, Groznik, A. and Krisper, M. (2001). Business renovation: From business process modelling to information system modelling. *Journal of Simulation*, 2(2), 41–50.

Robey, D., Ross, J. W. and Boudreau, M. C. (2002). Learning to implement enterprise systems: An exploratory study. *Journal of Management Information Systems*, 19(1), 17–46.

Sandberg, K. D. (2001). Reengineering tries a comeback — This time for growth, not just for cost savings. *Harvard Management Update*, 3–6.

Sarker, S. and Lee, A.S. (2003). Using a case study to test the role of three key social enablers in ERP implementation. *Information & Management*, 40(3), 813–829.

Tsou, D. and Hantos, P. (2005). A case study of a centrally managed ERP implementation for manufacturing plants of a global corporation. *International Journal of Internet & Enterprise Management*, 3(3), 304–311.

White Paper

Nikovski, D. and Kulev, V. (2006). Induction of Compact Decision Trees for Personalized Recommendation. *ACM Symposium on Applied Computing* (SAC).

Online Resources

Digital Opportunities for Development. http://learnlink.aed.org/Publications/ Sourcebook/home.htm

Guide to ERPs for Development. www.comminit.com/pdf/CKS_Guide_to_ERPs_ for_Development.pdf

http://en.wikipedia.org

Making a Go of It Alone: Some Companies Reengineer without Consultants. Reengineering Resource Center. http://www.reengineering.com/articles/aug96/ goalone.htm

CHAPTER 6

SYSTEM ARCHITECTURE

Quotation

System designing and architecture allow beginners to easily break and design complex software systems by using a modular-based development approach with a pattern, which we all practice in our day to day life.

Nirosh, 2006

Structure

♣ *Quick look at chapter themes*
♣ *Learning objectives*
♣ *Case study*: Falafel Software Delivers Complex ERP System with Test Complete and Visual Studio
♣ *Sketch of EIS system architecture*
   6.1 EIS as an Information Systems Project
   6.2 IS/IT Project Management Results
   6.3 System Architecture and EIS
   6.4 Open Source EIS
   6.5 Systems Design Aspects of EIS
      6.5.1 The Waterfall Model
      6.5.2 Prototyping
      6.5.3 The Spiral Model
      6.5.4 Other Options for Systems Development

♣ QUICK LOOK AT CHAPTER THEMES

The benefits of an EIS can only be realized from its installation. The design of the system is in great part determined by the vendor's off-the-shelf software. However, each EIS needs to have an architecture, a plan linking hardware, software, data, network, and user access.

♣ LEARNING OBJECTIVES

This chapter will discuss concepts, principles, and state-of-the-art methods in enterprise system architecture, together with architectural styles, architecture portrayal languages (ADL), software connectors, dynamism in architecture, and architecture-based testing and analysis. This will facilitate understanding the role of architecture in Enterprise Information System engineering, including phases of requirements analysis, design (including object-oriented design and related notations, such as UML), and implementation. Implementation of any information systems (IS) project is risky. EIS system implementations are especially risky, because of their size, and the magnitude of their impact on the organization. EIS systems have some unique features. First, if a vendor system is adopted, there is much less system design than in conventional IS projects, in that the software from the vendor is already programmed. Further, in most forms of EIS implementation there is usually a great deal of assistance: from the vendor, from consultants, and from a fairly extensive internal project management team. Third, there are opportunities to outsource even more of the EIS operation, or to use application service providers. This chapter covers the following:

* EIS as an information systems project.
* When/where architectural reuse may be employed.
* Relative use of implementation stratetgies.
* Fundamental enterprise architecture themes and concepts.
* Typical IS/IT project failure experience.
* Building a service-oriented architecture.
* Contrast a stakeholder- and view-based approach to documenting enterprise architecture.
* The role of architecture in achieving agility.
* System design and EIS.
* Open source software and impact of application service providers on EIS project design.

♣ CASE STUDY

Falafel[1] Software Delivers Complex ERP System with TestComplete[2] and Visual Studio

OVERVIEW

Falafel Software provides development, consulting and training services for big name companies all over the world. When they agreed to develop Velocity, a Web-based ERP system, for one of their key clients, they knew they had their work cut out for them. Microsoft solutions like ASP.NET, Active Directories and SQL Server would give them what they needed to implement the system's functionality, but they needed a testing system that would scale with this project and their company. It was also critical that the product was easy enough to learn quickly without sacrificing advanced features they would need when they gained more experience with automated testing.

The company chose TestComplete Enterprise, a comprehensive award-winning automated testing solution, to integrate all of their testing in one powerful, cost-effective solution. TestComplete's easy to use interface and point and click recording helped them get off to a quick start. Its standards-based scripting languages like C#Script and VBScript made it easy for them to take advantage of their existing knowledge and do advanced testing of every layer of the project from backend to user interface.

TestComplete helped Falafel deliver their project on-time and on-budget with confidence that it met their high standards for quality. They continue to use it today to maintain Velocity and to ensure the success of new projects.

---

[1] Falafel Software is a Silicon Valley software development company that includes some of the industry's top names, best-selling authors, industry speakers and former Microsoft and Borland engineers. Falafel helps their clients with all phases of the application development lifecycle, strategy, architecture and implementation.

[2] TestComplete is a comprehensive test automation solution with integrated support for a wide range of both internal and UI-based testing. Designed for use by developers and testers alike, TestComplete offers both visual and scripted test generation and robust test management facilities. TestComplete supports Microsoft Windows, NET, Delphi, Java, and Web applications.

Jesse Miller, lead tester at Falafel Software, has a lot to say about TestComplete. As head of Falafel's test team he's responsible for ensuring the quality and reliability of their software. He uses TestComplete to get the most out of his limited resources, ensure consistent results, and do more testing in less time.

"At Falafel, we build large scale NET applications, and it's critical that we deliver them on time and tested," says Miller. "We produce a lot of code and our test team couldn't keep up with development if we didn't have TestComplete."

SITUATION

Falafel's latest project is Velocity, a web-based ERP system they developed for one of their key clients. It's a big project, with modules like general ledger, AR, AP, purchase orders, inventory, warehouse management and more. The system handles the complete business flow from online orders through warehouse management and shipping, with reports and auditing to track the business process at every level.

Jesse's team is responsible for testing Velocity to ensure that it meets Falafel's high standards. "Velocity has so many complex screens and function points that we couldn't even begin to test it manually, even if we wanted to limit ourselves to manual testing." Jesse says, "So we knew it had to be automated testing."

"We wanted something scalable and easy to use that was cost-effective. We didn't want to spend half the testing budget if we didn't have to."

THE SOLUTION

"There was resistance at first because we were worried that doing auto-mated testing would slow us down. We thought we might have to learn a proprietary language and work in a closed environment."

The team took notice when they realized that TestComplete created tests in standard languages like C# Script and VB Script. "It was a pleasant surprise that TestComplete offers languages like C# Script. Our applications are written in C# and it makes it much easier for all of us to be working with similar languages."

TestComplete is an open environment. It lets test developers choose the language that best fits their team and their project. They can choose any of 5 scripting languages, VBScript, C# Script, JavaScript, C++ Script, or DelphiScript. And, tests are stored in standard text files so they can be managed with source code version control, just like application source code.

They completed their evaluation and decided to use TestComplete for Velocity and all their testing. "TestComplete has an unbelievable feature set. It can test our desktop applications, Web client applications, server load tests, database verification, and more. It was a great fit since we develop so many different kinds of applications on Windows."

Jesse emphasized the importance of TestComplete's cost-effectiveness. "TestComplete was our first choice because of features, but we couldn't ignore the price either. We licensed the entire team for less than it would have cost to get one seat of another product."

The team purchased TestComplete and implemented their first test within a week. Within 90 days, they had integrated it completely into their operations and had automated most of their tests for Velocity. "We use the test recorder to quickly make new tests. Those get added to our regression suite right away, then we copy them and use the recorded code as a base for more advanced techniques like data-driven testing."

How has TestComplete changed how they work? "I'd estimate that we're doing eight times the number of tests that we could have done without TestComplete. And since they're automated, I'm much more confident that the tests are being run correctly and no steps are missed."

"The test team also sees fewer bugs since we added tests to the build server. Developers get immediate feedback when their changes break the smoke tests and they don't have to wait to hear back from us. We also use TestComplete to record the steps to duplicate a bug, then we can recreate any problem automatically for our own testing and attach it to the bug report for the developer so they can use it themselves."

"TestComplete has saved us an enormous amount of time and money. We're working faster and doing more. I feel better shipping changes knowing how much our coverage has increased. TestComplete has made my job a lot easier."

UPDATE:

John Waters, Falafel's Chief Technology Officer, read this case study and wrote to add another important point:

"There is one thing of great value to me that wasn't mentioned in the case study.

Using TestComplete's automated load testing, we could measure the performance impact of SSL contra plain HTTP, WAN contra LAN, and changes to our caching strategies. In a way that provided meaningful metrics to us and our client, and it allowed us to make informed architectural decisions."

Source: AutomatedQA (2008).[3]

♣ SKETCH OF EIS SYSTEM ARCHITECTURE

An enterprise information system architecture is an elusive analysis of an enterprise system apart from the particulars of implementation, algorithms, and data. Enterprise architecture has turned out to be an area of foremost concentration in the software enlargement community. A number of architecture modeling notations and support tools, as well as new architectural styles, has materialized in current years. Architecture-based software expansion facilitates and directs the focus to coarser-grained building blocks and their interconnections rather than on the code level as in Figure 6.1. In short it is an Enterprise-level depiction of the portfolio of systems elements to achieve greater integration and more efficient deployment and exploitation of those elements.

Another objective of this chapter is to help the student understand the issues and decisions that must be made when managing an EIS project. Every project is different; there are different organizational contexts, infrastructures and strategies. Even so, methodical approaches are believed to have a better likelihood of EIS project implementation success. This is because technique draws on standards and prior learning and enables the reuse of resources and competencies. The dilemma is that no

---

[3] AutomatedQA offers software products and services for development and quality assurance projects worldwide. We create innovative, award-winning and affordable products for the entire software development lifecycle including TestComplete for test automation and AQtime, a sophisticated performance and memory profiler. AutomatedQA has an impressive list of customers ranging from huge teams in the world's largest organizations to progressive one-developer shops. AutomatedQA was founded in 1999 with headquarters in Las Vegas, Nevada, United States.

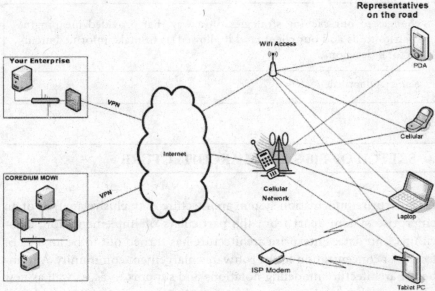

Figure 6.1: Enterprise Architecture.

Source: Coredium (2008).[4]

single method is widespread; no method fits all settings. A methods engineering approach considers human factors and applies appraisal modeling techniques. The knowledge management development team analyzes the business situation and, draws from an inventory of methods. We will describe general lifecycle and project management models for EIS systems. The issues are discussed and illustrated via academic and industry cases.

Figure 6.2 seeks to demonstrate how system architects can draw their ideas from a variety of sources and experiences, in conjunction with talking with stakeholders. The overall aim is to assemble an EIS that optimally provides information to the using organization.

---

[4] Coredium Inc was founded in 1998 with the purpose of optimizing the process linked to the order cycle management of companies who work in the manufacturing, distribution and retail industries.

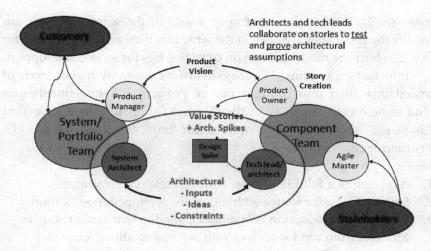

Figure 6.2:   Role Collaboration in Systems Architecture.
Source: Copyright 2008, Dean Leffingwell.

6.1 EIS AS AN INFORMATION SYSTEM PROJECT

The primary reason that EIS systems are adopted is to gain high-quality computing service for the organization. Vendors have spent a great deal of research in identifying better ways to provide organizational computing support. Research has indicated a very high payoff from high quality information systems. EIS systems are designed to be efficient, integrating computing within organizations. They are also intended to provide high quality. This quality is obtained through improved business processes, and also through linking to add-on software products.

Another major development in EIS has been open software systems. This idea, made famous by the Linux operating system, provides the opportunity to utilize more service-oriented systems, strongly supported by organizations such as IBM with their on-demand computing initiative and an industry focus on software as a service (SaaS), where vendors develop software posted to the Web and made available for customer use. Web delivery has been selected as a means to distribute a number of interesting enterprise system software, led by Compiere from France. Compiere (and many similar products) are not open source in the sense that users can modify the code. They are open in the sense that they are downloadable for free. The business model is based on collecting fees for service and support.

Information systems (IS) projects involve relatively higher levels of uncertainty than most other types of projects. EIS implementations tend to be on the large end of the IS project spectrum. As discussed in Chapter 3, there are many options for implementation of an EIS. Reordering that list a bit:

1. Adoption of a full EIS package from a single vendor source.
2. Single EIS vendor source with internally developed modifications.
3. Best-of-breed: adoption of modules from different vendor sources.
4. Modules from vendor sources with internal modifications.
5. In-house development.
6. In-house development supplemented by some vendor products.
7. Application service providers (ASP).

Barring number 7 on the above list, ASP, the easiest method is to adopt a system provided by a single vendor, without modifications (number 1 above). But this isn't necessarily the least expensive option, nor will it necessarily provide the greatest benefits to the firm. The reason to use the best-of-breed approach (number 3 above), using modules from different vendors, is that the functionality obtained from specific modules may be greater in one area for one vendor, but better in another module area (with respect to the needs of the specific adopting organization) from another vendor. EIS systems could be developed in-house (number 5 above). This is not recommended. If this method were adopted, a great deal of IS/IT project management effort would be necessary. As implied by variants numbered 2, 4, and 6, blends of each of these forms of EIS implementation have been applied as well. Finally, EIS could be outsourced (number 7 above), through application service providers. This can result in the lowest cost method of installation. As discussed later in this chapter, that may involve a lot of convenience at the cost of a loss of control.

Mabert *et al.* surveyed the strategic approach adopted in their sample of manufacturing firms who had implemented ERP systems. ASP implementation was not surveyed. Katerattanakul *et al.* replicated the study in

Table 6.1: Relative use of ERP Implementation Strategies.

Strategy	Percentage US	Percentage Korea
Single ERP package with modifications.	50	43
Single ERP package.	40	
Vendor packages with modifications.	5	
Best-of-breed.	4	27
In-house plus specialized packages.	1	14
Total in-house system.	0.5	16

Source: Mabert *et al.* (2000), Katerattanakul *et al.* (2006).[5]

Korea, reporting only four of these options. Their relative use in percentage is given in Table 6.1.

In the US, the dominant strategy in this sector (manufacturing) was to rely upon a single developer, with a large number of firms supplementing the system for internal needs. The concept of best-of-breed was not widely applied. Few firms developed their own ERP system. One reason for this reliance upon vendor plans for the most part is that it is much easier to control installation by following implementation procedures developed and tested by the vendors. The Korean study saw much greater use of best-of-breed approaches, mixing software from different vendors. There also was much greater use of in-house systems. The difference can be attributed to local conditions.

6.2 IS/IT PROJECT MANAGEMENT RESULTS

Project management is one of the most important fields in information systems. It is difficult to bring an information systems project to completion on time, within budget, and meeting specifications. A partner of KPMG Peat Marwick said that, based on a survey of 250 companies, some

[5] Mabert, V. A., Soni, A. and Venkataramanan, M. A. (2000). Enterprise resource planning survey of U.S. manufacturing firms. *Production and Inventory Management Journal*, 41(2), 52–58; Katerattanakul, P., Hong S. and Lee, J. (2006). Enterprise resource planning survey of Korean manufacturing firms. *Management Research News*, 29(12), 820–837.

30 percent of information systems projects exceeded the original budget and time frame by at least a factor of two, or did not conform to specifications.[6] A report issued by The Standish Group in 1994 (based on a survey of 365 companies with over 8,000 development projects) found that only 16 percent came in on time and within budget. For large companies, the success rate was only nine percent. It was also reported that only 42 percent of planned features and functions end up in the final version of the software.[7] A 1995 report of The Standish Group stated that over half the software development projects initiated by large companies would cost 189 percent more than originally estimated. American Express Financial Advisors experienced project budget overruns as high as 500 percent.[8] The Standish Group issued yet another report in 1997, reporting that in 1996 73 percent of U.S. software projects had been canceled, were over budget, or were late, but that this was much better than the corresponding 84 percent in 1995.[9] Meta Group, Inc. in 1997 reported that poor project planning and management had led to U.S. companies scrapping almost one-third of their new software projects at a loss of $80 billion annually. One out of every two projects ran more than 180 percent over budget for another $59 billion in losses.[10] Yet information systems projects offer great value for companies.

While EIS systems involve a little more structure, there are still problems encountered in implementing EIS. A typical problem is underestimation of the time to get an EIS system working.[11] However, there have been a number of efforts to make this type of installation less problematic. One major reason is that vendors have a vested interest in making EIS installation less risky and more predictable.

While implementation of the basic EIS software systems is becoming less problematic, the situation is complicated a bit by the opportunity to

[6] Booker, E. (1994). No silver bullets for IS projects. *Computerworld*, www.computerworld.com.

[7] Cafasso, R. (1994). Few IS projects come in on time, on budget. *Computerworld*, www.computerworld.com.

[8] King, J. (1995). Tough love reigns in IS projects. *Computerworld*, www.computerworld.com.

[9] King, J. (1997). IS reins in runaway projects. *Computerworld*, www.computerworld.com.

[10] King, J. (1997). Project management ills cost businesses plenty. *Computerworld*, www.computerworld.com.

[11] Romeo, J. (2001). ERP: On the rise again. *Network Computing*, p. 46.

enhance EIS. Enhancement tools include customer relationship management, supply chain management, and knowledge management. The Gartner Group has estimated that up to 30 percent of implementation in major enterprise applications involve the integration of such systems with EIS.[12] The increased use of application service providers is another complicating factor. However, while there will always be new challenges, there are many productivity tools available to make it easier to install EIS and related systems. The use of extensible markup language (XML) to streamline data access, and portals for making EIS data more accessible, make EIS installation and operation much less difficult. XML streamlines data access between applications. Many firms find it useful to include portals for end-user data access, and other enterprise application integration tools.

6.3 SYSTEM ARCHITECTURE AND EIS

A system architecture displays the layout of computer systems used to support an organization. Traditionally, EIS systems were focused internally, which eliminated many problems relative to security and compatibility with external systems. By using closed systems on dedicated servers (mainframe or client/server architecture), access to organizational data could be strictly controlled.

EIS systems that provide access to customers and suppliers (supply chains, for instance) need open system architecture.[13] Such applications lead to the use of EIS systems in e-commerce environments. EIS data in such systems can be distributed over many systems, and the exchange of data across such systems can be problematic. This creates a need for common standards. It also creates the need for systematic and rational design of EIS systems.

---

[12] Ibid.
[13] Hasselbring, W. (2000). Information system integration. *Communications of the ACM*, 43(6), 33–38; Fingar, P. (2000). Component-based frameworks for e-commerce. *Communications of the ACM*, 43(10), 61–66.

Hasselbring (2000) suggests a vertical structure of three architectural layers for an organizational information system.[14] The business architecture layer defines organizational hierarchy and workflows for business processes and rules. This layer is conceptual, expressed in terms meaningful to application users. The application architecture layer defines implementation of business concepts in terms of enterprise applications. This layer provides the glue between the application domain described by the business architecture with the technical solutions described in the technology architecture. The technology architecture layer defines the information and communication infrastructure, where IT does the work required by the business users.

When EISs are tied to external systems, there is a need to integrate independent EISs across organizations. This is usually done through messaging services. The SAP R/3 approach aims at enterprise integration via a single database, without boundaries between EISs. But messaging services are still required to integrate autonomous EIS systems. There are products specializing in application adapters, data transformations, and messaging services across EIS systems based on different vendor products.

6.4 OPEN SOURCE EIS

Web services provide a convenient way to access existing internal and external information resources. They use a number of technologies to build programming solutions for specific messaging and application integration problems.[15] However, building a new information system is in some ways like building a new house. Web services may be analogous to cement and bricks. Blueprint and engineering knowledge are more important. SOA gives the picture of what can be done with Web services. SOA exploits the business potential of Web services, which can lead to a type of

---

[14] Hasselbring (2000), op. cit.

[15] Brenner, M. R. and Unmehopa, M. R. (2007). Service-oriented architecture and Web services penetration in next-generation networks. *Bell Labs Technical Journal*, 12(2), 147–160.

convergence by enabling organizations to access better methods at lower cost through technology.

SOA is a strategy based on turning applications and information sources which reside in different organizations, different systems and different execution environments into "services" that can be accessed with a common interface regardless of the location or technical makeup of the function or piece of data. The common interface must be agreed upon within the environment of systems that can access or invoke that service. A service within SOA either provides information or facilitates a change to business data from one valid and consistent state to another one. Services are invoked through defined communication protocols. The pivotal part of SOA is how communication between different data formats can be accomplished. Web Services, which are independent of operational environment, allow this communication.

The goal of EIS is to integrate and consolidate all the old departments across an organization into one system that can meet and serve each department's unique needs and tasks. Therefore, every aspect of an organization's business process needs to have a unified application interface, which provides high competitiveness in the market. Enterprises have invested heavily on EIS acquisition while small businesses or entrepreneurs often could not afford it mainly due to its high upfront prices and lack of resources to maintain the system. To attack this niche market of EIS in the small to medium-sized business sector, vendors has developed transformed EISs by adopting the most advanced information technologies available. The most available business models of EIS include software as a service (SaaS), open source software (OSS) and service-oriented architecture (SOA).

SaaS offers EIS as a service that clients can access via the Internet. Smaller companies are spared the expenses associated with software installation, maintenance and upgrades. Mango Network, an Irving, Texas, software and services company is a channel of providing software and services for small and midsize wholesale and retail distributors. It combines the pure open-source business model and SaaS. Compiere, which is a pure open-source company, provides products and Mango sells them through SaaS. Mango charges annual fees based on a customer's revenue, rather than monthly fees based on the number of users.

The Organization for the Advancement of Structured Information Standards (OASIS) defines SOA as: A paradigm for organizing and utilizing distributed capabilities that may be under the control of different ownership domains. It provides a uniform means to offer, discover, interact with and use capabilities to produce desired effects consistent with measurable preconditions and expectations. SOA-driven EIS is not only beneficial to enterprises as many believe but also to SMBs.

OSS EISs allowed small and medium sized businesses access to EIS. The benefits of applying OSS are as follows[16]:

♦ Increased adaptability: Since EIS is not plug and play, implementation processes are necessary to match the company's business processes and local regulations. Having full access to the EIS source code is beneficial.

♦ Decreased reliance on a single supplier: Proprietary EISs depend highly on the services from vendors and distributors. Upgrading and maintaining service can be obtained from a single source.

♦ Reduced costs: Proprietary EIS licenses are expensive. OSS EIS' average implementation costs are at between one-six and one-third of the costs for typical proprietary EIS.

The majority of Web 2.0 business models can be explained in a production/filtering (P/F) model.[17] The basic structure of a successful Web 2.0 business model is used to understand open-source EIS business models. Value creation includes two processes: production (P) and filtering (F). Figure 6.3 shows clusters of the P-F model. The P process produces value and F process filters information based on customers' needs, a tailoring process. There were only a limited number of professionals who could participate in P or F steps in traditional industrial economic systems. P was limited to reporters in the press or developers of software firms and F was limited to editorial writers, managers and marketers. Most of the current

---

[16] Serrano, N. and Sarriegi, J. M. (2006). Open source software ERPs: A new alternative for an old need. *IEEE Software*, 94–97.

[17] Kim, T. M. (2008). *Economy*, Seoul: Hanbit Media.

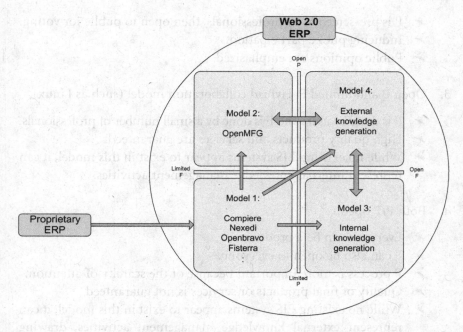

Figure 6.3:   The Clusters of the EIS P-F Model.[18]

Web 2.0 businesses belong to one of the following three types. When extending this model to open-source EISs, we limit the meaning of "open" only to "free-of-charge".

1.   Limited P model: Free software, no participation by users.

   ➢ All activities are done by the members/employees.
   ➢ Guarantees high quality of final products and services after the F process.

2.   Limited P and Open F: Competition model.

   ➢ P is done by a small number of professionals or Pro-Ams and F is done by public users.

---

[18] Figure developed by Sang-Huei Lee.

> ➤ F is pre-screened by professionals, then open to public for voting.
> ➤ Inducing public participation.
> ➤ Public opinions are emphasized.

3. Open P and limited F: Hybrid collaboration model (such as Linux).

> ➤ P is done by users and F is done by a small number of professionals.
> ➤ High quality products and services are guaranteed.
> ➤ While no existing EIS systems appear to exist in this model, it can represent internal knowledge management activities.

4. Both P/F open.

> ➤ Everyone can be a producer.
> ➤ F can also be open to everyone.
> ➤ F process is more important because of the scarcity of attention.
> ➤ Quality of final products or services is not guaranteed.
> ➤ While no existing EIS systems appear to exist in this model, it can represent external knowledge management activities, drawing upon Web 2.0 links for gaining additional understanding of organizational problems.

The most common business model of OSS is based on a simple idea — free for use, modification, resale and fee for services including implementation. Figure 6.3 shows that most EIS-related open-source software uses the Web for delivery of free software (Model 1). There is at least one product (OpenMFG) allowing users to participate in software development, but with software vendor filtering (Model 2). Open filtering models have not appeared to date.

Among the many open-source EIS vendors given in Model 1 in Figure 6.3, Compiere has most often appeared in many research articles and business reports. Compiere recorded more than 1.2 million downloads of its software and has more than 100 partners in 25 countries (Ferguson, 2008). They don't sell software but sell services — security and support. They do not allow just anyone to contribute code — the majority of code contributors are trained partners who understand the company's business model. This belongs to limited P/limited F model in P-F model of Web 2.0.

The EIS software OpenMFG allows community members including customers and partners to get the source code and extend and enhance it. The company, then, brings the enhancements into the product.[19] This could be an example of typical open P/limited F model.

We have not seen products fitting Models 3 and 4, but Web 2.0 development can lead to systems of value fitting these models. Both are open, offering a collaborative environment inductive to innovation. The difference between Models 3 and 4 is the degree of participation. Internal focus groups working on improved business process development would fit Model 3, while the inclusion of external ideas would fit Model 4.

6.5 SYSTEMS DESIGN ASPECTS OF EIS

EIS implementations usually involve installation of vendor software. Custom-designed EIS systems are sometimes built, which would be a major information systems project. On the other hand, installation of a vendor system is much simpler, but still is a significant information systems project. There are a number of techniques that have been developed to accomplish information systems projects. The standard approach is the waterfall model, a straightforward sequence of activities typically involved. For projects with higher levels of risk, alternative methods have been developed. Here we will give a brief overview of the waterfall model, which represents a sequence of activity within which a standard EIS installation might proceed, as well as the spiral model intended to provide support when high levels of risk are involved.

6.5.1 The Waterfall Model

The waterfall model is the basic standard for software development of all types, including EIS. The waterfall model recognizes feedback loops between stages of software development to minimize rework, as well as incorporating prototyping as a means to more thoroughly understand

---

[19] Ferguson, R. (2008). Open-source enterprise push. *eWeek.*

new applications. The waterfall model (named because each step follows its predecessor in sequence) consists of the following stages, each of which can involve reversion to the prior stage if attempts at validation uncover problems. The waterfall model has the advantages of encouraging planning before design, and distills system development into subgoals with milestones corresponding to completion of intermediate products. This allows project managers to more accurately track project progress, and provides project structure, as shown in Table 6.2.

The list shown is for a software life cycle product. There are variations in the stages for different types of projects, such as acquisition of software, implementation of a vendor system, or other kinds of projects. In EIS projects, feasibility analysis is a major concern due to the scope of investment involved, and the impact on future operations. Software plans and requirements are determined in large part by the implementation option selected. Product design is tied to business process reengineering efforts. Detailed design is expedited by vendor and consultant support for the most part, and their methodologies eliminate the need for most coding. (If the system is built in-house, a heavy coding burden would be required.) Integration is also expedited by vendor products. While design, coding, and integration

Table 6.2: Waterfall Model of Software Life Cycle Stages.

Stage	Feedback determinant
System feasibility	Validation
Software plans and requirements	Validation
Product design	Verification
Detailed design	Verification
Code	Unit test
Integration	Product verification
Implementation	System test
Operations and maintenance	Revalidation

Source: Boehm (1988).[20]

---

[20] Boehm, B. (1988). *Software Risk Management*, p. 27. Atlanta: Computer Society Press.

efforts would be less following pure vendor implementation options, the implementation effort would be high, as extensive training is required to get each member of the organization to adopt the best practices imposed by the system. Conversely, in-house systems would often be built around existing business practices, and thus implementation would likely have less impact for in-house systems. The impact on operations and maintenance is expected to have high payoff for systems adopting improved business practices.

Each stage involves a test, either validation or verification. Validation is the process of evaluating software to ensure compliance with specification requirements. (Is this the right product?) Verification is the process of determining whether or not the software component functions correctly. (Is the product built right?)

In the original waterfall model, problems accumulated over stages and not noticed until project completion resulted in very expensive code. User needs were often not met, resulting in rejection of products after they were built. Therefore, feedback loops were added, along with prototyping, to catch problems early. The waterfall model does not allow rapid response to the pervasiveness of change in information system projects. The orderly sequence of activities in the waterfall model does not accommodate new developments.

In-house implementation of EIS, and even implementations involving vendor systems with some customization, can be expected to follow the waterfall model. For complete in-house EIS development, higher levels of risk are present, and the spiral model below might be appropriate. Rapid prototyping, object-oriented processes, or rapid application development might also apply. However, that form of EIS implementation is expected to be rare. Far more common is use of vendor software directly, in which case the implementation process will be much more straightforward. The waterfall model still can apply, with the risk involved far less.

Prototyping is the process of developing a small working model of a program component or system with the intent of seeing what it can do. Thus it is a learning device, especially appropriate when users are not absolutely sure what they want in a system.

6.5.2 Prototyping

When dealing with systems which involve beneficial features that are both difficult to predict and difficult to price, the systems development approach has proven ineffective. What happens is that the hard, clear dollar benefits rarely are sufficient to justify adopting the system.

An evolutionary approach is useful for evaluating systems applied in unstructured environments, because users very often do not know what benefits or what features the system will provide until they see it in operation.[21] A prototyping approach involves building a small-scale mock-up system, allowing the user to try it out. The user could then ask for modifications based upon a better idea of what the system could do. Prototyping is a much less thoroughly planned approach, but is often appropriate for applications with low investment and low structure. This can result in much lower development cost and time, especially when there are many uncertainties about what the system should consist of.

Prototyping has uses in the installation of parts of EIS systems. It is especially appropriate when generating modifications to systems, when there is no complete assurance that the proposed change is not going to involve unexpected complications. In EIS systems, risk is present in some implementation options. The spiral model has been suggested as a methodology to deal with information system project risk. The spiral model methodology includes prototyping.

6.5.3 The Spiral Model

The spiral model[22] uses iterative prototypes. This approach was developed for software projects involving high levels of risk. This might be an appropriate method for EIS implementations involving significant in-house work. Implementation of EIS vendor software involves major iterations, with each iteration often involving revision, re-implementation, and

---

[21] Keen, P. G. W. (1980). Adaptive design for decision support systems. *Database*, 12(1–2), 15–25.

[22] Boehm, B. (1988), op. cit.

upgrades.[23] In the spiral model, risk analysis is performed for each portion of the system. Starting with a concept of system operation, a requirements plan is developed. Software requirements are generated and validated, followed by a development plan. Risk analysis is repeated, and a new prototype incorporating the new development plan is generated, followed by software product design, which is validated, verified, integrated, and tested. After another risk analysis, an improved prototype is developed with a more detailed design. Given this more complete information, coding proceeds, along with testing, integration, acceptance testing, and implementation. The spiral model is shown in Table 6.3.

Each cycle of the spiral begins with the identification of objectives, alternative means of implementing the particular stage of the product, and consideration of constraints. Each cycle involves risk analysis, an identification of what might go wrong, and a plan to deal with problems if they occur. Then prototypes are developed to demonstrate what the system can do at this stage. Models, in the form of simulation to determine risk, and benchmarks to test system modules, are applied. This is followed in each cycle by design considerations.

Table 6.3: The Spiral Model of Software Development.

Cycle 1	Cycle 2	Cycle 3	Cycle 4
Risk analysis	Risk analysis	Risk analysis	Risk analysis
Prototype models	Prototype models	Prototype models	Operational prototype
Operation concept	Software requirements	Software product design	Detailed design
			CODE
Requirements plan	Requirements validation	Design validation & verification	Unit test
Life-cycle plan	Development plan	Integration & test plan	Integration & test
			Acceptance test
			Implementation

Source: Boehm (1988), p. 64.

---

[23] Gable, G. G., Chan, T. and Tan, W.-G. (2001). Large packaged application software maintenance: A research framework. *Journal of Software Maintenance and Evolution: Research and Practice*, 13, 351–371.

Many risks exist in EIS projects. The management of these risks is critical to successful delivery of needed information system support. The spiral model emphasizes risk analysis to yield more consistent system performance.

The degree of complication in installing an EIS system depends primarily on the type of EIS system adopted. Full implementation of vendor software will involve the least risk, as the implementation technique that has been developed and thoroughly tested through experience by the vendor can be adopted. At the other extreme, building an EIS internally from scratch would be a mammoth undertaking full of risk, calling for a spiral approach. In between, the more modification to the vendor software that is involved, the greater the consideration of risk elements.

6.5.4 Other Options for Systems Development

EIS development includes modules, much the same idea as objects. Software development productivity tools include the use of object-oriented enterprise frameworks (OOEFs).[24] OOEFs are designed to reduce the complexity and cost of enterprise systems. They are meant to establish a formal set of criteria to be used in building or selecting an enterprise framework. Distributed object computing is a recognized way to build enterprise information architecture that can operate in advanced client/server, intranet, and Internet environments.[25] By using objects to build information systems, complexity is reduced because programmers do not need to know how an object works internally. They only need to know what the object is and the services it provides.

There are negatives to object-oriented technology. There is a steep learning curve. Business objects can become unwieldy when combined with large-scale commercial applications (which is what a vendor-provided EIS is). More plug-and-play application services, and reuse of components, are attractive. Java portability (write once, run anywhere) is useful, and the Extensible Markup Language (XML) is very useful in

---

[24] Fayad, M. E., Hamu, D. S. and Brugali, D. (2000). Enterprise frameworks, characteristics, criteria, and challenges. *Communications of the ACM*, 43(10), 39–46.
[25] Fingar, P. (2000), op. cit.

shared Internet file systems. Another productivity tool is the Unified Modeling Language (UML) that is designed to model components and guide construction, assembly, and reuse.

6.6   EXTERNAL EIS OPERATION AND SUPPORT

Recently it has become very popular to hire out large portions of information processing, or **outsourcing**. Outsourcing involves contracts with external vendors to operate your system on your premises. One purpose of outsourcing is downsizing. Unocal, like many other oil companies, pared their staff by 40 percent over a two-year period, with 130 layoffs in the information systems group.[26] Many functions can be outsourced, including data center management, telecommunications, disaster recovery, and legacy systems maintenance. This avoids the need to waste scarce resources, and can gain efficiencies by hiring vendors with expertise. Outsourcing can also be used for company Internet operations. Eastman Kodak, which began outsourcing in 1989, held on to its Internet activities because the environment was too dynamic, and its own plans were too uncertain. If plans are clearer, Internet functions that could be outsourced include connectivity, Web server hosting, firewall security, Web site development, and content development. These activities are complex, subject to change, and not particularly relevant to organizational core competencies.[27] Outsourcing makes sense when fast start-up is important, internal skills are lacking, and the vendor can provide strong features. Outsourcing for Internet operations is not as worthwhile if they are of strategic importance to the business, or requirements are ill-defined. Rarely is outsourcing used for everything involved within a project. For one thing, there will be need for internal training to implement the system, and to integrate it with the existing system.

---

[26] Moore, S. (1994). Unocal's outsourcing decision stirs up networking operations. *Computerworld*, www.computerworld.com.

[27] Anthes, G. H. (1997). Net outsourcing a risky proposition. *Computerworld*, www.computerworld.com.

The most popular way to outsource EIS and related systems is the use of **application service providers** (ASPs). An ASP is a company that leases software applications and distributes them via the Internet or private communications lines. In a way, this is like returning to the time-sharing approach in the early days of MIS. Boyd reported that most firms are not willing to outsource complex EIS or other complex applications, because of the need for high levels of integration by these systems.[28] However, ASPs can offer lower costs and increased flexibility.[29] They often provide a way to obtain more reliable and less expensive service than systems built in-house. This includes obtaining partial EIS services via ASP rather than developing a full-scale EIS system.

Cost savings from ASP are in software development and upgrading. Kavanagh estimates that costs of system implementation and maintenance would be the same for traditional approaches as for ASP.[30] Training costs would also be expected to be about the same. However, the cost of hardware and personnel would be eliminated, as would software upgrade costs. These cost savings would be expected to be far higher than the cost of the ASP. Kavanagh concludes that total operating cost for the ASP option over a five-year period would be about 30 percent less than for a conventional EIS model.

EIS is only one service offered through ASPs. Acquisition of customer relationship management services through an ASP often makes sense.

There are a number of risks in the ASP route to obtaining EIS services[31]:

1. Applications and data are controlled by others.
2. Service failures.
3. Confidentiality failure.
4. Performance issues.

---

[28] Boyd, J. (2000). Technical limitations hold back ASPs — Quality of service, security, app interoperability, responsiveness still question marks. *Internetweek*, 832, 12, 16.

[29] Apicella, M. (2000). Alternatives to the traditional ASP model. *Inforworld*, p. 65, www.infoworld.com.

[30] Kavanagh, S. (2001). Application service providers (ASPs): Can ASPs bring ERP to the masses? *Government Finance Review*, 17(4), 10–14.

[31] Apicella (2000), op. cit.

Leaving your applications in the hands of others involves the primary risk that your ASP may decide to discontinue product features that you were relying upon. They also might inadvertently leak information sensitive to your organization. Use of ASP relinquishes a degree of control. On the positive side, ASPs can develop core competencies in training and support that can be very costly for customer organizations. They also can agree to meet performance standards that are necessary to allow interaction with other systems, for e-commerce or supply-chain management purposes. Kavanagh found that EIS vendors have been committed to at least some sort of ASP effort.[32]

There are a number of alternative approaches available to obtain ASP support for EIS. The original vendor can deliver EIS through ASP, or third-party resellers can be utilized. Smaller EIS companies selling to a variety of markets may find a third-party, value-added reseller best able to meet their needs. Those EIS-using organizations specializing in only a few markets may be better off hosting the application themselves, because there is little the third party could add.

6.7 ORGANIZING FOR IMPLEMENTATION

Implementing an EIS is a major organizational project. There are various ways to organize for EIS implementation, shown in the Method column of Table 6.4. Regardless of the method adopted by an organization, there will be some project structure to create. An individual is appointed to be the project manager of this implementation. The effort can be carried by vendors, consultants, or in-house personnel to varying degrees. If a single vendor source is the method adopted, the vendor will provide people to coordinate the effort. Most organizations also feel the need to hire consultants. A major EIS implementation project concern is how to control the participation (and thus the cost) of such consultants.

The amount of effort depends a great deal on the form of implementation adopted. Table 6.4 compares this relative effort by entity.

---

[32] Kavanagh, S. (2001), op. cit.

Table 6.4:   Relative Implementation Effort.

Method	In-house	Vendor	Consultant
Single vendor source.	Significant.	Heavy.	Heavy.
Single vendor with modifications.	Significant +.	Heavy.	Heavy +.
Best-of-Breed.	Significant +.	Moderate.	Heavy +.
Multiple vendor modules with modifications.	Significant ++.	Moderate.	Heavy +.
In-house.	Excruciating.	None.	Might be useful.
In-house with modules.	Painful.	Moderate.	Might be useful.
Application service providers.	Light.	None.	To select.

Implementing an EIS is going to place a strain on in-house information systems groups. Consultants are expensive, but so are surgeons, and there are times where their expertise is needed.

Project sponsors can have a major impact on the success of any information system project. Project sponsors could be those who control purse strings, but also could be those who generate convincing arguments that lead decision-makers to adopt EIS systems. The concept of a project champion is someone who is an influential individual within an organization who applies his or her influence to make sure that a project has sufficient resources and attention to succeed. Project champions can come from the top of the organization, and in the case of EIS, very often the motivation to adopt an EIS system comes from chief executive officers. Project champions can come from other higher level people in an organization as well. The key feature is to provide enthusiastic interest in the project to overcome inevitable problems from undertaking such a large and pervasive system.

EIS implementation teams always include people from within the organization. What they do varies by the method of EIS implementation adopted. All systems involve heavy training efforts. The level of coordination activity will vary as indicated in Table 6.4. If a vendor product is involved, vendor support personnel will be actively involved. Consultants are always available at the call of the organization. The degree of consultant activity is heaviest if there are more complexities involved in the EIS implementation. For instance, mixing modules calls for a great deal of difficult coordination, and consultants can be very helpful.

The seven methods given in Table 6.4 have relative advantages and disadvantages. Table 6.5 compares these.

Table 6.6 focuses on relative method advantages on the specific aspects of time and budget, risk, access to technology, and security for organizational data.

Table 6.5: Relative Advantages of Implementation Methods.

Method	Relative advantages	Relative disadvantages
Single vendor source.	Fastest of controlled methods. Least amount of complications. Proven business processes.	Subject to vendor changes. Potential loss of any internally developed competitive advantages.
Single vendor with modifications.	More responsive to organizational methods.	Modifications involve high schedule risk.
Best-of-Breed.	Select preferred approaches for each function.	A highly risky method with many coordination problems.
Multiple vendor modules with modifications.	The most flexible approach.	The riskiest of all methods.
In-house.	Custom-designed to match organizational needs. Least change on the part of users.	A massive undertaking — high budget and time risk. Requires development of many expensive areas of expertise.
In-house with modules.	Custom-designed utilizing vendor products for selected applications.	Moderately high budget and time risk.
Application service providers.	Least budget, time risk. May provide access to latest vendor technology at relatively low cost.	Highly vulnerable to continued success of provider. Lowest degree of control over organizational data.

Table 6.6:　Relative Features of EIS Implementation Methods.

Method	Time & budget	Risk	Access to technology	Security
Single vendor source.	Very good.	Lowest risk.	Subject to vendor upgrades.	High.
Single vendor with modifications.	Good.	Modifications inherently risky.	Very good.	High
Best-of-Breed.	Poor.	Development of interfaces problematic.	Ideal.	High.
Multiple vendor modules with modifications.	Very poor.	Very high risk.	Theoretically very good.	High.
In-house.	Worst.	The worst kind of IS project.	Very risky — design all internally.	High.
In-house with modules.	Better than all in-house.	Very difficult IS project.	Less risky than all In-house.	High.
Application service providers.	Can be best.	Low project risk. Highly vulnerable to continued success of ASP.	Can be ideal, if ASP can afford to buy the best.	Very low.

Tables 6.5 and 6.6 include the features that explain why most EIS adopters utilize vendor systems with modifications. This method provides access to well-tested software while allowing some ability to maintain organizational competitive advantages through modifications. Many adopters use a single vendor source method, which is the fastest and cheapest way to develop an EIS within an organization. However, this approach means that you have an information system that is available to all customers of that vendor. The best-of-breed approach is rarely used, and so are in-house methods. They involve high levels of risk, and are appropriate only in special circumstances. Use of ASPs is relatively new. ASPs offer great reductions in time and budget risk in the short run, but entail future risks.

6.8 AVENTIS PHARMA HELLAS CASE

Customer:

Aventis Pharma Hellas

Challenge:

♦ Integrate Aventis Pharmas business processes with business partners in automating manual tasks that required information lookup and exchange, resulting in delays and inefficient use of resources.

♦ Provide a seamlessly integrated solution incorporating Aventis Pharmas current IT infrastructure (SAP/R3 ERP, Oracle RDBMS) with that of its partners (Oracle RDBMS, Oracle-based ERP, proprietary systems).

♦ Meet strict time-to-market business integration requirements.

Applications:

Aventis Pharma required robust solutions for automating the following business processes with its business partners:

♦ Payment/Check Management.

♦ Product returns handling.

♦ On-line order management.

♦ Monitoring and administration for the above applications.

Key Business Challenges:

Minimize handling delays and costs, minimize errors, and improve high-level view by management.

Key Technical Challenges:

♦ Seamless integration of the various EISs with minimum business partner impact.

♦ Minimization of IT solution complexity.

♦ Quick system response in communicating with the SAP ERP back end located in Germany.
♦ Easy maintenance and expandability.

Solution:

EBS designed and implemented a set of solutions, applying standard software engineering methodologies that allowed rapid development, integration and deployment in a multi-vendor and distributed IT environment. The products and technologies involved included IBMs Websphere Application Server, SAP Business Connector, XML/Webservices, and Oracle RDBMS. The delivered solution met the business goals with proven flexibility and can be easily expanded to accommodate changing business needs and additional requirements. Figure 6.4 shows the EBS architecture.

Technology:

Back End EISs: SAP R/3 ERP, Oracle-based ERP, Oracle RDBMS.
Application Server: IBM Websphere.
Integration: Web Services/SAP BC/Axis.
Software Architecture: Full J2EE* 1.3.1 3-tier approach.

*Java 2 Enterprise Edition

Value for Aventis:

♦ Reduced operational costs.
♦ Reduced costs of contracted services of business partners.
♦ Better quality of service for employees (real-time access to information) enabling them to make better informed decisions.

6.9 CONCLUSION

EIS implementations are complex because they force an organization to link manifold systems across business processes. For any large-scale imple-

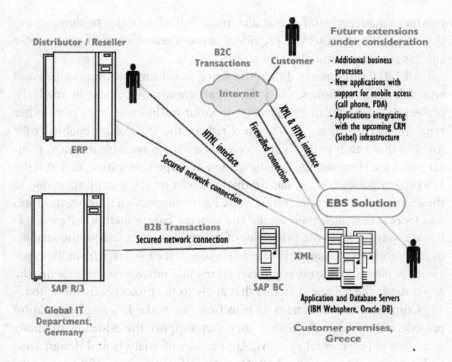

Figure 6.4: EBS Architecture.

Source: www.ebs.gr/en/aventis.html[33]

mentation project, business process and system information are incorporated in the enterprise-solution architecture. To comprehend the entirety of any organization's business processes, managers must define and document all core and support processes. EIS is an idea fundamentally based on obtaining quality software support. Implementation of an EIS is an IS/IT project. There are a number of ways to accomplish this, ranging from in-house development of the entire system (considered by most to be the most painful way), through direct adoption of an unmodified vendor

[33] EBS combines technology with innovation into solutions and services that enable companies to meet their goals. Whether you need new solutions or you want to leverage your current IT investment, EBS offers you enabling capabilities to increase your profit, streamline your operations, and increase your customer base.

product (the least painful, but also most inflexible way), to outsourcing through application service providers (a more recent phenomenon whose success is still questionable).

All IS/IT projects are difficult to bring in on time, within budget, and with full designed functionality. Risk is an important element in any IS/IT project. It is present in EIS projects too, but in different ways from other types of IS/IT projects. EIS has less risk in the technology-enabled BPR form, in that a clear path of what needs to be done is available for many project activities. However, the risk dimension of scope is very high, in that if the EIS project goes wrong, it has dramatic impact on the organization due to the scope of investment involved, as well as the impact on how organization members accomplish their work. The systems failure method offers a systematic way to apply the principles of the systems approach to the analysis of new project proposals. It is based on a simple idea — learn from the experience of others. While other projects clearly face different environments, the key is to see the pertinent factors that apply to the project being designed.

Consideration of system architecture can make EIS implementation projects more rational, in that they can support the addition of many attractive supplemental systems. Application of analysis and design control frameworks provides better means of controlling IS/IT projects, including EIS implementation. The traditional approach to an IS/IT project design is the waterfall model. If a direct implementation of a software vendor's system is adopted, this is probably sufficient, as there are relatively low levels of risk involved (the vendor has worked out the bugs of implementation). For EIS systems involving modification (or at the extreme of in-house implementation), high levels of risk would be involved, and Boehm's spiral model may be more appropriate. This model considers risk directly, and uses prototypes as a means to assess the success of the system in dealing with project risks.

Web services provide a more open system, which should lead to a better market for all participants in the long run. This open market can lead to innovation in enterprise systems. EIS can be viewed as a self-organizing system, whose components can be assembled in an open market accessed over the Web. The composition of Web services is an important strategic decision in the new software environment. The concept of bundling was demonstrated qualitatively through the EIS market. Vendors can improve their total profit if they open their systems to an open market for non-core components. Their clients can benefit by accessibility to the appropriate functionality of software best fitting their needs (and the right cost).

Web 2.0 provides a collaboration platform that can be used to generate better decision processes internally or externally to the organization. This activity is unstructured by its nature, and is best accomplished outside of the enterprise system. SOA provides a mechanism for implementing external business processes. SOA is a major element of new products by vendors such as SAP, who have been pushing NetWeaver, which promises to open SAP to easier integration and data exchange, making its replacement (MySAP.com) to the core R/3 system more functional.[34] Oracle is doing similar things with its Project Fusion. These also make it more expensive to upgrade, but EIS vendors are forcing some switching through maintenance support policies.[35]

Firms such as Compiere in France and Belgian Tiny ERP provide innovative access to enterprise systems through open source software. Instead of charging millions (many millions for large firms) like SAP and Oracle, open source software is free! One might wonder about their business model, but such vendors seem to be doing well providing service to users. This is massive innovation in the largest software market in the world. While traditional vendors charge more and more and upgrade their software (discontinuing service for old versions) to maximize their revenue streams, strategic innovation has hit even the EIS market through the same open source venue that brought us Linux.

Outsourcing application service providers offer a new way to share risk. While this approach seeks to shift the burden of EIS implementation and operation to others, it is not a foolproof approach. New risks are introduced relative to security, control, and what to do if the ASP provider fails.

---

[34] Callahan, D. (2005). SAP moves offerings. *eWeek*, 22(21).
[35] Ferguson, R. (2005). ERP friction leaves users cold. *eweek*, 22(4).

☆ KEYWORDS

☆ **Application Service Provider (ASP):** Organization that offers computing services for an organization at a fee. (Use ASP computing facilities.)

☆ **EIS Implementation Strategy:** Strategic approach adopted to implement an EIS system.

☆ **Object-Oriented Enterprise Frameworks (OOEF):** Formal set of criteria designed to systematically assist development or selection of an EIS using object-oriented technology.

☆ **Outsourcing:** Contracting with others external to the organization to operate an organization's computing on the organization's computer system.

☆ **Project:** A project is a temporary endeavor undertaken to achieve a particular aim.

☆ **Project Management:** Project Management is the application of knowledge, skills, tools and techniques to a broad range of activities in order to meet the requirements of the particular project.

☆ **Project Scheduling:** Project scheduling is where the project manager manages a good time line to maximize efficient use of resources.

☆ **Prototyping:** Development procedure involving iterative development of small-scale versions of a system with the intent of identifying needed modifications.

☆ **Software Life Cycle:** Stages typically involved in developing software, or installing software such as EIS.

☆ **Spiral Model:** Software development procedure designed to reduce risk through careful analysis of prototypes.

☆ **System Architecture:** Layout of computer systems used to provide an organization with an information system.

☆ **Waterfall Model:** Standard software development sequence of interrelated activities.

☆ TERMINOLOGY REVIEW

Review Questions

1. Identify a relative advantage for each of the seven EIS implementation methods given in this chapter.
2. Why would you expect such a heavy proportion of EIS systems reported by Mabert *et al.* to involve vendor packages?
3. What is the general track record of information system organizations with respect to completing projects on time and within budget?
4. How can the systems failure method lead to reduction of information system project risk?
5. Discuss the applicability of the stages of the waterfall model to implementation of an EIS vendor product.
6. For what type of EIS implementation might the spiral model be most appropriate?
7. Research the library and/or Internet for links between EIS and rapid application development, or joint application development.
8. Discuss some limitations of application service providers as a means to implement EIS.
9. Search the library and/or Internet for use of systems failure analysis or other systems approaches in information system project management, especially EIS.
10. What are the Input(s) of the Enterprise Information system?
11. What are the Processes of the Enterprise Information system?
12. What are the Output(s) of the Enterprise Information system?
13. What are the basic principle and components of enterprise modeling?
14. Show your understanding by the processes and logic of modeling a large and complex enterprise.
15. How would you apply the appropriate tools and methods in modeling enterprise architecture and information system?

16. Explain how you would identify the information and system requirements of such an enterprise?
17. What would you use to gain hands-on experience from designing enterprise system, writing system requirement and specification?
18. Why would we not leverage the skills of external members who have the experience to match the challenges internal teams face?

☆ COMPETENCY REVIEW

---

1. Assess the student's understanding of the basic software engineering concepts and your perception of several enterprise architecture terms and concepts.
2. Develop and analyze an architectural breakdown for the system described in the case study discussed in class.
3. Develop a partial architectural description of the software system from Assignment 2.
4. Develop a partial implementation of the architecture from Assignment 3 using the supplied architecture implementation infrastructure.
5. As a "systems architect", you will research a business and provide a designed solution for a "state-of-the-art" business information system that will provide excellent service for the next 10 years
6. As a CIO, it is your job to understand the business goals and objectives, now and in the future, and make decisions regarding the purchase and use of a wide array of business information systems.
7. Select a business for which you have an interest. Can it be a real business? Gather a lot of information about the business.
8. Perform a "systems analysis" (Systems Architect role): And find out the following things

   ➢ Determine how the business is organized.
   ➢ Major work areas and information processing needs and requirements.
   ➢ What type(s) of BIS is currently being used… research these systems.

> Identify current and future business needs.
> Research and analyze possible systems and technologies.
> Determine a "good fit" of possible new systems with business needs.
> Prepare your proposal (report).

9. Prepare a "business case" for your proposal (CIO role):

> Business needs and goals, now and in the future.
> Costs versus benefits.
> Decision and plan for "deployment".

☆ CHECK YOUR PROGRESS

Briefly comment on the following:

1. EIS applications and transactions are probably unlike anything else that you have running on your network. It is not safe to assume that the network will handle them well.

   ....

   ....

2. Every EIS deployment is different. The application modules are customized and the architecture of the system and distribution of computing resources will be unique to your environment.

   ....

   ....

3. It is critical to understand how your application performs on the network before beginning enterprise-wide deployment.

   ....

   ....

4. Test your network in advance to understand how these applications will perform and what impact they will have on existing applications. Pay particular attention to WAN links and heavily utilized LANs.

....

....

5. The location of computing resources may have a significant impact on how the application performs, particularly in three-tier environments. Understand the traffic flows between the client and the server as well as the server-to-server communication flows.

....

....

6. An opportunity to demonstrate how to apply appropriate technological systems and infrastructures to support a business information systems solution.

....

....

7. System architecture is a role collaboration.

....

....

8. The teams that code the system design the system.

....

....

☆ SUGGESTED READING

Books

Bass, L., Clements, P. and Kazman, R. (2003). *Software Architecture in Practice*, 2nd Ed. Addison Wesley Professional.

Kendall, K. and Kendall, J. (2005). *System Analysis and Design*, 6th Ed. Prentice Hall.

Marshall, C. (2000). *Enterprise Modeling with UML: Designing Successful Software Through Business Analysis*. Addison-Wesley.

Wasson, C. S. (2006). *System Analysis, Design, and Development: Concepts, Principles, and Practices*. Wiley.

Whitten, Bentley and Dittman (2005). *System Analysis and Design Methods*, 5th Ed. McGraw Hill.

Journal Article

Zachman, J. (1999). A framework for information systems architecture. *IBM Systems Journal*, 26(3), 276–292.

CHAPTER 7

SYSTEM INSTALLATION

Quotation

As commerce becomes more complicated, and companies look to increase automation and collaboration, data is now emerging as a major market battleground. Enterprise Information System management will become critical as companies move toward architecture that supports business efficiency and agility by design and installation.

White & Zrimsek

Structure

♣ *Quick look at chapter themes*
♣ *Learning objectives*
♣ *Case study:* Enterprise system installation throughout the One Vodafone initiative
♣ *Sketch of EIS initiation*
♣ *Introduction*

♣ QUICK LOOK AT CHAPTER THEMES

Globalization and Technology modernization present a new set of challenges to organizations, including increased competition, shrinking margins and increasing customer expectations. In the face of such challenges, it is vital for an organization to have a customer-centric business strategy. EIS implementation and installation is a step in this direction. EIS systems are very popular and widespread. Nonetheless, there are many reports about installation difficulties. On the other hand, vendors make radical claims of how easy installation is with their systems, if only customization is avoided. It seems to be true that vendor installation of their uncustomized systems is reasonably fast and trouble-free. However, that may force the

> *organization to change everything it does, creating many hidden costs that well may eradicate any benefits provided by the EIS. Conversely, massive customization has been reported to involve high cost and time overruns (along with lower hidden costs of operation). EIS installation is a crucial topic meriting close attention.*

♣ LEARNING OBJECTIVES

This chapter discusses the process for setting up and configuring enterprise systems. After reading this lesson you will be able to:

- ♣ Define EIS System installation.
- ♣ Explain and describe the EIS installation functions and architecture.
- ♣ Use the expressions unique to EIS installations.
- ♣ Explain the application integration server requirements in an EIS.
- ♣ Identify the critical factors in IS/IT projects.
- ♣ Identify strategic option for the implementation of EIS systems.
- ♣ Appreciate failure rates in general for IS/IT projects.
- ♣ Understand failure in EIS implementation.
- ♣ Analyze why EIS projects succeed and fail.

♣ CASE STUDY

Enterprise system installation throughout the One Vodafone initiative

About Vodafone: Vodafone has become one of the world's largest mobile communications communities 154.8 million customers, equity interests in 27 countries and partner networks in another 14 countries. To keep up with this demand, we wanted to deliver a single customer, partner and vendor proposition across the entire (and vast) group footprint. The successful project would result in the provision of a unified enterprise view to employees and shareholders; in fact, to all stakeholders.

Questions related to process: The process, the result of a deliberate act of reflection, was constructed from answers to common-sense business questions: Why enterprise architecture (EA)? What are its economic drivers and benefits? What is the context of the technology? Basically, what are the requirements and what should the enterprise architecture deliver to the organization? At the initiation stage, the principle aims of the One Vodafone program were the standardisation of design and processes, reducing duplication, centralizing certain functions, and sharing best practices. The plans are now established and work streams are already well advanced, for instance, the successful roaming initiative that Vodafone announced recently, as well as the introduction of new service platform hosting centers, which have been built in Germany and Italy.

Developments: A few other developments within the Vodafone enterprise also helped pave the way to its overall enterprise architecture. These were: the group target architecture framework, including but not limited to, specifications of the service-delivery platform architecture; the integrated IP multimedia subsystem; intelligent packet core and services architecture; and the group IT architecture.

This case study will attempt to identify and summarize best practices in enterprise architecture, using the experiences and knowledge we have accumulated throughout the duration of these initiatives. The narrative is based on a post-analysis of the existing experience at Vodafone and will follow the entire EA development process, recommending best practices at each phase.

Enterprise architecture: The problem and the solution: A combination of increasing market pressure and years of patching and point solutions has seen many enterprise systems grow somewhat organically. What we are often left with is similar to the pieces of a complex puzzle, which we have to fit together to operate efficiently. How do you make sure that its business objectives are achieved across siloed solutions? In short, how do all the components of the enterprise puzzle fit together? Increasing technological complexity, a daily rise in the amount of information we handle, and the ever quickening pace of change are expected to challenge the very existence of many enterprises in the next few years. One prediction is that EA will offer the enterprise the edge that it needs in the race for survival over the next decade. But, what is EA and, for that matter, what is architecture?

EA is the organization of the enterprise and its blueprint for change, road mapping, product design, business modelling comprehension, and organizational evolution. In simple terms, EA shows how the enterprise operates. We are all familiar with processes and programs such as EA, IT, service-oriented architecture (SOA), enterprise service bus (ESB), Web services, distributed component architecture, and business-process management (BPM). But, how are they all related to each other? Indeed, are they related at all?

Enterprise architecture is often associated with SOA or IT architecture. But, the scope of EA can be wider than that of SOA or indeed IT, as it may encompass non-service oriented manual or mechanical processes. An SOA paradigm may be applied to the whole enterprise, not only to the IT infrastructure. e.g., a "send bill" service may be implemented by a third-party paper process with well-defined interfaces.

Source: Adrian Grigoriu.[1]

♣ SKETCH OF EIS INITIATION

To compete in this highly competitive business world, companies need better information management. Conventional software is transforming into enterprise software, where the system is as smart as the applications. Enterprises are migrating to streamline their computer systems and business processes, even though many of them are unaware why they are making this swing. Gigantic business enterprises today rely more on the hardware and network infrastructure to support their business operations. EIS systems are the workhorse of enterprise computing. Numerous organizations have struggled to deploy them on time and within budget.

---

[1] Adrian Grigoriu is senior manager, emerging technologies at Vodafone UK. Adapted from the website http://www.eimagazine.com/xq/asp/sid.0/articleid.1EC6C304-A5CD-4F39-8F4E-7697A2D73A66/qx/display.htm. Ark Group, 2005.

♣ INTRODUCTION

EIS systems are adopted in the hope that they will improve the performance of an organization on a number of key performance indicators, such as profitability, efficiency, and improved accuracy in information system data and reports. EIS vendors typically promise gains of 10 to 15 percent in revenue, customer satisfaction, and other measures of value. The effort required to build these systems is significant. Meta Group found that the average EIS implementation takes 23 months with total ownership cost of $15 million.[2]

It is typical for firms adopting EIS to go through an initial period where they realize few improvements. Some firms even experience a decline in performance for a period. Major reasons for such declines are:

♦ Failure to thoroughly reengineer business processes.
♦ Management errors in system configuration.
♦ Failure to map changes to the system deriving from changing business needs.
♦ Mistakes in estimated processing power and data storage requirements.
♦ Insufficient training of end users.

In a perfect world, all of these factors would have been considered in planning, and taken care of prior to going live. In practice, it is nearly impossible to anticipate every factor.

When new EIS systems are installed, the way in which the organization does business is usually changed. Newly reengineered business processes have been designed to get more work done with fewer personnel. Caldwell (1988) reported three stages of change. In the first stage, there is a period of productivity decline while jobs are redefined, new procedures established, the EIS system is fine-tuned, and the organization

---

[2] Wheatley, M. (2000). ERP training stinks. *CIO Magazine*, www.cio.com/archive/060100_erp_content.html.

learns to process new streams of information. This first stage typically takes three to nine months. A second stage includes development of new skills, organizational changes, process integration, and addition of bolt-on technologies to expand the functionality of EIS systems. The third stage is where EIS pays off, with transformation of organizational operations to an efficient level.[3]

7.1 EIS INSTALLATION COST

The installation of EIS Systems takes into consideration three factors during installation procedure (Figure 7.1): People, Technology and Process.

♦ People: for whom all this is about.
♦ Technology: bridging the gap between humans and computing.
♦ Process: the modus operandi to execute installation properly.

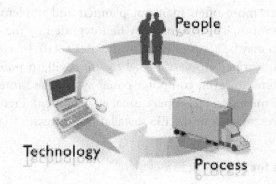

Figure 7.1: EIS Installation Factors.

Source: ERPINDIA.NET.[4]

---

[3] Caldwell, B. (1998). New IT agenda. *Informationweek*, 711, 30–38.
[4] ERPINDIA.NET is currently one of the most visited hubs on the Internet in its domain. These integrated sites help each individual user locate, retrieve and manage information tailored to his or her personal interests.

7.1.1 Installation Cost

Installation may take as little as a few months for very basic EIS implementations, but have taken years for large organizations in the past. The longer installation takes, the more it costs in terms of the organizational team, vendor team, and probably consultant team involved. During EIS installation, there are additional costs from disruption of information systems and operations including:

- ◆ Facilities costs: setting up the environment for the EIS system.
- ◆ Training costs: costs of organizing training for users of the system.
- ◆ Opportunity costs: It is the next best alternative cost. This includes costs of the business which has been lost or delayed while the system is being installed and normal operations are disrupted.
- ◆ Backup costs: the costs of backing up the old system so that recovery is possible if failures occur.

7.1.2 EIS Installation Process

EIS Systems are more often than not planned and implemented in the developer's premises. The systems may be integrated by the developer or this integration may be accomplished by the user's staff. In a few cases, systems may be integrated in place i.e. where they will, in point of fact, be used. Most often, however, computer-based systems are integrated separately, then are moved to their operational environment. Figure 7.2 gives a schematic representation of the EIS installation process.

7.1.3 Options for Installing EIS

There are three frequently used approaches to installing a new EIS system in an enterprise:

1. *Enterprise-wide full installation (big-bang)* — This approach was used very widely in the early days of EIS installations as many large corporations were trying to rapidly be Y2K-compliant. The principal challenge companies faced was getting all their employees to act as

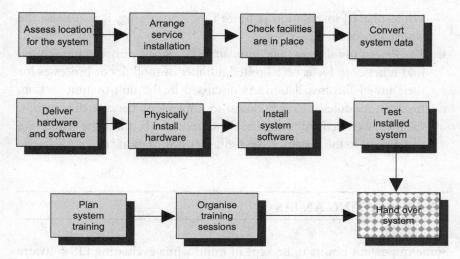

Figure 7.2: EIS Installation Process.

Source: Sommerville, I. (1998). Software Intensive Systems Engineering.

Note: Installation planning is a user's movement which is designed to make certain that the EIS system is installed with minimum interference to the user's business.

a team in using a new enterprise software system. If you are leaning towards this technique of installation, make the changeover easier by communicating the ways that the new EIS software will be an enhancement over existing software. Employees need to be trained in an effective manner. With strong top-management support and effective staff preparation, the EIS can be a valuable improvement for the organization.

2. *Unit by Unit (phased by unit)* — Large organizations with special requirements in particular organizational units usually find it better to implement an EIS in a phased manner, unit by unit. A pilot EIS installation should be established to demonstrate the value of the new system. It is wise to implement the pilot system very carefully, seeking as much assurance of success as possible in order to ease adoption in later phases. Phased installation also occurs by module quite often, again beginning with the easier to implement modules such as financials or accounting. Once the organization feels comfortable with these initial modules, more challenging modules can be attempted.

While phased installation is more time-consuming, it is usually the wisest approach.

3. *Key-Process Installation (pilot installation)* — Smaller organizations often find it better to focus on a limited number of modules or processes for their initial EIS installation. As discussed in the unit-by-unit section, financial modules are often easiest to implement, because they involve the most well-defined processes. Other modules by the same vendor are easy to add to the system, given limited customization.

7.2 EVALUATING AN EIS

Some important points to be kept in mind while evaluating EIS software include:

♦ Functional fit with the Company's business processes.
♦ Degree of integration between the various components of the EIS system.
♦ Flexibility and scalability.
♦ Complexity; user-friendliness.
♦ Quick implementation; shortened ROI period.
♦ Ability to support multi-site planning and control.
♦ Technology; client/server capabilities, database independence, security.
♦ Availability of regular upgrades.
♦ Amount of customization required.
♦ Local support infrastructure.
♦ Availability of reference sites.
♦ Total costs, including cost of license, training, implementation, maintenance, customization and hardware requirements.

7.3 CRITICAL SUCCESS FACTORS IN EIS

According to a Gartner report published in the year 2003, 40 percent of enterprises deploying EIS or ERP II systems during 2004 spent more time and money on implementation by at least 50 percent more than their original estimates. Numerous enterprises have suffered project failures due to unplanned or under-planned implementation projects. Reliably predicting costs and time required for implementation are two results of successful EIS planning. EIS implementation horror stories emphasize severe business consequences, but often the software vendors are not at fault. The key to a successful deployment is in the process. Too many organizations fail during the critical stage when they must design new business processes prior to software selection, purchase, and deployment. As more enterprises prefer to construct their corporate knowledge base around complex infrastructure solutions, the need to understand how to implement an EIS system successfully has become increasingly imperative.

A critical success factor is something that the organization must do well to heed. In terms of information system projects, a critical success factor is what a system must do to accomplish what it was designed to do. Three factors consistently appear as critical success factors for information systems projects: top management support, client consultation (user involvement), and clear project objectives.[5]

7.3.1 User Involvement

Effective user involvement is often difficult to attain. A large manufacturing firm adopted a system that affected 12 departments at five sites, and 280 users around the country. A project team was formed consisting of 15 consultants, 10 people from within the firm, and two project managers working for the firm. A committee of top managers was created to provide oversight, and met with the project team once a month. Weekly project meetings were held, chaired by the vice president for information systems. The project team encouraged user sign-offs at different phases of the project, such as software selection, and at the end of phases such as changes to system components and development of screens. Different levels of users were involved at different phases to get users to buy into the system. Training sessions were provided, as well as pilot sessions where

---

[5] Olson, D. L. (2001). *Introduction to Information Systems Project Management*. New York: Irwin/McGraw-Hill.

user suggestions were encouraged. However, the project was not a success. Four months after the system was installed, over 1,000 requests for changes in the system had been received. Even though many means of encouraging user involvement had been applied, poorly defined lines of responsibility and communication resulted in failure of communication between users and system designers. Users grew to feel that their input wasn't valued, and therefore they quit contributing.[6]

7.3.2 Phemonemon of User Failure

The phenomenon of user failure in cooperating with EIS systems is common. The percentage of EIS system failures was rated by one study as ranging from 40 to 60 percent,[7] and by another study as between 60 and 90 percent.[8] The last study defined failure as not attaining the return on investment claimed in the approval phase. There are many examples of EIS failure that have been reported. Some of these involve user factors. Others involve other complications. Motwani *et al.* reviewed four cases of EIS systems causing considerable problems for the organizations that adopted them[9]:

1. Hershey's — through adoption of their EIS, Hershey's had a 19 percent drop in quarterly profit, and a 29 percent increase in inventory blamed on the EIS order-processing system.[10]
2. The city of Oakland adopted an EIS project but, when implementing that system, generated erroneous paychecks for city employees.[11]

---

[6] Amoako-Gyampah K. and White, K. B. (1997). When is user involvement not user involvement? *Information Strategy*, 40–45.

[7] Langenwalter, G. (2000). *Enterprise Resources Planning and Beyond: Integrating Your Entire Organization.* Boca Raton, FL: St. Lucie Press.

[8] Ptak C. and Schragenheim, E. (2000). *ERP: Tools, Techniques, and Applications for Integrating the Supply Chain.* Boca Raton, FL: St. Lucie Press.

[9] Motwani, J., Mirchandani, D., Madan M. and Gunasekaran, A. (2002). Successful implementation of ERP projects: Evidence from two case studies. *International Journal of Production Economics*, 75, 83–96.

[10] Stedman, C. (1999). Failed ERP gamble haunts Hershey. *Computerworld*, 33(44), 1–2.

[11] Stedman, C. (1999). ERP project problems plague city payroll. *Computerworld*, 33(50), 38.

3. Miller Industries suffered an operating loss due to inefficiencies in its EIS system in its first quarter of implementation.[12]
4. WW Grainger Inc. saw its operating earnings drop $11 million, blamed on improper EIS implementation.[13]

7.3.3 Ten Categories of EIS Implementation Failures

Many studies have examined critical success factors in EIS implementation. Umble *et al.* (2003)[14] integrated these findings into **10 categories** of failure. Before we elaborate on these 10 implementation failures, it is better if we look at Figure 7.3:

The ten categories of failure given by Umble *et al.* are:

1. Clear understanding of strategic goals.
2. Commitment by top management.

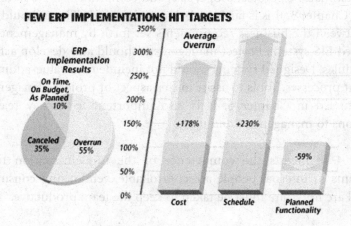

Figure 7.3:   ERP Implementation Results.

Source: Booz-Allen & Hamilton.

---

[12] Gilbert, A. (1999). ERP installations derail. *Informationweek*, 22, 77.
[13] Ibid.
[14] Umble, E. J., Haft, R. R. and Umble, M. M. (2003). Enterprise resource planning: Implementation procedures and critical success factors. *European Journal of Operational Research*, 146(2), 241–257.

3. Excellent project management.
4. A great implementation team.
5. Successful management of technical issues.
6. Organizational commitment to change.
7. Extensive education and training.
8. Data accuracy.
9. Focused performance measures.
10. Multi-site issues resolved.

Categories 1 and 2 are classical critical success factors for any IS project. (Clear statement of project objectives is inherently present in EIS implementations, and the scope of investment needs to be attended to by management.)

Category 3 underline the need for project management to include accurate estimates of project scope, size, and complexity. As we have discussed in Chapter 3, this is far from being a trivial task. There should be a match between the business requirements set forth by management and the selected EIS system. Project management should also develop achievable schedules. Designed systems should not include non-value-adding or redundant processes. Tools to assist in this aspect of project management were discussed in Chapter 6. It is also important to convey realistic expectations to management and users.

Category 4 highlights the competence of the implementation team. Assignments of internal people are controllable, vendor and consultant personnel are not. Care must be taken to keep the team productive.

Category 5 deals with the technical side of project management. Vendor and consultant personnel can help a great deal in this area of EIS installation.

Category 6 is associated with category 2, top management commitment. EIS systems will usually involve significant changes in the way in which almost everyone in the organization does their work. This requires people to change, something that we all tend to resist. In order to work with as little disruption to productivity as possible, it is necessary for the organization to be committed to carry through the project. Employees are also often quite concerned that the EIS system will eliminate their job (a not altogether unreasonable fear). Middle managers may also be concerned with the greater visibility into business operations provided by the EIS to top management. There will be a year or two of significant organizational change.

Category 7 focuses on the organization providing the needed training to employees, educating them on their role in the new system, and the training and skills development required to maximize the benefit of EIS.

Category 8 relates to internal data. It is very important that the EIS system deliver useful information. The Hershey case is a counterexample. If the new system provides bad data, the company will suffer major losses. Hershey survived this period. Most organizations would have difficulty doing that.

Category 9 concerns system design. The EIS should provide reports of critical information to all levels of management. If it does not provide management with the information that it needs, it obviously is not accomplishing its purpose.

Category 10 relates to the organizational network design. If each site has its own location-specific (or functional-specific) needs, the information system needs to be responsive. The greater the diversity of needs, the less attractive big-bang implementation is, and the more attractive a phased EIS implementation would be.

7.3.4 Management Commitment

A lot has been said about the competitive advantage provided by EIS. Consultants from the major accounting firms are often hired to bring the "best practices" into the industry.

First and foremost is top management commitment. The large investments necessary to implement EIS ensure that decisions are invariably made at top management level. This ensures top management involvement, but it does not guarantee top management's obligation. Here is an example. To be successful, the EIS team must consist of your "best" people. Until top management makes a deliberate decision to take out the "best" people for an extended period of time (several months) at the cost of "losing the best people" during implementation, EIS has little chance of success.

Management dedication involves the management of change. EIS will probably spin the organization "upside down" by unleashing lots of energy from vested interests. Unless top management is unswervingly committed, it is impracticable for any line manager to support the new system.

Another real test of top management commitment is the need to minimize customization, predominantly in the Indian and American context. One rationale why many computerization efforts in Indian and American organizations have predominantly not been successful is not having systems in place. EIS implementation is a golden chance to put such systems in position.

One more study by the Gartner[15] Group found application software (especially EIS) failure to be a major factor (31 percent) affecting the availability of a site. The second-highest factors were network software and traffic (16 percent). Other reasons for possible problems in the system were server hardware failure, storage failure, platform software failure, network hardware failure, power failure, database corruption, and operating system failure. Natural disasters such as earthquakes and floods were also found to be factors for downtime. Figure 7.4 displays another study's view of failure sources.

---

[15] Gartner, Inc. (NYSE: IT) is the world's leading information technology research and advisory company. It delivers the technology-related insight necessary for their clients to make the right decisions, every day. From CIOs and senior IT leaders in corporations and government agencies, to business leaders in high-tech and telecom enterprises and professional services firms, to technology investors, it is the indispensable partner to 60,000 clients in 10,000 distinct organizations. Through the resources of Gartner Research, Gartner Executive Programs, Gartner Consulting and Gartner Events, it works with every client to research, analyze and interpret the business of IT within the context of their individual role. Founded in 1979, Gartner is headquartered in Stamford, Connecticut, U.S.A., and has 4,000 associates, including 1,200 research analysts and consultants in 80 countries.

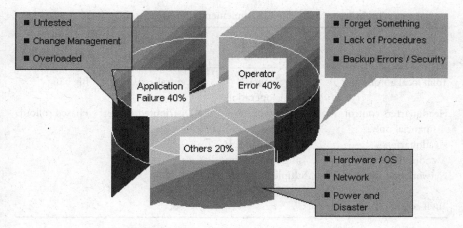

Figure 7.4: Microsoft's View of Failure Sources.
Source: Microsoft Corporation (2008).

7.4 IMPLEMENTATION STRATEGY OPTIONS

EIS implementations involve complications in business strategy, software configuration, technical platforms, and management execution. Markus *et al.* reviewed observations of practice in all four of these areas in multi-site EIS implementations. At least five ways to arrange relationships among business units were identified, four ways to configure software, and two ways to accomplish execution of an EIS system in multi-site implementations, as displayed in Table 7.1.

7.4.1 Control Strategy

An initial issue in multi-site EIS is scope. The scope of the system defines benefits expected from the EIS. If only a few financial modules are adopted, benefits from the other modules are not obtained, and the full scope of EIS benefits is not gained. But projects of larger scope require higher levels of coordination and top management support, as the impact is much more pervasive.

Table 7.1:   Multi-Site EIS Implementation Areas and Options.

Control strategy	Software configuration	Technical platform execution	Management
Total local autonomy.	Single financial/ single operation.	Centralized.	Big bang.
Headquarters control — financial only.	Single financial/ multiple operations.	Distributed.	Phased rollout.
Headquarters coordination.	Multiple financial/ single operation.		
Network coordination.	Multiple financial/ multiple operations.		
Total centralization.			

Source: Markus *et al*. (2000).[16]

There were five business strategy alternatives cited by Markus *et al*. One European multinational allowed its sub-units nearly **total local autonomy** in EIS adoption. This firm had different product subsidiaries operating in different countries. While this strategy does not take advantage of EIS potential, it does avoid conflict associated with centrally mandated changes, and also allows companies the ability to pursue independent initiatives, and reduces the risk of implementation project failure. When **headquarters control financial modules only**, business units were often observed to independently configure, implement, and maintain EIS software. If the activities of different business units are independent, this approach makes sense. It also allows application of the best-of-breed approach. Another pattern of implementation is for **headquarters coordination of operations**, with high degrees of local autonomy. This strategy seems to work best when benefits in some particular areas such as purchasing are available. The strategy of **network coordination of operations** allows local operations to access the information of other business units for lateral coordination without high levels of centralization. This approach works best when entities sell to each other as well as to external

[16] Markus, M. L., Tanis, C. and van Fenema, P. C. (2000). Multisite ERP implementations. *Communications of the ACM*, 43(4), 42–46.

customers. **Total centralization** works best when companies are more tightly coordinated. With respect to the impact of EIS effectiveness, theoretically a centralized EIS system used throughout the organization makes the most sense in order to gain EIS's potential benefits of integration. However, in practice, there are often overriding reasons why decentralization makes greater sense.

7.4.2 Technical Platform

For technology platforms, site refers to a combination of a central database and possibly multiple applications servers. Organizations with many units and locations may opt for a **centralized** architecture with remote access via telecommunications lines and PCs. Another extreme is to **distribute data and processing**. EIS configuration is easier and often cheaper if centralized. However, there may be advantages in distributed architecture relative to database size and performance, telecommunications costs, maintenance costs, and risk management.

7.4.3 Execution of EIS Systems

Execution of EIS systems can be accomplished in a number of different ways. The extremes are the "**big bang**" deployment, where on one magic day, the old system is unplugged and the new system turned on-line. Markus *et al.* (2000) cited use of this strategy by Quantum Corp. which shut down their operations worldwide for eight days to switch systems. This risky approach was motivated by that company's specific circumstances. The other extreme is **phased rollout**, with components of the system brought on-line serially, and operated and observed prior to moving on to implementation of the next phase. Markus *et al.* cited BICC Cables which adopted a lengthy process of consensus building in their global operation. The selected EIS system was implemented one step at a time, as BICC Cables wanted no more than three software versions in operation at any one time (old being replaced, new being installed, future version being tested at headquarters). This resulted in an environment with technology changes as often as every 12 months.

Table 7.2: Implementation Strategies Adopted.

Strategy	Time U.S.	Time Sweden	U.S. (%)	Sweden (%)
Big Bang	15 mths	14 mths	41	42
Phased rollout by site	30 mths	23 mths	23	20
Phased rollout by module	22 mths	20 mths	17	17
Mini big bang	17 mths	16 mths	17	20
Phased rollout by module & site	25 mths		2	

Source: Mabert et al. (2000), Olhager and Selldin (2003).[17]

Mabert et al. surveyed manufacturing users of EIS for implementation, and found results as shown in Table 7.2.

The Korean study[18] reported over 72 percent of the firms surveyed utilized a form of the big bang approach. The big bang approach is a dangerous approach for general IS/IT projects, but often makes sense in the context of EIS for smaller systems especially. The alternatives are to roll out a system, or to do a pilot study (here labeled mini big bang). Rolling out a system makes sense for larger firms where geographic dispersion is present, or in conglomerates with diverse functional groups. The data indicates that phased rollouts are often used, sometimes by both module and site. The pilot approach is less reliable in EIS contexts than it is for general IS/IT projects, because scalability is so often a problem in EIS implementations. The pilot test may work quite well, but the server system may be overwhelmed when the full computational load is applied.

The time required for installation varies a great deal depending upon installation strategy. There is obviously a longer time frame required for a rollout strategy. The duration averages identified in the surveys are probably related to organization size, in that smaller organizations are likely to use the big bang approach.

---

[17] Extracted from Mabert et al. (2000) based on 479 manufacturing users of EIS, and Olhager and Selldin (2003) based on 190 Swedish manufacturers using EIS.
[18] Katerattanakul, P., Hong, S. and Lee, J. (2006). Enterprise resource planning survey of Korean manufacturing firms. *Management Research News*, 29(12), 820–837.

7.5 LEVELS OF IS/IT PROJECT FAILURE

Project failure can come in many forms (budget overrun, schedule overrun, technical inadequacy). Lyytinen and Hirschheim (1987)[19] identified four major categories of project system failure. A fifth category, strategic/competitive failure, is added by the authors.

1. Corresponding failure.
2. Process failure.
3. Interaction failure.
4. Expectation failure.
5. Strategic/competitive failure.

7.5.1 Major Categories of Project System Failure

Obviously some of these categories of failure are more critical than others.

Corresponding failure alludes to the failure of the system to meet design objectives. This is a technical failure in that a computer program didn't do what it was intended to do. The Hershey EIS implementation to be covered in Chapter 8 was a failure of this type.

Process failure is a failure to bring in a project system on time and within budget. The system may technically work, but it is no longer economically justifiable, or at least not within current business plans. The FoxMeyer Drug EIS implementation discussed in Chapter 1 was an example of this category of failure.

Interaction failure occurs when a system is not used as much as planned. This can arise when a system is built to technical specifications within budget and on time, but the intended users do not use it. This can

---

[19] Lyytinen, K. and Hirschheim, R. (1987). Information systems failures — A survey and classification of the empirical literature. *Oxford Survey of Information Technology*, 4, 257–309.

be because of some bias on the users' part to continue to operate the old way, or because the planned system design really didn't effectively deal with the problem.

Expectation failure occurs when the system does not quite match up with the expectations of project stakeholders. The system may perform technically, and may be on time and within budget, and may be used, but may not do the job as management was led to expect.

Strategic/competitive failure comes about when systems work, and are used as designed, and even meet stakeholder expectations, but the organization is not able to compete successfully. We could argue that an EIS system would avoid this situation, but that would not be true. No computer system is a guarantee of success. In order for businesses to succeed, they have to have a good fundamental business purpose, providing their customers with something that their competitors can't.

Ewusi-Mensah and Przasnyski (1991) distinguished between total abandonment (complete termination of project activity before implementation), substantial abandonment (major simplification resulting in a project radically different from original specifications), and partial abandonment (reduction in original project scope without major changes in original specifications).[20] Dell Computer and Kellogg are examples of firms that totally abandoned EIS implementations, apparently applying successful alternatives. Sometimes managers became too committed to projects, extending their life when they should be canceled.[21] Project failure causes can be grouped into inadequate economic payoff, psychological factors (managerial persistence in expecting positive project prospects when they feel personally responsible), escalation factors (throwing good money after bad), social factors (including competitive rivalry), and organizational factors related to a project's political support.

---

[20] Ewusi-Mensa, K. and Przasnyski, Z. H. (1991). On information systems project abandonment: An exploratory study of organizational practices. *MIS Quarterly*, 15(1), 66–86.

[21] Keil, M. (1995). Pulling the plug: Software project management and the problem of project escalation. *MIS Quarterly*, 19(4), 422–447.

7.5.2 EIS Implementation Failure

EIS implementations tend to be large in size, require a long time to put in place, have high levels of complexity, and involve new technology. These are all characteristics of difficult IS/IT projects. A number of problems have been observed in implementing EIS systems.

Mabert *et al.*'s systematic analysis of survey data identify those key variables to successful EIS implementation.[22] Seven issues were considered.

1. Use of a single EIS package versus use of multiple packages is a major issue. Both approaches have been successfully implemented, and neither was found significant in either EIS implementation time or budget performance.
2. EIS systems can be implemented at one time across the organization (the Big Bang approach) or in phases (as well as other variations in between). Again, a variety of approaches have been used in successful EIS implementations, and the variants were not found significant for either time or budget performance.
3. The number of modules implemented was examined, with no significance found.
4. The order of module implementation also did not prove to be significant.
5. Application of major BPR initially as opposed to limited reengineering did not make a significant difference in time or budget.

The two variables that did prove significant were:

6. Modifications to the system, which were significant in both time and budget performance. If vendor systems are modified, it will cost more and take longer (but will likely provide a better system).
7. Use of accelerated implementation strategy, which was significant in implementing EIS systems on time (but not significant with respect to

---

[22] Mabert, V. A., Soni, A. and Venkataramanan, M. A. (2003). Enterprise resource planning: Managing the implementation process. *European Journal of Operational Research*, 146, 302–314.

budget). Vendors have been successful in expediting implementation of their systems.

The relative roles of CIOs and the information technology group are seriously neglected in many EIS implementations. Most EISs studied by Willcocks and Sykes (2000) accomplished the integration of data into a common data structure, which vastly improved the development of new software applications.[23] However, the primary benefit of an EIS is through improving the way in which the organization does business (business process reengineering — BPR). Many organizations were observed to fail on this aspect of EIS implementation (a case of interaction failure). This failure was driven by the need for major changes in human, cultural, and organizational relationships. Three factors were associated with EIS implementation failure. Table 7.3 displays these factors.

7.5.3 Technological Determinism

This scenario arises from the view of an EIS system as a packaged solution to all of an organization's technical and business problems. This often is the view adopted when the CIO is too technically focused, and the IT group is developed around technical skills. In such organizations, the IT function is seen as the prime owner of IT issues. EIS implementation results typically include general resistance and high rates of failure. Willcocks and Sykes found technological determinism to be common in

Table 7.3: Factors in EIS Implementation Failure.

Scenario	CIO/IT focus	Typical outcome
Technological determinism	Technical	Failure to gain business benefits
Supplier/consultant-driven	Disregarded	Cost overruns
Outdated relationships & capabilities	Insufficient talent	Chaos

Source: Willcocks and Sykes (2000).

---

[23] Willcocks, L. P. and Sykes, R. (2000). The role of the CIO and IT function in ERP. *Communications of the ACM*, 43(4), 22–28.

early implementations of EIS in the mid-1990s. Implementation of EIS in this model is typically handed over to the IT group, who focus on time and budget metrics, giving little attention to business benefits.

7.5.4 Supplier/Consultant-Driven

This type of EIS implementation commonly arises when senior business executives mandate EIS without significant consultation with the CIO and IT group. This can be because top management views EIS as a great strategic tool, or because of lack of trust in IT group abilities (and EIS is seen as a means of replacing them). In this sense, EIS is outsourced (either through vendors and consultants, or more recently through application service providers). This approach has been seen to suffer considerable cost overruns. Willcocks and Sykes reported one case where costs were 10 times what was estimated in the first feasibility study. Another feature is that the organization often does not buy into the system, which is viewed as imposed from above. While the focus is on business benefits, the means of attaining those benefits are not present.

7.5.5 Outdated Relationships and Capabilities

This scenario occurs when the CIO and IT group are insufficiently prepared to cope with the challenges of new technologies. The focus tends to be on cost minimization rather than on EIS as a strategic resource. The IT function is largely responsible for the EIS system, but lacks the technical skills to make it work. External suppliers are often hired to fill skills-gaps. Relationships with business users are not developed, and there is a failure to reorient business thinking to utilize EIS tools. Willcocks and Sykes found this third scenario to be the most commonly observed, even in some successful EIS implementations.

7.6 BREAK DOWNS OF EIS

When the EIS systems initiated in the 1990s were implemented, it meant the integration of manufacturing resource planning, or MRP, and several accounting and human resource management functions. At its heart was focus on inventories and demand through scheduling manufacturing operations, generating work orders, tracking labour and materials, and to tie manufacturing to other modules of the enterprise, such as sales and distribution, accounting, production monitoring, and reporting. EIS systems have broadened to embrace many supplementary functions. In addition to the core manufacturing and front office functions, EIS systems have expanded to incorporate elements of customer relationship management (CRM), warehouse management systems (WMS), electronic data interchange (EDI), supply chain management (SCM), knowledge management (KM) and even integrated quality management (IQM), which involves operations external to the enterprise. The term "EIS II" now identifies systems that put together these new features into ERP systems.

Still too many countless breakdowns: While systems have made tremendous gains in the past decade, there are still too many breakdowns. The following are fundamental principles for assuring implementation success:

♦ Select the most talented business manager in the enterprise as project manager.
♦ Make certain of senior executive commitment before proceeding.
♦ Make the EIS implementation a business transformation project, not an IT project.
♦ Manage issues promptly and decisively.
♦ Communicate often.
♦ Analyze the configured EIS software exhaustively, i.e. has it become redundant or are there better packages available in the market?
♦ Plan user training and assign sufficient resources to this activity.
♦ Set realistic user and executive expectations.
♦ Ensure that your technical infrastructure is competent before implementing an EIS solution.
♦ Don't customize the EIS system source code unless there are clear improvements to be gained.

Once the enterprise had implemented EIS systems, user should be keen about improving their business operations. We will drill down another level to make clear what works — and, just as important, what does not — in the real world using critical success tactics.

▽ **Breakdown 1:** Presumption that employees will lose rights and power after EIS installation

Critical Success Tactic: If people who are associated with the EIS systems were asked how many were keen to execute standard business processes across the enterprise, what do you imagine you would hear? Dead silence. At least, that is what has come about in enterprises that embarked on hefty EIS Systems implementations. These people are inclined to be strongly opposed to losing power of administrative operations. Employees have to administer a budget, recruit people, distribute payroll, and process purchase orders and so on. EIS Systems solutions make available a standard, homogeneous way of performing these functions, so the enterprise can reduce duplication, produce meaningful information and cut administrative costs (Kesharwani, 2003).[24] A solution is needed in which enterprise and employee both flourish by giving-up their self-centered attitude. The initiative could start with the leader at the top of the enterprise to get the message out.

▽ **Breakdown 2:** Emphasis on technology as the main factor for success at the expense of human factors

Critical Success Tactic: From the very beginning the emphasis should be on the real challenges, that is **people and procedure** would be very important in order to make the methodological challenges of implementation as trouble-free and user friendly. In fact, where

---

[24] Kesharwani, S. (2006). ERP systems: New Fangled approach to manage technology for competitive advantage. *Review of Professional Management*, 4(1), 52–58.

implementations have failed, 70 percent of the reasons arise from ignorance of the human side of the equation. Causes could be: insufficient training and preparation, inadequate or poor change management, deficient communication; low levels of user involvement, adversarial relationships with enterprise channel partners, incompetent project management, etc. So in order to avoid these types of breakdown the enterprise have to be more concerned about human SWOT (strength; weakness; opportunity & threat) from every aspect.

▽ **Breakdown 3:** Holding back on streamlining the Front End for Implementation and ignoring back-end activities

Critical Success Tactic: Always document current business processes i.e. back-end activities. Planning and organizing for an EIS Systems venture is an intricate and resource-consuming mission. But if you do not accomplish these activities — what we call "Phase Zero" — you are asking for trouble down the line. One of the key steps in planning is appraising how to do business in today's environment. This involves not only the procedures outlined in business manuals but the processes people are using in practice. The best way is to determine *how the work is truly being done.* Once the documentation is accomplished, sort processes into "competitive advantage" and "commodity." Those involving competitive advantage can give enterprises an edge over their business rivals; commodity processes can give an enterprise a solid standing in a market to compete and also help in building image. Thus, the key processes that run your business and add value, must be protected. For the remaining processes, which will make up the vast majority, the enterprise should accept the best practices built into the selected package.

▽ **Breakdown 4:** Trying to accomplish everything at one time instead of phased implementation

Critical Success Tactic: The **big bang** i.e. all-at-once approach to EIS systems implementation carries great risks as implementation of all the modules can disrupt the enterprise. It is better to implement a segment of the system at a time. Early successes gain support and momentum, and reveal problems that can be solved before moving on; training activities can be staged to make well-organized use of resources; **phased** implementation (one module at a time) puts a realistic load on the help desk and support staff, etc. EIS solutions can also be executed by business unit. Since EIS projects affect large numbers of people, and few enterprises have the competence to instruct everybody at once, the phased approach can spread out the burden on training resources. When an EIS system has been executed, the members accomplishing that phase can serve as mentors to train the next wave. Another problem arises when enterprises insist on including all functionality at the initial go-live date. Much concentration is needed in getting the system up and running with basic functionality. By keeping it trouble-free, success can be achieved, bring users on board and add supplementary features as you go along. *It is a little like driving a new vehicle: If you have to read the whole instruction booklet before driving, you may never leave the garage.* Remember, transformation does not take place the day you turn over the switch. This is a continuing process where the end-state visualization becomes clearer the closer you get to it. As you better comprehend what you have just implemented, your visualization will grow.

▽ **Breakdown 5:** Insufficient support for users

Critical Success Tactic: More attention should be given by the enterprise to the users in terms of support and sales promotion schemes. Everyone agrees that training is important, it is *how* you conduct training that determines what users learn and remember, as well as their attitude to the project. The natural tendency is to teach just the transaction: for example, how to enter an invoice. But users want to understand the business process, including how you move from purchase to payment. When you put the transaction in context, it is easier to relate to, understand and remember. Our experience also shows that simulations are not an effective way to teach. In fact, users are likely to rebel and demand hands-on experience with live data. They want to conduct real transactions in a "sandbox" system with real data. Finally, do not waste your money on reproducing large binders of useful information. Users will not read them. Instead, they want short, easy-to-scan documents that cover fundamentals.

▽ **Breakdown 6:** Underrating the essential resources and underestimating hidden cost

Critical Success Tactic: Take into account the numerous hidden costs. Every enterprise underestimates what it will take to implement an EIS. While the budget people vigilantly compute direct costs — software, tools, hardware and consultants — they fail to perceive countless indirect costs. Take human resources, for instance. An implementation will use much more organizational employee resources than the installation team. Most enterprises make the blunder of assuming that the project staff will accomplish the entire amount of work to be done prior to installation. In fact, the rest of the staff will have to take on those tasks. Realistic expectations are needed early on, letting managers and staff knows what is ahead so they can get ready to help. Few clients appreciate that they will need a requirements workshop for each business process that will be affected by the new system. Every workshop may take one-half to two days — adding up to thousands of staff hours. Whether it is computer-based or instructor-led classroom training, you can foresee each employee needing two hours, two days or two weeks of training. Hidden cost is very damaging and usually unexpected. Hidden costs have the shape of a rabbit during the planning of EIS systems becoming an elephant when the financial burden is evaluated and finally turning into a dinosaur in the final implementation. (Kesharwani 2003).[25]

▽ **Breakdown 7:** Expecting too much of best practices adoption

Critical Success Tactic: Be pragmatic in recognizing the accurate EIS package for your enterprise. Each ERP system solution includes best practices for administrating finances, human resources and procurement, that have been proven over time. But when appraising an EIS package, it is imperative to be realistic. The real issue is not how many finest practices are built into the package, but how many your enterprises will in fact put into practice, and how many compromises you will decide to adopt. Sometimes there is a rationale for not making an alteration, for legal or contractual reasons or the precedents of the past. In most cases, however, changes to the basic package are not essential. They are merely the enterprise's way of holding on to the familiar practices and processes of the past. Every modification to the software slows down the project, adds costs and problems in future upgrades. In other words, changes quickly increase your total cost of ownership. To get the most return on your investment, you need to appraise the options carefully, avoid modifications wherever feasible and set reasonable expectations for payback.

---

[25] Kesharwani, S. (2005). Enterprise Resource Planning Interactive Viaduct B/w Human & Computer. *Asia-Pacific Business Review*, 1(II), 72–82.

▽ **Breakdown 8:** Evaluate all external factors relevant to the implementation

---

Critical Success Tactic: Decision-makers must consider external factors that will impact the venture as any cut-off in the financials would instantly stop the venture and risk cancellation of the EIS installation project. **Budget strength:** An EIS System venture is a multi-year enterprise, crossing budget cycles. It is vital that funding be committed for the period of the venture. **Management transformation:** In governance, there may be a revolution in leadership and configuration over the course of the venture. The venture design should consider such timelines i.e. building in the major functionality before the administration changes. **Legal completion:** This is a good time to appraise some of the laws that have always been in black & white for years and to develop legal compliance requirements for the system — and to authenticate that the system meets the current legislative structure. **Labour contracts:** Determine when contracts are renegotiated and be attentive that the EIS implementation may speedily become a focus for employee unions. By considering the long term and planning ahead, you can construct a plan that overcomes these risks to a successful implementation.

▽ **Breakdown 9:** Failure to meet deadlines

Critical Success Tactic: Treat milestones as sacrosanct. Agencies, departments, divisions and programs will have reasons why they cannot meet deadlines. But once schedules slide, this creates an environment where it could occur again and again. It is vital to meet deadlines by requiring all project schedule changes to be approved by the steering committee, a group of high-level executives committed to the project's success. You can accelerate the process by giving project team leaders the authority to make day-to-day decisions

---

without an elaborate approval process. Leaders are needed who are willing to make tough calls to realize the benefits of and "burn the bridges" — making it clear that failure is not an option. EIS systems projects will define your operations for at least the next 10 years. While these multifaceted and resource-intensive projects are risky, the risk can be reduced through strong executive sponsorship, communication and involvement of stakeholders, and good project management. EIS is about transforming the way an organization does business, not installing software; an EIS project will need the help of agencies to facilitates process changes. If processes do not change, no benefits will be realized. Process changes require changes in roles and responsibilities and not all benefits will be realized on the go-live date. Process changes are ongoing, and benefits will accrue as changes are implemented.

7.7 FEATURES OF SUCCESSFUL EIS IMPLEMENTATION

The most successful approach was to develop key IT capabilities before adopting EIS. Feeny and Willcocks (1998) gave the nine core IT capabilities required for successful EIS implementation.[27] These factors were assessed as in Table 7.4.

This approach involves development of a competent internal IT organization, along with a systems view of the organization. A systems view enables better understanding of what IT is needed for, and how the organization's business processes can best be supported.

This list of core capabilities needs to be maintained in-house. If key skills are lacking, unless they are of a very short nature, Willcocks and Sykes recommend hiring the skills required rather than relying on long-term consultant relationships.

---

[27] Feeny, D. and Willcocks, L. (1998). Core IS capabilities for exploiting IT. *Sloan Management Review*, 39(3), 9–21.

Table 7.4: Core IT Capabilities needed for EIS Implementation Success.

Capability	Impact
IT leadership	Strategy, structures, processes & staff developed
Business systems thinking	Adopt systems view
Relationship building	Cooperate with business users
Architecture planning	Create needed technical platform
Technology fixing	Ability to troubleshoot
Informed buying	Compare vendor sources
Contract facilitation	Coordinate efforts
Contract monitoring	Hold suppliers accountable
Supplier development	Explore long-term mutual benefits

Source: Willcocks and Sykes (2000).

7.8 STRATEGIES TO ATTAIN SUCCESS

In addition to obtaining needed IT capabilities, Willcocks and Sykes suggested the following strategies to successfully implement an EIS system.

User vs. Specialist Focus: An EIS is intended to enable users to do their jobs better. Business process reengineering inherently leads to changing views of business requirements. Therefore, requirements lists tend to be unstable, and flexibility is required in EIS system implementation. This change can also outdate vendor software capabilities. Technology focus (whether internal IT or outsourcing) should be adopted only when the technological maturity required is high and detailed specifications can be developed.

Governance and Staffing: Willcocks and Syke consistently found that effective business innovations require high-level support and a project champion. This top support usually comes from the business side rather than the IT side. Project managers for EIS implementation projects need to be credible to top stakeholders, have a record of success, and be able to keep the project on its critical path. A multifunctional team is essential, including end users, in-house IT specialists, people with the ability to get diverse groups to work together, and specialists in IT and business needs.

Time-Box Philosophy: A short time frame for EIS implementation may seem clearly preferable. From a systems perspective, this time frame is ideally six to nine months. Often this may be identified as impractical. If so, it might be possible to decompose implementation into smaller projects, each with tangible business benefits. This approach to time discipline does a great deal in reducing project risk of failure to satisfy business requirements. This approach was referred to as converting "whales" (large unmanageable projects) into "dolphins" (smaller and more manageable projects) by Willcocks and Sykes.

One reason short EIS implementation projects are undesirable is the time required for employees to adjust to the new system. If employees have been working with different systems for extensive periods of time, there will be a longer transition period required to refocus the thinking of these employees.

Supplier/Consultant Role in EIS: Consultants can provide a great deal of knowledge and EIS experience. In highly innovative EIS systems supporting activities that the organization has as core competencies, it is best to strictly control outside consultants. The alternative is to outsource management of business innovation. This is counterproductive, because the consultant gains your expertise to sell to others.

7.9 CONCLUSION

EIS installation involves a number of critical factors needed for success. Some key elements are:

- Plan, prepare and plan some more.
- Add time to your *implementation* timeline when major business process change is part of the project; if possible, consider an implementation that meets current requirements first, followed by a phase 2 which adds the new processing requirements.
- Create a project war room containing work stations, Web access, documentation, training materials, white boards, etc; this is where all project work is done.

♦ Assess the corporate culture and track record with previous projects; implement project management procedures to deal with any negative cultural elements. Put the right people on the project team (leadership abilities, people who learn quickly, proper business or technical backgrounds, *willingness* to work hard).

♦ Ensure that you truly have upper management support; this support should be clearly visible.

The success of an EIS project is measured in terms of project completion on time, within budget, and by the functionality attained by the system. Factors consistently found critical in general IT projects are top management support, client consultation, and clearly stated project objectives. The scope of EIS projects almost ensures that top management support and clear project objectives are present before funding can be gained. Other important success factors in EIS projects include sound project management, change management, and technical implementation. Project success is expedited by careful consideration of business strategy, software configuration, technical platform architecture, and management execution. Client consultation often is not considered, and is probably a major factor in EIS implementation difficulties.

A number of different control strategies are available for EIS implementation. The degree of decentralization applied should match how the EIS system will be operated. It is possible to allow decentralized operation of EIS systems to include different modules. However, this decentralization should be reserved for those cases where different organizational elements have diverse operational problems. Similar considerations need to be given to the centralization of technical platforms. Finally, EIS systems can be brought into production all-at-once, or in phases. It is wiser to use a phased approach, except for very small and easy to control organizations.

There are many definitions of failure. The point is that expectations have to be managed. If too much is promised, failure will be inevitable at some level, regardless of the degree of success attained in implementing the EIS. The probabilities of success can be enhanced by constant communication among members of the installation team, as well as with top management to retain their support. It is also critical to keep users involved, and to impress upon them the benefits of the new EIS system.

Once an EIS system is installed, that is usually not the end of the story. There are two factors of concern. First is maintenance. There is a need to maintain any type of software, and EIS systems also involve a number of maintenance activities. Additionally, vendors will likely improve their software products over time, and if the technology-enabled approach has been adopted, the organization is subject to the need to consider migration to new versions of software. A second factor relates to training of organizational users. In order to be considered successful, EIS projects need to be implemented throughout an organization in an effective way, changing how the organization does its work. An important element of implementation is training, making sure that all users of the EIS system are aware of the need to utilize the system. This requires a great deal of information dissemination as well as a great deal of training.

ERP offers too much to ignore. It makes sense to reinstate a paper calendar or manifold old-fashioned accounting and spreadsheet software programs with an integrated system that stores and sorts the information flowing in from all areas of your plant floor, front office, and supply chain. A properly implemented ERP system can convey good results and dramatically changes your attitude towards reducing costs, running leaner, and making available good customer service.

☆ KEYWORDS

- ☆ **Big Bang Deployment:** Implementation of an EIS throughout the organization at one time.
- ☆ **Corresponding Failure:** Failure of a system to meet design objectives.
- ☆ **Critical Success Factors:** Those activities which the organization must do well to succeed.
- ☆ **Expectation Failure:** Failure of the system to perform as stakeholders expected.
- ☆ **Implementation Strategy:** Alternative ways to implement an EIS.
- ☆ **Interaction Failure:** Failure of the system to be used by those it was intended for.
- ☆ **Migration:** Upgrading to a new EIS system.

☆ **Phased Rollout:** Implementation of an EIS incrementally.

☆ **Process Failure:** Failure to implement project on time and within budget.

☆ **Specialist Focus:** EIS design focused on minimizing problems for the organizational information system.

☆ **Supplier/Consultant Driven:** EIS design driven by external agents.

☆ **System Migration:** Switch from one EIS system to another (mergers, acquisitions, growth, vendor upgrade).

☆ **Technological Determinism:** EIS design focused on system capabilities.

☆ **User Focus:** EIS design focused on giving users the tools needed to perform their work.

☆ TERMINOLOGY REVIEW

1. Explain how the ERP system reduces manpower.
2. Explain why communication is vital in the ERP context.
3. Give an EIS example of corresponding failure, process failure, interaction failure, and expectation failure.
4. How does ERP seem to be a dream for small organization? What is the misconception about ERP?
5. How do you achieve a successful ERP Implementation? Explain why ERP implementation also engenders a host of fears.
6. How does ERP systems software work in direct marketing?
7. In manufacturing practice (according to Mabert *et al.*), which is used more often: Big bang or phased rollout?
8. Markus *et al.* considered five business strategies, ranging from total local autonomy to total centralization. What did Markus *et al.* conclude relative to EIS implementation and this range of business strategies?
9. What advantages does a phased rollout approach have over a big bang EIS deployment?
10. What are the critical success factors for the implementation of ERP?
11. What are the five reasons for poor ERP results?
12. What is the future of ERP systems?

13. What are the ERP Software selection and implementation steps that can support your strategic and process objectives better?
14. What did Willcocks and Sykes mean by a supplier/consultant-driven EIS?
15. What did Willcocks and Sykes mean by technological determinism?
16. What is meant by cultural alternation?
17. What is meant by the costing of an ERP?
18. How are employees trained about EIS systems?
19. What is a critical success factor?
20. What is meant by EIS system migration?
21. What is the process of evaluating an ERP Software?
22. How are education and training of personnel used in respect to ERP system?
23. What problems can be expected from software-specific EIS training of employees?
24. When would it make the most sense to adopt a single financial EIS configuration in conjunction with multiple-operations EIS modules?
25. Why might a distributed data and processing technology platform be used with an EIS system?

☆ COMPETENCY REVIEW

1. Multiple Choice Questions

    1. Customization is a process
       (i) Time taken
       (iii) Both time taken costly

       (ii) Costly
       (iv) No one

    2. Communication is
       (i) one-way process
       (iii) three-way process

       (ii) two-way process
       (iv) four-way process

    3. Typically, how many times the cost of the product does implementation cost?
       (i) One time
       (iii) Four time

       (ii) Twice or thrice
       (iv) Equal

2. True or False

   1. ERP problems are performance-related.
   2. ERP terrorizes the delicate balance of knower and control.
   3. ERP is a cheap system.
   4. ERP requires highly efficient manpower.

3. Fill in the blanks

   a) ERP is also cultural _____
   b) Flow of communication _____ the amount of strem associate with the change.
   c) The major obstacles of ERP are its _____
   d) IT is just a part of _____
   e) _____ is a set of best practices for performing different duties in your company.
   f) _____ make the software more unstable and harder the maintain when it is finally does come to life.
   g) Balancing the expectation and fears is a very necessary part of the _____ process.

☆ SUGGESTED READING

Books

Adam, F. and Sammon, D. (2004). *The Enterprise Resource Planning Decade: Lessons Learned and Issues for the Future.* USA: Idea Group Publishing.

Curran, T. A. and Ladd, A. (2000). *SAP R/3, Business Blueprint.* 2nd Ed. Prentice Hall.

Davenport, T. (2000). *Mission Critical: Realizing the Promise of Enterprise Systems.* Harvard Business School Press.

Dinkar (2004). *Strategic Planning in Information Technology.* India: Viva Books.

Fowler, M. (2002). *Patterns of Enterprise Application Architecture.* Addison Wesley.

Hamilton, S. (2003). *Maximizing Your ERP System: A Practical Guide for Managers.* United States: McGraw-Hill.

Jacobs, F. R. and Whybark, D. C. (2003). *Why ERP? A primer on SAP implementation.* New York: McGraw-Hill.

Kesharwani, S. (2003). *ERP System Application, Experience & Upsurge.* India: Pragati Prakashan.

Norris, G. (2000). *E-Business and ERP: Transforming the Enterprise.* USA: John Wiley & Son.

O'Leary, D. E. (2000). *Enterprise Resource Planning Systems: Systems, Life Cycle, Electronic Commerce, and Risk.* United Kingdom: Cambridge, University Press.

Olson, D. L. (2004). *Managerial Issues of Enterprise Resource Planning Systems.* New York: McGraw Hill/Irwin.

Rikhardson, P., Kræmmergaard, P. and Møller, C. (2004). *Enterprise Resource Planning — Danske Erfaringer med Implementering og Anvendelse.* Børsens Forlag.

Sandoe, Corbitt, and Boykin (2001). *Enterprise Integration.* Wiley.

Shields, M. G. (2002). *E-Business and ERP: Rapid Implementation and Project Planning.* Canada: John Wiley & Sons.

Summer, M. (2004). *Enterprise Resource Planning.* Prentice Hall.

Wallace, T. W., Kremzar, M. H. and Kremzar, M. (2001). *ERP: Making It Happen: The Implementers' Guide to Success with Enterprise Resource Planning.* Canada: John Wiley & Sons.

Journal Articles

Akkermans, H. and van Helden, K. (2002), Vicious and virtuous cycles in ERP implementation: A case study of interrelations between critical success factors. *European Journal of Information Systems*, 11(1), 35–46.

Chen, I. J. (2001), Planning for ERP systems: Analysis and future trend. *Business Process Management Journal*, 7(5), 374–386.

Chung, S. H. and Snyder, C. A. (2000). ERP adoption: A technological evolution approach. *International Journal of Agile Management Systems*, 2(1), 24–32.

Clegg, S., Soliman, F. and Tantoush, T. (2001). Critical success factors for integration of CAD/CAM systems with ERP systems. *International Journal of Operation & Management*, 21(5/6), 609–621.

Haberman, F. and Scheer, A. W. (2000). Making ERP a Success. *Communications of the ACM*, 43(4), 56–61.

Kuang, J., Lau, L. S. and Nah, F. F. H. (2001). Critical factors for successful implementation of enterprise systems. *Business Process Management Journal*, 7(3), 285–296.

Markus, M. L. and Tanis, C. (2000). The enterprise systems experience — From adoption to success. Framing the Domains of IT Research: Glimpsing the Future Through the Past. *Pinnaflex Educational Resources*, 173–207.

Stensrud, E. (2001). Alternative approaches to effort prediction of ERP projects. *Information and Software Technology*, 43(7), 413–423.

White Papers and Conference Presentations

Corbitt, G., Hu, B., Parr, A., Seddon, P. B., Shanks, G. and Thanasankit, T. (2000). Differences in critical success factors in ERP systems implementation in Australia and China: A cultural analysis. In *Proceedings of the 8th European Conference on Information Systems*, 1–8.

Coffin, G. W. and Murray, M. G. (2001). A case study analysis of factors for success in ERP system implementations. In *Proceedings of the 7th Americas Conference on Information Systems*, Boston, USA, 1012–1018.

Nelson, K. and Somers, T. (2001). The impact of critical success factors across the stages of enterprise resource planning implementations. In *Proceedings of 34th Hawaii International Conference on Systems Sciences*, Maui, Hawaii, 1–10.

Parr A. and Shanks G. (2000). A taxonomy of ERP implementation approaches. *Proceedings of the 33rd Hawaii International conference on System Sciences*.

Smyth, R. W. (2001a). Challenges to successful ERP use (Research in progress). In *Proceedings of the 9th European Conference on Information Systems*, University of Maribour, Slovenia, 1227–1231.

Smyth, R. W. (2001b). Threats to ERP success: A case study. In *Proceedings of the 5th Pacific Asia Conference on Information Systems*, Seoul, Korea, 1141–1151.

Steenkamp, M., van Eeden, J. and van Leipzig, K. (2000). A model for the Evaluation of ERP Systems within the South African industry. In *Proceedings of the USP Conference on ERP: E-Enterprise 2000: Structures and Systems*, Haifa, Israel, 10.

Internet sources

Esteves, J. (2002). Management of critical success factors in SAP implementations. http://www.lsi.upc.es/-jesteves/thesis_research.htm (accessed on 6 February 2002).

IIIT (n.d.). Critical Success Factors for ERP Implementation. http://www.iiitb.ac. in/ss'o20homepage/papers/critical.html (accessed on 18 March 2001).

Stedman, C. (2000). ERP woes cut Grainger Profits. http://www.computen-vorld.com/cwUPrinter_Friendly_VersioN0,121,NAV47_ST0429, (accessed on 18 March 2001).

Trimble, P. S. (2000). The key to ERP success. http://www.fcw.comffcw/articles 12000/0313ffcw-mgt-erp-03-13-OO.asp, (accessed on 19 December 2001).

CHAPTER 8

USER TRAINING

☆ Keywords
☆ Terminology Review
☆ Competency Review
☆ Suggested Reading

♣ QUICK LOOK AT CHAPTER THEMES

Enterprise systems promise competitive advantage to those organizations that are early adopters. In today's highly competitive global environment, efficiency is needed in all aspects of business, including information systems. It is paramount to have the best software, and personnel who know how to effectively use it. There are many costs to implementing an enterprise system, including vendor software, hardware, and consultants. Implementation also involves training expenses, and the hidden costs of lost productivity in the first months or year of operation. The better the training program implemented, making sure that employees understand what the enterprise system is supposed to do for the organization, and how they can use it in doing their jobs, the less hidden costs and the sooner the organization can reap the benefits of the more efficient system.

♣ LEARNING OBJECTIVES

EIS user training is one of the most significant costs in the implementation of the software. The training will update the inherent skills of employees for managing the enterprise system. As per the wikipedia, "The term *training* refers to the acquisition of knowledge, skills, and competencies as a result of the teaching of vocational or practical skills and knowledge that relate to specific useful competencies. It forms the core of apprenticeships and provides the backbone of content at technical colleges and polytechnics." This chapter covers:

- ♣ How to provide training to users.
- ♣ How to facilitate cost reduction and cycle time reduction.
- ♣ How to enhance productivity and improve efficiency.
- ♣ How training facilitates quality improvement and customer services improvement.
- ♣ How to facilitate improvements in resource management.
- ♣ How to track & report training outcomes.
- ♣ How to better plan training.
- ♣ How training supports business growth.
- ♣ How training can be enhanced by EIS consultants.
- ♣ How to facilitate interactive training & interactive exercises.
- ♣ How to identify roles and responsibilities of IT, functional and consulting team members.

♣ CASE STUDY

Lancashire County Council

"Helped by the excellent ERP consultancy and knowledge transfer provided by Fujitsu, the new Oracle system has given us the tools we need to increase efficiency." Adrian Cutts — Executive Director of Resources, Lancashire County Council.

As part of its 40,000-strong workforce the Council has a very capable technical team, so when it decided to upgrade and standardize its core systems infrastructure around the Oracle eBusiness Suite, the Council chose not to simply contract out the work. "Most people get consultants in to do a job and when it goes live everyone rubs their hands with glee at how good it is," says project manager Pete Ripley, Principal Accountant (Corporate Financial Systems), Lancashire County Council. "However, if you've not had any direct involvement in the process, the problem then is how do you support it? So, we said that as a large organization we have the resources to implement and support the system, but what we don't have is the detailed knowledge — all the tips and tricks that you gain from years of implementing and using a system. So that's what we decided to buy!"

Solution: Following a competitive procurement through the government procurement catalogue, GCat, Lancashire County Council chose Fujitsu to provide the enterprise resource planning (ERP) consultancy and knowledge transfer services it needed to successfully build and deploy the new Oracle Financials and Procurement suite of applications needed to satisfy the needs of the Council, Lancashire Police and Lancashire Fire & Rescue Service. "We did a lot of evaluation of the capability of each supplier that we shortlisted," comments Pete Ripley, "and we chose Fujitsu because what came through was a flexibility and willingness to work together with us and help achieve our aims rather that a strict, contract-based approach."

Under the contract, Fujitsu was responsible for providing in-depth training to the Council's staff for all of the key components of the Oracle system, including General Ledger, Accounts Payable, Accounts Receivable, Core Purchasing & iProcurement and Cash Management. Fujitsu also effected the knowledge transfer to the Council staff regarding the use of its iTrade solution and, critically, all of the methods it would typically employ to handle a wide range of bespoke developments, such as direct debits in Accounts Receivable, invoice load in Accounts Payable, PO approval workflow, and BACS output. As well as providing 100 days of "learning events" geared to different modules and aspects of the system, Fujitsu also developed a version of the system that could be used as a demonstration tool to help the training process. Pete Ripley continues, *"The quality of the learning events run by Fujitsu was generally very good and we were very pleased with the quality of the training and the materials that we got to work on."*

Lancashire County Council was then able to develop and install a second test version of the system with Fujitsu providing any necessary support and advice. Finally the Council built the production version of the system from scratch, with very little involvement from Fujitsu. It also conducted extensive user acceptance testing before the new services eventually went live in a staged rollout, with ongoing support from Fujitsu, firstly in Lancashire Police, then the Council and lastly the Lancashire Fire Service. "When the Oracle system first went live we were confident that it would work well, which it did and it's been a huge success," explains Pete Ripley. "As a result, we're now looking at replacing other key systems and Fujitsu is well placed to help us do that, because we've shown that this approach works and we're keen to follow it again in the future. Anyone can read or use a manual, but by learning the practical tips and tricks you can maximize and future proof the return on your investment." Adrian Cutts, Executive Director of Resources, Lancashire County Council, comments, "Helped by the excellent ERP consultancy and knowledge transfer provided by Fujitsu, the new Oracle system was implemented without incident and has given us the tools we need to increase efficiency. The more we save on back office functions, the more resources we can divert to improving the education and social services we provide to the public, which is really what we're here for."

Benefits: The ERP knowledge transfer and support services provided by Fujitsu have enabled Lancashire County Council to:

◆ **Minimize risk** — a complex implementation was successfully planned and executed on time and without incident, with comprehensive system scoping, piloting, testing, training and knowledge transfer.
◆ **Increase productivity** — can now take advantage of the system's significantly improved functionality to streamline operations and improve resource usage.
◆ **Reduce costs** — the new system has enforced the use of corporate contracts, so reducing the costs of standard purchases.
◆ **Optimize system availability** — effective system design is ensuring optimised application performance and reliability.
◆ **Enhance flexibility** — the Oracle platform can be extended in the future to include new functional areas for greater efficiency and operational synergy.

"Under Fujitsu's expert guidance we have put in an ERP system that is undoubtedly making people more efficient across the organization," says Pete Ripley. "However, the biggest savings so far are coming from our improved procurement processes, where using corporate contracts and automated processes means we're reducing the costs of our purchases and there's much less manual authorization and paper-chasing. We're now keen to make progress on the income side as we think Oracle will help us get a grip on that and reduce bad debt."

Approach: The success of the Oracle implementation is largely due to the detailed project preparation and planning that was undertaken in the first phase of the project. This included the creation of an initial project plan covering all of the knowledge transfer deliverables and a high level outline of the pre- and post-production activities. "As one of Lancashire's biggest purchasers, the consequences of not being able to pay our suppliers could be dire for some smaller firms," adds Pete Ripley. "So, our general philosophy was that we would only implement the new Oracle system when we were ready and happy that it was a zero-risk option. As a result, rather than setting a fairly arbitrary, fixed deadline, we had built a comprehensive project plan with Fujitsu, which included detailed estimates of the work and resources needed to get the job done. We then just did the maths to work out how long it would all take with the resources that could be allocated — and tested the system to death! Our management were prepared to take this approach, which meant it took longer to go live, but it did mean that they expected the system to be right, from the go-live. And it was."

Expertise: With over 30 years experience of supporting the needs of customers, Fujitsu has a proven track record in providing complex systems integration and management services that reduce costs, improve productivity and customer services and deliver a compelling return on investment. In particular, Fujitsu has more than 4,000 SAP and Oracle specialists worldwide and extensive experience in creating practical ERP solutions and supporting customers with a hands-on approach.

"I have to say that we didn't know quite what to expect with the knowledge transfer approach that we took," comments Pete Ripley, "but we were certainly impressed by the Fujitsu consultants and their attitude. They very much became part of the team. "What pleased me, in particular, is that we drew up a contract that was really just our best guess as to how things would turn out. However, it became clear that some things weren't necessary, because we had acquired the in-house knowledge to do them ourselves. So, rather than slavishly following the contract, Fujitsu swapped around the services to deliver the best value for us, which is unusual in an IT supplier. This put Fujitsu in a very positive light with the Council, because it showed that it was more interested in our success and in developing a long-term relationship."

Source: URL [http://www.fujitsu.com/uk/casestudies/fs_lancashire-2008.html] © FUJITSU 2008.

♣ SKETCH OF EIS INITIATION

Speedy technology changes, tighter budgets and deadlines are forcing corporations to be exceedingly discriminatory about technical training for their EIS users. A growing demand for training that supports companies in their quest to develop their employee's intellectual capital is fueling change in the market place. The guru mantra behind EIS is well put by Satish Joshi, Chief Technology Officer, Patni Computer Systems Ltd that "EIS consulting, training and solutions are people's business, where inter-personal and intrapersonal skills are equally important — besides basic qualifications and certifications". EIS software packages help organizations in effective management of resources such as machines, material, man-power, inventory, etc. An amalgamated database serves the needs and requirements of various departments, leading to optimized functioning. The endeavor of a business in using an Enterprise Information System is to support all its departments with a common platform, such that the departments can contribute to information and communicate with each other.

Staff proficiency requires more than just training. An organization should always link their business objectives to their staff development plan. This also helps to bring about the four elements of the Investors in People customary.

It is paramount that key project personnel recognize the principles of EIS and their application to particular areas of the organization, so that training for users can be most effective. IT personnel need to be able to execute technical work and provide needed user support. Project leaders/middle management need to understand the big picture of the EIS and how it will affect each area of the organization. Executives also need to understand the big picture, what systems are capable of and can't do and what are the priorities and trade-offs.

EIS/ERP brings together fragmented operations found in legacy systems. By widespread information sharing of an integrated set of appli-cation modules, EIS/ERP can speed processes across the business. Training makes this possible.

♣ INTRODUCTION

Before the arrival of integrated systems, diverse departments within an organization developed their own computer systems, each operating independently using its own applications and data. One of India's best-known business leaders, Mr. N. R. Narayana Murthy says: "Ensure that each person gets to train intensively during the year. Follow best practices from around the world, give the players the best facilities and make them work really hard — eight hours a day. If anyone refuses to practice or follow the rules, axe him immediately. Follow these principles and you're bound to have a world-beating team". In many ways, the same applies to Enterprise Information System Users and vendors.

EIS training includes both that specified by the vendors for employees as well as customer users, or in-house training by the users for their employees. All require the same preparation and homework. Figure 8.1 shows a possible sequence of EIS training activities.

Training is most advantageously directed at those who will be using the system in their daily work. Unless you physically use the computer, it may not be necessary for you to be acquainted with how to enter data of work orders, for example. Systems training are more frequently than not

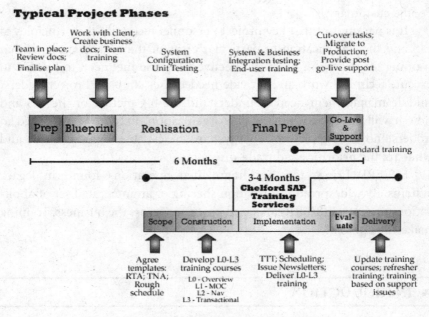

Figure 8.1: Possible EIS Training Activity Sequence.

Source: SAP's Training of Enterprise System Project phase.

given by the software vendor. It comes as part of the package and they are the best people to give it. If they are also offering education, it may be prudent to ensure it is not merely a high level overview of their own interpretation. If it is, it might overlook some of the fundamental business issues of the organization. It would be as if you might end up understanding how aerodynamics affects only one particular type of aircraft.

8.1 ABOUT USER'S TRAINING

Training is imparted to the users to give them understanding of product features and techniques. The late Management Guru Peter Drucker was asked: "What is the most imperative impact of Information Technology on business?" He replied: "Information technology forces you to organize your processes more logically."[1] In any ERP implementation, it is generally understood that training is a key component of organizational change management and of the overall success of the ERP implementation. However, there is a subtle and distinct difference between training and training effectively.

The computer can handle only things to which the answer is 'yes' or 'no.' It cannot handle maybe. It is not the computerization that is important; it is the discipline that it brings to your business processes. The activities of selecting and installing an EIS system have received a great deal of attention. However, there are many important issues remaining in making EIS systems work. User training has shown up as a critical success factor in the implementation of an EIS in many studies (Ngai and Law, 2008, for one recent example).[2] Duplaga and Astani (2003)[3] found training to be the top ERP/EIS problem in their study of 30 manufacturing firms. There is a strong tendency to underestimating the magnitude

---

[1] Kimberling, E. (2007). ERP training: More than software transactions. *ERP and Business Consultant*, posted 9/23/2007.
[2] Ngai, E. W. T. and Law, C. C. H. (2008). Examining the critical success factors in the adoption of enterprise resource planning systems. *Computers in Industry*, 59(6), 548–564.
[3] Duplaga, E. A. and Astani, M. (2003). Implementing ERP in manufacturing. *Information Systems Management*, 20(3), 68–75.

required in such a training program. Training is typically underestimated, and is often the first target for budget cutting.[4] There is usually a period of about one year where the trauma of the new system is very difficult to bear by all concerned. This difficult period is easier to cope with if a thorough training program has been adopted. Furthermore, those organizations that do a poor job of training have been found to have poorer performing enterprise systems.[5]

Good training programs can pay off in many ways. Gartner has claimed that each hour of effective training is worth five hours to the organization because well-trained users take less than a quarter of the time to reach productive performance levels, they require less assistance from help sources, and they spend less time correcting errors.[6]

Thus EIS/ERP training programs focus on transactional training. EIS/ERP software companies and implementation teams are normally superior at generating credentials and delivering training that teaches how to perform transactions. On the other hand, running a business entails much more than simply performing transactions. As an alternative, EIS/ERP training programs should focus on new business processes.

8.1.1 The Need for a Training Programme

Every EIS implementation project needs to take training into account. One of the most effective ways to accomplish this is delivering a "train the trainer" approach, where the EIS consultants will instruct key customer staff, who in turn will train their operatives. This has the benefit of delivering end-user training in an operational environment. A negative feature is that delivery may be impromptu and ineffective, may not be well supported with training materials, and may not be repeatable after system go-live. It will be dependent on local staff and there may not be facilities for self-learning.

---

[4] Slater, D. (1998). The hidden costs of enterprise software. *CIO Magazine*, 123–129.
[5] Tsai, W.-H. and Hung, S.-J. (2008). E-commerce implementation: An empirical study of the performance of enterprise resource planning systems using the organizational learning model. *International Journal of Management*, 25(2), 348–352.
[6] Aldrich, C. (2000). The justification of IT training. *Gartner Research Note, DF-11-3614.*

8.2 THE MAGNITUDE OF TRAINING

Every organization has training programmes of their own for new recruits, irrespective of work experience and educational qualifications. "Training programmes are imperative, as there is always a deficiency of trained and experienced professionals. Training facilitates the gaining of practical experience and supplementary understanding, which will help them in their work. Though training freshly recruited staff is costly, it is a long-term investment," says Chetan Pathak, Vice President, Enterprise Solutions, Ramco Systems (India) Ltd, a company that provides enterprise IT solutions and services.

"At Wipro, we have an internal Talent Transformation Cell, where we train people recruited to work with EIS/ERP systems on platforms of vendors such as Oracle, SAP, MS Dynamics, etc. After the training, they get certified in their respective modules and are exposed to hands-on projects to learn the functional aspects of business design and adopt best practices in the EIS/ERP package," says Krishna Kumar Tirumalai S, Head, SAP Delivery, Wipro Infotech Ltd.

For in-depth and hands-on expertise, companies also conduct training programs addressing specific roles in EIS/ERP. "We have a career development framework, through which specific training is delivered to the candidate, depending on the job experience the candidate has acquired over the years and on his or her aspiration and capability," says Suman K. Mazumder, Director, Application Services Global Delivery, IBM India.

This training period varies depending upon the role of the individual and the organization. On-the-job training is also common in many organizations, and some are flexible enough to allow employees to pursue education related to their job function.

"EIS/ERP consultants need to keep themselves updated with new applications and evolving technologies. Quitting their official obligations and pursuing full-time study is not a wise choice. The concept of part-time module courses has therefore evolved to help them keep pace with changing trends," says Anand Ekambaram, Director, Education Services, SAP India Ltd.

Careers for ERP professionals lie in product development, implementation, maintenance, and consulting. Within these, there are multiple options available. Industry verticals often refer an ERP professional as a consultant based on his or her role and area of expertise in that organization. The ERP employment scenario offers career options that can be classified under Functional, Technical, and Training.

8.2.1 Training in Functional Areas

Career options here need in-depth understanding along with experience of physical implementation in various functions of the business process. "By relevant experience and sound knowledge of functions like finance, human resources, materials management, quality control, production planning, manufacturing processes, etc., a person can excel in an ERP career. Also, the full life-cycle experience of the implementation of the ERP package in one or more functional modules is necessary," says B. Chandrashekhar, Vice President and Delivery Head (SAP, Oracle and Siebel), Datamatics Limited, a company that provides offshore outsourcing software services.

The ERP functional consultant interacts with the client organization — he understands their business processes, requirements, and problems. He then analyzes and builds the process flow of the functions, and recommends a cost-effective implementation of an ERP solution package.

8.2.2 Training in Technical Areas

In ERP software companies, the individual can be involved in development of various applications on different platforms — an ERP package or specific modules within a package. They work on ERP applications like mySAP, Oracle 11i, PeopleSoft, and J. D. Edwards, to name a few. These professionals — often referred to as consultants — document the requirements of the business and integrate them to form an ERP implementation plan that incorporate in the clients' business process models. In organizations that provide consulting services, the technical professionals are also required to help with the implementation and maintenance.

The Training Area: After relevant industry experience and pursuing training through vendor-specific courses, training can be a good career option. Organizations looking to train their freshly-recruited ERP staff always need training professionals. The latter would need to be experienced in working on different platforms and has knowledge of many domains.

Freelancing: Many ERP professionals provide freelance consulting to client organizations. It is mostly small or medium businesses who hire freelance consultants for implementation or maintenance of their ERP system. As a freelancer, one can perform any role from the bottom to the top level, depending, of course, upon the years of experience and specialization.

8.3 TRAINING EXAMPLE

Marathon Oil Company is a large oil-processing firm that implemented their EIS/ERP in the late 1990s.[7] They were part of the pre-Y2K generation of EIS/ERP users. They were able to successfully install their system within 18 months. This installation was easier than those of many others, because the computer platforms housing the system were relatively standardized. The enterprise system was selected to upgrade information systems to a higher level rather than to fix problems. Marathon's system linked financial, human resources, procurement, and management reporting, with linkages to oil and gas technical systems.

The Marathon installation process began with forming a cross-functional team to assess current business processes. A SAP system was selected based upon their well-developed software in the oil and gas industry. Marathon developed a business case focusing on software functionality, including gains from implementation of best practices. Marathon studied failed efforts by other organizations, and identified factors critical to successful enterprise system implementation.

Marathon recognized the high degree of change management required. "When you move to SAP, you are changing the way people work.

[7] Stapleton, G. and Rezak, C. J. (2004). Change management underpins a successful ERP implementation at Marathon Oil. *Journal of Organizational Excellence*, 15–22.

You are challenging their principles, their beliefs, and the way they have done things for many, many years."[8] Marathon sought to transfer ownership from the project team to end users of the system, relying on three fundamental elements:

♦ **Knowledge transfer** to ensure the employees knew what to do with the new system.
♦ **Responsibility transfer** to ensure that employees are fully participatory.
♦ **Vision transfer** to aid employees in translating new tools and processes into improved business results.

Marathon relied on a number of tools to deliver their training. **One-way channels** included newsletters, road shows, town meetings, a Web site, and personal appearances by key leaders to inform employees of what was developing in their IT. **Interactive communication** included workshops, meetings to deal with specific issues, conference calls, and collaborative Web sites. **Hands-on interaction** was also developed, including **sandboxes** enabling users to play with the system using simulated data prior to using the real system.

Marathon was able to implement their system, consisting of eight modules, in 13 months, which at that time was considered a record for SAP installations. The implementation varied from the normal in that employee skills and commitments were leveraged throughout the organization by careful change management. The focus on business functions and processes rather than on how to use SAP was credited with much of the implementation success. Employees were trained on how the new system would impact how they did their jobs, and their comments were solicited and formed the basis to some system changes.

8.3.1 Training Problems

EIS software itself is rarely the source of implementation problems. Poor training of users is usually the source of most implementation problems.

---

[8] Dunn, J. (2002). CIO of Nestle Company, quoted in *CIO magazine*.

Organizations with higher proportions of new employees may find implementation of EIS easier. Firms with many employees with many years of experience within the firm prior to EIS implementation require greater levels of change. Conversely, managerial and professional employees are often easier to convince of the positive impact of EIS on organizational effectiveness.[9] Further, the degree of change required within the organization can have an impact on EIS installation timing. If the system is implemented too quickly, this may not provide sufficient time for the organizational climate to change.

A major issue in training is the focus. Vendors and consultants have developed extensive training programs for enterprise system installations. However, these training programs by their nature focus on how to use the software. This is an ineffective focus, because the impact of job change is more important to system users.[10] It has been found that it is far more important to center EIS training on understanding the system concept and spirit, and the changes in the specific business processes users will face.[11] This type of training is much more difficult to design and deliver, as it is specific to individual jobs within each organization.

Rarely do EIS implementations run smoothly. Some of the pitfalls organizations typically face are:

♦ Placing employees in software-specific training, without attention to business processes.
♦ Training focusing on command sequences without explanation of the purpose.
♦ Skimping on training time.
♦ Tendency of new users to solve problems the old way rather than learn the new system.

---

[9] Abdinnour-Helm, S., Lengnick-Hall, M. L. and Lengnick-Hall, C. A. (2003). Pre-implementation attitudes and organizational readiness for implementing an Enterprise Resource Planning System. *European Journal of Operational Research*, 146, 258–273.
[10] Scott, J. E. (2005). Post-implementation usability of ERP training manuals: The user's perspective. *Information Systems Management*, 67–77.
[11] Yu, C.-S. (2005). Causes influencing the effectiveness of the post-implementation ERP system. *Industrial Management & Data Systems*, 105(1), 115–132.

8.3.2 Training Media

Some of the reasons training in new EIS systems is difficult include user diversity, the complexity of the new system, and the variety of training methods available. By their nature, EIS systems are going to radically change how many people do their jobs. The theory of EIS is to integrate computer support to all aspects of the business, naturally leading to user diversity. These people also are busy, especially in coping with the requirements of the new system. Training users in new EIS systems can be extremely expensive, usually over 10 percent of total EIS system cost.

Experience has demonstrated to companies the importance of training. The need for flexibility in timing and place as well as the need for training in specific functions rather than the comprehensive EIS system have made it important to have flexible training schedules. This has led to an entire industry providing EIS training. There are many delivery formats available, including:

♦ Web-based virtual training.
♦ Computer-based training.
♦ Video courses.
♦ Self-study books.
♦ Training manuals.
♦ Pop-up help screens.
♦ Classroom training.
♦ Sandboxes, or prototype systems using simulated data for hands-on orientation.

Many large companies have been created with the sole purpose of training organizational employees in using their enterprise systems.[12] These firms have charged fees around $200 and up per hour in the early 2000s. Not all organizations need to go outside to obtain necessary training, however. Many organizations work with vendors to accomplish the two important tasks of 1) showing users how to interact with the EIS, and 2) showing users

---

[12] Dowlatshahi, S. (2005). Strategic success factors in enterprise resource-planning design and implementation: A case-study approach. *International Journal of Production Research,* 43(18), 3745–3771.

how to do their jobs within the new system. Obviously, the more the system is customized, the less burdensome this training is. However, as we have seen earlier, the more customization, the greater the cost of system implementation. Organizations have to carefully balance these conflicting factors.

Utilizing electronic forms is highly cost effective, and has been reported to be as low as 2.5 percent of traditional training costs (Dwyer, 2001).[13] Web-based training is most efficient in terms of cost, but usually is best at training users in how to use vendor systems rather than the specific tasks users will perform to do their jobs.

Ways to improve enterprise system training cited by Scott[14] include:

♦ Focusing documentation on organization-specific business processes.
♦ Role-based training providing knowledge integration tailored to user needs.
♦ Making frequently asked questions (FAQs) available online.
♦ Print more static content in manuals, while posting more dynamic content online.
♦ Include advanced search capabilities in online versions of content.
♦ Restrict the size of manuals by having versions for "getting started," "reference manual," and "advanced manual."

Vathanophas (2007)[15] argued that enterprise system training should be conducted during business hours to indicate its importance. He saw three levels of training, where consultants and vendors can first train IT staff, who in turn train individual departmental representatives (sometimes called **superusers**), who finally deliver training to their compatriots within their departments.

The scope of training is demonstrated by the experiences of Pratt and Whitney, Canada (P&WC) in 1998.[16] They trained 110 employees from

---

[13] Dwyer, J. (2001). In a different class. *Works Management*, 54, 46.
[14] Scott, J. (2005). op. cit.
[15] Vathanophas, V. (2007). Business process approach towards an inter-organizational enterprise system. *Business Process Management Journal*, 13(3), 433–450.
[16] Tchokogué, A., Bareil, C. and Duguay, C. R. (2005). Key lessons from the implementation of an ERP at Pratt & Whitney Canada. *International Journal of Production Economics*, 95, 151–163.

their six most affected departments as internal trainers (superusers). The year 1998 saw P&WC convert their facilities into a massive classroom, training over three thousand employees in both technical aspects (system navigation and task training) delivered by consultants as well as providing business-oriented training (processes and tasks). P&WC created over 150 manuals to cover diverse user needs.

8.3.3 Training Plan

Fulla (2007)[17] recommended the following steps to attain successful change management during enterprise system implementation:

1. **Identify the project sponsor and executive team** — this ensures the presence of top management commitment that repeatedly is cited as a critical success factor.
2. **Ensure that all in the organization are aware of the enterprise system installation** — sharing project information establishes a sense of trust and develops an environment based on full disclosure.
3. **Communicate the value of the enterprise system** — if employees see that the system is beneficial to the organization, that will go a long way to gaining their commitment and acceptance of the system.
4. **Establish project goals to define key business drivers** — citing gains from elimination of data redundancy and greater access to analytics can validate the value of the enterprise system to the organization.
5. **Inform key individuals about the project and concerns of its progress** — managers and key end users should regularly be given the opportunity to discuss concerns about the system installation. This is especially important when organizations have multiple sites.
6. **Establish a project plan including resources required** — clear statement of project timelines provide a basis for project management coordination with vendors for training and rollout implementation.
7. **The people factor** — enterprise systems change how people do their jobs. Experienced employees have invested much of their careers in

---

[17] Fulla, S. (2007). Change management: Ensuring success in your ERP implementation. *Government Finance Review*, 23(2), 34–40.

learning old organizational procedures, and there is strong inertia to overcome in their cases. Other employees may be uncomfortable with technology, and require additional care. Training programs need to convince experienced employees and also need to be user-friendly to keep all key employees in tune with the new system.

8. **Multiple and ongoing training media** — vendors offer system training prior to system rollout, but as we have emphasized, that is only part of the required training focus. Long-term training is needed to provide greater in-depth coverage of business process content. Furthermore, the organization will need to train new hires in the future.

9. **Review performance and compliance** — once the enterprise system is brought on-line, it is necessary to check that it is properly being used, or the benefits expected will not occur.

8.4 CONCLUSION

Training is a key component of a successful enterprise system installation. Training needs to be considered in the initial project budget. Typically, it is underestimated by significant amounts. There are two major elements of enterprise system training. The first is focused on how to use the system, and this type of training is well-developed by vendors and consultants. The second is on organization-specific business processes. This second form of training has proven to be far more important than the first. Vendors and consultants can't be expected to deliver training programs covering organization-specific processes unless the installed system has no customization. Usually, effective systems that match organizational needs do have customization, and the organization itself will have to develop this form of training. (They will want to if it covers core competencies that yield competitive advantage to the organization.)

An effective means to organize training is to have experts (vendors or consultants) train IT staff. IT staff in turn train a set of superusers from departments within the organization, who then relay the knowledge they obtain to general organizational users.

There are many different media available to deliver enterprise system training. One-way media can be used to inform users of the system's value to the organization. Two-way media are usually more effective in teaching users how to use the system. Hands-on interaction with sandbox systems can be highly effective in training users of their specific job requirements.

Through careful planning and delivery of training, the success rate of enterprise systems installations can be vastly improved.

Today's EIS market is a mixed bag of enormous expectations, unbelievable results, and wealthy rewards and in some cases debatable enthusiasm. It will be another two to three years before the dust settles and a balanced view will materialize. Let us hope this happens.

☆ KEYWORDS

☆ **Knowledge transfer** to ensure the employees knew what to do with the new system.
☆ **Responsibility transfer** to ensure that employees are fully participating.
☆ **Sandbox**: small scale version of EIS system using historical data used for training outside of actual operations.
☆ **Vision transfer** to aid employees in translating new tools and processes into improved business results.

☆ TERMINOLOGY REVIEW

a) How do you set up and run an EIS Training Lab?
b) What are the innovative value-added training modules of EIS?
c) How do enterprise information system address performance management and training processes for education of users of EIS software?
d) When all is said and done, the team must thoroughly exercise the system in order to know and assess its strengths, weaknesses and different ways they can solve problems with it, in order to iron out bugs, procedural weaknesses, needed EIS Implementation.

☆ COMPETENCY REVIEW

1. **Pragmatic Questions**

   a) EIS Software Training facilitates stated performance goals, in line with the organizational perspective, and targeted job competencies.

   b) EIS Software Training can provide managers with a model for clear language and a basis for developing the narrative portion of the review. It helps in identifying legally sensitive and inappropriate language.

   c) How HR managers can easily create training roadmap for their companies, departments and individuals.

   d) The role of the IT organization is critical to the success of the implementation as it requires training and skills to develop and support the new system while maintaining the legacy system until the go-live date.

2. **Briefly Comment on the following statements:**

   a. Training is imparted by real-time EIS consultants.

   ....

   ....

   b. With just a few clicks, managers can track the individual's training schedule.

   ....

   ....

   c. High cost and inefficient traditional training process

   ....

   ....

d. Virtual Learning System provides a low-cost, high efficiency system where employees can learn anytime while they are at work.

....

....

e. Any organization needs a comprehensive generic business systems *education* program to ensure that people are aware of the state of the art.

....

....

f. The individual joins the global race by enhancing his skills in EIS.

....

....

☆ SUGGESTED READING

Books

Eden, C., Jones, S. and Sims, D. (1983). *Messing About In Problems. An Informal Structured Approach to their Identification and Management.* Oxford: Pergamon Press.

Schönefeld, M. and Vering, O. (2000). *Enhancing ERP-Efficiency through Workflow-Services.*

Shang, S. S. C. and Seddon, P. B. (2000). *A Comprehensive Framework for Classifying the Benefits of ERP Systems.*

Scott, J. E. (2000). *Implementing Enterprise Resource Planning Systems: The Role of Learning from Failure.* Information Systems Frontiers.

Journal Articles

Holland, C. P. and Light, B. (1999). A critical success factors model for ERP implementation. *IEEE Software*, 16, 30–36.

Shtub, A. (2001). A framework for teaching and training in the Enterprise Resource Planning (ERP) era. *International Journal of Production Research*, 39(3).

Umble, E. J. and Umble, M. M. (2002). Avoiding ERP implementation failure. *Industrial Management*, 44(1), 25.

Umble, E. J., Haft, R. R. *et al.* (2003). Enterprise resource planning: Implementation procedures and critical success factors. *European Journal of Operational Research*, 146(2), 241–257.

Verville, J. C. and Halingten, A. (2003). Analysis of the decision process for selecting ERP software: The case of Keller Manufacturing. *Integrated Manufacturing System*, 14(5), 423–432.

Weston Jr., F. D. T. and Weston, T. (2003). ERP II: The extended enterprise system. *Business Horizons*, 46(6), 49–55.

Zeng, Y., Chiang, R. H. L. *et al.* (2003). Enterprise integration with advanced information technologies: ERP and data warehousing. *Information Management & Computer Security*, 11(3).

White Papers and Conference Papers

Relaxation training may cut hypertension medication among elderly. Thaindian News.

Dong, L., Neufeld, D. and Higgins, C. (2002). The Iceberg on the Sea: What Do You See? *Proceedings of the 8th Americas Conference on Information Systems*, 857–864.

Volkoff, O. and Sawyer, S. (2001). ERP implementation teams, consultants, and information sharing. *7th Americas Conference on Information Systems*.

Wang, J. H. W. Y. M. (2003). Enterprise resource planning experience in Taiwan: An empirical study and comparative analysis. *Proceedings of the 36th Annual Hawaii International Conference on System Sciences*.

Yakovlev, I. V. and Anderson, M. L. (2001). Lessons from an ERP implementation. *IT Professional*.

Zhang, L., Lee, M. K. O. *et al.* (2003). Critical success factors of enterprise resource planning systems implementation success in China. *Proceedings of the 36th Annual Hawaii International Conference on System Sciences.*

Online Resource

Swanson, E. B. (2000). Information Systems as Buzz.

CHAPTER 9

SYSTEM MAINTENANCE

Quotation

Reinventing your business doesn't happen overnight, but three years after a major systems overhaul and maintenance.

David Braue, ZDNet Australia

Structure

♣ *Quick look at chapter themes*
♣ *Learning objectives*
♣ *Case study:* Tofan Grup, Romania — The Shift to Systems Integration
   9.1. Classification of EIS/ERP Maintenance Activities
   9.2. EIS/ERP System Migration
   9.3. EIS/ERP Upgrades
   9.4. Critical Success Factors
   9.5 Conclusion
☆ Keywords
☆ Terminology Review
☆ Suggested Reading

♣ QUICK LOOK AT CHAPTER THEMES

> *Three years ago, PeopleSoft acquired JD Edwards for more than US$1.7 billion. In 2004, Oracle nabbed PeopleSoft for US$10 billion. The idea of EIS is to have a stable integrated system. However, software providers have a product life cycle offering improved versions periodically. This creates a problem for EIS users, because vendors want to discontinue service on old versions to encourage purchase of their improved versions, while users would like to obtain as much value from their investment as possible. Maintenance and upgrades of EIS software is a critically important consideration.*
>
> *Rapidly changing technology and economic climate has made IT investment highly risky. Organizational investment in EIS offers a great deal of value, but benefits and costs must be evaluated in light of specific circumstances. Even after an EIS has been obtained, important decisions must still be made.*

♣ LEARNING OBJECTIVES

EIS maintenance includes a variety of components. Precautionary system maintenance focuses on avoiding system downtimes and failures. We will present other forms of EIS maintenance in this chapter, including:

- ♣ Discussion of different types of EIS maintenance.
- ♣ EIS system migration and the operation of organizational EIS.
- ♣ How EIS upgrades affect using organizations.
- ♣ Critical Success Factors.

♣ CASE STUDY

Tofan Grup, Romania — The Shift to Systems Integration

A leading Romanian tire manufacturer runs production control systems powered by the Microsoft BackOffice technologies, gaining competitive edge and building efficiencies into the local corporate culture.

Situation: Tofan Grup is the leading producer and distributor of tires in Romania, generating annual sales in excess of 150 million USD on local and international markets. The headquarters coordinate five production plants — Danubiana Bucuresti, Victoria Floresti, Silvania Zalau, Rotras Turnu-Severin and Tofan Recap — whose activities cover all tire manufacturing essentials. The management developed a strategic vision in order to better support and control the production planning and tracking operations. In the context of the growing local market and faced with the increased qualitative requirements imposed by customers abroad, the isolated, out-of-date applications, that were inconsistently used, had to be replaced by an integrated solution, able to manage the production process, from the planning phase all the way down to sales completion.

Solution: In order to use an IT solution at its highest potential, Tofan Grup had already chosen to deploy, in the entire organization, the ISIS ERP system. Running on Microsoft BackOffice technologies and developed by Omnis Group, a Romanian software company, this system was implemented to support Tofan's commercial operations, based on common catalogs and a central accounting platform. The SQL Server 2000 replication mechanism provides the means to transfer and consolidate data generated and used by all organizational units.

The technological platform strengths, the modularity and flexibility of the ISIS solution, together with its openness and unique orientation towards the local economical and cultural context, turned this implementation into a major success. The local management and the strategic partner — Nomura Securities — decided to extend the system implementation scope in the area of the tire manufacturing process.

"Witnessing the versatility proved by the open standards and by the component-based technologies embedded in the Microsoft platform, we understood that our ISIS implementation could break down the barriers that were still separating some of our business areas. We had to link all departments taking part in the production process, inside a system that already provided corporate-wide integration for our distribution operations", says Cristinel Popa, Vice-President of Tofan Grup.

The ISIS–Production solution components are based on the Windows DNA for Manufacturing technology, supporting complete management of the production workflow and business decisions based on accurate and timely information. It is an efficient way to get faster time-to-market and an edge over the competition.

Implementation: The ISIS–Production system components were deployed in the production facilities of each plant. The network was extended to tie together most of the data points on the production flow. Users operate on Windows 98 and Windows 2000 Professional workstations, connected on optical fibre cable to the central server of each plant, which runs Windows 2000 Server and hosts the SQL Server 2000 database. These servers are interconnected through the main server installed at the headquarters, which manages all replication processes and grants corporate-wide data consolidation. Communication is provided by VSAT, radio relays and modems connected on phone lines.

The objectives were set in order to address priority production areas that were subject to former computerized procedures. Users in technical departments, at all production plants, were trained to enter complete tire building technical specifications into the system first. It was then possible to accurately evaluate, based on a production plan, the types and quantities of necessary raw materials. The same technical specs were also used to estimate the value of the unfinished production — an important factor that influences production costs.

"The excellent scalability features of the Microsoft platform helped us to quickly achieve outstanding results in the physical and logical integration of production-specific data processing into our ISIS implementation", states Mr. Popa. "It gives us complete confidence in controlling the business".

The system deployment, from office production planning down to the factory floor operations, as well as extensive user training seminars, were conducted by the solution developer, Omnis Group. Its local expertise, project management and proactive communication capabilities, turned the implementation into a winning business partnership experience.

Benefits: Common raw materials and tire catalogs, as well as common customer and supplier catalogs, are used across the entire corporation.

Up-to-date tire building technical specs can easily be maintained, allowing accurate production planning. The system tracks the transfers of materials and by-products between all production departments — mixing, calendering, diagonal cutting, extrusion, bead building, assembly and curing.

ISIS–Production is seamlessly integrated with the other components of the ISIS ERP solution. Information processed in Sales, Stock Management, Fixed Assets, Maintenance and Repairs, Utilities, Payroll, is consolidated in the accounting platform, offering a tool for the evaluation of production costs per cost centre and per type of tire.

Windows DNA for Manufacturing delivers the basic technology that links operations within the corporation. This infrastructure brought productivity improvements and the headroom needed for organizational growth.

The future: The principle of mass customization calls for the integration of modern MRP functionalities — just-in-time manufacturing, manufacturing line-feed at point-of-fit, advanced inventory and shipping functions. At the same time, the market requires integration with other systems and applications, tools to connect partners, employees, external contractors, customers and suppliers in various collaborations, both inside the corporation and across the Internet. Microsoft .NET for Manufacturing will supply products and services that will bring Web integration to the level of assembly lines, equipment and machines powered by Windows CE 3.0. ISIS–Production will represent a key player in this new time-critical, Internet-enabled world of manufacturing IT solutions.

Source: Omnis Group LTD (2008).[1]

---

[1] Omnis Group was founded in 1990 as the first private company in Romania to develop software solutions on top of the most advanced technology platforms. Since then, the company has gained a solid technological expertise, in the process of building and implementing software systems, solutions and services, while sustaining successful collaborations with international partners.

9.1 CLASSIFICATION OF EIS/ERP MAINTENANCE ACTIVITIES

A system is a set of related parts coordinated to accomplish a set of goals. The function of a system is to convert or process the inputs to achieve useful outputs. For example, car is a system. Figure 9.1 displays a type of system.

Another activity that tends to receive insufficient attention is EIS/ERP system maintenance. All computer systems need to be maintained. Nah et al.[2] have classified EIS/ERP maintenance tasks, as outlined in Table 9.1.

Maintenance activities can include corrective actions for problems that are detected, adaptive procedures as new feature requirements are generated, perfective maintenance as new software upgrades are developed, and preventive maintenance to deal with routine administrative

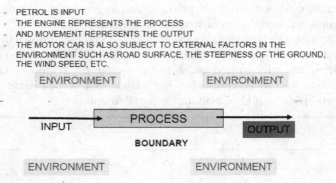

Figure 9.1: A System and Components.

Source: www.dnserp.com[3]

---

[2] Nah, F. F.-H., Faja, S. and Cata, T. (2001). Characteristics of EIS/ERP software maintenance: A multiple case study. *Journal of Software Maintenance and Evolution: Research and Practice*, 13, 399–414.

[3] DNS e-BUSINESS CONSULTANCY is a business services company offering a range of consulting and technology solutions/services across domains. Committed to enabling excellence, DNS e-BUSINESS collaborates with its clients to help substantially raise the level of their performance and profitability, and enter the world of e-Business.

Table 9.1:   Classification of EIS/ERP Maintenance Activities.

Maintenance class	Typical tasks	Descriptions
Corrective	♦ Application of vendor additions.	Incorporate vendor patches and objects.
	♦ Troubleshooting.	Fix problems submitted by users.
Adaptive	♦ Transfers.	Implement new features.
	♦ Testing.	Test after change.
	♦ Modifications/enhancements.	Internal customization.
	♦ Authorizations.	Password maintenance.
	♦ Interface tuning.	Implement interfaces with other software.
Perfective	♦ Version upgrade.	Justification, planning, and implementation of new versions.
Preventive	♦ Administration.	Monitor response times, thresholds, file sizes, backups, error logs.
	♦ Work-flow monitoring.	Track flow of maintenance activities.

Source: Nah *et al.* (2001).

functions of a computer system. Additionally, activities of training users and providing help are important, as well as coordinating with vendors, consultants, and other external organizations. Figure 9.2 displays how system maintenance fits into an overall software implementation. This is important for understanding the need for long-term budget planning of any software implementation including EIS.

The degree of maintenance activity is expected to vary with system cycle, much as with other software. Initially, the focus is on adaptive, corrective, and preventive maintenance. These maintenance classes decline in volume with time, while perfective maintenance activities increase. The greatest volume of maintenance activity would be generated by version upgrades. This creates a natural opposition in interests, as using firms will prefer system stability, while EIS/ERP vendors will emphasize the need for

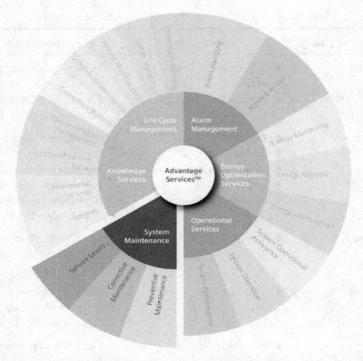

Figure 9.2: Systems Maintenance in Overall Software Implementation.
Source: Siemens AG (2008).[4]

upgrades to improve system efficiency and capacity (while also improving vendor cash flow).

9.2 EIS/ERP SYSTEM MIGRATION

Implementing EIS/ERP conceptually implies the adoption of best practice processes. However, as EIS/ERP systems evolve, new versions are regularly

[4] Siemens AG (Berlin and Munich) is a global powerhouse in electronics and electrical engineering, operating in the industry, energy and healthcare sectors. Siemens AG (Berlin and Munich) is a global powerhouse in electronics and electrical engineering, operating in the industry, energy and healthcare sectors. For over 160 years, Siemens has stood for technical achievements, innovation, quality, reliability and internationality.

developed. There will be times when organizations decide it is time to adopt changes, either minor modifications or ultimately EIS/ERP system replacement (Kremers and van Dissel).[5] Vendors find EIS/ERP migration important because of a number of reasons. First, the older the installed system, the higher the switching cost for the organization. To ensure long-term relationships with customers, EIS/ERP vendors need to upgrade their systems. Second, it is easier to support and service a smaller number of software versions. Thus, by upgrading older systems for customers, vendors simplify their maintenance headaches, as well as providing better value to customers. Third, migrations can lead to increased sales for more seats on new software applications, as well as through sales of add-on products supported by new versions but not supported by older versions.

Adding functionality was cited by Kremers and van Dissel as the most common reason for updating EIS/ERP systems. Technical reasons included compliance with new standards and dissatisfaction with technical performance, as well as a desire to keep EIS/ERP systems current. Sometimes vendors discontinued support for installed versions, providing another technical reason for switching. There also was some response for switching because of organizational issues. Customers encountered a number of problems. Fifty percent of the responses indicated time problems in implementing the new version, 31 percent technical problems with the new version, and 25 percent problems with costs. Other negative experiences reported were strain on the organization and quality of migration support tools. Still, many organizations found migration something that had to be done.

9.3 EIS/ERP UPGRADES

EIS/ERP upgrades are mainly intended to take advantage of new technologies and business strategies to ensure that the organization keeps up with the latest business development trends. Therefore, the decision to upgrade EIS/ERP is usually not driven by code deterioration or anticipated reduction

---

[5] Kremers, M. and van Dissel, H. (2000). ERP system migrations. *Communications of the ACM*, 43(4), 53–56.

in maintenance costs alone, but by different purposes. According to an AMR study,[6] 55 percent of upgrades were voluntary business improvements triggered by the need for new functionality, expansion or consolidation of systems; 24 percent of upgrades were triggered by technology stack changes; 15 percent of upgrades were forced by de-support of the running version of software to avoid vendor support termination[7]; and six percent of upgrades were triggered by bug fixes or statutory changes.

The cost of EIS/ERP upgrades is high.[8] Swanton cited the cost of each upgrade including: 50 percent of the original software license fee and 20 percent of the original implementation cost per user, which means over 6 million dollars for a 5,000-user system. Typically, each EIS/ERP upgrade requires eight to nine months of effort with a team the equivalent of one full-time employee per 35 business users. The EIS/ERP-adopting organization does not have to develop and re-write the EIS/ERP system itself but rather it replaces (or upgrades) the old version with a readily available new version from the EIS/ERP vendor. However, a lack of experience may cause the costs and length of the upgrade project to approach or even exceed those of the original EIS/ERP implementation effort. Collins[9] listed some general benefits for organizations from EIS/ERP upgrades:

♦ Eligibility for Help Desk Support: Most EIS/ERP software vendors stop providing technical support 12 to 18 months after the next version becomes available. Therefore, keeping upgrades with the pace of EIS/ERP vendors will guarantee the support for the system from the vendors.

♦ Solutions for Outstanding "Bugs" or Design Weaknesses: It is impossible to guarantee spotless and error-free EIS/ERP systems after the implementations even though vendors will conduct many different

[6] Swanton, B. (2004). Build ERP upgrade costs into the business change program — not the IT budget. *Computer Weekly*, 28–28.

[7] Craig, R. (1999). Laurier enterprise system upgrade. *International Conference of Information Systems*, Charlotte, USA.

[8] Montgomery, N. (2004). Build your business case for upgrades by adding functionality. *Computer Weekly*, 16–16.

[9] Collins, K. (1999). Strategy and execution of ERP upgrades. *Government Finance Review*, 15(4), 43–47.

testing processes to eliminate errors in the system before the leasing time. The majority of software bugs are resolved and delivered either fix-by-fix, or all-at-once as part of the next release version of the EIS/ERP package. In this case, upgrades will be beneficial to the organizations in problem-solving.

♦ New, Expanded, or Improved Features: EIS/ERP software provides organizations the knowledge and strength (i.e. best practices) from the vendors. EIS/ERP upgrades provide organizations future enhancement from the vendors to give the organizations better opportunities to catch up the current business development, improve their processes and build more efficient business models with new functions, new features and new processing styles provided in the upgraded EIS/ERP versions. Figure 9.3 shows some possible upgrade cycles.

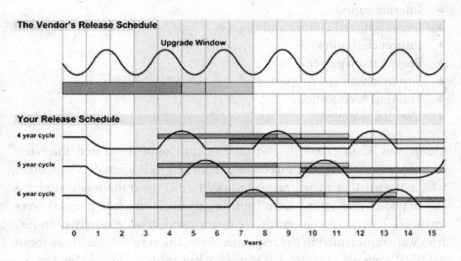

Figure 9.3: ERP Upgrade Cycles.

Source: Army Business Transformation.[10]

---

[10] The Army Business Transformation Vision describes how the Army in the future applies proven business principles to the Army's business problems, and achieves efficiencies. The means to achieve those efficiencies are embedded in the *Business Transformation Strategic Framework*. The three focus areas and five enablers that comprise the framework are formed of the best practices and methods of American enterprise, and will provide the boundaries, structure, and standards to help ensure its success.

9.4 CRITICAL SUCCESS FACTORS

Critical success factors (CSFs) in EIS/ERP implementation have been studied fairly extensively. Some of these CSFs are expected to be less important in EIS/ERP upgrade projects, due to experience gained with the systems by organizations adopting these systems. Critical success factors which lead to successful information systems projects have been found to include:

◆ Business process reengineering.
◆ Business vision.
◆ Communication.
◆ External support.
◆ Internal support.
◆ Organizational culture and change.
◆ Project champion.
◆ Project management.
◆ Top management support.
◆ Training & education.
◆ User involvement.

Olson and Zhao (2007)[11] used an in-depth semi-structured interview technique to examine the success factors in EIS/ERP upgrade. Companies who reported that their organization's EIS/ERP upgrade was completed the previous year (some were finishing up their upgrade project) were included. Fifteen IT managers were interviewed. A wide variety of industries were represented in the responses. In addition to the questions about EIS/ERP upgrade projects, CIOs were asked to rank the relative importance of critical success factors in each project phase. Table 9.2 reviews characteristics of organizations interviewed.

More details about these upgrade projects are given in Table 9.3. The vendor for each organization is given, with the year of upgrade and the

---

[11] Olson, D. L. and Zhao, F. (2007). CIO's perspectives of critical success factors in ERP upgrade projects. *Enterprise Information Systems*, 1(1), 129–138.

Table 9.2: Sample Demographics.

Organization	Industry sector	Annual gross revenue	Number of employees	EIS/ERP vendor
A	Industrial Manufacturing	9 Billion	60,000	JD Edwards
B	Public Sector	1 Billion	3,000	JD Edwards
C	Consumer Products	3 Billion	6,500	Oracle
D	High Technology	1.1 Billion	2,000	Oracle
E	Agriculture	100 Million	200	Oracle
F	Education	500 Million	6,000	PeopleSoft
G	Healthcare	850 Million	6,000	PeopleSoft
H	Education	800 Million	11,000	SAP
I	Industrial Manufacturing	2.6 Billion	24,400	SAP
J	Industrial Manufacturing	19 Billion	84,000	SAP
K	High Technology	200 Million	200	SAP
L	Utilities	200 Million	1,100	SAP
M	Banking	1 Billion	86,000	mySAP
N	Distillery	2.7 Billion	3,400	mySAP
O	Industrial Manufacturing	100 Million	100	Syspro

upgrade project's duration. The reasons given for the upgrade are provided as well as problems encountered during the upgrade project.

These upgrade projects took between 2.5 months (a local system, with no customization) to 11 months (a more complex organizational structure with heavy training requirements). Customization may be needed by organizations, but will incur costs in time (and thus money). The assessment phase was often quite short, ranging from two weeks to a month typically, although larger organizations took longer because of the need to obtain corporate approval. Planning and action phases were relatively consistent. We would conclude that upgrade projects involve lower levels of risk and uncertainty (and thus variance) than initial installations because the organization is very familiar with what the system should do. The renewal phase (putting the system on-line) was very short, typically less than two weeks. With proper project management, overnight or a weekend would suffice.

The reasons for upgrade included 11 cases where some new functionality was desired (to include things like supporting Web access). There

Table 9.3: Upgrade Project Reasons.

	Vendor	Upgrade	Months	Why	Problems
A	JDE	2004	5	End of service pending New functionality (Web)	Scalability, solved by JDE
B	JDE One World	2005	9	End of service pending New functionality	Customization needed
C	Oracle	2005	5	Web functionality	Customization for CRM, dropped project
D	Oracle	2005	7	Web functionality	None
E	Oracle to 11i	2004	6	Web functionality	Dropped unhelpful consultant
F	PeopleSoft	2004	9	End of service pending New functionality	None
G	PeopleSoft	2004	7	Integrate modules	None
H	SAP	2004/5	11	End of service pending Better vendor support	Training scheduling (many users)
I	SAP to 4.6B	2003	5	New functionality End of service pending	None
J	SAP to 4.7	2004	4	Fix bug	Problems with TMS add-on
K	SAP (mySAP)	2005	3	Web functionality	None
L	SAP to 4.7	2004	3	Better vendor support	Testing (some repeats)
M	mySAP	2005	5	New functionality	None
N	mySAP	2004	8	e-business, currency	None
O	Syspro Impact	2003	6	New functionality	Needed patch to FedEx, UPS

were five cases among the fifteen where the vendor had announced discontinuance of service. Two cases cited the desire to obtain better vendor support. Another case cited the need to fix a bug in the existing system, and another to integrate modules.

There were far fewer problems involved in upgrade projects than are typically reported in initial EIS/ERP installations. This is to be expected, due to the experience gained with the system by the organization. Customization was a problem in two cases, one where customization was needed to provide adequate service (case B), and another (case C) where customization to implement a CRM add-on led to dropping this additional desired functionality. A problematic consultant was a problem in case E. There also were problems with a TMS add-on in case J, and needed links to delivery vendors was a problem overcome in case O. Scalability was initially a problem in case A, but was resolved by the vendor. Some repeated testing was reported in one case, and the difficulty of dealing with massive retraining reported in another. Thus a variety of different problems can be expected in EIS/ERP upgrade projects, but for the most part these challenges are easier to overcome than is the case in initial implementation projects.

1. EIS/ERP upgrade projects are easier to control than initial installation projects, because organizations have gained experience (often the hard way) and the organizational users have a better idea of what to expect.
2. Vendor marketing drives many upgrades. Beatty and Williams argue that this is due to vendor product improvement, which we admit undoubtedly plays a role. Vendor greed might also be a factor. Therefore, organizations should consider alternatives such as application service providers, based upon a sound business case analysis.
3. Upgrade phases are important to consider, with some factors being more important in one phase than they are in others (shown in Table 9.3).

The 15 organizations were quite consistent in their selection of critical success factors by phase. Business vision was selected by most organizations in the assessment phase. Top management support was selected by 12 of the 15 organizations in this phase. Four organizations also selected communication.

In the planning phase, there was unanimity that project management was the most important success factor. Communication was selected as second in importance by 14 of the organizations. Six selected external support, which would emphasize the need to work with vendors.

In the action phase, project management continued to be selected as important (12 of 15 organizations). User involvement was also usually cited as important in the action phase (12 out of 15 organizations). Two organizations identified the need for a positive organizational culture. They were the multinational organizations. The other organizations were smaller in geographical scope. In addition, seven organizations emphasized the need for training. Customization was tabbed by three organizations, and one included the value of a project champion.

The renewal phase was quite short in most of the cases. All organizations (even those currently undergoing their upgrade projects) cited the need (or expectation) that user involvement was important. Five also cited the need for external support (from vendors). Only two emphasized communication which help users understand the new policies after the upgrades.

Of the expected list of upgrade critical success factors, business process reengineering and internal supports were not mentioned by any of the 15 organizations. Evidently, BPR is already accomplished in the original project, and wasn't as critical in the upgrade projects. Internal support was probably developed to the extent needed by the organization's prior experience.

9.5 CONCLUSION

One of the benefits you will notice upon the implementation of an enterprise resource planning system is that cost will go down while productivity will go up. As previously stated, employees will no longer need to wait on other employees and departments because all the information can be accessed by anyone. This allows employees to perform their jobs faster, which in turn provides them with the opportunity to take on more tasks. In addition, a company will notice fewer maintenance calls and repairs. Since there would be only one program instead of multiple programs, then the amount of maintenance a company will experience automatically goes down. The lower amount of maintenance can also be seen in terms of money. Many times, when a product needs maintenance, work has to stop until after the maintenance is complete. This can be costly; however, if a company has fewer maintenance calls and repairs, then the number of costly work delays is also diminished.

EIS/ERP upgrade projects have grown in importance, as vendors are seeking to generate revenue through improved systems. The reticence of vendors to support old systems was noted by multiple organizations in this study. (The value of improved functionality was also noted.)

Upgrade projects seem to be much more controllable than initial EIS/ERP installation projects. This should be expected due to the experience organizations gain with their original systems. All the organizations seemed to do something that fit the theoretical model of an upgrade project that we used. Assessment, planning, and action phases were present to at least some degree. The renewal phase noted by the 15 organizations involved very smooth turnover. A limitation of the study is that future implications were not yet available in all cases (problems may crop up later), although all organizations credited strong planning and project management as ways to assure smooth transitions.

EIS/ERP upgrade projects were shown to be less problematic that initial EIS/ERP installations, which in retrospect, may seem obvious. However, the 15 cases clearly show that some factors are more critical in different phases. And clearly careful planning is needed to attain success. It is recommended that future studies apply quantitative methods to evaluate the results from this qualitative study.

However, should you need corrective maintenance in the event a component is faulty, or needs repairing, our qualified specialists swiftly take the necessary measures, be it replacing a component, supplying spare parts or recovering lost data. Together with you, we define the appropriate service levels such as guaranteed response time, extended hours or even 7/24 on call.

The important point with respect to maintenance is that EIS offers 24×7 support and maintenance services which facilitate in reducing the total cost of ownership and frees up critical IT resources for its clients.

Enterprise Systems maintenance plays a vital role in defining Service Level Agreements at the outset of a maintenance assignment so that its clients are assured of assistance from a defined services level.

☆ KEYWORDS

☆ **Analysis and design:** Transforms the requirements into a design of the system-to-be and adapts that design to match the implementation environment, designing it for performance. The analyst can discover flaws in design. Change requests are generated and applied. Business entities in the business modeling discipline are also an input to identifying analysis and design solutions.

☆ **Business modeling:** Provides guidance for the analyst on how to understand and visually depict a business.

☆ **Configuration and change management:** Supports the analyst with the process of change, ensuring that changes are effectively documented and accepted during the lifecycle of the project. This also allows the analyst and those in other roles to do impact analysis.

☆ **Corporate Strategy:** Degree of strategic fit of a business function to the selected corporate strategies is measured by executives of a firm. This can be abstracted to "Strategic Fit".

☆ **Deployment:** Describes the activities associated with ensuring that the software product and related materials are available for end users. The analyst produces the software requirements specification, which is one of the key input to development end user support and training materials.

☆ **Design:** Data structures, software architecture, interface representations, algorithmic.

☆ **Environment:** Develops and maintains the supporting artifacts that the analyst uses during requirements management and modeling.

☆ **Implementation:** Defines the organization of code, implements classes and objects, tests the resulting implementation elements, and integrates them into an executable system. This discipline includes developer testing — that is, testing done by developers to verify that each developed element behaves as intended. This behavior derives ultimately, although often indirectly, from requirements captured by the analyst.

☆ **Project management:** Plans the project and each iteration and phase of the project. The requirements artifacts, particularly the requirements management plan, are important input to the planning activities. The driving forces behind the assessment and management activities are the requirements.

☆ **Requirements:** Involves finding, maintaining and managing requirements for the business application. The business models developed in the business modeling discipline are a key input to these activities.

☆ **Test:** Validates the system against (amongst other things) the requirements, ensuring that the system works properly. Requirements artifacts provided by the analyst are the basis for the definition of the evaluation activities.

☆ TERMINOLOGY REVIEW

1. What are the driving forces for the system change to an EIS/ERP architecture?
2. Is there a strategic plan in place to guide the deployment of the new EIS/ERP system?
3. What are the specific principles that guided system development as part of the strategic plan?
4. Looking back at the implementation process, what are those factors that critically determined implementation success or failure?
5. On a post-implementation basis, what actions are taken to enhance system functionality, review the system's service potential, or evaluate user acceptance?
6. Could specific success factors be identified that were discovered during the post-implementation phase of the system life cycle? What tools are used for their measurement, if any?
7. What is a potential functionality of an Enterprise System in our organization?

8. What can the system cover?
9. What are the advantages of such a system maintenance?
10. What is the possible structure of an Enterprise System for the company?
11. What should we consider in implementing the new integrated system?
12. What are the factors affecting the selection of implementation projects?

☆ SUGGESTED READING

Journals

Akkermans, H. and Van Helden, K. (2002). Vicious and virtuous cycles in ERP implementation: A case study of interrelations between critical success factors. *European Journal of Information Systems*, 11(1), 35–46.

Al-Mashari, M. (2003). Enterprise resource planning (ERP) systems: A research agenda. *Industrial Management and Data Systems*, 103(1), 22–27.

Al-Mashari, M., Al-Mudimigh, A. and Zairi, M. (2003). Enterprise resource planning: A taxonomy of critical factors. *European Journal of Operational Research*, 146(2), 352–364.

Ang, J. and Teo, T. S. H. (2000). Management Issues in Data Warehousing: Insights from the Housing and Development Board. *Decision Support Systems*, 29(1), 11–20.

Chenn, J. (2001). Planning for ERP systems: Analysis and future trend. *Business Process Management Journal*, 7(5), 374–386.

Davenport, T. (2000). Mission Critical: Realizing the Promise of Enterprise Systems. Boston: Harvard Business School Press.

Kumar, K. and Hillegersberg, J. (2000). ERP experiences and evolution. *Communications of the ACM*, 43(4), 23–26.

Nah, F. F., Lau, J. L. and Kuang, J. (2001). Critical factors of successful implementation of enterprise systems. *Business Process Management Journal*, 7(3), 285–296.

White Papers

DeLone, W. H. and McLean, E. R. (2002). Information Systems Success Revisited. *Proceedings of the 35th Hawaii International Conference on System Sciences.*

Zhang, L., Zhang, Z. and Banerjee, P. (2002). Critical Success Factors of Enterprise Resource Planning Systems Implementation Success in China. *36th Hawaii International Conference on System Sciences.*

Online Resources

http://www.knacksystems.com/support.html
http://enriqsoft.blogspot.com/2007/12/system-mechanic-7543.html

CHAPTER 10

BUSINESS INTELLIGENCE SYSTEMS AND EIS

Quotation

Today the cutting edge technologies reside with consumers. From there, this technology filters into the enterprise. This fundamental shift means application vendors will have to give users what they want: Sophisticated applications in an easy-to-understand wrapper.

Don Campbell

Structure

♣ QUICK LOOK AT CHAPTER THEMES

Over the years, data sources grow in number and size. Managers, supervisors and executive teams have obtained key information from many EIS applications. As per the wikipedia,[1] 2006, "Business intelligence entails the gathering of data from internal and external

---

[1] The Free Encyclopedia, http://en.wikipedia.org (accessed 17 July 2006).

data sources, as well as the storing and analysis thereof to make it accessible to assist in better decision-making." *Business intelligence (BI) is arguably the most important enterprise application in an organization. BI is the technology and practice of applying information to make decisions. In this way, BI is different than data warehousing, which is more about storing information. It is also more comprehensive than data mining. Information shows its real value when many people can use and share it. This is the goal of business intelligence.[2] Figure 10.1 gives a brief idea about the BI with the help of a diagram.*

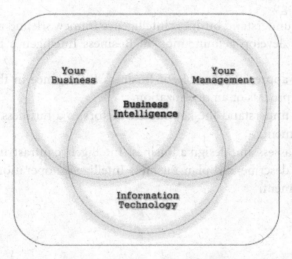

Figure 10.1:   BI the Intersection of IT, Management, Business.

Source: sju-online[3]

---

[2] Cognos, an IBM company, is the world leader in business intelligence (BI) and performance management solutions. It provides world-class enterprise BI, planning and consolidation software and services to help companies plan, understand and manage financial and operational performance. Cognos brings together technology, analytical applications, best practices, and a broad network of partners to give customers a complete performance solution. It provides an open and adaptive solution that leverages an organization's ERP, packaged applications, and database investments.

[3] http://www.sju-online.com/programs/business-intelligence-masters.asp

♣ LEARNING OBJECTIVES

The objective of this chapter is to give students an understanding of various aspects of business intelligence systems and knowledge management with a managerial focus. Specifically, the areas include:

- ♣ Concepts to understand the role of business intelligence in the fields of marketing, finance, human resources, and production.
- ♣ How to gain fundamental understanding of Business Intelligence technologies.
- ♣ How to develop a decision-making approach to business intelligence technology.
- ♣ How to understand business intelligence framework and architecture.
- ♣ How to develop a foundation in Business Intelligence for Business Analysis.
- ♣ How to appreciate the role of Business Intelligence in the decision-making process of an organization.
- ♣ How to understand the key success factors in a business intelligence environment.
- ♣ How to assess and design a Business Intelligence infrastructure.
- ♣ How to describe and plan Business Intelligence operations and their management.

♣ CASE STUDY

National Scorecard Transforms How Best Buy Does Business

Best Buy[4] is North America's number-one specialty retailer of consumer electronics, personal computers, entertainment software and appliances. With over 700 stores nationwide and rapid growth continuing, Best Buy needed an application that was simple to use, delivered consistent information on which to run the business, and was intuitive enough to be used by everyone in the company.

SUMMARY

With disparate data sources and fragmented reports, a solution was needed to align 90,000 employees in making decisions based on timely, consistent information. The result was a national scorecard that now serves as a single source graphical representation of information that unifies priorities, tracking and reporting on key business areas.

ABOUT LANCET

Lancet has been able to retain top-notch employees due to our award-winning work environment. Our culture fosters open discussion, teamwork and creativity with a constant emphasis on training and growth. Many clients have found our style to be pleasantly contagious; they hear our feedback in the form of business advice and we encourage and welcome their feedback. Lancet has created a process for interaction and idea exchange among our employees, allowing us to continue learning as individuals and as a company. When you hire a Lancet employee, you get the benefit of the whole Lancet team, including formalized quality assurance, support and an internal knowledge base. Our employees are enthusiastic and not only thrive on learning and mastering new technologies, but also on sharing their knowledge with one another and our clients.

---

[4] Best Buy Co., Inc. is a specialty retailer of consumer electronics in the United States accounting for 19% of the market. Best Buy is sometimes called the "big blue box" because of the prominent design on Best Buy stores. One can go through the website at http://www.bestbuy.com/.

THE SITUATION

Historically, Best Buy had several disparate data sources with various users having access to relatively small sets of metrics producing fragmented reports while the demand for information and more complex ad-hoc reporting continued to increase exponentially. The data that would satisfy the demand was neither contained nor accessible within one data source, nor could employees access key information. And, out-of-the-box analysis software was not sophisticated enough to provide the ad-hoc drilling needed to make decisions based on root cause analysis. With no way to access and analyze the information essential to drive this fast-paced transaction-oriented business, Best Buy turned to Lancet for help.

THE SOLUTION

For seven years, Best Buy looked for a partner that was business savvy with IT vision and technical expertise to deliver an application that would feed critical information to every channel in the company, driving daily workflow, and do it all at a low cost of ownership. There was no centralized data repository, no clear path from key information to its root cause for analysis, no way to custom drill, nor a way to perform ad-hoc inquiries and get reports to retail without putting IT processes at risk. "Lancet was the only company we found that could realize our vision. They brought strategy, thought-leadership and business intelligence expertise," said Brad Elo, Director, Margin Enhancement Strategies. With years of business intelligence experience, Lancet worked with Best Buy's internal team to develop the technology strategy that delivered on Best Buy's vision. They also played a key role in executing the plan — mapping out logical connections and creating a custom functional, workflow-based drilling architecture and ad-hoc reporting system for the enterprise-wide national scorecard which has become a cornerstone application within Best Buy because of the way it has transformed the business. The resulting solution allows the business to get the information they need directly without going to IT, resulting in lower costs while maintaining the security and integrity of the production systems. In addition, the complexities and technical challenges are easily managed behind the scenes while employees are presented with a front-end that is simple to use and intuitive yet extremely powerful. "Lancet continues to play a key role in the project, including long term vision for the application," adds Elo.

THE RESULTS

Companywide, the national scorecard is the key to Best Buy's marketing and company intelligence. It is the single source that aligns and unifies the retail organization's priorities, tracking and reporting on key business areas, presenting information to users at all levels in the company in a format that is meaningful to them. The application touches every aspect of the business and keeps all 90,000 employees informed and focused on the same consistent information across the enterprise. Everyday these reports guide proactive behaviors essential to keeping Best Buy in the forefront of the fast-paced, consumer electronics retail business. Each week, over 1 million reports are generated that present accurate snapshots of the business from all angles. For the first time, employees at the stores can get useful customer information and understand what items or categories are "hot," answering key questions about what customers need and how sales associates can better interact in order to enhance the customer experience and foster passionate customer loyalty. Best Buy is more proactive and responds rapidly because trends can easily be identified. Problem areas or issues can be set to, "What If," scenarios, and access to data and response time is immediate. Plus, the data resources are so unified and rich that drilling anywhere is possible. Operations can see up-to-date labor allocation, usage, and spending. Sales performance metrics are readily accessible and time spent in front of the computer has been reduced, allowing store personnel more time with the customers. Retail behavior can be immediately adjusted and better paths to action are employed. With accurate, consistent information at their fingertips, employees know what to do and what not to do everyday. The return on investment is astonishing. For each $1 spent on the scorecard application, Best Buy yields a $4 return. Says Elo, "Lancet turned our vision into reality, transforming the way we do business — from the CEO to store management to customer specialists — with insight into information that helps us proactively manage our business while delivering a four-fold return on investment." The possibilities for the future of the national scorecard are endless and Lancet will play an integral part. "Our national scorecard has proved itself to be the most strategic application in the company. It keeps all 90,000 employees focused on the key business drivers that give us the competitive advantage not possible before. Working with Lancet is a big win for Best Buy," concludes Elo.

Source: Lancet Software.[5]

♣ SKETCH OF BI RELEVANCE TO EIS

In today's rapidly moving and progressively more digital world, it is necessary to comprehend advancing technologies in order to accomplish anything. Business leaders need the capability to accumulate and digest information concerning customers, suppliers and competitors, and to formulate decisions that positively influence their company's performance. Enterprise systems offer powerful tools to better measure and control organizational operations. Many organizations have found that this valuable tool can be enhanced to provide even greater value through the addition of powerful business intelligence systems. Business intelligence guru Ralph Kimball defines business intelligence as "a generic term to describe leveraging the organization's information assets for making better business decisions."[6] Business intelligence in this context is supported by storing data (data warehouse and related systems) and conducting studies using this data to solve business problems (one means to do this is through data-mining). Figure 10.2 describes a view of how business intelligence can be built.

One of the most popular forms of data mining in EIS systems is support of customer relationship management (CRM). Data warehouses are one of the most popular extensions to EIS systems, with over two-thirds

---

[5] Lancet Software was founded in 1997 to provide business intelligence services. It has successfully completed hundreds of business intelligence and web development projects with its partners. © Copyright 2008.
[6] Kimball, R. and Ross, M. (2002). *The Data Warehouse Toolkit*, 2nd Ed. New York, NY: John Wiley and Sons.

Building Business Intelligence

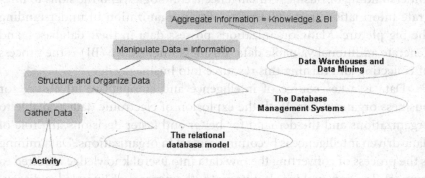

Figure 10.2:   Building Business Intelligence.

Source: Exonous (2004).[7]

of U.S. manufacturers adopting or planning such systems (and slightly less than two-thirds of Swedish manufacturers doing the same).[8] This chapter discusses forms of data storage available. It also introduces data mining concepts, and reviews typical data mining applications within EIS systems.

♣ INTRODUCTION

Engaging in e-commerce is not a decision that should be made without first gaining knowledge about the firm and its relationships with its customers, competitors, suppliers, and other external entities. Business Intelligence (BI) is the activity of gathering information about the elements in the environment that interact with the firm. Business Intelligence endows you with a diverse business education in the field of technology and decision sciences and helps you to develop the capability to generate

---

[7] http://exonous.typepadc.com/mis/2004/03/building_busine.html
[8] Mabert, V. M., Soni, A. and Venkataramanan, M. A. (2000). Enterprise resource planning survey of US manufacturing firms. *Production and Inventory Management Journal*, 41(20), 52–58; Olhager J. and Selldin, E. (2003). Enterprise resource planning survey of Swedish manufacturing firms. *European Journal of Operational Research*, 146, 365–373.

business models for forecasting and business analysis, a fundamental understanding of Business Intelligence technologies, and the skills to integrate information from all aspects of the organization in understanding the big picture. Many organizations possess data in their databases, and generate additional valuable data. Business Intelligence (BI) is the process of collecting and turning this resource into business value.

Data is a key source of intelligence and competitive advantage for business organizations. With the explosion of electronic data available to organizations and the demand for better and faster decisions, the role of data-driven intelligence is becoming central in organizations. Data mining is the process of converting the raw data into useful knowledge required to support decision-making. It automates the process of knowledge discovery, providing us with greatly enhanced productivity in our search for useful information than we would be otherwise. It also increases the confidence with which we can make business decisions. In this age of the so-called information democracy, each employee of a company has the right to appropriate access to information. This alone (and there are many other reasons) turns the entire company into a potential business intelligence user base. This chapter will examine the value of information in a competitive environment from the perspectives of various types of business information, cost and management of information, developments on the Internet, and the role of governments. In addition, discerning client needs, and the packaging of information for client use are considered. The chapter will begin with the definition of business information, and work through specific types of information including company research, industry research and understanding statistics. The latter half of the chapter will focus on giving students an overview of the important trends in business research: competitive intelligence, knowledge management, and learning how to make a business case to support the decision to implement expensive information products. Virtually every business organization these days is in the process of exploring and implementing data mining solutions to core business problems. This chapter is essential for anyone interested in understanding how to get the maximum value from data, especially when abundant data are available. Application areas covered include marketing, customer relationship management, financial forecasting, risk management, personalization, Web searching, and other topics.

10.1 ALL ABOUT BI

There are a number of definitions of Business intelligence:

♦ BI as a term that encompasses a broad range of analytical software and solutions for gathering, consolidating, analyzing and providing access to information in a way that is supposed to let an enterprise's users make better business decisions.[9]

♦ BI benefits that facilitate the connections in the new-form organization, bringing real-time information to centralized repositories and support analytics that can be exploited at every horizontal and vertical level within and outside the firm.[10]

♦ BI includes an effective data warehouse and also a reactive component capable of monitoring the time-critical operational processes to allow tactical and operational decision-makers to tune their actions according to the company strategy.[11]

♦ BI as the result of in-depth analysis of detailed business data, including database and application technologies, as well as analysis practices.[12]

♦ BI as a technically much broader tool, including potentially knowledge management, ERP, decision support systems and data mining.[13]

[9] Adelman, S., Moss, L. and Barbusinski, L. (2002). I found several definitions of BI. *DM Review*, www.dmreview.com/article_sub.cfm?articleId (accessed 10 Sep 2008).

[10] Malhotra, Y. (2000). From information management to knowledge management: Beyond hi-tech hidebound systems. In *Knowledge Management*, Srikantaiah, T. K. and Koenig, M. E. D. (eds.), Medford, NJ: Information Today.

[11] Golfareelli, M., Rizzi, S. and Cella, L. (2004). Beyond data warehousing: What's next in business intelligence? *Proceedings of DOLAP-04*, Washington, DC, USA. www.acm.org (accessed May 17, 2006).

[12] Gangadharan, G. R. and Swamy, N. S. (2004). Business intelligence systems: Design and implementation strategies. *Proceedings of 26th International Conference on Information Technology Interfaces*, Cavtat, Croatia. http://ieeexplore.ieee.org/xpls/abs_all. jsp?arnumber=?1372391 (accessed March 15, 2007).

[13] Gangadharan, G. R. and Swamy, N. S. (2004), Business intelligence systems: Design and implementation strategies. *Proceedings of 26th International Conference on Information Technology Interfaces*, Cavtat, Croatia. http://ieeexplore.ieee.org/xpls/abs_all. jsp?arnumber=?1372391 (accessed March 15, 2007).

Roadmap to embrace Business Intelligence

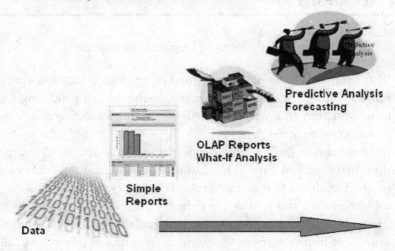

Figure 10.3: Roadmap to Business Intelligence.

Source: Analytics works (2006).[14]

Figure 10.3 sketches the evolution of business intelligence from simple data to support business decision-making.

10.1.1 What is Business Intelligence?

Business Intelligence (BI) is about getting the right information to the right decision-makers at the right time. It is an enterprise-wide platform that supports reporting, analysis and decision-making. BI leads to fact-based decision-making and a "single version of the truth." It also includes reporting and analytics. It facilitates organizational improvement through providing business insights to all employees leading to better, faster, more relevant decisions in the areas of:

♦ Advanced Analytics.
♦ Self Service Reporting.

---

[14] Analyticsworks is a professional services firm that helps medium and large enterprises leverage the business intelligence to make better decisions. http://www.analyticsworks.com

- End-User Analysis.
- Business Performance Management.
- Operational Applications.
- Embedded Analytics.

Business Intelligence is the process of intelligence gathering applied to business. This can be viewed as consisting of four stages in business intelligence development. The first three steps are often repeated several times before the fourth step is taken and the cycle completed, as shown in Figure 10.4.

The term "Business Intelligence" and its acronym "BI" are so pervasive in today's data-intensive lexicon that it's a challenge to know just what to make of it. If you add in all the new trendy terminology such as business process management (BPM), data mining, data warehousing, business process automation, decision support systems, query and reporting systems, enterprise performance management, executive information systems (EIS), business activity monitoring (BAM), modeling and visualization,

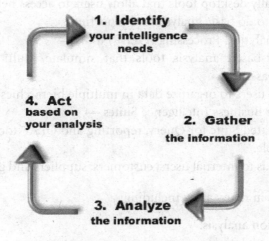

Figure 10.4: Business Intelligence Stages.

Source: FAQ (2006).[15]

---

[15] FAQ is to provide a one-stop Business Intelligence service business be the collection, analysis or distribution of information. http://www.faq.co.za/genl/index.shtm Copyright © 2000–2006

and so forth, your head can start spinning. A Technology Evaluation Center article by Mukhles Zaman entitled in "Business Intelligence: Its Ins and Outs" said in its Technology Evaluation 10 January 2005 issues. BI is neither a product nor a system. It is an umbrella term that combines architecture, applications, and databases. It enables the real-time, interactive access, analysis, and manipulation of information, which provides the business community with easy access to business data. BI analyzes historical data — the data businesses generate through transactions or by other kinds of business activities — and helps businesses by analyzing the past and present business situations and performances. By giving this valuable insight, BI helps decision-makers make more informed decisions and supplies end users with critical business information on their customers or partners, including information on behaviors and trends." To put it in simpler terms, BI makes the right information available in the right format to the right person at the right time. There are a variety of tools enabling BI including:

- ◆ Query and Reporting Tools —
    - ➤ Typically desktop tools that allow users to access networked databases to do basic analysis and reporting.
- ◆ Online Analytical Processing (OLAP) tools —
    - ➤ Server-based analysis tools that simulate Multi Dimensional Databases.
    - ➤ Allow users to organize data in multiple hierarchies.
- ◆ Enterprise Business Intelligence Suites —
    - ➤ Integrated Suite for Query, reporting and OLAP tools.
    - ➤ Scalable.
    - ➤ Extends to internal users, customers, suppliers and general public.

We can use BI in many areas including:

- ◆ Competition analysis.
- ◆ Customer analytics.
- ◆ Enhanced Customer Relationship Management.
- ◆ Better decision-making.
- ◆ Market examination.
- ◆ Risk scrutiny.
- ◆ Site selection.
- ◆ Territory management.

10.1.2 Business Intelligence System Architecture

A phrase coined by (or at least popularized by) Gartner Group defines BI as any computerized process used to extract and/or analyze business data. The organization engenders Business Intelligence (BI) by entering raw transactional data into a Data Mart or Data Warehouse, and generates decision support systems capabilities by means of Query, OLAP and Data Mining access tools. Components of BI can include Data Mart, Data Warehouse, OLAP and Data Mining models which are described in the following paragraphs. The architecture of BI is shown in Figure 10.5.

A successful BI architecture has four parts, as given below:

1. **Information Architecture:** The information architecture defines what business application systems are needed to access, report, and analyze

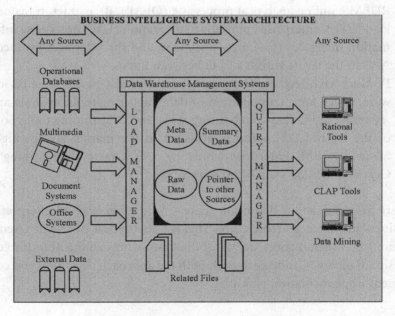

Figure 10.5:   Business Intelligence Architecture.

Source: Dataquest.[16]

---

[16] DQIndia website is the online version of the print magazine Dataquest, referred to as the Bible of Indian IT. http://dqindia.ciol.com/.

information to enable business decision-making. It includes BI systems and business analytics applications used for reporting and analysis.

2. **Data Architecture:** The data architecture defines the data, source systems, and framework for transforming data into useful information. It begins with the sources (the information provider) and ends with the business user (the information consumer). It includes defining information requirements; determining the source of data; defining business rules and transformations; and moving, storing, formatting, and enabling access to the data. Transformations are used to create dimensions, i.e., create a common product, customer, and employee reference data; reformat data between source systems to enable common processing; handle data quality issues; and prepare data content, context, and structure for reporting and analysis.

3. **Technical Architecture:** The technical architecture defines the technology of the products and infrastructure. Technologies include RDBMS, online analytical processing (OLAP), BI, extract, transform, load (ETL), enterprise application integration (EAI), enterprise information interfaces (EII), networks, OSs, and the interfaces/protocols/APIs in the layers within and in between them.

4. **Product Architecture:** The product architecture includes the BI software, which are a combination of data-capturing tools, analysis-and-reporting tools, data-warehousing tools, and data-mining tools. Some of the BI and DM software available in the market are Intelligent Miner by IBM, Enterprise Miner by SAS, Oracle Data Mining by Oracle, and SPSS Data Mining by SPSS.

Apart from the above definition there is one other way of interpreting Business intelligence architecture. This is a theoretical BI sketch given in Figure 10.6 which is constructive for illustrating how all the BI technology fits simultaneously, and assists with both the approach definition and consequent implementation planning.

10.1.3 Business Intelligence Vendors

Many products are used in business intelligence. Some of these are listed in Table 10.1.

Other vendors include companies displayed in Figure 10.7.

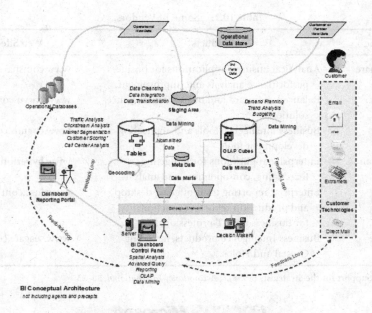

Figure 10.6:   BI Conceptual Architecture.

Source: Electrosmart Ltd (2008).[17]

Some features of various vendors include:

1. SAP

SAP NetWeaver 2004s BI has the following most important new features:

♦ The Enterprise Services Architecture (ESA).
♦ The Enterprise Data Warehouse (EDW).
♦ Real-time data warehousing (DWH).
♦ Information lifecycle management and the use of nearline storage.
♦ Clustering, partitioning (repartitioning), and remodeling functions.
♦ The new extraction, transformation, and loading (ETL) process including transformation rules and data-transfer process (DTP).
♦ The Business Intelligence Accelerator (BIA) including its search and classification functions (TREX).

---

[17] The BI vision is documented in a BI strategy document to ensure that implementation of specific technology or a data structure remains focused on the BI objectives for a particular organisation. http://www.thebusinessintelligenceguide.com/bi_strategy/BI_Strategy_Document.php.

Table 10.1: Some BI Vendors.

Name	Products	Web Site
Comshare	Analytical business applications for business performance analysis and improvement.	www.comsharc.com
CorVu	Balanced scorecard and business intelligence solutions.	www.corvu.com
Cognos	Business intelligence tools and application development tools.	www.cognos.com
Hyperian	Enterprise applications for budgeting, forecasting, consolidation, and analysis.	www.hyperion.com
IQ	Enterprise reporting tools offering desktop and production reporting functionality for business and IT professionals.	www.iqsc.com
Seagate	Business Intelligence products, including Crystal and Holos.	www.seagate.com

Source: Support for the Strategists (1998).[18] *Accountancy International*, 50–53.

Figure 10.7: List of additional BI vendors.

Source: Avocado Security (2007).[19]

---

[18] Integrated Information System (IIS) and *Management Accounting*, www.cbs.dk

[19] Avocado Security is the first provider of cross-platform BI & Security On-Demand service. Avocado Security's business intelligence optimization platform help clients reach new untapped potential. To enable security and business intelligence information sharing across the organization, Avocado Security provides a web based On-Demand platform. http://www.avocadosecurity.com

- Advanced analytics applications.
- BI-integrated planning.
- Composite Application Framework (CAF) and barrier-free applications including.
- Visual Composer.
- Data Warehousing Workbench (DWB).
- NetWeaver architecture and within the closed-loop process (see Figure 10.8).

2. Microsoft

- Make it affordable:
  - ➢ Centers around a belief that today's BI tools are specialized and expensive.
  - ➢ Microsoft will focus on affordability and lower TCO.

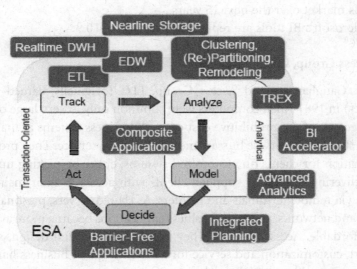

Figure 10.8:   The Most Important Features of SAP NetWeaver 2004 BI.

Source: SAP NetWeaver 2004s Business Intelligence.[20]

---

[20] SAP NetWeaver is SAP's integrated technology platform and is the technical foundation for all SAP applications since the SAP Business Suite SAP NetWeaver is marketed as a service-oriented application and integration platform. SAP NetWeaver provides the development and runtime environment for SAP applications and can be used for custom development and integration with other applications and systems. www.sap.com/platform/netweaver/index.epx

- ◆ Leverage the Microsoft investment already made by clients:
  - ➤ End-to-end solution leveraging Microsoft SQL Server™, Microsoft Office®, Microsoft Office SharePoint® Server and Performance Management Applications.
  - ➤ Focus on the end-user's experience with Microsoft Office and the desire to "Stop Building Tools for Analysts."
- ◆ Long-term Commitment:
  - ➤ "We are dead serious about Bi," — Steve Ballmer, CEO, Microsoft Microsoft BI Conference, 11 May 2007, Seattle, WA.

Dan Vesset of IDC has commented: "Microsoft's BI Tools revenue growth in 2005 was more than 25 percent, growing at more than twice the rate of the overall market. ... Microsoft's impact on the BI tools market cannot be overemphasized. This impact will mark an evolutionary change that has been put into motion by the database vendors overall and will reshape the BI tools market over the next 15 years."

Microsoft's BI tools are represented by Figure 10.9.

3. Access Group, LLC

Patrick Gaughan formed Access Group, LLC (originally named Access Services) in 1981 when computers were common only in very large companies. Because of the prohibitive cost of small business systems at that time, Access started as a service bureau and time-sharing service. They processed information for clients on customized systems, either by picking up input and delivering output, or supplied clients with access to their mainframe system via remote terminals and printers. As shared servers, personal computers and networks, and open business applications became more available and affordable, Access adapted. They grew to provide full design, supply, support, customization and service for a broad scope of business hardware and software, with a specialty niche in manufacturing systems. Now, close to 25 years later, almost every skill, tool and product used by Access Group has changed — most of them numerous times as in the following:

- ◆ Every client is a partner.
- ◆ Every need must be addressed with a combination of experience and a fresh perspective.

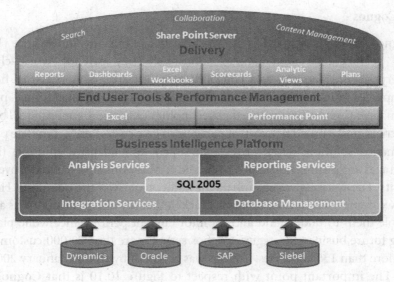

Figure 10.9:   Microsoft BI Architecture.
Source: Microsoft Dynamics (2008).[21]

♦ Every challenge requires a quick response and thorough solution.
♦ Every user must be a reference.
♦ Its pride must result directly from what its clients achieve.

Since 1981 Access Group has assisted hundreds of organizations in installing and utilizing computer systems and technology to improve their performance and to enhance their competitive edge. Access Group has matured and prospered as its clients have succeeded. They advise, guide, train and assist clients throughout changes in the essential systems and best practices that add to their success. Access Group continues to press forward and transform its capabilities, tools, and services to support the varying needs of its clients. For a quarter of a century, in an industry too often known for missed dates and over-sold promises, it has upheld its core value — Access Builds Success.

---

[21] Microsoft Dynamics is a line of business software owned and developed by Microsoft, though the percentage products were originally created by other companies and known by various other names. Dynamics was earlier known by the codename "Project Green". www.microsoft.com/dynamics

4. Cognos

Cognos, an IBM company, is the world leader in business intelligence (BI) and performance management solutions. They provide world-class enterprise BI, planning and consolidation software and services to help companies plan, understand and manage financial and operational performance. Cognos brings together technology, analytical applications, best practices, and a broad network of partners to give customers a complete performance solution. They provide an open and adaptive solution that leverages an organization's ERP, packaged applications, and database investments. The system gives customers the ability to answer the questions: How are we doing? Why are we on or off track? What should we do about it? and enable them to understand and monitor current performance while planning future business strategies. Cognos serves more than 23,000 customers in more than 135 countries. Cognos was acquired by IBM in January 2008.

The important point with respect to Figure 10.10 is that **Cognos 8** is the only BI product that delivers the entire range of BI capabilities

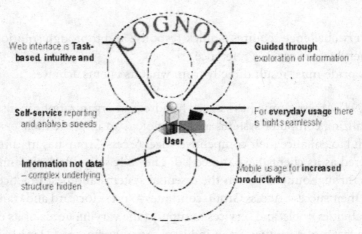

Figure 10.10: Cognos 8 Business Intelligence.

Source: LSA Solutions (2005).[22]

---

[22] LSA was founded in 1996 and is a services-focused, solution specialist Cognos Partner for the Cognos Performance Management suite. LSA Solutions specializes in enterprise-wide Corporate Performance Management (CPM) solutions that help businesses to align business strategies with their execution, measurement and communication. http://www.lsa-solutions.co.uk

covering: Business reporting, Business analysis, Score carding, Dashboards, Business event management etc.

5. Analyticsworks

Analyticsworks is a professional services firm that helps medium and large enterprises leverage business intelligence to make better decisions. Analyticsworks is founded by an experienced team of e-Commerce, retail, consumer finance, technology professionals with years of data analysis and strategy experience. They specialize in initiating business intelligence practice within organizations and delivering valuable solutions generating results quickly, creating immediate and lasting value. Key differentiators include in-depth understanding of vertical relationships, bringing the concept of centers of excellence within the analytics domain and using the best class open source technologies to justify ROI and minimize the total cost of ownership of the BI implementation. Analyticsworks has a high-energy environment that encourages continuous learning. Analyticsworks blends the best of a consulting firm and technical savvy of a service company with the innovative spirit of entrepreneurs.

10.2 DATA STORAGE SYSTEMS

The advent of digit technology has brought with it an increased demand for data storage. There has been tremendous progress in computer storage of data. This area of technology is clearly one where the capacity to do things has outstripped the ways in which business has been able to apply them. However, many applications are being found for this new capacity. One major user of massive storage capacity is EIS systems, which have large storage requirements due to their comprehensive nature.

Accurate information in real time facilitates expansion. Data Storage is the structure that stores private or community data for trouble-free access at whichever time and place. A data-storing and repossession system is consistent, well-organized, error-free and fast, serving diverse applications. To deal with the difficulty of supporting diverse needs,

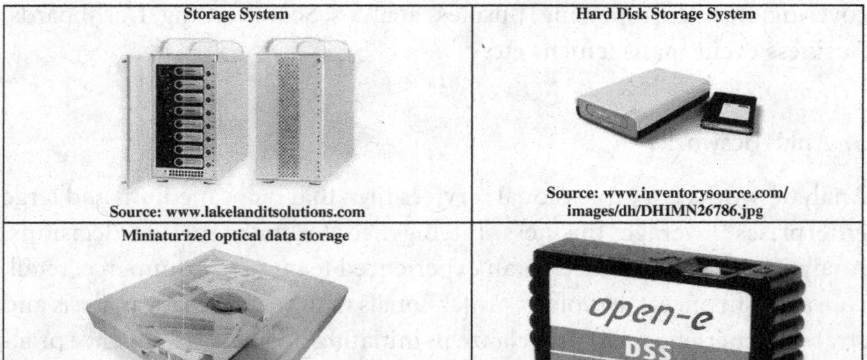

Storage System	Hard Disk Storage System
Source: www.lakelanditsolutions.com	Source: www.inventorysource.com/ images/dh/DHIMN26786.jpg
Miniaturized optical data storage	
Source: http://www.infotech.oulu.fi/ Annual/2002/pics/OPME_datastorage.jpg	Source: http://www.gigaserver.nl/ images/attributes/dss_module_big.jpg
CD and DVD storage management system	Secure data storage system.
Source: www.krome.co.nz/images	Source: http://ecx.images-amazon.com/ images/I/31XPG0RV8PL._SL500_AA280_.jpg

Figure 10.11: Diverse Data Storage Systems.

various categories of data storage systems are accessible including Data Backup Storage, Offsite Data Storage, Media Data Storage and many others as shown in Figure 10.11.

10.2.1 Data Warehousing

Data warehousing is an orderly and accessible repository of known facts and related data that is used as a basis for making better management decisions. Another more complete definition is: "a subject-oriented, integrated, time-variant, and non-volatile collection of data in support of management's decision-making process."[23] Data warehouses provide ready access to information about a company's business, products, and customers. This makes it possible to organize data by subject rather than by process. These systems are used to store massive quantities of data from a variety of sources in an integrated way. The data is identified by a particular time period. Non-volatile means that the data added to the data warehouse is stable after initial formatting and cleaning, and not removed. An additional feature is efficiency, allowing quick retrieval of specific types of data. EISs generate massive amounts of data, and often data warehouses are used to support EISs. Data warehouse systems generally store data in fine granular form which other related systems such as data marts, OLAP, and other forms of decision support systems can summarize or aggregate. Data warehouses also include a metadata repository holding data about the data stored, which ensures data integrity and speedy retrieval. They also have extraction/transformation/loading (ETL) tools enabling data extraction for specific applications. Figure 10.12 shows data warehouses as a centerpoint for storage for many systems.

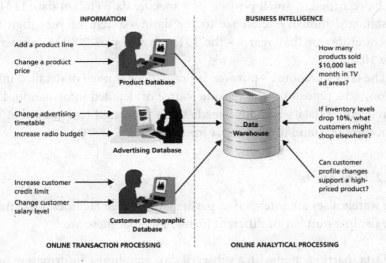

Figure 10.12:   Data warehouse linkages with Information and BI.
Source: Exonous (2004).[24]

---

[23] Inmon, W. (2000). Data mart does not equal data warehouse. DMReview.com.
[24] http://exonous.typepad.com/mis/business_intelligence.jpg

Within data warehouses, data is classified and organized around subjects meaningful to the company such as customers, employees, or products. The data is gathered from operational systems (in addition to EIS generated data, data can be generated by bar-code readers at cash registers, information from e-commerce, daily reports, etc.) and external data sources (industry volumes, economic data, etc.). Data from different sources (shipping, marketing, billing) are integrated to a common format. Transformation also includes filtering data to eliminate unnecessary details, cleaning the data to eliminate incorrect data or duplications, and consolidating data from multiple sources. This transformation, part of the data warehouse management rather than the data mining process, makes accessing data more efficient. To demonstrate these concepts, consider toys sold over the Internet. Many toys are sold each day, with detailed information kept on each sale. The company is organized into regions, and it assigns an item number to each product. Lot numbers are assigned by the source. The data warehouse would deal with **granular** data, information in its rawest form. Within the data warehouse, each transaction may be recorded. A small portion of a specific date (Julian date 1131 — the standard industry reference to the dating system of year digit and sequential day of that year — the 131st day of year 2001) is shown in Table 10.2.

The data warehouse's purpose is permanent storage of detailed information. This repository is a reliable source of detailed information. Data entered into a data warehouse needs to be processed to ensure that it is clean, complete, and in the proper format.

10.2.2 Data Marts

Data warehouses are intended as permanent storage facilities. Data marts can exist in a number of different forms. Three of these are:[25]

1. Data marts created with a subset of data warehouse information, usually focusing on information needed by a specific set of users.

---

[25] Browning D. and Mundy, J. (2001). *Data warehouse design considerations*. Microsoft Corporation, www.msn.com.

Table 10.2: Data Warehouse Example.

Key	Date	Customer	Name	City	Region	Product	Item #	Quant	Lot #	Price	Source	Cost
7332	1131	C129	Kim	Seoul	Intl	Cell phone	B019	120	XY482	39.99	Samsung	10.50
7333	1131	C320	McGraw	Santa Fe	SW	IPOD cord	A001	1	BA2441	18.62	Ericsson	2.50
7334	1131	C320	McGraw	Santa Fe	SW	Camera phone	A059	1	CAB12	59.95	Motorola	13.25
7335	1131	C320	McGraw	Santa Fe	SW	Phone charger	B008	1	F431	8.62	Ericsson	0.62
7336	1131	C289	Terry	Richmond	SE	Nokia decal	C373	576	AZ26	3.59	Nokia	0.25
7337	1131	C151	Doyle	New York	NE	IPOD cord	A001	20	BA436	18.62	Ericsson	2.50
7338	1131	C151	Doyle	New York	NE	Phone charger	B008	200	F431	8.62	Ericsson	0.62
7339	1131	C238	Devlin	Austin	SW	Camera phone	A059	3	CAB12	59.95	Motorola	13.25
7340	1131	C241	Kelly	Orlando	SE	Camera	A007	1	RA69	231.12	Motorola	36.67

2. Free-standing data marts independent of data warehouses, making them a quick and less expensive (although less powerful) means of implementing the data warehouse idea.
3. A prototype for a future full-scale data warehouse.

Data, once stored in a data warehouse, is usually not changed without a compelling reason. In order to apply data mining, an intermediate storage form is used. Data marts are sometimes used to extract specific items of information for data mining analysis (type 1 above). Data marts have a number of advantages. First, they are available for data miners to work with, transforming information to create new variables (such as ratios, or coded data suitable for a specific application) without fear that these transformations will contaminate the data warehouse. Second, only that information expected to be pertinent to the specific data mining analysis is extracted. This vastly reduces the computer time required to process the data, as data marts are expected to contain small subsets of the data warehouse's contents and to have ample space available to generate additional data by transformation. Possible data warehouse linkages are displayed in Figure 10.13.

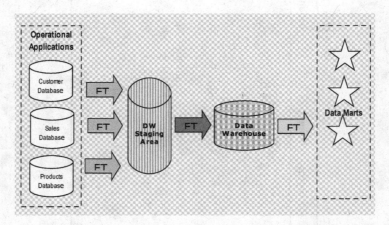

Figure 10.13: Data warehouse linkages with Information and BI.
Source: Data-warehouses.net[26]

---

[26] data-warehouses.net/architecture/datamarts.html

A data mart is interested in data relating to a question under study. For instance, a firm might be interested in examining the characteristics of customers who buy their products. The firm would be interested in response to advertising by mail, advertising by Internet, or advertising by print media. The firm would be interested in who buys by region, as well as the profitability by product, and the effectiveness of advertising in increasing sales by product. The data warehouse would contain much useful information related to these questions.

As with all centralized data systems, technical expertise is required to operate a data mart. However, there is a slight difference in its application from that of a data warehouse. A data warehouse would have permanent staff to operate that system, with an ongoing responsibility to clean and maintain data, and to ensure data integrity and security. A data mart, on the other hand, is typically applied to shorter-term projects, usually with the intent of collecting data for a specific study.

Analysts have choices to make about manipulating currently available information, generating additional information, or purchasing information from vendors. Information available from the data warehouse could include sales volume and profitability figures by time and region. Data marts could extract this data, aggregate it in a form useful for data mining, and keep only that information important for the study at hand (and possibly specify a time frame). But the data warehouse does not include the advertising media that triggered sales. This information would have to be generated by survey. Survey results could be added to the data mart. For observations where survey information is not obtained, the observation might be deleted, or it might be retained with a code for missing data. Additional observations or variable information might be available by purchase from information vendors. A subset of data mart entries for non-vehicular toy products is shown in Table 10.3.

Using raw data from the data warehouse, profit rates are calculated based on multiplying volume by the difference between price and cost, and inserting this in the appropriate data mart column. Customers listed in Figure 10.2 were contacted by survey to identify their media of product introduction. Survey results are appended within the data mart. The data warehouse provided the first five observations presented. External sources were used to supplement the data warehouse results. The last four

Table 10.3: Example of a Data Mart.

Customer #	Region	Item #	Qty.	Profit	Source	Media
C320	Southwest	A001	1	16.12	Ericsson	Internet
C320	Southwest	B008	1	8.00	Ericsson	Print
C289	Mideast	C373	576	3075.84	Nokia	Internet
C151	Northeast	A001	20	322.40	Ericsson	Internet
C151	Northeast	B008	200	1600.00	Ericsson	Internet
X	Northeast	D412	24	1248.00	Vendor	Internet
X	Midwest	B429	1	8.77	Vendor	Mail
X	Northwest	B231	12	36.36	Vendor	Print
X	Northwest	A622	1	17.25	Vendor	Print

observations presented are from this source, and they have no customer number. The items from these sources are keyed to this organization's catalog of products, or to the nearest equivalent. Profit is estimated for these additional entries based on this organization's prices and costs. The purpose of the data mart here is to feed data mining.

10.2.3 On-Line Analytic Processing

Another type of application to exploit data warehouses might not be as primitive in terms of the analysis conducted, but is tremendously fast in response and enables executives to make timely decisions: on-line analytical processing (OLAP). OLAP systems are multi-dimensional databases. These systems allow analysts to display data in one or more of a number of different dimensions, such as time, geographic region, product, organizational department, customer, or other factors. While data warehouses focus on efficiently storing vast quantities of data, OLAP systems are designed to make it easy to analyze data.

OLAP systems allow firms to deliver access to data and report generating tools throughout their organization in virtual time. The ability to access OLAP packages has allowed Lockheed Martin Tactical Aircraft Systems to make data widely available for analysts. The OLAP system provided a single source to find program and business-management metrics, staffing information, risk and technical measurements, sales and cost forecasting, and overhead information.

An OLAP application would focus more on analyzing trends or other aspects of organizational operations. It may obtain much of its information from the data warehouse. The OLAP application extracts granular information that is of interest to the users being supported, aggregates this information, and makes the information easily accessible on a number of dimensions. This information could be accessed to make a report by product, as shown in Table 10.4.

Tables, even if joining data from several sources, limit the review of information. Often, executives need to view information in multiple combinations of two dimensions. For example, an executive might want to see a summary of the quantity of each product sold in each region. Then, she might want to view the total quantities of each product sold within each city of a region. In addition, she might want to view quantities sold of a specific product in all cities of all regions. OLAP is specially designed to answer queries such as these. OLAP applications let a user rotate virtual "cubes" of information, whereby each side of the cube provides another two dimensions of relevant information. Figure 10.14 displays the operation of an OLAP system.

The purpose of OLAP here is summarizing data with a report focus. OLAP products have spreadsheet computational capability, as well as organization of data by selected dimensions (by region, by quarter).

10.2.4 Data Quality

Data warehouse projects can fail for a number of reasons. One of the most common reasons is users' refusal to accept the validity of data obtained from a data warehouse (Wu, 2000).[27] This is an issue of data integrity. Such problems can arise because of one or more of the following:

◆ Corruption of data or missing data from the original sources.
◆ Failure of the software transferring data into or out of the data warehouse.
◆ Failure of the data-cleansing process to resolve data inconsistencies.

---

[27] Wu, J. (2000). Ensuring data integrity (Parts 1, 2, and 3). *DM Review*. www.datawarehouse.com.

Table 10.4: Example of an OLAP.

Product	Region	Q IV Last Year	Quarter I	Quarter II	Quarter III	Quarter IV	Revenue This Year	Profit This Year
Cell phone	Northeast	326	122	98	82	125	15,235	6,875
	Southeast	258	68	42	39	51	7,536	3,168
	Midwest	412	151	112	106	165	19,871	8,168
	Southwest	168	39	26	25	32	4,536	1,832
	Northwest	151	36	31	30	35	4,986	2,126
	International	56	65	73	86	92	11,965	3,965
	Total	1,371	481	382	368	500	64,129	26,134

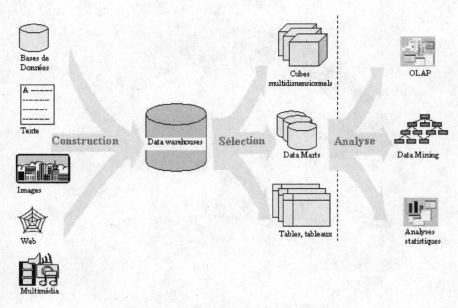

Figure 10.14:   Execution of OLAP.

Source: www.bdd.univ-lyon2.fr

Figure 10.15 shows the integration of quality in the data gathering process.

In the initial stages of data warehouse use, it is critical that data proves to be reliable. Once a reputation is lost, it is very difficult to recover. The information system staff operating the data warehouse must verify the integrity of data, ensuring that when data is loaded into the data warehouse, it is stored as planned. It is also necessary that the systems used to extract data from the data warehouse function properly. This is accomplished through cleaning up new data to do things such as removing redundancies, filling in blanks and missing fields, and organizing data into consistent formats.

10.2.5 Data Integrity

Data integrity requires that meaningless, corrupt, or redundant data not be entered into the data warehouse. Controls can be implemented prior to

Figure 10.15: Data Quality Integration Platform.
Source: 1105 Media, Inc. (2005).[28]

loading data, in the data migration, cleansing, transforming, and loading processes. This is the most efficient stage to prevent meaningless, corrupt, or redundant data from entering the system. Figure 10.16 shows a schematic representation of IT control aimed at attaining data quality.

An example of multiple variations for two of the variables in the example of a data warehouse is shown in Table 10.5.

---

[28] TDWI (The Data Warehousing Institute™) provides education, training, certification, news, and research for executives and information technology (IT) professionals worldwide. Founded in 1995, TDWI is the premier educational institute for business intelligence and data warehousing.

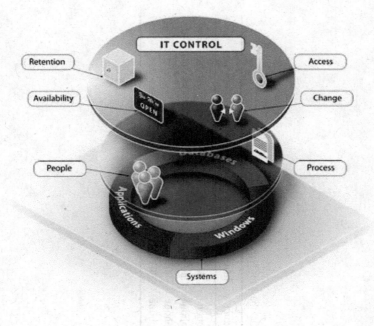

Figure 10.16: Data Integrity through Quality Control.

Source: www.kccaretech.com.[29]

In this case, the name variable includes three variations of the same customer. The second is a misspelling. The third is correctly spelled, but it includes a more complete definition. Since the name "Kim" is fairly common, it would probably be best to use the form "JD Kim," although this decision would be dependent upon the use of the variable. The process of developing unique variable values is **data standardization**.

10.2.6 Matching

Matching involves associating variables. For instance, in this database, the variable "Customer" is clearly associated with a unique "Name." We can see that the Customer variable includes a misread value (C729 rather than

---

[29] Kccaretech provides full support in billing and claims services. www.kccaretech.com

Table 10.5: Extract from Database for Name Kim.

Key	Date	Customer	Name	City	Region	Product	Item #	Qty.	Lot #	Price	Source	Cost
7332	1131	C129	Kim	Seoul	Intl	Cell phone	B019	120	XY482	39.99	Samsung	10.50
7671	1131	C129	Kimm	Inchon	Intl	Cell phone	B019	12	ZZ1243	41.16	Ericsson	10.66
7822	1131	C729	JD Kim	Seoul	Intl	Cell phone	B019	144	TU642	37.65	Samsung	10.12
7865	1131	C129	Kim	Seoul	Intl	Cell phone	B019	1	VV336	38.86	Samsung	8.67

C129) in the third row. It is often difficult to detect such errors, especially in conjunction with other problems such as variations in name spellings.

It is necessary for efficient data warehouse operation that the database contain the minimal number of consistent entries for each variable. As discussed above, one name entry for "JD Kim" needs to be identified. The overall system needs to be adjusted to reflect these choices. Software used to introduce new data into the data warehouse needs to check that the appropriate spellings and entry values are used. This also includes matching companies with addresses, an obvious opportunity for variety. Care needs to be taken to keep up with changes, such as telephone area code changes, or new zip codes. Personnel turnover makes maintaining proper contact names an interesting challenge. Means to guarantee data quality begin with ensuring that the data extraction process operates correctly. A framework for error identification and correction as well as reconciliation needs to be operating when the data warehouse is created. Data validation and testing tools are needed to monitor data quality and resolve problems as they arise.

Once data is stored in the data warehouse, controls can be applied to detect accuracy and completeness. Quick reviews should be performed soon after data is loaded to make sure that the correct numbers of records were loaded. It is useful to check aggregate totals as a means of verifying a degree of accuracy. More detailed validation efforts are often performed during data warehouse implementation. Ownership and accountability for particular data are assigned to a specific person or organization. Detailed validation checks whether data is complete and correct, whether business rules are followed, and whether the transformation processes of consolidation, filtering, cleaning, and aggregating are done properly. Validation also checks to make sure that data was loaded correctly. Data also is checked to make sure that entries are within tolerance levels. Any errors detected should be investigated to determine cause, so that appropriate changes can be made to the overall system. Data marts are products designed to select particular data from data warehouses (as well as from external sources) to be used for analysis, especially data mining. OLAP products come in a variety of product forms, but all are intended to give users the ability to design reports that give them insight into their operational environment. Table 10.6 compares the three database products discussed in broad terms.

Table 10.6: Comparison of Database Products Related to EIS.

Product	Use	Duration	Granularity
Data warehouse	Repository	Permanent	Finest
Data mart	Specific study	Temporary	Aggregate
OLAP	Report and analysis	Repetitive	Summary

Data quality is very important in ensuring the accuracy needed for successful system use. Data needs to be checked for accuracy before entry into the data warehouse. In an ideal system, if accurate data is entered, there should be little problem during subsequent operations. Realistically, there are many required changes to data, which makes administration of a data warehouse challenging. Data warehouses are capable of storing vast quantities of data. However, their implementation is not trivial. Missing and miscoded data have to be cleaned up, and variables often come in a variety of types, such as nominal data with no numeric content, dates, counts, averages, and many other forms. Relationships may be difficult to identify because of weak relations, often masked by other relationships. There are a number of publications available to explain more about data warehouses.[30] Now that we have established that the vast amounts of information generated by EIS systems can be efficiently stored and retrieved, we turn to ideas about how to utilize this information.

10.3 DATA MINING OVERVIEW

Data mining refers to the analysis of the large quantities of data that are stored in computers.[31] For example, grocery stores have large amounts of data generated by purchases. Bar coding has made grocery checkout very convenient. Grocery stores and other retail stores are able to quickly

---

[30] Inmon, W. H. (2005). *Building the Data Warehouse*, 4th ed. New York: Wiley; Silvers, F. (2008). *Building and Maintaining a Data Warehouse*. Philadelphia: Auerbach.
[31] Berry, M. J. A. (2002). *Mastering Data Mining*. New York: John Wiley & Sons; Olson D. L. and Shi, Y. (2007). *Introduction to Business Data Mining*. Boston: McGraw-Hill/Irwin.

process purchases, and use computers to accurately determine product prices. These same computers can help the stores with their inventory management, by instantaneously determining the quantity of items of each product on hand. They are also able to apply computer technology to contact their vendors so that they do not run out of the things that are in demand. Computers allow the store's accounting system to more accurately measure costs, and determine the profit that store stockholders are concerned about. All information is available based upon the bar coding information attached to each product. The benefits of bar coding are not only providing faster checkout service. The entire business management process can use the information generated.

Data mining can use bar code information to make better business decisions. Data mining is not limited to retail inventory control through bar coding. It is also widely used by banking firms in soliciting credit card customers, by insurance and telecommunication companies in detecting fraud, by manufacturing firms in quality control, and many other applications. One of the most prominent applications of data mining is support of **customer relationship management (CRM)**. Great Atlantic & Pacific grocery stores use data mining to target customers and centralize buying. Fingerhut has become very successful in **micromarketing**, targeting small groups of highly responsive customers. Media companies such as R. R. Donnelly & Sons provide consumer and life style data, as well as customized individual publications to firms that use data mining for catalog marketing. Data mining requires identification of a problem, along with collection of data that can lead to better understanding, and computer models to provide statistical or other means of analysis. There are two general types of data mining studies. **Hypothesis testing** involves expressing a theory about the relationship between actions and outcomes. In a simple form, there is a hypothesis that advertising will yield greater profit. This relationship has long been studied by retailing firms in the context of their specific operations. Data mining can be applied to identify relationships based on large quantities of data, which could include testing the response rates to various types of advertising on the sales and profitability of specific product lines. The second form of data mining study is **knowledge discovery**. In this form of analysis, a preconceived notion may not be present, but rather be seen by looking at the data. This may be supported by visualization tools which display data, or through fundamental statistical analysis such as correlation analysis.

Data mining has been called exploratory data analysis. Masses of data (generated from cash registers, from scanning, from topic-specific databases throughout the company) are explored, analyzed, reduced, and reused. Searches are performed across different models proposed for predicting sales, marketing response, and profit. Classical statistical approaches are modified in data mining, due to the lack of time for systematic exploration through classical statistical methods. However, some of the tools developed by the field of statistical analysis are harnessed through automatic control (with some key human guidance) in dealing with data. Data mining can be conducted with a variety of statistical and data manipulation tools. For large projects, data mining tools need to be versatile, scalable, capable of accurately predicting responses between actions and results, and capable of automatic implementation. **Versatile** refers to the ability of the tool to apply a wide variety of models. **Scalable** implies the ability to efficiently analyze large and even very large data sets. Automation is sought, but its application is relative. Some analytic functions are often automated, but human setup prior to implementing procedures is required. In fact, analyst judgment is critical to successful implementation of data mining. Proper selection of data to include in searches is critical. Too many variables produce too much output, while too few can overlook key relationships in the data.

10.3.1 Typical Benefits of Data Mining

Data mining is expanding rapidly with many benefits to business. Most of these gains involve relatively minor advantages. Two of the most profitable application areas have been by direct marketing organizations (to identify those with marginally greater probabilities of responding to different forms of marketing media) and banks (who use data mining to more accurately predict the likelihood of people to respond to offers of different services offered by the bank). Many companies are using this technology to identify their blue-chip customers so that they can provide them the service needed to retain them (customer relationship management). Figure 10.17 gives one view of the process of data mining with respect to data access.

Data Mining

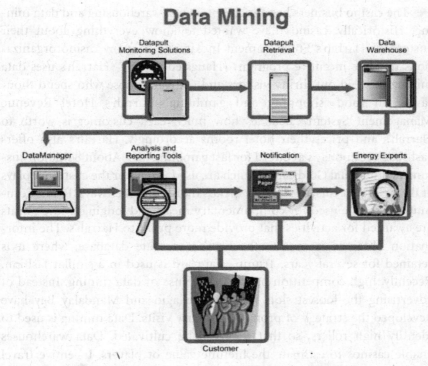

Figure 10.17: Data Mining Process linked to Data Warehouse.
Source: Datapult Limited Partnership (2000).[32]

Bank of America in San Francisco found that a small proportion of its customers determined bank profitability (20 percent in their case). Bank of America developed profiles of its top accounts to target services. They also were able to assess the likelihood that particular customers would take their business to a competitor (**churn**, in telephone business terminology, which we will see again later in this chapter).

---

[32] Datapult Data Mining Services transform data into information. Information that provides knowledge for reducing operating costs and minimizing equipment maintenance costs. Data Mining Services provide customers with tools to quickly sift through the clutter of vast amounts of data to identify potential areas of improvement. In addition, Datapult's capabilities include a dedicated staff of Energy Experts to help identify opportunities and to provide energy use and maintenance consultation. At the customer's option, Datapult Energy Experts will "mine" their usage data for valuable information to uncover savings opportunities.

The casino business has also adopted data warehousing and data mining. Historically, casinos have wanted to know everything about their customers. Harrah's Entertainment Inc. is one of many casino organizations that use incentive programs (Haugsted, 2007).[33] Harrah's uses data mining to weed out thrifty visitors and cultivates those who spend thousands on food, shopping and gambling. Harrah's Hotel Revenue Management System calculates how much each customer is worth to Harrah's and prices their hotel rooms accordingly. Harrah's also offers cash-back coupons as a reward for fast gambling play. About 8 million customers hold Total Gold cards, which are used whenever the customer plays at the casino, or eats, or stays, or spends money in other ways. Points accumulated can be used for complimentary meals and lodging. More points are awarded for activities that provide more profit to Harrah's. The information obtained is sent to the firm's corporate database, where it is retained for several years. Trump's Taj Card is used in a similar fashion. Recently, high competition has led to the use of data mining. Instead of advertising the loosest slots in town, Bellagio and Mandalay Bay have developed the strategy of promoting luxury visits. Data mining is used to identify high rollers, so that they can be cultivated. Data warehouses enable casinos to estimate the lifetime value of players. Incentive travel programs, in-house promotions, corporate business, and customer follow-up are tools used to maintain the most profitable customers. Casino gaming is one of the richest data sets available. Very specific individual profiles can be developed. Some customers are identified as those who should be encouraged to play longer. Other customers are identified as those who are discouraged from playing.

10.3.2 Business Data Mining Applications

There are many uses for data mining in business. A variety of techniques are applied to a diverse set of problems. See Table 10.7.

Data mining offers retailers in general, and grocery stores specifically, valuable predictive information from mountains of data. Grocery stores in

---

[33] Haugsted, L. (2007). Freebies help Harrah's ward off flashy rivals. *Multichannel News*, 28(30), 20; _____ (2004). Off-the-charts results. *Baseline* 31, 26–32.

Table 10.7:   Data Mining Applications.

Area	Applications
Retailing	Market basket analysis, affinity positioning, cross-selling
Banking	Customer Relationship Management
Credit Card Management	Lift, churn
Insurance	Fraud detection
Telecommunications	Churn (customer turnover)
Telemarketing	On-line caller information
Human Resource Management	Churn (employee turnover)

particular generate mountains of cash register data that require automated tools for analysis. Software is marketed to service a spectrum of users. In the past, it was assumed that cash register data was so massive that it couldn't be quickly analyzed. However, current technology enables grocers to look at customers who have defected from a store, their purchase history, and characteristics of other potential defectors. Targeted marketing programs are beginning to be successfully used by grocers. Single-store operations may be able to operate with PC software for as little as $4,000. Free Internet software is emerging as well. Most larger chain operations will have to spend up to $750,000 for data mining operations.

10.4 DIFFERENCE BETWEEN DATA WAREHOUSE AND BUSINESS INTELLIGENCE

A data warehouse incorporates enterprise-wide corporate data in a single repository, whereas Business Intelligence incorporates analysis and reporting tools that utilize information available in the Data Warehouse. Business Intelligence involves the process of analyzing large amounts of data in order to extract new kinds of useful information such as implicit relationships between different pieces of data. The differentiation between Data Warehouse and Business Intelligence can be very well explained with the help of Figure 10.18.

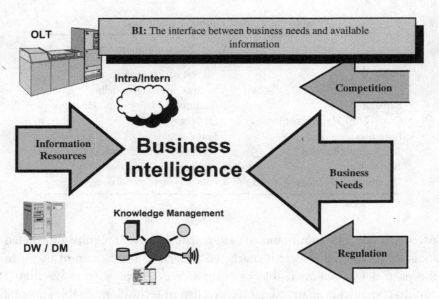

Figure 10.18: Relationship of Data Warehouses and Business Intelligence.
Source: Enterprise Group Ltd (1999).[34]

10.5 CUSTOMER RELATIONSHIP MANAGEMENT

The banking industry was one of the first users of data mining. Understanding the value a customer provides the firm makes it possible to rationally evaluate if extra expenditure is appropriate in order to keep the customer. An analyst at The Tower Group predicted that spending by U.S. banks on customer relationship management (CRM) will climb to $9 billion by the end of 1999, and grow at 11 percent per year thereafter. Deloitte Consulting found that only 31 percent of senior bank executives were confident that their current distribution mix anticipated customer needs. Figure 10.19 describes how business intelligence links organizational systems with profit-generating uses.

---

[34] Enterprise Group Limited (EGL) operated as a Business Intelligence (BI), technology and management consulting form from 1992 to 2003. EGL served clients worldwide, with a focus on the United States of America and Western Europe. EGL's BI practice focused on Global 1000 firms, while the technology and management practices primarily served high technology start-up companies. www.egltd.com.

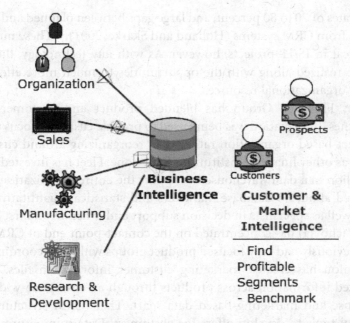

Organization

Sales

Manufacturing

Research &
Development

Business
Intelligence

Prospects

Customers

Customer &
Market
Intelligence

- Find
Profitable
Segments
- Benchmark

Figure 10.19: Business Intelligence as a Link between Organizations and Profitability.
Source: David Harper.[35]

Support of customer relationship management is the form of data mining most commonly associated with EIS. CRM allows businesses to identify the profitability of specific customers, and to increase chances of retaining them. This is accomplished by having all relevant information readily available that is needed for planning, product, and service through-out the customer life cycle. Oracle purchased Siebel Systems and has made that leading CRM add-on package a module in the Oracle enterprise system. SAP also supports CRM as a module in their newer versions of their enterprise system software. However, as with any innovative application of technology, there are growing pains. Ernst & Young studies noted CRM

[35] David Harper is a Contributing Editor and an Investopedia Advisor. In addition to being a writer for Investopedia, David Harper, CFA, FRM is a contributing editor for the Investopedia Advisor. David is Principal of Investor Alternatives LLC, a firm dedicated to research, consulting (e.g., derivatives valuation) and financial education. He publishes *The Bionic Turtle*, a set of study aids designed to help people prepare for financial exams.

failure rates of 70 to 80 percent, and large gaps between planned and actual benefits from CRM systems (Holland and Skarke, 2001).[36] These numbers are typical in IS/IT projects, however. As with any technology, the risks must be realized along with the opportunities to much more effectively manage organizational resources.

Fleet Financial Group has blended product and customer-based approaches. Information was being used to provide customer focus within a product-based organization rather than reorganizing around customer groups, as other financial institutions have done. Fleet has invested about $30 million in a data warehouse to support the entire organization. They also hired about 60 database marketers and statistical/quantitative analysts as well as specialists in decision support and other areas. First Union (now Wachovia) has concentrated on the contact-point end of CRM. The bank previously had very focused product groups with little coordination. First Union has created marketing customer information files, which integrated information across products through an enterprise-wide data warehouse and marketing-based data mart. Their CRM structure uses statistical tools to develop offers for customers. Data mining provides a way for banks to identify patterns. This is valuable in assessing loan applications, as well as in target marketing. Credit unions use data mining to track member profitability, as well as monitoring the effectiveness of marketing programs and sales representatives. They are also used in member care, seeking to identify what credit union customers want in the way of services.

10.5.1 Credit Card Management

The credit card industry has proven very profitable. It has attracted many card issuers, and many customers carry four or five cards. A common practice is balance surfing, where the card user pays an old balance with a new card. These are not considered attractive customers, and one of the uses of data warehousing and data mining is to identify balance surfers. The profitability of the industry has also attracted those who wish to push

---

[36] Holland, W. and Skarke, G. (2001). Is your IT system VESTed? *Strategic Finance*, 83(6), 34–37.

the edge of credit risk from both the customer and the card issuer perspective.

Data mining tools used by banks include credit scoring. A key is a consolidated data warehouse, covering all products, including demand deposits, savings, loans, credit cards, insurance, annuities, retirement programs, securities underwriting, and every other product banks provide. Credit scoring used to be conducted by bank loan officers who considered a few tested variables, such as employment, income, age, assets, debt, and loan history. Credit scoring applies statistical and mathematical models including many more variables on a much larger scale. Credit scoring provides a number for each applicant by multiplying a set of weighted numbers determined by the data mining analysis times ratings for that applicant. These credit scores can be used to make accept/reject recommendations, as well as to establish the size of a credit line.

Customers who usually use ATM machines can be presented with electronic sales pitches of products this particular customer is likely to be interested in. If a database indicates a new address for a customer with high credit scores, this customer may have traded up to a new, larger house, and may be a prime target for an increased credit line, a higher-end credit card, or a home improvement loan, which can be offered in a card statement mailing. Databases can also be used to support telephone representatives when customers call. The representative's computer screen can indicate the customer's characteristics as well as products the customer may be interested in.

The new wave of technology is broadening the application of database use and targeted marketing strategies. In the early 1990s, nearly all credit card issuers were using mass-marketing to expand their cardholder bases. However, with so many cards available, broad-based marketing campaigns have not been as effective as they initially were. Card issuers are more carefully examining the expected net present value of each customer. Data warehouses provide the information giving issuers the ability to try to more accurately predict what the customer is interested in, as well as their potential value to the issuer. Desktop campaign management software is used by the more advanced credit card issuers, utilizing data mining tools such as neural networks to recognize customer behavior patterns to predict their future relationship with the bank.

10.5.2 Insurance

The insurance industry utilizes data mining for marketing, just as retailing and banking organizations do. But they also have specialty applications. Farmers Insurance Group has developed a system for underwriting that generates millions of dollars in higher revenues and lower claims. The system allows the firm to better understand narrow market niches, and to predict losses for specific lines of insurance. One discovery was that it could lower its rates on sports cars, which increased their market share for this product line significantly. Farmers uses seven databases and 35 million records.

Unfortunately, our complex society leads to some inappropriate business actions, including insurance fraud. Specialists in this underground industry often use multiple personas to bilk insurance companies, especially in the automobile insurance environment. There are a number of specialty data mining software tools for various applications of fraud detection. By linking names, telephone numbers, streets, birthdays, and other information with slight variations, patterns can be identified indicating fraud. The similarity search engine has been found to be able to identify up to seven times more fraud than exact-match systems.

10.5.3 Telecommunications

Deregulation of the telephone industry has led to widespread competition. Telephone service carriers fight hard for customers. The problem is that once a customer is obtained, it is attacked by competitors, and retention of customers is very difficult. The phenomenon of a customer switching carriers is referred to as **churn**, a fundamental concept in telemarketing as well as in other fields.

A director of product marketing for a communications company considered that one-third of churn is due to poor call quality, and up to one-half is due to poor equipment. That firm has a wireless telephone performance monitor tracking telephones with poor performances (Reeves, 1998).[37] This system reduced churn by an estimated 61 percent,

---

[37] Reeves, B. (1998). All in the family. *Wireless Review*, 15(7), 42–50.

amounting to about three percent of the firm's overall subscribers over the course of a year. Given an average business volume of $150 per month, this churn reduction was estimated to be worth $580,000 in revenue a year. The firm's cellular fraud prevention system monitors traffic to spot problems with faulty telephones. When a telephone begins to go bad, telemarketing personnel are alerted to contact the customer and suggest bringing the equipment in for service.

Another way to reduce churn is to protect customers from subscription and cloning fraud. A number of cloning fraud prevention systems are marketed. These systems provide verification that is transparent to legitimate subscribers. Subscription fraud has been estimated to have an economic impact of $1.1 billion. Deadbeat accounts and service shutoffs are used to screen potentially fraudulent applicants. Churn is a concept that is used by many retail marketing operations. Banks widely use churn information to drive their promotions. Once data mining identifies customers by characteristic, direct mailing and telemarketing are used to present the bank's promotional program. The mortgage market saw massive refinancing in the early 1990s. Banks were quick to recognize that they needed to keep their mortgage customers happy if they wanted to retain their business. This has led to banks contacting current customers if those customers hold a mortgage at a rate significantly above the market rate. While they may cut their own lucrative financial packages, banks realize that if they don't offer a better service to borrowers, a competitor will.

10.5.4 Telemarketing

Telephone providers obviously are among the many marketing operations utilizing telemarketing. MCI Communications has utilized a strategy of **data marts**, extracting data on prospective customers from a data warehouse. This data is typically applied in a two-month program, after which the data mart is shut down. The data system required a multimillion-dollar investment in data marts and parallel hardware to support it. This operation was staffed by 45 people.

Segmentation involves grouping data with common characteristics, such as the set of customers who respond to new promotions, the set of customers who respond to discounts, or the set of customers who respond to new product offers. This information is used to determine the group of customers offered a new service, or to predict the set of customers most likely to commit fraud. Data mining can be used to determine segments. Once segments have been defined, on-line analytic processing (**OLAP**) tools can be used to explore them in greater depth. The MCI system has been used for trend-spotting. If a prospect turns down one frequent-flier pitch enough times, the program can suggest a different approach, such as switching airlines. On the data mart, data can be updated by the user. Data marts for a specific application are designed to include only the information needed for the specific promotion. However, it is important that all required information be included, so initial design of the data mart is crucial. Too much data slows the system, while too little causes problems requiring additional data.

10.5.5 Human Resource Management

Business intelligence is a way to truly understand markets, competitors, and processes. Software technology such as data warehouses, data marts, and data mining or on-line analytical processing (OLAP) makes it possible to sift through data in order to spot trends and patterns that can be used by the firm to improve profitability. In the human resources field, this analysis can lead to identification of individuals who are liable to leave the company unless additional compensation or benefits are provided.

Data mining can be used to expand upon things that are already known. A firm might know that 20 percent of its employees use 80 percent of services offered, but may not know which particular individuals are in that 20 percent. Business intelligence provides a means of identifying segments so that programs can be devised to cut costs and increase productivity.

10.5.6 Data Mining Tools

There are many statistical and analytic software tools marketed to provide data mining. One of the most widely used products is SAS Institute's Enterprise Miner. But many other products also are being used. These products use one or more of a number of analytic approaches. The major categories of methods applied are regression, decision trees, neural networks, cluster detection, and market basket analysis. The market supplying software for both data warehousing and data mining is growing very rapidly. Vendors selling data access tools include IBM, SAS Institute Inc., Microsoft, Brio Technology Inc., Oracle, and others. IBM's Intelligent Mining Toolkit has a set of algorithms available for data mining to identify hidden relationships, trends, and patterns. SAS's System for Information Delivery integrates executive information systems, statistical tools for data analysis, and neural network tools.

10.5.7 Real Practice

Our example of real practice reviews Wal-Mart's highly successful data warehouse system, which has been a key element in Wal-Mart's dominance of their business field. Wal-Mart was founded in 1962. Forty years later it dominated the retail market in the U.S. One of the primary reasons for this dominance has been the use of information technology, used in great part to support Wal-Mart's core competency of supply chain distribution over its many outlets. Wal-Mart uses a data warehouse consisting of 101 terabytes in 2001, believed to be the world's largest database.[38] The original investment for this data warehouse was over $4 billion.

The initial Wal-Mart data warehouse was stocked with point of sale and shipment data. This has been supplemented with inventory, forecast, demographic, markdown, return, and market basket information. Data about competition was also included, with over 65 million transactions processed per week. This data warehouse included 65 weeks of data by item, by store, and by day.

The purpose of this information was to support decision-making. Buyers, merchandisers, logistics personnel, and forecasters had direct access to the data warehouse, as did over 3,500 vendor partners. The system handled up to 35,000 queries per week, with benefits per query estimated to be over $12,000 per query. Power users ran up to 1,000 queries per day.

---

[38] Foote, K. P. S. and Rishnamurthi, M. (2001). Forecasting using data warehousing model: Wal-Mart's experience. *The Journal of Business Forecasting*, 13–17.

10.5.8 Caveats

Data mining involves the application of statistics and artificial intelligence. In business, one of the most popular forms of data mining is support to customer relationship management (CRM). While CRM is very promising, it has often been found to be less effective than hoped. Patton (2001)[39] found that up to 70 percent of CRM projects did not produce measurable business benefits. CRM systems can cost up to $70 million to develop, with additional expenses incurred during implementation. Patton cited problems with applications at Monster.com, Mshow, and CopperCom. One reason cited for problems in implementing CRM was that its users, marketing personnel for the most part, were not as computer-familiar as were accounting and production personnel. At Mshow, the sales force refused to use a new CRM system. At CopperCom, a $500,000 CRM project was reduced in size due to lack of support from an applications service provider. On the other hand, Siebel Systems, the largest provider of CRM software, reported that the vast majority of its customers were happy with their product. Even Fingerhut, a pioneer at using data mining for business, has seen their operations shut down after being absorbed by a large sales organization.

Many of the problems in CRM expectations have been blamed on over zealous sales pitches. CRM offers a lot of opportunities to operate more efficiently. However, they are not silver bullets, and benefits are not unlimited. As with any system, prior evaluation of benefits is very difficult, and investment in CRM systems needs to be based on sound analysis and judgment.

10.6 ONLINE ANALYTICAL PROCESSING

Another type of application to exploit data warehouses might not be as primitive in terms of the analysis conducted, but is tremendously fast in response and enables executives to make timely decisions: online analytical

---

[39] Patton, S. (2001). The truth about CRM. *CIO Magazine*, www.cio.com/archive/050101/truth_content.html.

processing (OLAP). Tables, even if joining data from several sources, limit the review of information. Often, executives need to view information in multiple combinations of two dimensions. For example, an executive might want to see a summary of the quantity of each product sold in each region. Then, she might want to view the total quantities of each product sold within each city of a region. In addition, she might want to view quantities sold of a specific product in all cities of all regions. OLAP is specially designed to answer queries such as these. OLAP applications let a user rotate virtual "cubes" of information, whereby each side of the cube provides another two dimensions of relevant information.

10.7 QUESTIONS AND ANSWERS RELEVANT TO BI

1. I have heard of Competitive Intelligence. How is Business Intelligence different?

Competitive Intelligence is one aspect of Business Intelligence. Competitive Intelligence is limited to information about competitors and how that affects strategy, tactics and operations. Business Intelligence includes that, but also uses information about overall industry conditions, political situations, and internal operations.

2. How does Business Intelligence relate to Knowledge Management?

We define Knowledge Management as the way that organizations create, capture and re-use knowledge to achieve organizational objectives. There's some overlap between the two terms, but there seem to be some differences of application in most cases. Business Intelligence uses many of the tools of Knowledge Management (things like data mining, for example) but concentrates more on strategic and tactical recommendations than Knowledge Management.

3. What are the three key steps in Business Intelligence?

The three key steps in Business Intelligence are gathering, analysis and recommendation. For most organizations, this is most effective if it's a part of regular ongoing business practice.

4. Should Business Intelligence be a staff function, or should I use an outsider?

The answer to that is an absolute "it depends." Larger businesses often have staff resources that can do most of the data gathering and analysis. They will often benefit though from having an outside perspective during the analysis phase. Smaller businesses almost never have the internal staff resources to do an effective Business Intelligence job. The exception to this is if there is a person (often the CEO) who does the BI work because he or she likes it. Smaller businesses and independent business professionals can usually benefit from outside help with information gathering and with analysis and recommendation.

5. Who is Business Intelligence for?

Business Intelligence is for businesses that want to drive intelligent decision-making throughout their organizations and make it easy for everyone in the organization to collaborate, analyze, share, and act on business information from a centrally managed, more secure source. With its attractive price for the Enterprise model, Business Intelligence supports IT professionals, information workers, and developers, and empowers organizations of all sizes.

10.8 ALL ABOUT ITeS

As per the encyclopedia.thefreedictionary.com, ITeS stands for "Information technology enabled services, or ITeS, a form of outsourced service which has emerged due to involvement of IT in various fields such as banking and finance, telecommunications, insurance, etc. Some of the examples of ITeS are medical transcription, back-office accounting, insurance claim, credit card processing and many more." IT Enabled Services are human-concentrated services that are transported over telecommunication networks or the Internet to a variety of business segment. ITeS significantly augments the employment opportunities. According to Carl Gunnarsen, "ITeS stands for IT-enabled services that major corporations are now adapting into their businesses." For a company to be considered ITeS-powered, it should have:

1. The kind of services that are being offered through the use of telecommunication. It can also be through networking and other forms of electronic media.
2. Services that make use of information technology from the process up to the delivery of the product.

ITeS makes possible the following:

♦ Outsourcing of processes that can be enabled with information technology.
♦ Delivered from/to remote areas through the telecom and Internet medium.
♦ Transfer of ownership and management of the process from the customer to the service provider, e.g., functions like finance, HR (human resource), administration, healthcare, telecommunication, engineering etc.

Figure 10.20 shows the uses of ITeS.

Some ITeS are:

♦ e-Governance.
♦ Call Centers.
♦ Data Management.
♦ Medical [Telemedicine and Transcription].
♦ Data Digitization.
♦ Website Services.

ITeS are applied to many areas of work including:

♦ Program Management.
♦ Enterprise IT Policy and Planning.
♦ Enterprise Design.

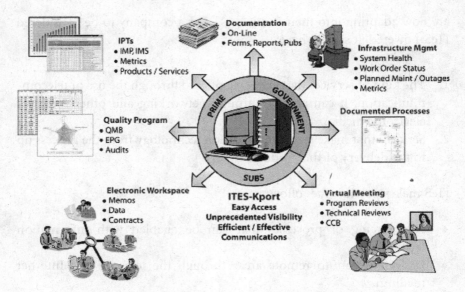

Figure 10.20: Diagrammatical Explanation of ITeS.

Source: Tim Rouch, Northrop Grumman Corporation (2005).[40]

- ◆ Integration and Consolidation.
- ◆ Information Assurance.
- ◆ Business Process Re-engineering.
- ◆ Requirements Analysis.
- ◆ Market Research and Prototyping.
- ◆ Information and Knowledge Engineering.
- ◆ Development of Software Interfaces and Software Configuration.
- ◆ Product Integration.
- ◆ Test and Evaluation.
- ◆ IT Infrastructure Systems Integration.
- ◆ Seat Management/Asset Management & Managed Services.
- ◆ Technology Insertion.

---

[40] Northrop Grumman Corporation (Northrop Grummer) is engaged into manufacturing of products, services, acrospace, electronics and shipbuilding services.

In order to operate ITeS, the following basic skills are required:

- Basic Computer knowledge (for general processes).
- Excellent Communication Skills (neutral Accent, clear speech, good grammar & language etc.).
- Customer Interaction Skills (customer handling skills, telephone etiquette, empathy and listening skills etc.).
- Understanding of target groups and their cultures.
- Positive attitudes like:

  ➢ commitment to understanding customers.
  ➢ solving their problems.
  ➢ motivation to work hard.

- Process training is given in-house by ITeS companies but basic skills like communication and interaction skills etc. are expected attributes of the employment candidate and form the criteria of screening for ITeS jobs.

Table 10.8 lists skills required by functional activity.

There are many areas promising high growth in the use of ITeS:

- Customer Analytics and CRM.
- HR Outsourcing.
- Legal transcript support.
- Knowledge process outsourcing —
  ➢ Market research.
  ➢ Equity research.
  ➢ Engineering design.
  ➢ Animation and simulation.
  ➢ R & D (non-IT areas).

- Financial Services outsourcing ... already witnessing explosive growth —

  ➢ Insurance underwriting.
  ➢ Fund management.

Table 10.8: Skills Requirements by Function.

Function	Skills required
Call center	Good communication and language skills, accent understanding team leadership, basic computing skills
Remote customer interaction	Language and accent understanding
Date search, Integration	Computing, language and analytical skills
Human Resource Services	Country-specific HR policies, rules and regulations
Remote education	Subject knowledge, computing and language skills
Engineering and design	Technical and engineering design and computing skills
Translation, medical transcription and Localization	Language understanding, basic computing (word processing knowledge) and understanding of various medical terminologies
Animation	Drawing and creative skills, computer graphic skills
Finance and accounting	International/country-specific accounting rules
Market Research	Understanding statistical sales and marketing concepts
Network Consultancy and management	Understanding different network configurations and support equipment, technical/computing skills

> ➤ Risk assessment and actuarial analytics.
> ➤ Commodities processing services.
> ➤ Debt collection and recovery.
> ➤ Equity research.
> ➤ Financial data mining and modeling.
> ➤ Corporate & Market research.

ITeS were designed to help customers meet enterprise standards at every level while meeting local customer requirements. ITeS puts control of the contractor in the hands of the local customer who can continue to work with one contractor as a program matures or changes scope. (ITeS becomes your vehicle.) ITeS can be used for almost anything from hardware to services. Figure 10.21 shows some of the driving forces behind ITeS.

Table 10.9 lists companies who are providing services under the ITeS banner.

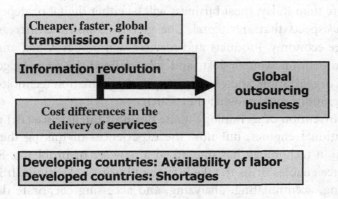

Figure 10.21:   Driving Forces behind ITeS.

Table 10.9:   ITeS Providers.

Accenture National Security Services	HP
Advanced Systems Technology	Linden International
American Systems Corporation	Microsoft Corporation
Applied Information Sciences, Inc.	MORI Associates, Inc.
Base Technologies, Inc.	Multimax
Capstone	NETCONN Solutions
CEXEC, Inc.	Optimus Corporation
CISCO Systems, Inc.	PAVL
Communications Technologies, Inc.	PKMM
Data Systems Analysts, Inc.	RAM
Dell	Securify, Inc.
DeVA Systems, Inc.	Smart Technology, Inc.
DigitalNet	Solid Network Solutions
EDO	Strategic Enterprise Systems, Inc.
EDS	Techni-Core Engineering
Federated Data	TelosOK
Frontier	Titan
Hoppmann	T-Systems

10.9 CONCLUSION

During the last 10 to 15 years, business management has changed intensely around the world. Business is increasingly becoming *digital*. In the future, even more than today, most business will be either digital or depend critically on aspects that are digital. The global economy is increasingly a *knowledge* economy. Products and services will be developed and delivered, competition won or lost, and jobs defined, by knowledge — its creation, organization, and communication. Information technologies are pervasive, and transform what they touch.

The invention of technology made Business Intelligence (BI) possible over relational engines, but now the experiences of linking them with information technology has unearthed a new set of problems. Business intelligence enables firms to take informed business decisions. It involves assembling, accumulating, analyzing, and accessing corporate data. For this purpose, it uses a variety of tools including query and reporting tools, OLAP, DM and DSS. Business intelligence is increasingly being identified as a mission-critical, firm-wide technology which helps firms to create business advantage and reap the rewards of expensive applications such as CRM and SCM (Supply Chain Management).

This chapter has introduced the concepts of data warehousing and business intelligence as enhancements to EIS systems. EIS systems and business intelligence operations are mutually supportive. Both can exist without the other, but both can be much more profitable if used together. Data warehouses are often used as efficient storage units for larger EIS systems. They also provide the ability to support business intelligence in the form of data mining. Data mining has proven to be extremely effective in improving many business operations. The process of data mining relies heavily on information technology, in the form of data storage support (data warehouses, data marts, and/or online analytic processing tools) as well as software to analyze the data (data mining software). However, the process of data mining is far more than simply applying these data mining software tools to a firm's data. Intelligence is required on the part of the analyst in selection of model types, in selection and transformation of the data relating to the specific problem, and in interpreting results.

By going through this lesson, you are now able to:

♦ Know how technical components of Business Intelligence (software, a wide variety of technical equipment) are managed in theory.
♦ Develop an ability to transfer and relate the formal knowledge of theory to practice.
♦ Initiate and execute independently various types of projects, many of which are IT-related.
♦ Understand business intelligence as learning in action.
♦ Understand modern information technology and its business opportunities.

You are thus equipped with the valuable, sought-after skills that will give you an advantage as a prospective employee.

☆ KEYWORDS

☆ **Analytical Model:** A structure and process for analyzing a dataset. For example, a decision tree is a model for the classification of a dataset.
☆ **Business Intelligence (BI):** The activity of gathering information about the elements in the environment that interacts with your firm.
☆ **Churn:** Customer turnover to competitor promotional programs.
☆ **Customer Relationship Management (CRM):** Software with the purpose of monitoring customer requirements and aiding organizations in maintaining their business. Data mining support of CRM includes identification of the value of a customer profile.
☆ **Data Integrity:** Absence of meaningless, corrupt, or redundant data.
☆ **Data Mart:** Either smaller scale data warehouse, or database product gathering data for a specific study.
☆ **Data Mining:** Use of statistics or artificial intelligence to confirm hypotheses or to identify patterns.

☆ **Data Quality:** Accuracy and completeness of data with proper formatting.

☆ **Data Redundancy:** The same data being shuffled from one place to the next, leading to massive amounts of data being repeated and taking up significant amounts of storage and processing power.

☆ **Data Standardization:** Process of developing unique variable values.

☆ **Data Warehouse:** The data warehouse is the place where transactional source data are specifically structured for query and analysis performance and ease of use. It is also known as subject-oriented, integrated, time-variant, and non-volatile collection of data.

☆ **Granular data:** Degree of detail in data.

☆ **Hypothesis Testing:** Systematic statistical testing of a proposed relationship.

☆ **Integrated data:** The data from various subject areas should be rationalized with one another.

☆ **Knowledge Discovery:** Examining data without preconceived notions of relationships.

☆ **Matching:** Association of variables within a database.

☆ **Micromarketing:** Targeting promotional campaigns based on information about customer's likelihood of response.

☆ **Online Analytical Processing (OLAP):** Refers to array-oriented database applications that allow users to view, navigate, manipulate, and analyze multi-dimensional databases.

☆ **Scalable:** Ability of the system to cope with increases in volume.

☆ **Subject-oriented:** Data is organized around a major object or process of an organization. Classic examples include subject area databases for customer, material, vendor, and transaction.

☆ **Time-variant:** Record is accurate only as at a specific moment in time. In some cases, the moment in time is a single moment. In other cases, it is a span of time. In any case, the values of data found in a data warehouse are accurate and relevant only to a specific moment in time.

☆ **Versatility:** Ability of the system to apply a wide variety of data mining models.

☆ TERMINOLOGY REVIEW

1. Discuss the role of BI in business today.
2. Discuss the role of BI and DM in the various fields of management, such as marketing, human resource, finance, and production.
3. Explain the purpose of an (info cube/cube) and dimensions. How do two components relate to each other? Why is it important to identify an organization's key performance indicators before developing a BI solution?
4. The Business Intelligence solution has been designed to interoperate with data that exists in virtually any enterprise data source, Explain.
5. How does BI work with existing servers and databases?
6. What are the system requirements for Business Intelligence?
7. How does Business Intelligence fit in with the Operating system?
8. How much does Business Intelligence cost?
9. What is Business Intelligence and what does it do?
10. What if I have a small (fewer than 100-person) company? Can I still use Business Intelligence?
11. What is a typical way an organization might use Business Intelligence?
12. What programs are included in Business Intelligence? Is Business Intelligence available as a single product in a box?
13. Describe a data warehouse. What does that have to do with EIS?
14. What is data granularity?
15. What are data marts typically used for in CRM?
16. What is an On-Line Analytic Processing System, and what relation does it have with data mining?
17. What is meant by data quality?
18. What is meant by data integrity?
19. What is meant by data standardization?
20. Describe micromarketing, and its relationship with data mining.
21. What is the difference between hypothesis testing and knowledge discovery?
22. What does scalable mean in information systems?
23. What is the difference between IT and ITeS?

24. What does ITeS mean?
25. Which types of work are available in ITeS industry?
26. What do I need to enter the ITeS arena?
27. What is meant by churn in data mining?
28. How does an organization get intelligence from cross-pollination of business information? The lists below provide an example of the questions that result from the hybrid mix of customer and competitor information.

☆ COMPETENCY REVIEW

A. Student Activity

1. To run a company with just traditional BI tools would be like driving a car and looking only into the rear-view mirror. Although you can see everything that happens, you don't see it until it has happened, which might be too late. Comment.
2. Business Intelligence includes two major components: the business intelligence platform and end-user tools. Justify your answer with illustrations.
3. Experience is about creating something that people want to use. People are happier with a EIS software product when they enjoy using it. For instance, Ted refers to Tableau as "a radically new product." I've seen it and it's a GREAT experience, with some GREAT visualization but there's nothing REVOLUTIONARY about it except for the experience. It's not in the cloud, it's not scaling beyond the petabytes, it's not even a web product (it's a windows desktop APP). Not revolutionary, just GREAT to use.
4. Search the library and/or the Internet for applications of CRM in EIS.
5. Search the library and/or the Internet for applications of data warehouses in EIS.
6. What happens when software becomes a commodity? There's usually a mid-market but you start to see players emerge at two ends of a spectrum.

7. Business intelligence is arguably the most important enterprise application in your company. But questions abound: How can you get more workers using it? What are the new frontiers? And how simple can you make it?

B. Explain the Following Statements with Relevance to Businesses Intelligence

1. The good side of the 80/20 rule still applies. Experience-based doesn't always mean 100% high end, every bell and whistle.
2. Focus on features that matter to the user doing a job. If a feature is needed to help a customer nail a part of their using your product, add it and make it better than they expect. Lacking features isn't a bad thing if you keep adding them — for instance, the iPhone was deficient in features (no GPS, battery was a pain, etc.) but users were patient.
3. Provide a high quality product that is as much about using as performing. The experienced-based product says that it's not enough to have a product that does what you want, but it has to be something you ENJOY using.
4. User and Experience is KING. Usability is not something that is a feature to implement, it's the thing that informs, prioritizes and determines what features are implemented.

C. Briefly Comment on the Following

a. The business intelligence that results from cross-pollination establishes reason and basis, the knowledge for actions.

....

....

b. A business is operated with the objective of making a profit from the sale of goods or services.

....

....

c. Business Intelligence enables comprehension, understanding and profit from experience.

....

....

d. Business intelligence is not a single entity; it is decomposed into business information.

....

....

☆ SUGGESTED READING

Books

Berson, A., Smith, S. and Thearling, K. (2002). *Building Data Mining Applications for CRM*. Delhi: Tata McGraw-Hill.

Delmater, R. and Hancock, M. (2001). *Data Mining Explained: A Managers' Guide to Customer-Centric Business Intelligence*. Digital Press.

Fusaro, (2004). None of Our Business. *Harvard Business Review*.

Green, A. (2004). Prioritization of sources of intangible assets for use in enterprise balance scorecard valuation models of information technology (IT) firms. Unpublished doctoral dissertation, George Washington University, Washington, DC.

Kimball, R. and Ross, M. (2002). *The Data Warehouse Toolkit*, 2nd Ed. New York: John Wiley and Sons.

Moss, L. T. and Atre, S. (2003). *Business Intelligence Roadmap: The Complete Project Lifecycle for Decision Support Applications*. Boston, MA: Addison Wesley Longman.

Oracle (2001). *Oracle CRM for higher education*. CA: Oracle Corporation.

Watson, Wixom, Hoffer, Anderson-Lehman, Reynolds (2005). Real-time Business Intelligence: Best Practices at Continental Airlines. *Winter* 23(1).

Weaver, M. (ed.) (2001). *The Canadian B2b Research Sourcebook: Your Essential Guide.* Ottawa: Canadian Library Association.

Whitten, J. L., Bently, L. D. and Dittman, K. C. (2004). *Sytems Analysis and Design Methods,* 5th Ed. New York: McGraw Hill.

Journal Articles

Alstete, J. W. and Beutell, N. J. (2004). Performance indicators in online distance learning courses: A study of management education. *Quality Assurance in Education,* 12(1), 6–14.

Azvine, B., Cui, Z. and Nauck, D. (2005). Towards real-time business intelligence. *BT Technology Journal,* 23(3), 214–225.

Azvine, B., Cui, Z., Nauck, D. and Majeed, B. (2007). Real time business intelligence for the adaptive enterprise. *The 8th IEEE International Conference on and Enterprise Computing, E-Commerce, and E-Services,* 29.

Grigoria, D., Casatib, F., Castellanosb, M., Dayalb, U., Sayalb, M. and Shan, M. C. (2004). Business process intelligence. *Computers in Industry,* 53, 321–343.

Luhn, H. P. (1958). A Business Intelligence System (PDF). *IBM Journal.* Retrieved on 10 July 2008.

Viitanen, M. and Pirttimaki, V. (2006). Business intelligence for strategic management in a technology-oriented company. *International Journal of Technology Intelligence and Planning,* 2(4), 329–343.

Williams, S. and Williams, N. (2004). The business value of business intelligence. *Business Intelligence Journal,* 8, 4.

White Papers and Conference Papers

Brobst, S. and Ballinger, C. (2000). Active data warehousing. White Paper NCR Corporation.

Kadayam, S. (2002). New business intelligence: The promise of knowledge management, the ROI of business intelligence. www.kmworld.com/publications/whitepapers/KM2/kadayam.pdf.

Kumar, S. and Deshmukh, S. (2005). Business intelligence: delivering business value through supply chain analytics. Infosys White Paper.

Mulcahy, (2001). ABCs of Business Intelligence. *CIO Magazine.*

Online Resources

Golfareelli, M., Rizzi, S. and Cella, L. (2004), Beyond data warehousing: What's next in business intelligence? *Proceedings of DOLAP-04*, Washington, DC, USA, www.acm.org (accessed 7 September 2008).

Lawton, G. (2006). Making business intelligence more useful. *Computer.* http://doi. ieeecomputersociety.org/.10.1109/MC.2006.318 (accessed 6 September 2008).

McKnight, W. (2002). Ask the CRM expert. http://expertanswercenter.techtarget. com/eac/knowledgebaseAnswer/0,295199,sid63_gci974430,00.html

Power, D. J. (2007). A Brief History of Decision Support Systems, version 4.0. dssresources.com. retrieved on 7 October 2008.

Raden, N. (2003). Exploring the business imperative of real-time analytics. Teradata White Paper.

CHAPTER 11

EIS AND SUPPLY CHAINS

Quotation

Supply Chain Management is not a business function, rather it is a new business model necessary for an organization's success and everyone in the organization needs to be involved.

scm-institute.org, Florida

Structure

- ♣ *Quick look at chapter themes*
- ♣ *Learning objectives*
- ♣ *Case study:* Wipro with SAP AG: Equipping Sanyo to meet fluctuating consumer demand
- ♣ *Sketch of EIS in SCM*
- ♣ Introduction
  - 11.1 Concept of Supply Chain Management
    - 11.1.1 SCM Streams
  - 11.2 Supply Chains are Alliances
  - 11.3 Advantages of Supply Chains
  - 11.4 Advanced Planning Systems
  - 11.5 On-Line Market Places
    - 11.5.1 Examples of On-Line Marketplaces
  - 11.6 Lean Manufacturing
    - 11.6.1 Role of Lean in EIS

♣ QUICK LOOK AT CHAPTER THEMES

Logistics and supply chain management is unique and, to some degree, represents a paradox because it is concerned with one of the oldest and also the most newly discovered business activities. Supply chain system activities — communication, inventory management, and warehousing, transportation, and facility location — have existed since the start of commercial activity. It is difficult to visualize any product that could reach a customer without logistical support. Yet it is only over the last few years that firms have started focusing on logistics and supply chain management as a source of competitive advantage. There is a realization that no company can do any better than its logistics system. This becomes even more important given that product life cycles are shrinking and competition is intense. Logistics and supply chain management today represents a great challenge as well as a tremendous opportunity for most firms. Another term that has appeared in the business jargon recently is demand chain. From our perspective, we will use the phrases logistics management, supply chain management and demand chain management inter-

> *changeably. Thus we can say that, in a nutshell, SCM applications can potentially improve the time-to-market of products, reduce costs, and enhance administrative procedures and plan for future needs.*

♣ LEARNING OBJECTIVES

Optimizing the supply chain is a major task in today's global business world. Supply chain incompetence is a key cause of unnecessary costs and poor performance. Successful supply chain end-to-end projects demand a complex blend of process, IT and financial skills and qualified and trained people at virtually every level. As a result, they can take a few years and create hope disruptions, even though the result is often highly successful. After going through this chapter you will be able to:

- ♣ Describe what supply chains are, and what advantages they provide.
- ♣ Understand how blocks of a supply chain network are built.
- ♣ Understand the business processes obtained from EIS aid supply chains.
- ♣ Understand types of supply chains and examples.
- ♣ Understand strategic, tactical, and operational decisions in supply chains.
- ♣ Understand supply chain performance measures.
- ♣ Understand supply chain inventory management.
- ♣ Understand ERP and supply chains, supply chain automation, and supply chain integration.
- ♣ Describe advanced planning systems to support supply chains.
- ♣ Discuss the role of on-line marketplaces in supply chains.
- ♣ Review the concept of lean manufacturing in the context of ERP.
- ♣ Evaluate available technologies and identify system needs.
- ♣ Maximize the results of the integration investment.
- ♣ Understand how to apply a variety of lean assessment tools in an ERP.
- ♣ Introduce the concept of value-driven supply chains and its integration with manufacturing and process operations.

♣ CASE STUDY

Wipro with SAP AG: Equipping Sanyo to meet fluctuating consumer demand

THE IDEA

Better collaboration and quicker decision-making to address fluctuating consumer demand.

REALIZING RETURN

An integrated SAP R/3 system in eight locations and five countries creating a seamless information network.

THE CLIENT

Sanyo is the world's leading manufacturer of rechargeable batteries. Headquartered in Japan, Sanyo has operations in North America, Europe, Japan and Asia Pacific.

BEFORE

Eight locations in five countries, with three languages (English, Taiwanese and Mandarin) were involved in inter-company transactions in the Asia Pacific. Each location followed their own business process model, capturing data differently in disparate AS400 legacy systems. The market is characterized by widely fluctuating demand cycles. Slow decision-making meant Sanyo was unable to respond to changes in consumer demand quickly. This in turn led to cost inefficiencies across business units in the region.

HOW WIPRO HELPED

Sanyo's long term objective was to enable quick and effective management decision-making across their batteries and cell operations. Here's how we addressed this need:

Implemented SAP R/3 across eight locations — the modules that were implemented included financial accounting & controlling, sales & distribution, materials management, and production planning. This involved reengineering more than 30 business processes across functions.

Since six of the eight locations were tightly coupled through inter-company transactions, their Go-Live dates could not be separated. We proposed a phased rollout approach. Six locations went live together in Phase I, followed by the other two locations.

Got a global MIS system going

The MIS system ensured that a universal set of accurate data was available for decision-making. This provided for:

- ♣ Common data definitions and standards.
- ♣ Standardized process models.
- ♣ A global set of business rules to be acknowledged and followed across operations.

Set up an Organizational Change Management (OCM) framework

An OCM framework was integrated into the project plan to risk the shift from AS400-driven, non-standard processes to structured definitive process paths in SAP. OCM also ensured stakeholder commitment at the locations, and an understanding among the business users of what to expect after SAP went live.

Bridged multiple countries, languages and cultures

The multi-cultural Wipro team handled:

- ♣ SAP implementation in Mandarin, Cantonese and English.
- ♣ Multi-lingual data conversions with cross-location master data.
- ♣ A Big Bang Go-Live for Greater China.
- ♣ A diverse user community that spoke multiple languages and had different cultural and working styles.
- ♣ The adoption of a global Asian template that still allowed for localized requirements.

Countered SARS

Hong Kong and Singapore were affected by SARS (Severe Acute Respiratory Syndrome) in March–April 2003. Robust disaster and business continuity planning ensured there were no delays in the launch of the project. The entire implementation was carried out on time and on budget within 12 months.

AFTER

Process quality improvement

- ♣ Interacted sales and manufacturing lead to real-time visibility in the supply chain.
- ♣ Sanyo can adjust quickly to changing customer demand cycles without affecting downstream production execution processes.
- ♣ Clear visibility of inventory quantities at any stage of the supply chain.
- ♣ More effective planning for future demand quantities.

Improved costing systems

- ♣ Consistent and standardized understanding of cost component structures across all implementation locations.
- ♣ Better reporting capabilities on profitability of specific product lines.

THE TECHNOLOGY

- ♣ SAP R/3 Rel. 4.6C SR2.
- ♣ Oracle 8.1.7.0.0.
- ♣ OS: AIX 5L Regatta.
- ♣ Server IBM P670, with ESS.
- ♣ 3-system landscape — DEV, QA, PROD.
- ♣ 3 user languages — simplified Chinese or Mandarin (Login language ZH), Traditional Chinese or Taiwanese (login language ZF), English (login language EN), tackled using Asian Unification Blended Code Page.

Source: www.wipro.com/eas Copyright © Wipro Technologies, (2005).[1]

---

[1] Wipro Technologies is the No. 1 provider of integrated business, technology and process solutions on a global delivery platform. Wipro Technologies is a global services provider delivering technology-driven business solutions that meet the strategic objectives of their clients. Wipro has more than 40 "Centers of Excellence" that create solutions around specific needs of industries. Wipro delivers unmatched business value to customers through a combination of process excellence, quality frameworks and service delivery innovation. Wipro is the World's first CMMi Level 5 certified software services company and the first outside USA to receive the IEEE Software Process Award.

♣ SKETCH OF EIS IN SCM

Today's global market combines rigorous competition, leading to lower profit margins, and opportunities to tap rapidly growing customer prospects. A successful supply chain participant requires information on everything from supply chain inventories, to production planning and shop-floor scheduling, to customer demographics and preferences. The ability of organizations to accumulate, scrutinize, and allocate this information has become a basic operating prerequisite for global supply chain operations. An EIS can facilitate organizational utilization of their manufacturing assets and give their customers the visibility they need. An EIS system can enable manufacturers to gain significant insight and competitive advantage beyond simply managing internal business processes.

♣ INTRODUCTION

To succeed in today's business, it is necessary to accurately assess consumer demand. At the venture level, the design of the value chain is linked with the efficient management of a supply chain. An effective supply chain must be configured to distribute customer value while also maintaining decisive price tag advantages. To diminish system-wide costs, firms increasingly rely on innovative tools for modeling complex supply chain relationships to accomplish the firm's logistics and operations requirements. This chapter initially focuses on the elementary principles underlying supply chains, using insights from both operations management and logistics. It discusses the likely impact from increasingly restrictive environmental standards, technology changes and other global trends that can be expected in the future.

If we link the definition of SCM with what is shown in Figure 11.1, it is coordinating and integrating information and materiel flows both within and among companies. It is said that the ultimate goal of any effectual supply chain management system is to reduce inventory (with the stipulation that products are obtainable when desired).

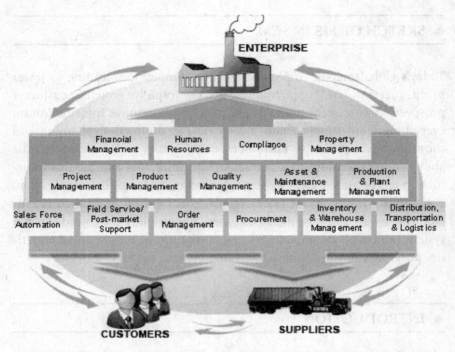

Figure 11.1:   Enterprise, Customer and Supplier Relationships with EIS Software.
Source: www.symphonysv.com[2]

11.1   CONCEPT OF SUPPLY CHAIN MANAGEMENT

Supply chain management (SCM) helps businesses to enhance and understand the activities that provide component level material for their finished products. According to Tom Blackstock,[3] "If you are in supply chain management today, then complexity is a cancer that you have to

---

[2] Symphony Services is dedicated to helping clients compress time to market, achieve higher innovation yields, and improve productivity to increase the value from their R&D investments. From strategic consulting guidance to complete product lifecycle capabilities, Symphony is distinguished by a singular focus on product development and collaborative, end-to-end solutions. http://www.symphonysv.com.

[3] Tom Blackstock, Vice President, Supply Chain Operations, Coca-Cola North America.

fight, and process management is the weapon. This framework develops a robust model of supply chain management processes and properly defines them so that they can be managed. It has enabled our organization to understand that supply chain management is too important to be just a function. Instead it's everybody's job." For example, in the retail sector, wholesaler relationships are vital, and in the automotive industry, part supplier relationships can influence the manufacturer's capability to construct a car on time. By focusing on SCM, corporations can get significantly better operational efficiency. SCM seeks to help businesses control costs by uncovering the difficulties in their key relationships (e.g., with internal suppliers and external vendors). The fundamental issue is the necessity to understand customer demand and bring the supply side of the business into conformity with this customer demand. By doing this, organizations can reduce or even prevent costly overruns and/or product shortages. Figure 11.2 demonstrates the role the Internet can play in SCM.

Supply Chain Management

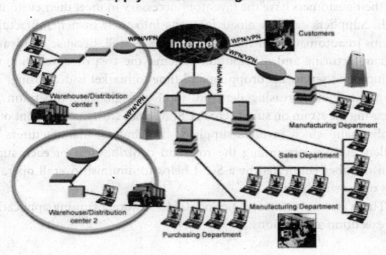

Figure 11.2: Supply Chain Management Linked by the Internet.
Source: Radix (2008).[4]

---

[4] Radix provides a platform to enhance good customer relationship while mitigating time spent with under- and/or non-performing customers. http://radix_technologies.com.

11.1.1 SCM Streams

A supply chain management stream can be divided into three main streams, i.e., the product, information and finances.

- **Stream 1: Product** — The progress of goods from a supplier to a customer, as well as any customer returns or service needs.
- **Stream 2: Information** — Transmitting orders and updating delivery status.
- **Stream 3: Financial** — Credit terms, payment schedules, and shipment and title ownership arrangements.

SCM software achieves these outcomes in diverse ways. Fundamentally, SCM links suppliers to databases that show forecasts, current inventory, shipping, or logistics timeframes within the customer organization. By giving suppliers such access, they can better meet their customers' demands. For example, the supplier can adjust shipping to make certain that their customers have the inventory necessary to meet their customers' needs. Suppliers can download forecasts into their own manufacturing systems to automate their internal processes as well. Because of advances in manufacturing and distribution systems, the cost of developing new products and services is dropping and time to market is decreasing. This has resulted in increasing demand, local and global competition and increasing the strain on supply chains. SCM deals with management of the supply chain which involves suppliers, distributors, manufacturers and resellers etc. Understanding the role and contributions of each supply chain member connected by a SCM helps to diminish overall operating costs of the supply chain.

There are two primary types of SCM software: planning applications and execution applications.

- Planning applications use highly developed algorithms to establish the optimal plan.
- Execution applications trace goods, the management of materials, and financial information involving all parties.

Some SCM applications are found in unwrapped data models that support the sharing of data both internally and externally to the enterprise (this is called the extended enterprise, and includes key suppliers, manufacturers, and end customers of a definite company). This shared data may be stored in miscellaneous database systems, or data warehouses, at several dissimilar sites and companies.

11.2   SUPPLY CHAINS ARE ALLIANCES

Today's business requires coordination of the stream of materiel flow from material source throughout the sequence of production activities needed to manufacture the final product, and deliver it to consumers. Coordination across organizations is required to produce, test, package and deliver products at desired quality with speed and accuracy. Supply chains are collections of organizations that work together to provide raw materials, which are converted into products, and delivered to retail outlets where customers can obtain them. In the past, monopolies would sometimes seek vertical integration so that they could control the entire supply chain (Standard Oil went a long way towards total vertical integration; steel companies also attained at least something approaching it). The Dutch East India companies are an early example of a global supply chain.[5] Military logistics systems are the epitome of a supply chain. The value of a supply chain is control and efficiency. Standard Oil a century ago and the military today have sought control. Today's higher degree of specialization gains efficiency through specialization. This appears in various forms, including outsourcing. The idea behind outsourcing is that there are specialists throughout the supply chain who can do a better job of the specific function they perform.

Figure 11.3 is a diagram of the supply-chain management for an apparel company (management of orders, stock and distribution). This type of alliance enhances the functioning of an organization.

---

[5] Kumar, K. (2001). Technology for supporting supply. *Communications of the ACM*, 44(6), 58–61.

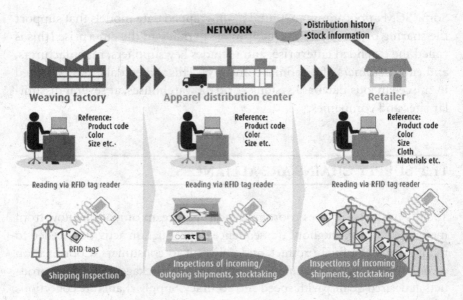

Figure 11.3: Diagram of a Supply Chain Network.
Source: Ministry of Internal Affairs and Communications (2007).[6]

In pure vertical integration, the idea was to closely coordinate the supply chain internally. Automobile firms in the 1970s and 1980s often tied vendors and retail outlets together into closely coordinated supply chains for purposes of gaining production efficiency (appearing in the form of just-in-time manufacturing). Today, computer technology makes it possible to obtain many of the same benefits of coordination across organizations. With the advent of ERP systems, along with telecommunications technology, supply chains have provided increased efficiency.

---

[6] Since the development of the "u-Japan Policy Package" in December 2004, MIC has been steadily implementing the Policy Package. In response to the latest trends, MIC has developed the "u-Japan Promotion Program 2006" with the purposes of i) identifying detailed ICT policies, ii) ensuring the comprehensive promotion of the "u-Japan Policy Package," and iii) specifying priority areas meeting current circumstances. Hereafter, the "u-Japan Policy Package" will be managed through the plan-do-check-action cycle. The "u-Japan Promotion Program 2006" (Japanese-language version) is available at: http://www.soumu.go.jp/joho_tsusin/eng/index.html

While far from universal, almost 20 percent of U.S. manufacturers in one survey had implemented supply chain extensions into their ERP systems. Less than one-third had no plans for such extensions (as opposed to 46 percent in a related Swedish study).[7]

11.3 ADVANTAGES OF SUPPLY CHAINS

Supply chains can provide competitive advantage from a combination of cost and value.[8] On the cost side, production efficiencies can provide output less expensively. At the delivery end, added value may be gained through logistics efficiencies that lead to lower costs, better coordination of advertising campaigns, enhanced service from larger scale operations, or other means. One of the most important motivations for manufacturing firms to implement ERP has been to improve interactions and communication with suppliers and customers.[9] Thus, ERP has a role in supporting supply chain activities. It has been reported in a study of over 400 Midwestern manufacturers that 20 percent of the firms surveyed had already implemented supply chain extensions to their ERP systems, and another 25 percent were planning to.[10] Figure 11.4 shows some of the functions needed to accomplish supply chain coordination by a French organization.

[7] Mabert, V. M., Soni, A. and Venkataramanan, M. A. (2000). Enterprise resource planning survey of US manufacturing firms. *Production and Inventory Management Journal,* 41(20), 52–58; Olhager, J. and Selldin, E. (2003). Enterprise resource planning survey of Swedish manufacturing firms. *European Journal of Operational Research,* 146, 365–373.

[8] Christaanse, E. and Kumar, K. (2000). ICT-enabled coordination of dynamic supply webs. *International Journal of Physical Distribution and Logistics Management,* 30(3–4), 268–275.

[9] Mabert, V. A., Soni, A. and Venkataramanan, M. A. (2000). Enterprise resource planning survey of U.S. manufacturing firms. *Production and Inventory Management Journal,* 41(2), 52–58.

[10] Ibid.

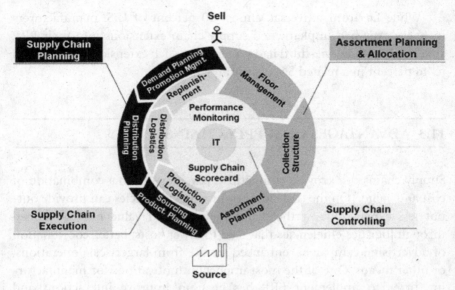

Figure 11.4: Bata SSA France Optimized Supply Chain.

Source: j&m Management Consulting AG (2006).[11]

Other supply chain advantages include the following features:

1. They reduce ambiguity, because the core organization can deal with the supply faster, thus reducing the cost of over production and management.
2. They help in horizontal performance, better response time and hence improve the quality and quantity of goods and services, because of speedy collection & retrieval of data. Hence, supply chain systems increase productivity by reducing unjustified use of resources.

---

[11] Bata is the world's best-known internationally operating retail chain for shoes and accessories. Its European headquarters is in Lausanne, Switzerland. The national company of Bata SAS France has started a campaign in collaboration with j&m Management Consulting AG, to optimize its supply chain. The project's drivers and goals center on increasing collection numbers, achieving a quicker and better supply of goods and replacing products more frequently. The overall aim is to align the company's systems even more closely with customer requirements. www.jnm.de

3. SCM also helps to develop products based on user requirements. This helps in accomplishing conflicting goals of lower inventory investment and lower unit cost.

Typical ERP installations can also impose some restrictions on communication. Internally focused ERP systems can constrain supply chain coordination.[12] ERP systems should be able to provide useful integration over supply chains in the long run, but in the short run could hinder logistical operations.[13] ERP systems make integrated information available within organizations that adopt them. However, unless all business units in the supply chain use the same system, ERP systems can be barriers to communication. Some suggest that units across supply chains would benefit by adopting a single vendor.[14] (This could work well in the long run, but imposes very high costs on vendors if they are required to spend millions of dollars on a system in order to do business with one client. That is precisely what some automobile manufacturers have done in the past.) Many of the problems of communicating across ERP systems relate to data incompatibility, as well as different software tools.

Part of the problem relates to system openness. Supply chains require open systems. ERP systems were developed on the assumption that a relatively small proportion of the workforce would need access to information.[15] This led to a pricing mechanism where license fees for each user were set at a high level. Edwards *et al.* gave a framework of three enterprise categories, shown in Table 11.1.

While, theoretically, open supply chains linked across organizations would have major advantages, currently this degree of openness is rare. Edwards *et al.* found that six of the 11 companies they interviewed felt that their transaction processing systems hindered linkage development. There are benefits to be gained, however. Those organizations moving toward

---

[12] Davenport, T. (1998). Putting the enterprise into the enterprise system. *Harvard Business Review*, 76(4), 121–131.
[13] Bowersox, D. J., Closs, D. J. and Stank, T. P. (1999). 21st century logistics: Making supply chain integration a reality. *Supply Chain Management Review*, 3(3).
[14] Baron, T. (1999). One vendor, one solution. *InformationWeek*, 760, 108–112.
[15] Edwards, P., Peters, M. and Sharman, G. (2001). The effectiveness of information systems in supporting the extended supply chain. *Journal of Business Logistics*, 22(1), 1–28.

Table 11.1: Characteristics of Different Categories of Organizational Openness.

	Extended enterprise	Cooperative enterprise	Traditional company
Profile	Agile	Lean	Profit focus
Strategy	Adaptive	Value-maximizing	Cost-minimizing
Goal emphasis	Flexibility	Effectiveness	Efficiency
Operations	Collaborative, open	Selective sharing	Limited sharing
Planning	Joint performance measures	Moving from push to pull	Push-orientation
Relationships	Extended alliances	Qualified relationships	Limited sharing
Technology	Linked systems, Internet ERP	ERP and selected SCM software	No linkage of ERP

Source: Edwards *et al.* (2001).

more open systems have been reported to gain advantages in ordering and logistics operations.[16] The Internet offers a rich information infrastructure making negotiation, knowledge-sharing, and transaction processing much easier and faster. Traditional firms can be pushed aside by more effective and competitive Internet-based supply chain groups.[17]

11.4 ADVANCED PLANNING SYSTEMS

Computer technology makes it possible for improvements at both the cost and value ends of the supply chain. Demand uncertainties can be better managed through improved inventory demand forecasting, reduction of inventories, and improved transportation costs through optimization of coordinated activities across the supply chain. **Advanced planning systems** (APS) provide decision support by using operational data to analyze material flows throughout the supply chain. Increased computing power enables more sophisticated analysis. APS products are shown in Table 11.2.

---

[16] Curry, J. and Kenney, M. (1999). Beating the clock: Corporate responses to rapid change in the PC industry. *California Management Review*, 42(1).
[17] Tapscott, D. (1999). *Creating Value in the Network Economy*, Boston: Harvard Business Press.

Table 11.2:   APS Software Suppliers.

i2	Consulting, and managed services
Manugistics	Resource planning and supply chain management
Numetrix	Provide optimization gateway to business customers
CAPS logistics	Decision optimization software for supply chain and logistics planning and scheduling
BAAN	SCM components
J. D. Edwards	SCM components
Oracle	11i
PeopleSoft	Enterprise Performance Management
SAP	SAP APO

Source: Baron (1999) and Kumar (2001)[18] and the respective URLs of the vendors.

Advanced planning systems use historical demand data as the basis of forecasts that are used to manage future demand. However, in order to optimize systems, a certain level of stability is required. John D. Rockefeller was able to manipulate demand for petroleum products over 100 years ago. Demand manipulation is still possible in some markets today, but is much more difficult. The idea of supply chain optimization is more difficult to implement in conditions of constant product innovation, highly volatile global demand, and increased product customization (such as applied by Dell and other computer vendors allowing customers to custom-design their computer systems on-line). This turbulent market environment makes it difficult to obtain extensive pertinent demand history. It is easy to collect data, but demand changes too rapidly to take advantage of it for extended periods of time.

There is a trend on the part of ERP vendors to expand their functionality to provide services formerly supplied by supply chain vendors such as Manugistics and i2 Technologies.[19] SAP has introduced mySAP.com, which is an open collaborative system integrating SAP and non-SAP software. SAP APO supports supply chain activities such as forecasting, scheduling, and other logistics-related activities. PeopleSoft has Enterprise Performance Management to support decisions at many levels. J. D. Edwards products

---

[18] Baron, T. (1999), op. cit., and Kumar, K. (2007), op. cit.
[19] Baron, T. (1999), op. cit.

have support for planning and execution. Oracle's 11i Advanced Planning and Scheduling system was designed to automate customer, supplier, and firm interactions. Vendors are moving toward greater integration of supply chain products.

In dynamic market environments, supply chain software may not be able to attain optimization, but there is still a great deal of benefit to be obtained from coordination of supply chain partners. IT also provides rapid coordination that can be even more beneficial than optimization in a stable supply chain environment. Technology makes it possible to find new partners at short notice in response to new market developments.[20]

11.5 ON-LINE MARKET PLACES

Open Internet marketplaces are becoming more widespread in use. These exchange mechanisms benefit suppliers and purchasers by providing a more competitive environment with broader access. E-marketplaces aggregate buyers, sellers, content, and business services. They also provide a single point of integration for interaction of buyers and sellers. A buyer can log on to an e-marketplace, issue a request for proposal, and be flooded with bids. This creates a problem of bid comparison and interpretation. Online marketplaces also provide services to help sift through large numbers of bids. Different types of OLM are listed in Table 11.3.

11.5.1 Example of On-Line Marketplaces

Figure 11.5 gives the reader an idea about Gojaba.com which is a marketplace for used, rare and out-of-print books that connects booklovers with independent sellers. Buyers can find signed books, first editions or simply used books in a few seconds and buy them from booksellers around the world. Booksellers can promote their business by listing and selling books on Gojaba.com.

---

[20] Moshowitz, A. (1997). Virtual organization. *Communications of the ACM*, 40(9), 30–37.

Table 11.3: Types of On-Line Marketplaces.

TARGET MARKET

Vertical	Deep and narrow product access
Multi-vertical	Multiple vertical sites
Horizontal	Broader, more extensive linkage to sites

TRANSACTION METHOD

Auction-based	Exchange seeking simultaneous bids
Future contract variants	For risk reduction
Pure auction systems	To establish prices for buyers
Reverse auctions	To establish prices for sellers
Metacatalogs	Reduce search costs
Mall-based	Access multiple suppliers at single site

Source: Manetti (2001).[21]

Figure 11.5: Gojaba.com On-Line Marketplace.
Source: Gojaba Inc. (2008).[22]

Table 11.3 lists some on-line marketplace types.

Vertical OLMs have narrow but deep product lines. Multi-vertical OLMs access multiple sources of product lines in the same way. These site types are particularly useful for those seeking products that are difficult to

[21] Gojaba.com launched in February 2008 in Sweden and Russia, in June in Brazil and in July in Poland. Gojaba.com plans to expand into new markets soon. Gojaba Inc. is an independent subsidiary of AbeBooks, the world's largest on-line marketplace for new, used, rare and out-of-print books.

[22] Manetti, J. (2001). How technology is transforming manufacturing. *Communications of the ACM*, 42(1), 54–64.

find. Horizontal OLMs deal with a broader set of products and more extensive linkage to buyer purchasing systems. A number of EIS/ERP vendors have horizontal OLMs, such as mySAP and Oracle exchange. OLMs also can be grouped by transaction methods. Auction-based OLMs are commonly used. One use of auction-based OLMs is as an exchange seeking simultaneous bids and offers to determine efficient prices. Future contract variants allow buyers to lock in supplies or hedge prices. Pure auctions seek only bids to establish prices for unique products. Reverse auctions do the same, only from the perspective of offers rather than bids. Metacatalogs focus on reducing search costs rather than on pricing. Mall-based OLMs allow buyers to surf a single site, with visits to individual areas representing different suppliers.

Advanced planning systems and on-line marketplaces represent two applications of technologies making supply chains more efficient. Lean manufacturing was originally proposed as a way to make supply chains efficient as a strategy not supported by information technology. EIS/ERP vendors are seeking to show how their systems can support lean manufacturing ideas.

11.6 LEAN MANUFACTURING

In 1990 James Womack wrote a book called *The Machine That Changed The World*. Womack's book was a clear description of the history of automobile manufacturing combined with a study of Japanese, American, and European automotive assembly plants. The "lean manufacturing" concept was popularized in American factories in large part by the Massachusetts Institute of Technology study of the pressures faced by mass production as described in Womack's book (Lean Manufacturing Guide.Com).[23] Lean manufacturing is a bundle of techniques pioneered by Toyota in the 1950s.

---

[23] This is a free resource site. It does not sell any services or products. This URL is designed to help you find questions to some of the most common questions about lean manufacturing — also known as just-in-time manufacturing. Lean Manufacturing Guide.com

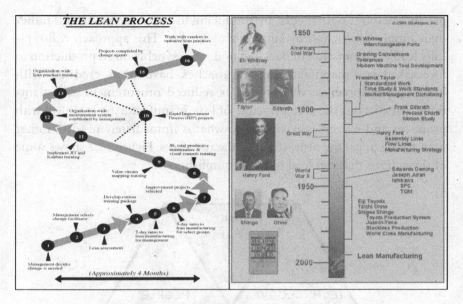

Figure 11.6: Views of the Evolution of the Lean Process.
Source: www.leanplus.com (2006).[24] Strategos, Inc. (2005).[25]

It has become a common philosophical approach to supply chain organizational design in the automobile industry. If we go into the basic definition of lean manufacturing, it is a strategy for achieving elimination of all waste of time and resources in the total business process. Lean is in relation to doing extra with less: Less time, inventory, space, people, and money. Lean is about momentum and getting it accurate the first time. Figure 11.6 gives an idea of the evolution of the lean philosophy.

The key principles of lean manufacturing are to cut out waste by eliminating activities that do not add value, by making sure that this principle is applied throughout the supply chain, by creating continuous flows of

---

[24] Leadership Excellence International, Inc. was founded in 1995 with the vision of being the catalyst for eliminating hidden waste in manufacturing, assembly, customer service, and distribution operations.

[25] The Strategos team has helped clients understand and improve business and manufacturing operations. Based in Kansas City, Missouri, USA. Strategos global affiliates each bring a unique international, experiential and topical perspective. www.strategosinc.com

product without bottlenecks, by producing to order (demand-pull rather than supply-push), and by emphasizing quality. This approach will typically lead to elimination of backlogs and more synchronized production to forecast. Lean manufacturing approaches have been credited with improved customer service as well as reduced procurement and plant-floor costs.[26] Thus the core principle of lean manufacturing is to deal with processes and resources according to what is immediately needed, rather than trying to get the utmost out of the resources. Figure 11.7 shows some of the actions that can lead to its accomplishment.

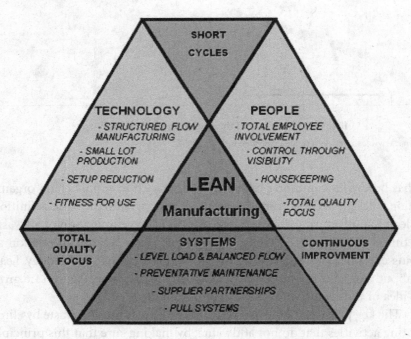

Figure 11.7: Means to Accomplish Lean Manufacturing.
Source: www.buker.com.[27]

---

[26] Bradford, M., Mayfield, T. and Toney, C. (2001). Does ERP fit in a lean world? *Strategic Finance*, 82(11), 28–34.

[27] Buker, Inc., founded in 1979, is an international management education and consulting firm. The Buker organization works with manufacturing and distribution firms committed to World Class and Best in Class performance.

Initial EIS/ERP applications often did little to obtain efficiency on plant floors. Problems with early EIS/ERP systems were complex bills of materials, inefficient work flows, and unnecessary data collection. Switching plant floor management in EIS/ERP systems to demand-pull (lean manufacturing) was cited as overcoming these limitations.[28]

There are differences in emphasis between EIS/ERP and lean manufacturing. EIS/ERP emphasizes planning based on sales forecasts. Lean manufacturing ties production to actual customer orders. (Dell Computer uses a lean approach, and gave this as the reason for dropping their planned SAP installation as discussed in Chapter 2.) Lean manufacturing emphasizes continuous improvement.[29] EIS/ERP tracks every activity and material price which often generates many non-value-added transactions, contrary to the lean philosophy's emphasis on speedy and smooth production. Some EIS/ERP users have dealt with this difference in philosophy by turning off EIS/ERP logs and reports that involve push motivation rather than pull.[30] Other companies prefer change of EIS/ERP software. Many EIS/ERP vendors have identified lean features of their systems, but not all customers have been convinced of EIS/ERP comprehensive support to lean ideas. Bradford *et al.* surveyed 14 EIS/ERP vendors, all of whom indicated that their product supported as least one lean manufacturing feature. Specific lean manufacturing features that vendors have included are demand smoothing, mathematical models to synchronize daily production to demand, Kanban replenishment calculation, and exception reporting. Bradford's overall assessment of EIS/ERP vendor products for their ability to support the lean business strategies in discrete and continuous manufacturing environments is summarized in Table 11.4.[31]

11.6.1 Role of Lean in EIS

The philosophy of lean manufacturing has had a great impact on enterprise excellence, as demonstrated in Figure 11.8.

---

[28] Ibid.
[29] Bartholomew, D. (1999). Lean vs. ERP. *Industry Week*, 248(14), 24–30.
[30] Bradford *et al.* (2007), op. cit.
[31] Ibid.

Table 11.4: Lean Business Strategies.

DISCRETE MANUFACTURING PROCESSES

Build-to-Stock	Customer orders filled from existing finished good inventory
Configure-to-Order	Products assembled to order from pre-built components
Assemble-to-Order	Batch formulated to fill a specific order from pre-built components
Engineer-to-Order	Each order designed to customer specifications

CONTINUOUS MANUFACTURING PROCESSES

Make-to-Stock	Customer orders filled from existing inventory
Configure-to-Order	Batches mixed in common, but packaged and processed to fill specific orders
Make-to-Order	Batch is formulated to specific order

Source: Bradford *et al.* (2001).

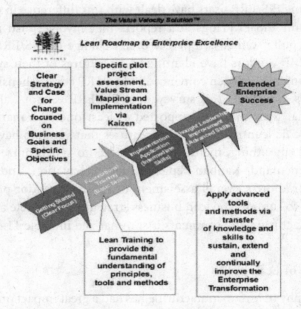

Figure 11.8: Role of Lean Philosophy in Improving Enterprise Excellence.

Source: www.7pines.com[32]

---

[32] Seven Pines is the better business and had an expertise in helping clients significantly improve profitability and organizational effectiveness through three interrelated services: It facilitate an organization in Business Process Improvement, Strategic Change Leadership Execution and Supply Chain Management.

The J. D. Edwards' EIS/ERP system supports mixed-model scheduling, demand-pull production, flexible material and capacity planning, distribution scheduling, and supply chain information sharing and analysis. The J. D. Edwards' OneWorld EIS/ERP system supports quality management, shop floor management, product data management, forecasting, and material planning, all of which relate to lean manufacturing.

Many modern EIS/ERP systems allow users to configure more than one of these business strategies. Most EIS/ERP vendors were found to support all but the engineer-to-order strategy, which was found in less than half of the EIS/ERP vendors surveyed by Bradford *et al.*[33] While it appears that EIS/ERP vendors are moving to provide greater support to lean manufacturing, the current state of systems has not yet achieved that ideal. The limitations of current EIS/ERP software led Bartholomew (1999) to view EIS/ERP and lean manufacturing to be competing approaches to plant operations. Bartholomew's view is supported by the actions of Dell Computer which has used customer demand as the basis of its system, the pull approach. As discussed in Chapter 3, Dell discarded a proposed EIS/ERP system after two years of study, concluding that the EIS/ERP approach was too inflexible for their demand-pull system.

11.7 KEY TRENDS IN SUPPLY CHAIN MANAGEMENT

The past few decades have seen a spectacular change in how business is conducted around the world. Firms have moved away from a hierarchical, one-dimensional supply chain to a disjointed network of joint ventures across organizations. This global phenomenon causes ripple effects throughout the old supply networks. Countless businesses, facing challenges arising from this change, are driven to participate in this new way of doing business. This creates opportunities for new supply chain services. The combination of information and system technologies and market necessities have led to new, supply chain designs. Akkermans *et al.* (2003) conducted a Delphi workshop of 23 Dutch supply chain executives of

---

[33] Bradford *et al.* (2001), op. cit.

European multinational firms.[34] That study reached consensus of over 50 percent on only two issues:

1. Further integration of activities between suppliers and customers across the entire chain (87 percent support).
2. How to maintain flexibility in EIS/ERP systems to deal with changing supply chain needs (57 percent support).
3. Mass customization (39 percent support).

Current EIS/ERP systems require greater openness to support the first issue. Vendors have moved to increase their ability to support Internet operations. However, there is an inherent trade-off in centralized, controlled, internally focused EIS/ERP systems and the openness of systems required to adequately support supply chain connectivity. This relates to both of the two most important issues identified. EIS/ERP systems do support mass customization by providing standard interfaces (given that the same system is used by all supply chain participants). Figure 11.9 shows how information technology can lead to improved supply chain management.

11.7.1 Research on EIS/ERP Integration with SCM

Implementing new software into your company's core businesses processes is painful. EIS/ERP came of age in the early 90's. Large firms had to have the functionality promised by EIS/ERP packages. Since then, as Web and Internet technologies have matured, EIS/ERP packages have come into their own on the front end, and Supply Chain Management packages, on the back end. One of the most important factors in the rise and collapse of the dotcoms was their failure to recognize the magnitude of sound Enterprise Resource Planning & Supply Chain Management. The capability to deliver on time may be the only differentiator between companies in an arena where the competitor is only a mouse click away. EIS/ERP has revolutionized the business environment. Fortune 1000 firms

---

[34] Akkermans, H. A., Bogerd, P., Yücesan, E. and van Wassenhove, L. N. (2003). The impact of ERP on supply chain management: Exploratory findings from a European Delphi study. *European Journal of Operational Research*, 146, 284–301.

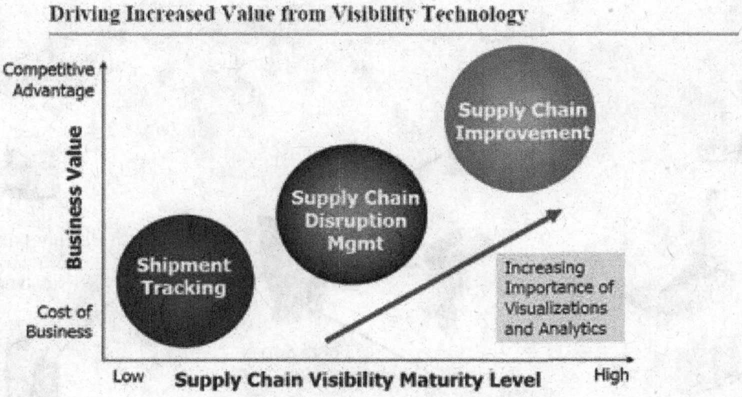

Driving Increased Value from Visibility Technology

Figure 11.9:   Supply Chain Technology.

Source: Aberdeen Group (2008).[35]

have or will install EIS/ERP systems, which will boost the global EIS/ERP market from 675 billion to 2250 billion rupees, over the next 5 years. So far, EIS/ERP sounds like a great idea. Yet, switching to an EIS/ERP system is a bit like constructing a new residence to replace an aged cottage. You know you need it, and you can envisage how much more functionality the new residence will have, but the old cottage is paid for and hard to give up. In addition there is bound to be interference during the construction process and some surprises along the way. Success in today's manufacturing environment is no longer measured merely on the basis of how proficiently your plants can manufacture products. Rather, success is increasingly measured by how effectively and efficiently you can consistently congregate customer requirements meeting those ever-changing requirements demands strong EIS solutions for your business — solutions built for manufacturers by experts that understand manufacturers i.e., EIS/ERP with SCM. What is needed is an established enterprise software solution integrating communications across supply chains.

---

[35] AberdeenGroup is the leading provider of fact-based research focused on the global technology-driven value chain. Founded in 1988, Aberdeen has established the market leading position as the "voice that matters" when it comes to understanding the measurable results being delivered by technology in business. www.aberdeen.com

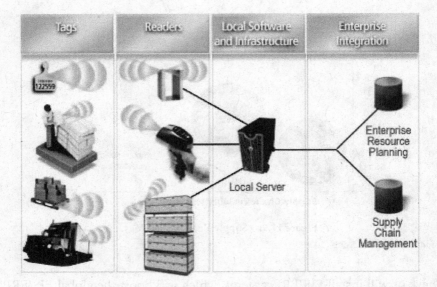

Figure 11.10: EIS Integrating ERP and SCM.

Source: IDA Singapore (2008).[36]

Figure 11.10 gives a clear idea about how the EIS/ERP and SCM can be synchronized.

11.8 MAGNITUDE OF EIS IN SCM

Traditionally EIS tools were not considered for SCM and thus, the information flow between various members of the supply chain was slow. This was because until the late 1990s, the concentration of organizations was on

---

[36] The Infocomm Development Authority of Singapore (IDA) cultivates a vibrant and competitive infocomm industry in Singapore — one that attracts foreign investment and sustains long-term GDP growth through innovative infocomm technology development, deployment and usage in Singapore — in order to enhance the global economic competitiveness of Singapore. IDA seeks to achieve this objective in its roles as the infocomm industry champion, the national infocomm master-planner and developer, and the Government CIO. http://www.ida.gov.sg

improving internal efficiency alone. Organizations however, soon realized that although internal efficiency is important, its benefit would be limited unless complemented by increased efficiency across the supply chain. They also realized that accurate flow of real-time information across the supply chain was key to success in the emerging business climate characterized by rapid advances in technology, shorter product life cycles, etc. Therefore, organizations started integrating EIS applications with SCM software. This ensures that efficiency was achieved across the supply chain and there is a seamless flow of information. EIS became a vital link in the integrated supply chain as it serves as the integrated planning and control system.

In summary, EIS applications help in effectively delivering SCM in the following ways:

♦ **Share data:** They can create opportunities to share data across supply chain members which can help managers in making better decisions. They also make available wider scope to supply chain managers by providing access to much broader information.
♦ **Real-time information:** EIS/ERP systems can provide real-time information which can be a great help in supply chain decisions. For example, ordering raw materials can be based on the inventory details provided by the EIS/ERP systems.

11.8.1 Web-Enabled EIS/ERP and Its Impact on SCM

Web-based technologies have revolutionized the way business is conducted and supply chain management and EIS/ERP are no exceptions. In order to leverage the benefits offered by this new technology enabler, EIS/ERP systems are being "web-enabled." The Internet allows linking websites to back-end systems like EIS/ERP and providing connections to a host of external parties. The benefits of such a system are that customers have direct access to the supplier's EIS/ERP system and the vendors in turn can provide real-time information about inventory, pricing, order and shipping status. The Internet thus provides an interface between the EIS/ERP system and the supply chain members allowing real-time flow of reliable and consistent information. To illustrate, the web-enabling EIS/ERP allows customers to go on-line, configure their own products, get the price and know immediately whether the configured product is in stock. This is made possible because the customer's request directly accesses the EIS/ERP system of the supplier.

11.8.2 EIS vs SCM

The difference between EIS systems (e.g. SAP, Baan, Peoplesoft) and SCM systems has been subject to debate. One reason is that the EIS vendors are adding additional SCM functionality to their products while SCM vendors are also expanding their functionality, encroaching on the area handled by the EIS vendors. With the vendors of EIS systems and SCM systems adding new and more functionality, the divergences between them have been distorted. For example, major EIS vendors are introducing advanced planning and optimization as an integrated component (also a component in SCM) of their system. In Table 11.5, we try to show the main differences between EIS and SCM systems at this time.

Table 11.5:   Comparison of EIS and SCM.

Point of comparison	EIS	SCM
1. Comprehensiveness	More elaborative	Moderately less
2. Sourcing tables	Somewhat fixed	Self-motivated
3. Complexity	High	Reasonably lower
4. Functionality	Moderately more stable	More alteration
5. Processing speed	Slower	Quicker
6. Managing of constraints	Considered in isolation	Synchronized handling
7. Implementation	Pre-Implementation Services — Process Mapping & Gap Analysis / Solution Fit Assessment / Scoping & Sizing	Post-Implementation Services — User Training / Enhancements / Maintenance support

Source: sonata-software.com[37]

---

[37] Sonata Software, headquartered in Bangalore, India, is a leading IT Consulting and Services company. Sonata's customers span the US, Europe and Asia-Pacific. Its portfolio of services include IT Consulting, Application Development, Application Management, Managed Testing, Business Intelligence, Infrastructure Management and Outsourced Product Development. Sonata is listed on the Indian Stock Exchanges and is SEI CMM Level 5 certified.

11.8.3 Product Lifecycle Management (PLM)

Product lifecycle management (PLM) is the process of managing the entire lifecycle of a product from its conception through design and manufacture to service and disposal (CIMdata).[38] According to www.plm-technology.com[39] "PLM is about driving business processes and innovation through the lifecycle, and not simply the automation of individual processes such as design and manufacturing. In other words, to move to PLM, we need to move away from the mindset of seeing things from a computer-aided tools perspective." PLM is the progression of organizing the complete lifecycle of a product from its outset through blueprint and assembly to service and disposal. It is one of the four cornerstones of a corporation's information technology configuration. Every company needs to deal with communications and information with their customers (CRM — Customer Relationship Management) and their suppliers (SCM — Supply Chain Management) and the resources within the enterprise (ERP — Enterprise Resource Planning) or Enterprise Information System. The concept is demonstrated in Figure 11.11.

The important point with respect to PLM is that it considers management of a product from its beginning to the end of its development and manufacture, principally from a business/engineering point of view; while Product life cycle management (PLM) focuses on the life of a product in the market with emphasis on business/commercial costs and sales procedures. This concept is demonstrated in Figure 11.12.

Figure 11.13 shows PLM augmenting communication and teamwork across individual departments within a company, facilitating cost control while getting products to market faster.

---

[38] CIMdata is a non-biased, independent, global consulting firm that has established itself as a world-leading source of information and guidance to both industrial organizations and suppliers of PLM technologies and services. The advantages to our clients are significant, since it leverages what is learnt from one group to help the other navigate an ever-changing environment. The fact that it is completely independent assures the highest level of confidentiality and objectivity.

[39] PLM Technology, Rosenholmveien 25, 1410 Kolbotn/P.O. Box 62, 1411 Kolbotn. www. post@plm-technology.com

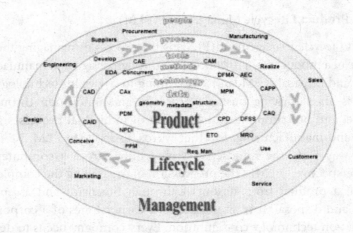

Figure 11.11:   Product Lifecycle Management Demonstrated.

Source: Wikipedia.org

11.9 FUTURE RESEARCH

The supply chain in a big business starts with the procurement of raw materials on one end and ends with the delivery of finished products to customers on the other. Depending on the nature of the business, managing the supply chain can be challenging and multifaceted. Supervising a supply chain involves making accurate decisions throughout the supply chain. SCM includes business processes, information flow, information processing, and connecting raw materials and finished goods. SCM software comes in four types. Supply-chain planning software, supply chain execution software, specialized sourcing and procurement software, and an amalgamation of these which vendors like i2 Technologies call end-to-end supply chain solutions. While supply-chain planning software uses advanced mathematical modeling and forecasting methods for planning the coordinated activities across the supply chain, supply chain execution software automates the dissimilar activities along the supply chain. The most influential part of an SCM solution is "demand planning" which determines how much product one needs to make to gratify customer demand under all probable outside constraints and uncertainties. Any

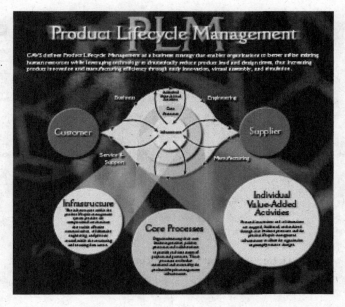

Figure 11.12:   Diagram of how PLM Facilitates EIS and SCM Integration.
Source: www.cavs.msstate.edu[40]

supply-chain software depends a great deal on exterior input like customer orders, sales data, stock positions at warehouses and the approximating and interior input that come in from an assortment of functional systems like sales, manufacturing, and finance.

While this is achievable with a legacy system, it is better to have all the information coming from an EIS application. That is, while EIS is strictly speaking not a pre-requisite for SCM, it is beneficial for the effective function of an SCM system. Supply chains cross the boundaries of the organization to suppliers and distribution partners. SCM software

---

[40] CAVS is an interdisciplinary center. It provides engineering, research, development, and technology transfer teams focused on complex problems, such as those encountered in technologies designed to improve human mobility. The development efforts provide short-term solutions relevant to regional manufacturers while the core research builds longer-term knowledge needed for sustained economic development. At the same time students gain valuable project experience that complements their formal classroom learning. http://www.cavs.msstate.edu

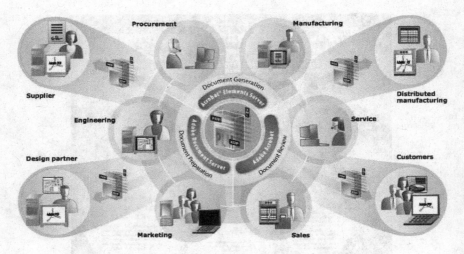

Figure 11.13: Adobe Intelligent Document Platform as a PLM.

Source: www.adobe.com[41]

functionality therefore works best when it includes the complete extended enterprise which is known as EIS. All of the SCM solutions are Web-enabled. Middle-aged organizations have been able to unify their comprehensive supply chains mutually using a single SCM system. Before choosing a SCM product, the company has to develop the complete supply-chain process diagram after re-designing key business processes. In the subsequent step of data flow diagramming, input and output to

[41] Adobe founders Chuck Geschke and John Warnock shared a vision for publishing and graphic arts that would forever change how people create and engage with information. The two men met in the late 1970s while working at the renowned Xerox Palo Alto Research Center (PARC), where they researched device-independent graphic systems and printing. Adobe revolutionizes how the world engages with ideas and information. For 25 years, the company's award-winning software and technologies have redefined business, entertainment, and personal communications by setting new standards for producing and delivering content that engages people virtually anywhere at anytime. From rich images in print, video, and film to dynamic digital content for a variety of media, the impact of Adobe solutions is evident across industries and felt by anyone who creates, views, and interacts with information. With a reputation for excellence and a portfolio of many of the most respected and recognizable software brands, Adobe is one of the world's largest and most diversified software companies. http://www.adobe.com

and from the processes in the supply chain are determined. Key functions akin to demand planning, scheduling, distribution planning, inventory management, accomplishment planning, outbound logistics, collaborator amalgamation, warehouse management, transportation management are examined and ranked according to virtual consequence. In reality organizations usually have a pre-determined supply chain plan based on historical experience. The diagnosis about supply chain bottlenecks can be determined at this stage. Once key functionalities are determined, diverse products are studied, compared, and pilot-tested for their respective strengths in these areas and the final selection can be based on the most suitable fit. A SCM project requires more functional experts and external consultants than technical professionals to see it through productively. When SCM products first appeared on the market, vendors began to influence technologies such as commemorative modeling and advanced optimization algorithms to provide customers with tools that gave greater value. These solutions principally appear in two areas: supply-chain planning and supply-chain execution.

Although many of these initial solutions have evolved to the point of commoditization, new applications and enhancements to current solutions are maturing to provide more cost savings and to enable more agile supply-chain structures. Many of these solutions are just appearing, and should presently be treated as immature. The pricing model of most Enterprise applications integration is dissimilar from that of long-established software. Not only do you pay originally for the number of seats you require, you also end up making annual payments towards maintenance of the software. The price of an EIS License has come down dramatically over the years, as vendors face saturation levels in larger organizations and move on to sell to smaller ones. SCM is yet to tag on that trend, and the installed base continues to be much smaller as opposed to ERP.

The future role of ERP systems may be much greater than the reasons for which they have conventionally been adopted. With the emergence of wave after wave of new technologies, the accessibility of an effective infrastructure may be one of the most important factors that facilitate and uphold future competitive advantage. Moreover, the lessons learned in the process of establishing this architecture may be invaluable for technological innovations in the future.

11.10 CONCLUSION

In the past, vertical integration was a way to gain efficiency in supply chains. Today, vertical integration does not work as well, because specialty organizations have developed to perform specific tasks very efficiently. Efficiency is gained today through supply chains linking specialists throughout the vertical business hierarchy.

EIS/ERP systems were initially focused on integrating internal operations. Their high investment cost and often rigid procedures made them barriers to effective supply chain linkage. However, there is evidence of recent trends toward more open systems that allow closer coordination across supply chains. One way to accomplish this efficiency would be for all elements in a supply chain adopting the same EIS/ERP vendor products, as well as software enhancements. However, this is not economically viable for most supply chain components. Many suppliers may not have the millions necessary to invest in technology adopted by the core company in the supply chain.

In this chapter we viewed the supply chain from the point of view of a general manager. Logistics and supply chain management is all about managing the hand-offs in a supply chain — hand-offs of either information or product. The design of a logistics system is critically linked to the objectives of the supply chain. Our goal is to understand how logistical decisions impact the performance of the firm as well as the entire supply chain. The key is understanding the link between supply chain structures and logistical capabilities in a firm or supply chain.

Other approaches are toward open EIS/ERP software. Advanced Planning Systems were originally developed to enhance the ability of firms to deal with other organizations in their supply chain. More recently, there are trends toward EIS/ERP vendors to provide this functionality within their products, especially through Internet technology. Lean manufacturing is another philosophy related to gaining efficiency in production operations. While the concepts of lean manufacturing initially seem in conflict with the idea of EIS/ERP, there have been imaginative developments allowing EIS/ERP systems to support lean manufacturing.

ERP deployment, management, and evolution are significant operational concerns in today's cost-conscious business climate. The performance of enterprise applications designed to streamline ERP processes and operations is dependent on the fundamental network infrastructure. Companies should take a holistic view of their mission-critical applications and networking environments and include best-in-class networking solutions.

Enterprises have long made flamboyant statements about getting closer to their customers and streamlining operations. ERP, CRM, and SCM applications and the organizations implementing them are in part, "bringing teeth" to those superior intentions. It is not a trouble-free process, however. In reality, the highly publicized failures of these initiatives have brought concern in some minds about these applications and their possible benefits. However, more and more organizations are moving ahead with these initiatives, and the successful organizations will gain from higher margins, better customer relations, and improved back office operations.

☆ KEYWORDS

☆ **Advanced Planning Systems (APS):** Software to analyze material flows throughout a supply chain.

☆ **Flexible Manufacturing System:** A process designed to re-balance the production line, rapidly matching output to changes in demand.

☆ **Lean Manufacturing:** Philosophical approach for efficient supply chain organization without bottlenecks.

☆ **Lean Means "Manufacturing Without Waste."** Waste ("muda" in Japanese) has many forms. Material, time, idle equipment, and inventory are examples. Most companies waste 70–90 percent of their available resources. Even the best Lean Manufacturers probably waste 30 percent.

☆ **On-Line Marketplaces:** Systems connecting parties potentially interested in a supply chain.

☆ **Supply Chain:** Network of organizations working together to produce a product, from raw materials to delivered goods. Is a network of supplier, manufacturing, assembly, distribution, and logistics facilities that perform the functions of procurement of materials, transformation of these materials into intermediate and finished products, and the distribution of these products to customers. Supply chains arise in both manufacturing and service organizations.

☆ **Supply Chain Management:** A systems approach to managing the entire flow of information, materials, and services from raw materials suppliers through factories and warehouses to the end customer. SCM is different from Supply Management which emphasizes only the buyer-supplier relationship. The use of information technology to endow automated intelligence to a network of cash registers, delivery vehicles, distribution centers, factories and raw-material suppliers.

☆ TERMINOLOGY REVIEW

1. What advantages do supply chain relationships provide to participating businesses?
2. According to Edwards, what feature of traditional EIS/ERP systems was incompatible with supply chain relationships?
3. Describe an advanced planning system.
4. Search the library and/or the Internet for advanced planning systems.
5. What are on-line marketplaces?
6. Search the library and/or the Internet for applications of on-line marketplaces related to EIS/ERP.
7. Describe lean manufacturing.
8. Understand the effect of supply chain on business operations.
9. Apply theory and practices to the design and management of supply chains.
10. Be able to formulate basic supply network distribution models.
11. Express familiarity with different forecasting tools and understand their use.
12. Develop models for planning and managing inventories.
13. Understand the importance of transportation and logistics in the supply chain and become familiar with ways in which transportation problems are modeled.

14. How does supply chain management evolve? Explain in brief the concepts of SCM.
15. Distinguish between ERP & SCM.
16. A supply chain management is a business approach that focuses on integration and partnerships, in order to meet customer's needs on a timely basis with relevant and high quality products, produced and delivered in a cost effective manner. Explain.
17. With SCM, you can get the right goods and services to where they are needed at the right time, in the right quantity and at an acceptable cost. Explain.
18. Manage inventory efficiently and pool inventory risks across time, products, channels, and geography.
19. Design supply chain contracts for effective governance of supply chain relationships.
20. Diagnose information integration problems across the supply chain and their consequent impacts in deploying physical and financial resources.
21. Evaluate alternate information-sharing and lead-time compression strategies, and supply chain coordination structures, and their organizational and performance implications.
22. Align supply chain integration strategy with the uncertainty conditions of supply and demand.
23. Optimally position the push-pull boundary to leverage economies of scale and economies of scope.
24. Evaluate strategic alliances for logistics and retailer-supplier relationships, such as vendor managed inventory.
25. Design implementation processes for partnerships, such as vendor managed inventory, that involve information sharing and shared governance of processes and infrastructure.
26. Evaluate outsourcing decisions by applying the buy-make framework.
27. How do you manage the benefits and risks of outsourcing?
28. Design e-procurement strategies for a firm's procurement portfolio of products and services.
29. Evaluate how the logistics process can be constrained by product design, and the implications of constraint reduction on logistics performance and market responsiveness.

30. Determine when and how a supplier should be integrated into the new product development process.
31. Apply strategic pricing for revenue management.
32. Determine the IT infrastructure requirements and IT integration strategy for supply chain management.
33. Determine the decision support system requirements for supply chain management.
34. Evaluate the risks and advantages of international supply chains.
35. Determine how you can implement enterprise resource planning (ERP) and distribution resource planning (DRP) and how these software packages can help your organization.
36. What is "logistical management" or "logistics"?
37. What are the Trends in logistics costs and performance?
38. What are the Objectives of logistical management?
39. How does a typical supply chain work? Explain with examples.
40. What are the processes involved in supply chains? Explain about the drivers of supply chain performance.
41. By understanding the supply chain management processes and how they should be implemented, management will better understand the value of more integrated supply chains and how this integration will lead to increased shareholder value and a sustainable competitive advantage. Discuss.
42. A lean organization emphasizes the prevention of waste: any extra time, labor or material spent producing a product that does not add value to it. Explain.
43. How do the components of Lean reduce waste and work together as a system?
44. What is Lean Manufacturing and where did it come from?
45. Today's companies manage supply and demand in a business climate characterized by instability. In response, they seek Supply Chain Management. Explain.
46. Supply Chain Management Solution enables you to develop accurate forecasts by creating a collaborative environment for multiple individuals, groups and partners. Elaborate with an example.

☆ COMPETENCY REVIEW

A. Student Activity

1. Companies are building on their ERP systems and integrated systems philosophy to practice SCM. In doing this, the company looks at itself as part of a larger process that includes customers and suppliers. By using information more efficiently along the entire chain, significant cost savings can result. Justify your answer with the help of an illustration.

2. Compare customer relationship management and SCM. How are they similar? How are they different? In answering, consider the kinds of technologies used in each.

3. Search the library and/or the Internet for applications of lean manufacturing. Try to find EIS/ERP relationships.

4. Search the library and/or the Internet for linkages between supply chains and EIS/ERP.

5. Search the library and/or the Internet for the Hershey's EIS/ERP case.

6. More and more firms are discovering that excellent management of supply chain resources is a way to reduce costs and achieve competitive advantage. Many of the value chain areas involved in supply chain management are covered extensively in required and elective courses for the Supply Chain Management degree.

B. Briefly Comment on the Following:

1. One of the primary objectives of SC management is to minimize the total supply chain cost which is subject to various service requirements.

....

....

2. The management of this network of relationships is supply chain management.

....

....

3. Successful supply chain management requires cross-functional integration within the firm and across the network of firms that comprise the supply chain.

....

....

4. It is focused on the improvements in performance that results from better management of key relationships.

....

....

5. A lean enterprise fosters our company culture in which all employees continually improve their skill levels and production processes.

....

....

6. Because lean systems are customer-focused and -driven, a lean enterprise's products and services are created and delivered in the right amounts, to the right location, at the right time and in the right condition.

....

....

7. A lean system allows production of a wide variety of products, efficient and rapid changeover as needed and efficient response to fluctuation in demand and increased quality.

....

....

8. Through the use of SCM, we can achieve better information engineering.

   ....

   ....

9. Every firm is unique. Each has its individual set of processes, technologies, culture, markets and strategy (implicit or explicit).

   ....

   ....

10. People and cultural considerations have equal importance with technology in the complex, probabilistic, and time-dependent socio-technical system known as a business.

    ....

    ....

11. In simple terms, supply chain improvements have resulted in reduced inventory levels, reduced logistics costs, and streamlined payments.

    ....

    ....

☆ SUGGESTED READING

Books

Brady, J., Monk, E. and Wagner, B. (2001). *Concepts in Enterprise Resource Planning*. Thomson Learning.

Chopra, S. and Meindl, P. (2004). *Supply Chain Management? Strategy, Planning and Operation*, 2nd Ed. Pearson Education.

Chopra, S. and Meindl, P. (2001). *Supply Chain Management: Strategy, Planning, and Operation*. NJ: Prentice-Hall.

Curran, T. A. and Ladd, A. (2000). *SAP R/3 Blueprint.* Prentice Hall.

de Kok, A. G. and Graves, S. C. (eds.) (2003). *Supply Chain Management: Design, Coordination and Operation.* Elsevier.

Kesharwani, S. (2003). *ERP Systems Application Experience & Upsurge.* India: Pragati Prakashan.

Lithicum D. (2001). *B2B Application Integration: e-Business Enable Your Enterprise.* Addison-Wesley.

Nagurney, A. (2006). *Supply Chain Network Economics: Dynamics of Prices, Flows, and Profits.* Edward Elgar Publishing.

Norris, G. (2000). *E-Business and ERP: Transforming the Enterprise.* USA: John Wiley & Sons.

O'Leary, D. (2000). *Enterprise Resource Planning Systems: Systems, Live Cycle, Electronic Commerce, and Risk.* Cambridge University Press.

Raghuram, G. and Rangaraj, N. (2000). *Logistics and Supply Chain Management: Cases and Concepts.* New Delhi: Macmillan.

Shapiro, J. F. (2001). *Modeling the Supply Chain.* Duxbury.

Shields, M. G. (2002). *E-Business and ERP: Rapid Implementation and Project Planning.* Canada: John Wiley & Sons.

Simchi-Levi, D., Kaminski P. and Simchi-Levi, E. (2003). *Designing and Managing the Supply Chain: Concepts, Strategies and Case Studies*, 2nd Ed. Irwin McGraw-Hill.

Woods, John A. and Marien, E. J. (2001). *The Supply Chain Yearbook.* New York: McGraw-Hill.

Journal Articles

Anderson, D. L., Britt, F. F. and Favre, D. J. (1997). The Seven Principles of Supply Chain Management. *Supply Chain Management Review*, 31–41. Also available at: www.manufacturing.net/scm/.

Aron, L. J. (1997). Speeding Cycle Times — The Mattress Industry Wakes Up. *Inbound Logistics*, 29–38.

Cooke, J. A. (2004). High Wire Act. *Logistics Management*, 32–38.

Cooke, J. A. (2004). Sole Sourcing. *Logistics Management*, 33–35.

Davis, T. (1993). Effective Supply Chain Management. *Sloan Management Review*, 35–46.

Garrett, D. (1997). Internet Versus Intranet Development. *DM Review*, 7(4), 40–43.

Gill, P. and Abend, J. (1997). Wal-Mart: The Supply Chain Heavyweight Champ. *Supply Chain Management Review*, 12–20.

Holmes, J. (1997). 5 Hot Spots of Supply Chain Management. *Inbound Logistics*, 40–44.

Jones, M. C. (2001). Organizational Knowledge Sharing and ERP: An Exploratory Assessment. In *Proceedings of the Seventh Americas Conference on Information Systems*, Strong, D. M., Straub, D. and DeGross, I. I. (eds.), 1030–1032.

Joseph, G. and George, A. (2002). ERP, Learning Communities, and Curriculum Integration. *Journal of Information Systems Education*, 13(1), 51–58.

Koch, C. (2002). The ABCs of ERP. *CIO Magazine*. http://www.cio.com/research/erp/edit/erpbasics.html.

Lacefield, S. K. (2005). Shippers See Inventory Rising. *Logistics Management*, 59–64.

Lee, A. and Lee, J. (2000). An ERP Implementation Case Study from a Knowledge Transfer Perspective. *Journal of Information Technology*, 15(4), 281–288.

Machuca, J. A. D. and Barajas, R. P. (2004). The Impact of Electronic Data Interchange on Reducing Bullwhip Effect and Supply Chain Inventory Costs. *Transportation Research Part E*, 40, 209–228.

McCrea, B. (2001). Playing the Waiting Game. *Logistics Management*, 69–72.

Richardson, H. (2004). Cross-Docking — Moving Products Directly from Inbound to Outbound — Can be a Strategic Weapon in a Successful Supply Chain Design. *Inbound Logistics*.

Soh, C., Kien, S. S. and Tay-Yap, J. (2000). Cultural Fits and Misfits: Is ERP a Universal Solution. *Communications of the ACM*, 43(4), 47–51.

Stackpole, B. (2003). There's a New App in Town. *CIO Magazine*.

Worthen, B. (2002). Nestle's ERP Odyssey. *CIO Magazine*. http://www.cio.com/archive/051502/nestle.html.

White Papers

AT&T Business (2004). The Critical Role of Networking in Enterprise Resource Planning. httpa/oracle.ittoolbox.com/documentG/document.asp?i=2862 (accessed 7 January 2005).

Butts, S. (2002). What is PLM. *Cad Digest*.

Carr, D. L. (2004). Pilot Air Freight: The Sky's the Limit. *Baseline*.

Hill, S. (2006). A Winning Strategy. *Manufacturing Business Technology*.

Hoffman, W. (2005). Shippers Still Reject RFID. *Traffic World*, p. 12.

Kerr, J. (2004). Yamaha Tunes Up its Import Operations. *Logistics Management*, 51–56.

Napolitano, M. I. (2005). Get Ready for RFID. *Logistics Management*, 83–88.

Opperman, G. (2005). The Five Kinds of Inventory: Invisible to Customers, Crucial to Profits, Crucial to the Bottom Line. *Inbound Logistics*.

O'Reilly, J. (2005). Track to the Future. *Inbound Logistics*.

Pan, S. L., Newell, S., Huang, J. C. and Cheung, A. W. K. (2001). Knowledge Integration as a Key Problem in an ERP Implementation. In *Proceedings of the 22nd International Conference on Information Systems*, 17–19.

Parr, A. and Shanks, G. (2000). Taxonomy of ERP Implementation Approaches. *33rd Hawaii International Conference on System Sciences* (HICSS), Maui, Hawaii.

Rehring, E. (2005). Wal-Mart Tags RFID Benefits. *Traffic World*, p. 10.

Shanahan, J. (2004). Ports Go High Tech. *Logistics Management*, Ports Supplement, S73–S77.

Teresko, J. (2004). The PLM Revolution. *Industry Week*.

Online Resources

Carey, N. (2006). Railroads and High-tech Logistics. Reuters, Information Week. http://www.informationweek.com/story/showArticle.jhtml?articleID= 184400022.

Federated Enterprise Offers a Breakthrough for Supply Chain Collaboration. (R) 2/24/2003

Global Intermodal Freight Transport System (GIFTS) brochures. http://gifts. newapplication.it.

North Carolina State University, Supply Chain Resource Cooperative, College of Management. http://scrc.ncsu.edu/

Stanford University, Global Supply Chain Management Forum, Graduate School of Business. http://www.gsb.stanford.edu/scforum/

University of San Diego, Supply Chain Institute, School of Business Administration. http://www.sandiego.edu/business/centers/supply_chain_management/index. php

Virtual Product Innovation (VPI): IBM's Mainstream Advantage for PLM. (R) 4/24/2003

CHAPTER 12

ADVANCED TECHNOLOGY

Quotation

Technology is dominated by two types of people: those who comprehend what they do not manage, and those who manage what they do not recognize.

— Archibald Putt

Structure

♣ *Quick look at chapter themes*
♣ *Learning objectives*
♣ *Case study:* Avago Technologies Overhauls EIS at Record Speed and on Budget with Oracle Enterprise System Software
♣ *Sketch of Advanced Technology*
♣ Introduction
   12.1 Open Architecture and EIS/ERP Bolt-Ons
       12.1.1 Example of an Optimization Bolt-On
   12.2 Middleware
       12.2.1 Middleware Definition and Features
       12.2.2 Middleware as an Enabling Engine
       12.2.3 Middleware Enhancement
   12.3 Security and EIS
       12.3.1 Security Threats by Type
       12.3.2 Adoption of Different Types of Secutrity

♣ QUICK LOOK AT CHAPTER THEMES

Consistent Web-delivered enterprise information system applications enable organizations to plan based upon accurate measures of organizational performance. Technology is a instrument to give support to us in our efforts to hold up. European Communities 2004 stated that, "The emergence of technology platforms represents an important development in addressing some of the major economic, technological or societal challenges." Today technology is, without doubt, a necessary tool to function in the marketplace. The aim of the enterprise information system is to apply technology to make organizations competitively efficient and capable of applying modern management principles based upon informed judgment.

♣ LEARNING OBJECTIVES

Technology platforms have as their primary objective a coherent and unified approach to tackling major economic, technological or societal challenges of vital importance. This chapter highlights security issues and raises awareness of security requirements in an EIS Environment. Students will learn how to apply concepts, strategies, and various tools to promote security of an EIS. They will understand aspects of EIS vulnerability, evaluating security of database tables, see the value of separation of duties and isolating critical authorizations that pose risks to system security. In this chapter, students will learn to:

- ♣ Develop enterprise information system policies for the use of technology.
- ♣ Provide instruction in the use of communication technology.
- ♣ Consider different views of future ERP development.
- ♣ Present the idea of middleware to allow enhancement of ERP.
- ♣ Discuss trends toward open EIS.
- ♣ Discuss security aspects of EIS.
- ♣ Articulate the security functions within the EIS.

♣ CASE STUDY

Avago Technologies Overhauls EIS at Record Speed and on Budget with Oracle Enterprise System Software

About Avago[1]

Avago Technologies may well be the world's oldest startup. We began as HP's components division back in the 60s — and thrived there for three decades. When HP spun off Agilent Technologies in 1999, we became Agilent's semiconductor products group: expanding into new markets and applications with products that would help revolutionize global communications. Then, in late 2005, KKR and Silver Lake Partners acquired our group changed its name to Avago Technologies. Overnight, Avago Technologies became the largest privately-held independent semiconductor company in the world. And the only new company in Silicon Valley with a 40-year track record. While it may be fairly easy to change a company name

---

[1] Avago Technologies provides an extensive range of analog, mixed-signal and opto-electronic components and subsystems to tens of thousands of manufacturers around the world. The company's products serve four end markets: industrial and automotive, wired networking, wireless communications, and computer peripherals. Avago Technologies Singapore. www.avagotech.com

on a paycheck, changing your software to reflect your current company — and severing ties with your previous company — is far from easy. But, in 2006, Avago — which manufactures analog mixed-signal and optoelectronic components and subsystems for the industrial and automotive, wired infrastructure, wireless communications, and computer peripherals markets and is co-headquartered in Singapore, and San Jose, California — was trying to do just that. The company needed to separate all of its applications and systems from Agilent's infrastructure while upgrading its software to streamline operations, expand its ERP footprint, and leverage the latest versions of several Oracle applications at the same time. "Avago's primary objective was to become totally independent from Agilent's systems, and improve our own capabilities and system performance," explained Hong Siew Lim, project manager for the ERP governance and support division arm of Avago, based in Penang, Malaysia. "We basically had an eight-month implementation plan with a major big bang separation from Agilent — from a system and infrastructure standpoint. We upgraded our software, and at the same time we were expanding our footprint and continuing to maintain our leadership in supply chain performance." It would be a tall order, and one the company would need some help with, considering the short time period in which the project needed to be completed.

Summary
- ♣ Industry: High Technology.
- ♣ Annual Revenue: US$1.8 billion.
- ♣ Employees: 6,500.
- ♣ Oracle Products & Services:

  Oracle Advanced Planning Suite.
  Oracle Financials.
  Oracle Procurement.
  Oracle Order Management.
  Oracle Shop Floor Management.
  Oracle Warehouse Management.
  Oracle Logistics.
  Oracle Product Lifecycle.
  Management.
  Oracle Sourcing.
  Oracle Real Application Clusters.

- ♣ Implementer: Oracle Consulting.

Key Benefits

Completed rollout ahead of deadline and within budget as a result of thorough project management by Oracle Consulting.

Cut advanced planning time from 12 hours to six hours.

Enabled quick problem resolution by employing pre-emptive thinking and extensive contingency planning.

Implemented global, future-focused solutions in response to local issues.

Strategy of Oracle

"Oracle[2] Consulting was in place strategically. They had the knowledge, the expertise, and the management skills to drive the project through to completion. They helped us manage the project and brought leadership to the table. They were strong pillars within our overall business team." — Hong Siew Lim, Project Manager, ERP Governance and Support Division, Avago Technologies.

A Big Bang

Avago Technologies began 2006 with Oracle ERP and legacy systems that hosted a significant number of applications. Its New Year's resolution was to install the latest version of Oracle E-Business Suite, reducing the number of applications to a more manageable size. One of the company's main goals was to provide real-time information throughout its supply chain, explained Hock-Leng Lee, end-to-end lead at Avago.

"We wanted a single system that could return customer information within a few minutes — inventory, orders, and related documents. We wanted our customers to have the best service possible, no matter how they contacted us," he said.

While the benefits were obvious, Avago executives knew that it would take a lot of planning, hard work, and more people than they had, so they looked outside the company for additional expertise. They found it, said Lee, with Oracle Consulting.

Accelerated Learning

From the first day working with Oracle Consulting on the 2006 project, Lee said he realized they had made a good decision. The consulting team

---

[2] Copyright © 2007, Oracle. Oracle is a registered trademark of Oracle Corporation and/or its affiliates. Other names may be trademarks of their respective owners.

quickly became an extension of the Avago IT team. In fact, when the project managers organized the implementation, they grouped both consultants and employees into 36 functional sub-groups, each with different tasks. Each team was given autonomy to work on their individual pieces of the larger project, but the company also created a cross-functional team that ensured everyone was working towards the same goals. Those cross-functional teams had Avago employees as well as Oracle Consulting employees. This was necessary given the volume of people and complexity involved. Avago was dealing with more than 20 different partners, including HP and other third-party application providers, over 150 Avago employees, and more than 50 Oracle consultants.

"It was a challenge because many of the partners had different backgrounds. We co-located the teams in Singapore and the U.S., but we also had teams in Malaysia and Europe. It was a worldwide team that was very much involved in the day-to-day operations of the project," explained Lim. If the consultants hadn't worked as part of that team, everything would have fallen apart. The Oracle Consulting team was both structured and flexible, blending in where needed, and asserting their knowledge when they were called on to support big decisions. They weren't afraid to ask questions, and they were genuinely curious about the plans that were being put into place by Avago executives, said Lee. "They weren't afraid to challenge our approach with another potential solution. That new solution may have been different than what we originally asked for, but it gave us the same functionality and would work better for our business because it was scalable or more user-friendly," he said. The Oracle Consulting team was also there when there were issues, ready and willing to not only help solve problems, but also to think ahead to prevent future ones, said Lee.

"This is where our executives were pretty impressed with the lead Oracle consultant, Mohit Ghatak, who was working with us. He asked questions that didn't just relate to that particular scenario or problem. He asked how we wanted to use our software in the future," he explained. "The consultant took the effort to actually expand his questions to encompass global usage. I was impressed that he was not just looking at input for the problem that we had, and then addressing it and coming back with the result. He actually took part in thinking through the whole solution."

Talking the Talk

As with any business relationship, Avago's leadership knew how and when to communicate with the consultants is key to a project's success. "It has to be a two-way process," said Lim. "It's very important that the company makes sure the commitment and the communication is there or the project won't succeed." Avago had the added issues of time, language, and culture barriers. With teams comprised of so many different nationalities and competencies, everyone had to be willing to adapt and grow. People also had to be willing to get their hands dirty. "In the past when we had consultants come in from third parties, they would spend a lot of time documenting the process, but most of their time was spent on the technical side," said Lim. "There was a limit to how far they would go for us. With Oracle Consulting, they were helping us with the solution design, but they were also getting right down to the nitty-gritty, going beyond what was required." This lead to camaraderie within the team, said Lim. "When there was a problem, there was very little finger-pointing. Instead, people would say, 'Let's try to address and resolve it.' Everyone was trying to learn from the issues and each other so they could avoid having problems happen repeatedly." Again, Avago executives contributed to this congenial atmosphere by giving the teams all the tools they needed. The Avago employees didn't push everything off on the Oracle consultants, and the consultants didn't mind doing whatever was needed to make the project a success because they could make decisions and act on them accordingly. Everyone had the power to quickly resolve roadblocks, rather than getting mired down in seemingly intractable problems. "Every team had the ability, whenever there was an issue, to escalate it as high as they needed to," Lim said. "We kept track of everything to ensure that issues that were escalated were owned by the right people. But we really could address problems quickly because we had contingency plans in place ahead of time and the leadership of Oracle Consulting to put them into play as soon as they saw they were needed."

New Name, New Game Face

In the end Avago's team not only hit its deadline ahead of plan, but succeeded in implementing its new infrastructure without going over budget. On 5 August 2006, the company turned off its old legacy systems and went live with Oracle E-Business Suite 11.5.10. The new software and hardware let the company cut its advanced planning run time by 50% — dropping from 12 to six hours — and improve productivity by automating processes that were previously done manually or enabling full integration within Oracle ERP. But most importantly, the company is able to maintain its best-in-class delivery and supply chain performance to its customers. "Oracle Consulting was in place strategically. They had the knowledge, the expertise, and the management skills to drive the project through to completion," he said. "They ensured that we looked at the project in totality — not just in silo-based functions. They helped us manage the project and brought leadership to the table. They were strong pillars within our overall business team."

Why Oracle?

Avago Technologies (as part of Agilent Technologies) chose Oracle Consulting in 2000–2002 when it initially installed several Oracle ERP applications, so they knew the organization had what it took to implement software from the ground up. This time, however, the process would be more arduous, but Avago executives were confident because they knew no other company had as much expertise and experience implementing Oracle products, explained Lim. "In 2000, we knew that the people who would know the most about Oracle ERP and Oracle E-Business Suite 11i would be consultants within Oracle," he said. "It was decided at that point that we needed and wanted the key consultants who were the most knowledgeable about the ERP modules in Oracle E-Business Suite 11i, especially since we were implementing relatively new modules — for example, the Oracle Advanced Planning Suite modules. At that time, in 2000, Oracle Advanced Planning Suite was a very new product, so we really needed someone who had lots of experience installing and integrating it. Since the company handled that implementation so well, engaging them in 2006 was the obvious choice." Lee agreed, "We knew we could work faster and smarter if we worked with Oracle Consulting rather than going with a third-party consulting firm," he said. "We have a rather complex business process that touches almost every function — from customer-facing applications to manufacturing to our employees — so we knew we needed someone who would do things right the first time." Company executives also wanted consultants who were familiar with the semiconductor business — how its environment develops and changes, and how its supply chain works. They got that and more, both Lee and Lim said.

♣ SKETCH OF ADVANCED TECHNOLOGY

One of the benefits of EIS software (and COTS software in broader terms) is that customers can quickly obtain the software needed to perform functions required by their special circumstances. This saves time and money, and puts the maintenance accountability and risk on the vendor rather than on the customer.

While going through the preceding chapters it is clear (see Figure 12.1) that EIS is an extended ERP drawing its advanced technology from its preceding counterparts.

The intention is to apply the EIS software "out of the box" as much as possible. Customizations may better fit an organization's needs, but complicate installation, safeguards, and upgrades because the customizations have to be handled as exceptions to the ordinary vendor course of action. So the challenge is getting the software to provide solutions to specific needs of the organization without customizing to the point where the benefits of EIS fade away.

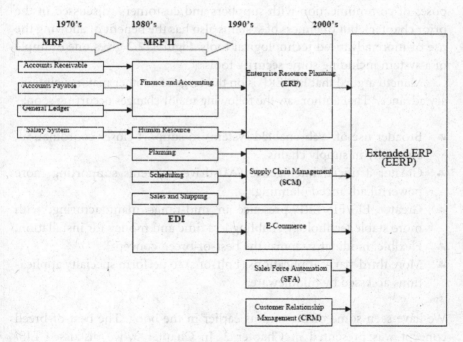

Figure 12.1:   Evolution of EIS.

Source: www.erp.org.tw.

♣ INTRODUCTION

There are many useful tools developed by information technology, including PDAs (personal digital assistants) and pocket PCs as well as other means of mobile computer access, wireless systems for making PDAs connectable to the Internet, and other forms of technology that expand our ability to do many things. These technology tools have had and will continue to have impact on EISs. The fundamental idea behind EISs was to integrate all business reporting systems within an organization. SAP pioneered products that were inherently secure, because they were focused internally. However, the advance of technology has made it apparent that there are many reasons to prefer open systems. Not only is this for purposes of communication with suppliers and customers (discussed in the prior chapter), but openness of systems also has the benefit of allowing the use of more advanced technological tools. Figure 12.2 gives one example of a system including some security tools.

Manetti argued that EIS/ERP is on the verge of another major evolutionary advance.[3] That author saw the following major changes occurring soon:

- ♣ Broader use of Web-enabled systems to support closer coordination, especially in supply chains.
- ♣ Greater artificial intelligence (AI)-driven systems supporting more powerful advanced planning.
- ♣ Greater EIS/EIS/ERP presence in mid-range manufacturing, with more stable technology enabling less time and money for installation.
- ♣ Flexible, modular systems (the best-of-breed concept).
- ♣ More third-party applications (bolt-ons) to perform specialty applications accessed by middleware.

We have seen some of these ideas earlier in the book. The best-of-breed concept was presented in Chapter 2. In Chapter 3, we discussed EIS/EIS/ERP implementation, and the trend toward easing implementation

---

[3] Manetti, J. (2001). How technology is transforming manufacturing. *Production and Inventory Management Journal*, 42(1), 54–64.

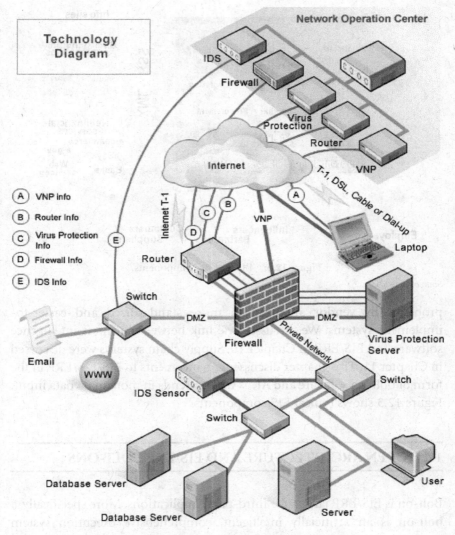

Technology Diagram

Network Operation Center

IDS
Firewall
Virus Protection
Router
VNP
Internet
Internet T-1
T-1, DSL, Cable or Dial-up
Laptop

(A) VNP info
(B) Router Info
(C) Virus Protection Info
(D) Firewall Info
(E) IDS Info

VNP
Router
Switch
DMZ
DMZ
Firewall
Private Network
Virus Protection Server
Email
WWW
IDS Sensor
Switch
Switch
Database Server
Database Server
Server
User

Figure 12.2: Example of System Security Devices.

Source: www.tiersolution.com[4]

---

[4] Tiersolution inc. was founded in 1997 in Silicon Valley by a team of software developers who saw a need for a dedicated solutions provider in the areas of Object Oriented Design and distributed architecture. TierSolution provides companies and organizations with world-class specialists who use the latest technologies. www.tiersolution.com

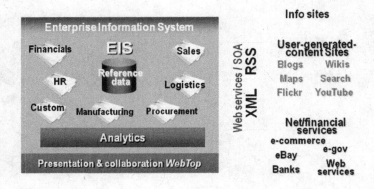

Figure 12.3: EIS and Its Components.

Source: Sage (2008).[5]

problems by vendor attention to more standardized and easier-to-implement systems. We discussed the link between business intelligence software and EIS/ERP in Chapter 10. Supply chain systems were discussed in Chapter 11. This chapter discusses enhancements to EIS/EIS/ERP in the form of bolt-on software and AI, as well as trends in more open data input. Figure 12.3 shows typical EIS components.

12.1 OPEN ARCHITECTURE AND EIS/ERP BOLT-ONS

Bolt-on is EIS/ERP jargon for third-party applications. More specifically, a **bolt-on** is an artificially intelligent, comprehensive execution system

---

[5] Sage ERP X3 is a full-service enterprise management software system for mid-to-large businesses aimed at meeting the most elaborate business processes, while remaining cost-effective, quick to implement and simple to use. It integrates all the enterprise's information and business processes within one single software system and database, allowing users to get an extensive view of their activity in real time, no matter where data has been created or stored. The system manages Finance, Sales, Inventory, CRM, Purchasing and Manufacturing operations globally and streamlines all of the enterprise's processes.

providing very specific functionality or technology to complement EIS/ERP software.[6] Bolt-ons employ client-specific business rules to meet unique needs. There are many useful applications of this type. The usual means of connection to other organizations with EISs is through software components. Most software had historically been delivered as monolithic code focusing on its originally intended application.[7] A much easier approach is the idea of componentization, where separate, encapsulated software code is written that is easier to manage, upgrade, and connect to host systems. Open systems are systems that can easily accept modifications or additions, or linkages to external software. Components make open systems possible.

Figure 12.4 displays how an EIS integrates core ERP with legacy applications through a Business-to-Business gateway.

Since the underlying philosophy in early EISs was internal integration, there was initially little apparent value in developing open systems. However, the EIS/ERP user market soon identified the benefits of best-of-breed selection of modules, sometimes across vendors. Vendors then

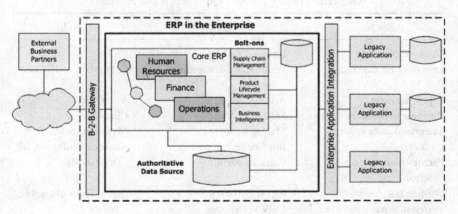

Figure 12.4: EIS in the Enterprise Diagram.

Source: www.army.mil/armybtkc/focus/sa/erp_ent_i1.htm

---

[6] Glazer, J. (1998). Make the choice between bolt-on and middleware solutions. *Automatic I.D. News*, 14(8), 46–48.

[7] Sprott, D. (2000). Componentizing the enterprise: Application packages. *Communications of the ACM*, 43(4), 63–69.

realized the need to componentize their applications. The focus shifted from internal design coherence to the ability to communicate with external software. Service-based architecture were created enabling business transactions and data transfer from outside the core application.

The types of software and related features of bolt-on software are shown in Table 12.1.

It can be seen from Table 12.1 that both EIS/ERP vendors (BAAN and J.D. Edwards) and other software providers (the rest of the vendors listed) are involved in developing bolt-on products to enhance EISs. Some of these products reflect the focus on materials planning, originally found in MRP (demand planning, inventory management products, order tracking). Others extend support to that originally provided by MRP-II software (factory planning and scheduling). Others focus on intranet and Internet communication (e-procurement, business to business products, on-line collaboration). The last two types of systems (warehouse management, data mining systems) are a bit different, in that they support business intelligence.

Table 12.1: Example of Bolt-On Products and Providers.

Bolt-On	Example	Vendor
Demand planning	Demand planner	BAAN
Inventory management	Warehouse Management System	Catalyst
E-procurement	Ariba Network	Ariba, Inc.
Business to business	MANAGE:Mfg	Cincom
Integrated suite systems	Manugistics 6	Manugistics, Inc.
Order tracking	Intelliprise	American Software, Inc.
Factory planning & scheduling	Capacity planning	J.D. Edwards
On-line collaboration	Aspen OnLine	Aspen Technology, Inc.
Warehouse management	CSW Warehouse Management System	Cambar
Data mining systems	Enterprise Miner	SAS Institute

Source: Mabert *et al.*, 2000.[8]

---

[8] Mabert, V. A. Soni, A. and Venkataramanan, M. A. (2001). Enterprise resource planning: Common myths versus evolving reality. *Business Horizons*, 44(3), 69–76.

12.1.1 Example of an Optimization Bolt-On

Optimization is a powerful tool that planning systems sometimes include as a feature. The following example demonstrates how a custom-built EIS was augmented by optimization software in a complex production scheduling/inventory management environment.

Figure 12.5 shows the iNet Business Optimization Platform for SAP. Optimization in this sense is optimization of the system architecture. This platform of .NET based business optimization services is designed to support the rapid extension and enhancement of SAP systems by letting information workers use the familiar Microsoft tools in support of

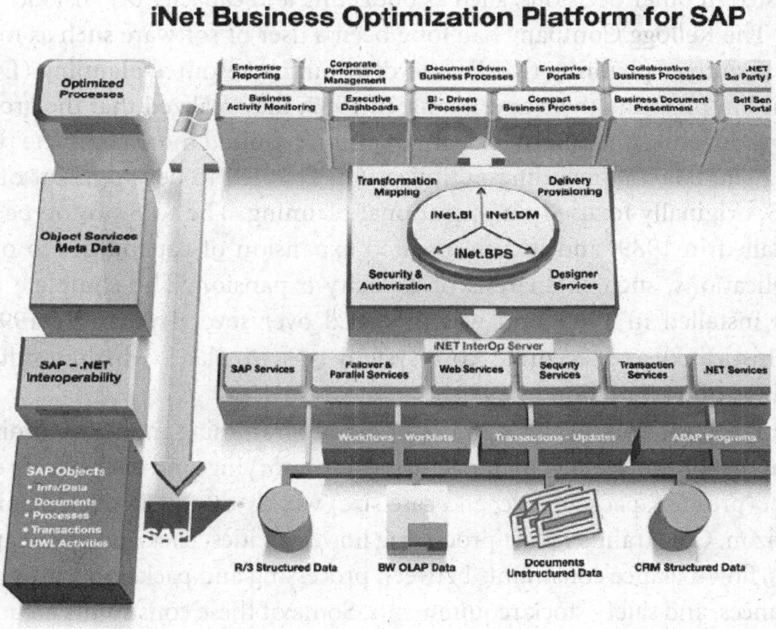

Figure 12.5: SAP iNet Business Optimization Platform.

Source: www.erp-link.com[9]

---

[9] ERP-Link was founded in 1998 to provide solutions to companies wishing to implement, or enhance SAP back-office systems. ERP-Link's founding principals already had over 15 years' expertise in enterprise systems and the application of leading edge technology to the biggest IT challenges companies were trying to address.

back-end SAP business functions and to offer a rapid .NET based development capability for extending and enhancing SAP system with their linkage to 3rd Party Business Solutions and .NET extended business processes.

The Kellogg Company developed their own internal enterprise resource planning (EIS/ERP) system to forecast demand, take orders from customers, coordinate purchases of raw material, produce over 100 food products, and distribute these products.[10] To complement this EIS/ERP, Kellogg utilized a large-scale linear programming that they named the Kellogg Planning System (KPS) to help develop weekly production, inventory, and distribution decisions for the various food products it produced. This system also assisted in other decisions, such as budgeting and capacity expansion.

The Kellogg Company had long been a user of software such as material resources planning (MRP) and distribution resource planning (DRP) to aid in planning their operations. In 1987, they realized that the growth in product line and international expansion required more complete planning and control including optimization. That led to development of the KPS, originally focused on operational planning. The KPS prototype was installed in 1989, and its use inspired expansion of capabilities to other applications, such as analysis of capacity expansion. The complete KPS was installed in 1990, and was modified over several years. By 1994, a sophisticated and accurate cost system was in place, which produced savings of $4.5 million in 1995.

The basic core of the KPS is a linear programming model minimizing total cost of purchasing, manufacturing, inventorying, and distributing each item (product, package size, and case size) weekly over a 30-week planning horizon. Constraints reflect processing line capacities, packaging line capacities, flow-balance constraints between processing and packaging, inventory balances, and safety stock requirements. Some of these constraints are modeled as elastic, meaning that they can be violated at a price (overtime, for instance). Other constraints impose restrictions reflecting Kellogg policies.

Raw materials are not modeled, but some intermediate products are. Input data that is relatively constant over time includes product codes,

---

[10] Brown, G. Keegan, J. Vigus, B. and Wood, K. (2001). The Kellogg Company optimizes production, inventory, and distribution. *Interfaces*, 31(6), 1–15.

relationships of intermediate and final products, and product-facility possibilities. Costs include inventory cost, shipping cost, and penalties for unmet demands, safety stock, and overuse of production facilities. More variable input include production capacities by shift, costs by time of year, estimated demands, and target safety stocks.

The model has about 700,000 variables and 100,000 constraints, with 4 million non-zero coefficients. This is a very large linear programming model. Technically, the model would be more precise were mixed-integer restrictions imposed, but the continuous linear programming model taxes solution capabilities too much to add this refinement. The continuous model takes several hours to run. Solutions are viewed as beginning production plans that managers modify to reflect integer restrictions.

There is also a great deal of uncertainty associated with the long-term inventory aspects of the model. Again, technically this could be modeled as a stochastic (and nonlinear) model, but such a model would require an unwieldy amount of data, and would be very difficult to solve. Therefore, probabilistic features of the real problem are dealt with through imposition of safety stocks. The output of the model is used in a rolling-horizon environment, where production and packaging decisions are fixed in the first week from prior decisions, and model output is used to establish plans for the second week out.

There are other types of software bolt-ons that can be added to EIS systems. Examples include auction management software, shopping cart management software, and credit authorization software. There is no end to the variety of products that the marketplace develops to utilize computers to do business better. Growth in the acquisition of components from multiple sources seems inevitable. Some firms may avoid the addition of such software, but competitive pressures will probably require adoption of some.

12.2 MIDDLEWARE

A noteworthy hindrance to modernism is the growing information system complication that takes place from incongruent technologies, gamut of information and detached service infrastructures. Supplementary challenges take account of constant transformation, the necessity to organize and decrease costs, demanding requirements for fulfillment, and a lack of tolerable service visibility and control. Middleware services help an organization to faultlessly integrate the application layer with the infrastructure layer to optimize the Information system and environment. This generates higher ROI on information system investments, and yields greater business value and innovation from the information system.

12.2.1 Middleware Definition and Features

Even though there are numerous definitions for middleware, it has been used to describe some different variants. In the past, some services, such as CRM, were provided by separate vendors from the ERP, requiring middleware to make software from different vendors work together. Recently, there is a strong trend towards EIS vendors providing such functionality within their system (such as Oracle purchasing Siebel Systems, and making CRM a module within the Oracle EIS). Some other services, such as TCP/IP protocol that is a branch of network, may be provided through middleware or as a middleware layer. The function of middleware is to deal with dispersed infrastructures and to construct simpler programming environments for application developers.

Another view of middleware is the notion of being at the center of a system. This is perhaps where the expression "middleware" originated. The conventional classification of an EIS is "the software that makes the hardware functional". Correspondingly, middleware can be thought of as the software that makes a distributed system programmable. Just as a stripped computer without an enterprise information system could be programmed with enormous difficulty, programming a distributed system is a wide-ranging operation. Middleware is occasionally referred to as "plumbing" because it hooks up parts of a dispersed application with data pipes and then passes data between them. It is also called "stick" technology from time to time, for the reason that it is repeatedly used to tie together legacy systems transparently. Transparency in this circumstance means that it is indistinguishable to the function developer and at the implementation echelon.

12.2.2 Middleware as an Enabling Engine

External applications to EISs were initially accessed through application programming interfaces (APIs) which can access ERP data. APIs are pieces of computer code at low level, which is time-consuming, costly, and difficult to maintain. A more recent trend has been the development of software with the specific purpose of accessing application packages to ERP. **Middleware** is an enabling engine to tie applications together. Middleware removes the need for APIs. Kara divided EIS/ERP middleware vendors into data-oriented products (supporting EIS/ERP integration through sharing data sources) and messaging-oriented vendors (who support direct data sharing between programs without the need of data files or databases).[11] Data-oriented vendor products extract and transform data, and then exchange data files between EIS packages and other applications. Middleware can transform data into standard formats readable by source and host systems. Most middleware products also serve to avoid problems of hub-and-spoke bottlenecks in single server computer architecture by providing load balancing in their execution environments if multiple servers are present. Figure 12.6 shows the relationship of middleware to the systems it links.

A major change in EISs has been the emergence of Web-delivered EIS. J.D. Edwards has designed their EIS product for that mode of delivery. SAP's mySAP.com is also oriented to Web delivery, and all vendors have moved that way. Kumar and van Hillegersberg expect expansion to multimedia documents, including engineering drawings, scanned documents, and audiovisual products.[12] Mullin noted a similar trend in the chemical industry (a big user of EIS), as well as increased emphasis on customer service and marketing rather than on internal transaction processing.[13] Every vendor has developed a **portal**, which provides linkage to sites of interest to specific users.

---

[11] Kara, D. (1999). ERP integration. *InformationWeek*, 3A–6A.

[12] Kumar, K. and van Hillegersberg, J. (2000). ERP experiences and evolution. *Communications of the ACM*, 43(4), 23–26.

[13] Mullin, R. (1999). Priorities shift away from ERP. *Chemical Week*, 44–45.

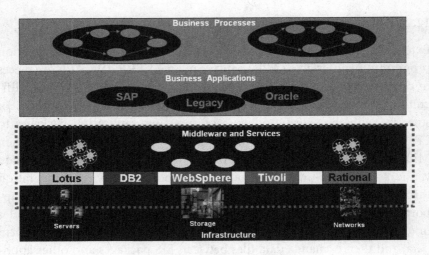

Figure 12.6: Middleware Linkages.

Source: www-935.ibm.com[14]

12.2.3 Middleware Enhancement

Table 12.2 gives one source's view of how middleware can give benefit to EIS users.

Middleware can support many forms of data acquisition. This includes bar-code data collection and radio frequency data collection. When Web systems are used, the term Web portal applies to software providing user-friendly access to data. Portals can act as middleware, giving organization members the ability to find technical information about engineering specifications, status information about promised shipments, and data about product prices and availability. Portals provide user-friendly access to data. Osram Sylvania developed a company-built portal for human resources information using Lotus Domino.[15] All EIS vendors also provide portals (see Table 12.3), although each tends to emphasize something different.

---

[14] IBM has been present in India since 1992 (re-entry, after an exit in the 1970s). Since inception, IBM in India has expanded its operations considerably with regional headquarters in Bangalore and offices in 14 cities including regional offices in New Delhi, Mumbai, Kolkata and Chennai. Today, the company has established itself as one of the leaders in the Indian Information Technology (IT) Industry.

[15] Michel, R. (2001). ERP gets redefined. *MSI*, 19(2), 36–44.

Table 12.2: Benefits of Middleware.

How Middleware services can help clients achieve significant benefits

Create an agile infrastructure that enables business process integration.
Increase business flexibility and decrease IT complexity.
Reduce the costs of business integration.
Simplify integration through IBM lifecycle methodologies and tool expertise.
Improve the management of infrastructures.
Improve time to value and make the most of existing technology skills.
Increase visibility and improve management and quality of IT services.
Create an IT infrastructure designed to address regulatory requirements.
Increase the value of existing IT investments.
Enhance information availability, quality and value.

Source: http://www-935.ibm.com/services/in/index.wss/itservice/gts/z1025998?source=cppITservices

Table 12.3: Portals Developed by Major ERP Vendors.

Vendor	Portal	Function
BAAN	IBAAN	Application integration
J.D. Edwards	ActivEra Portal	Single interface access to ERP, e-mail, spreadsheets, Internet data
	With CPqD Technologies and Systems	Telecommunications support to operations
Oracle	11i	Connect to business intelligence tools
	Oracle Portal Partner Initiative	Partnership of enterprise information providers (closed system)
PeopleSoft	PeopleSoft Business Network	Customers can tie applications to build online communities
	PeopleSoft Enterprise Portals	Data integration and aggregation targeted by employee
SAP	mySAP-Employee Workplace	Travel reservation, on-line procurement, etc.
	Business-to-Consumer Selling	Tools to build Internet storefront
	Business-to-Business Selling	Share production data
Lawson	Insight II Seaport	File, data warehouse, e-mail, Internet

Source: Stein and Davis (1999) and Stein (1999).[16]

---

[16] Stein, T. and Davis, B. (1999). Portal push: ERP vendors join the rush of software companies with plans to deliver gateways that integrate applications with other data sources. *Information Week*, 190–191, www.informationweek.com; Stein, T. (1999). ERP points to portals. *Information Week*, p. 26.

Table 12.4:   Portals Developed by Other Vendors.

Type	Third-party vendor	Function
Business Intelligence	Cognos	Access to data warehouses, data mining, and other business intelligence tools
	Information advantage	
	SAS Institute	
Documentation Management	Documentatum	Manage text
Others	Glyphica	Integrate ERP data into various applications
	Plumtree software	
	Viador	

Source: Stein and Davis (1999).[17]

The motivation for EIS vendors with respect to portals is to maintain a presence in a dynamic market. EIS vendor portals can focus attention to their products. Portals are also offered by third-party vendors, as shown in Table 12.4. Companies that are not EIS vendors provide portals to provide access to information in files, data warehouses, e-mail systems, the Internet, and many other applications.

Portals provide value to supply chain environments, feeding data across the entire supply chain and tapping into the power of an EIS. For instance, Gillette had a private exchange allowing suppliers and customers to view forecasts and actual orders to monitor production target performance. A portal provides a unified interface to various data sources.[18]

While adopting an EIS provides a competitive advantage, it also introduces concerns about security. Initial EISs were very closed, with limited numbers of organizational employees having access to the system. However, the strong trend toward more open EISs to gain advantages from supply chain connectivity and other features changes this circumstance dramatically.

---

[17] Stein, T. and Davis, B. (1999), op. cit.
[18] Greengard, S. (2001). New connections: Manufacturers are opening up ERP systems to enhance communication with business partners. *Industryweek*, 21–24, www.industry-week.com.

12.3 SECURITY AND EIS

Over the past two decades, the development of technology has accelerated. Security standards are critical to EIS. These standards apply to all EIS activities. EIS security must be a deep-seated premeditated driver of an organization's business to protect against theft and hostile acts.

Security is considered foremost in matters of national welfare. In the military, elaborate systems to safeguard information have always been important. Knowledge of enemy plans has been critical in influencing the course of human history. In classical business operations, just as in governmental and military operations, there have long been security issues concerned with physical protection. This physical protection could be of human access to buildings and information stored in critical rooms, much the same as banks were secured. With the advent of computer systems, this security expanded to data, wherever or in what form data was stored. There also has always been a concern about the security of individuals. In a military context, patrols are often sent out to capture enemy personnel with critical information. Business operations are not always as dramatic, although firms have been known to hire individuals with key information away from competitors, and the personality of the newly hired individual was undoubtedly not the only reason for the new job opportunity. The figure (Figure 12.7) below gives a clear view of the modus-operandi of security in enterprise information systems. It shows an archetypal dispersed mySAP ERP implementation and deliverance scenario. It illustrates how SAP servers require Software Distribution Servers to deliver SAP GUI and IPSec VPNs to provide secure remote access, requiring additional layers of management, security, and bandwidth.

12.3.1 Security Threats by Type

Computer systems involve a new level of detailed complexity, providing many opportunities to obtain key competitive information. Information is stored on computers and, with the advent of networks, is in most cases accessible by networks. There are many threats to the security of information

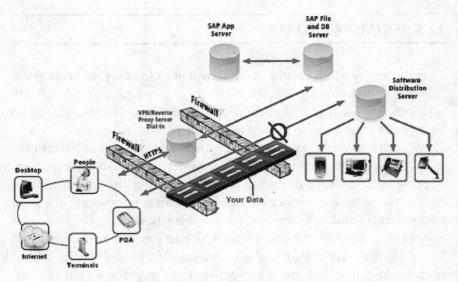

Figure 12.7: A View of Security Architecture.

Source: www.citrix.com[19]

found on EISs. Threats across all three forms of access are addressed in Table 12.5.

The traditional forms of physical spying can still be applied. This can include any form of unauthorized access to information. Social engineering is a term used to identify con games, using trickery to get those with critical information to reveal it. But the most common forms of security threats to EIS are those made possible because of computer technology. This can include invasive electronic entry, through some form of tapping or hacking. Unfortunately, some of this activity occurs from simple mischief and maliciousness, in the form of computer viruses. Viruses have been very irritating in recent times, making international headlines at a seemingly increasing rate.

---

[19] More than 215,000 organizations worldwide rely on Citrix to deliver any application to users anywhere with the best performance, highest security and lowest cost. Customers include 100 percent of the Fortune 100 companies and 99 percent of the Fortune Global 500, as well as hundreds of thousands of small businesses and presumes. Citrix has approximately 6,200 partners in more than 100 countries. Annual revenue in 2006 was $1.1 billion.

Table 12.5: Security Threats by Type.

Type of security	Threat
Physical	Theft, damage, copying Unauthorized access to information Natural disasters or accident
Social	Tricks to gain information
Network	Telephone taps Dial-up entry Internet hacking Viruses

In addition to these security risks faced by all computer systems, there are two aspects of security that are critical to EIS. One aspect concerns the quality of data generated and housed on the EIS. Data warehouses, discussed in Chapter 10, provide tools to ensure data quality. The other aspect is control over who can access data.

One major benefit of a Web-delivered system is the flexibility afforded to users through the ability to log into the EIS from any terminal (not only throughout the company, but also at airport terminals, hotels, or client offices). However, Liebmann reports that this creates a serious problem from the perspective of security.[20] One difficulty is that providers use forms of caching to improve performance. There is a serious risk arising from the user walking away from the terminal prior to deleting the cache. This can be cured by software designed to turn off caches once the need for them has gone. Another form of control that can be effective is a login page showing only those applications that the user is authorized to view. Some systems also provide access to HTML code that can reveal link information. The Web page access system can preclude user access of this HTML code.

While moving to the Web may make tight control more difficult, this is not insurmountable. A digital certificate sign-on can act as one security measure, with logon to a directory protocol permitting access to authorized EIS applications.[21] The ability to maintain EIS security in a Web

---

[20] Liebmann, L. (2001). ERP's housekeeping headaches. *InternetWeek*, 866, 37–38.
[21] Tiazkun, S. and Dunlap, C. (1999). Security strategies refined as ERP apps move to Web. *Computer Reseller News*, 5–6, www.crn.com.

environment is mandatory, given that all EIS vendors are responding to demand to provide Web products. Figure 12.8 demonstrates different types of security.

12.3.2 Adoption of Different Types of Security

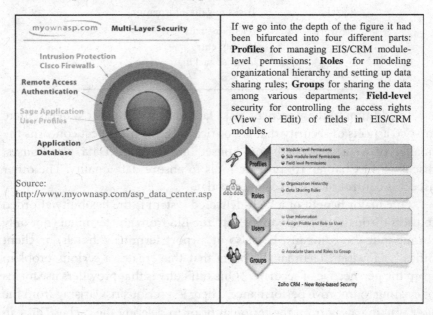

If we go into the depth of the figure it had been bifurcated into four different parts: **Profiles** for managing EIS/CRM module-level permissions; **Roles** for modeling organizational hierarchy and setting up data sharing rules; **Groups** for sharing the data among various departments; **Field-level** security for controlling the access rights (View or Edit) of fields in EIS/CRM modules.

Figure 12.8: Different types of security adopted by the user and vendors to regulate EIS.
Source: http://www.zolilog.com/tag/smb/

12.4 CONCLUSION

Since the beginning of the digital revolution, public and private organizations, leaders, and experts have dedicated noteworthy resources to developing the EIS security field, yet risks continue to exist. EIS security professionals must be equipped to meet the challenges that exist today and in the future.

The evolution of EIS has been meteoric. Prior to the early 1990s, EIS was mostly a vision on the part of SAP. During the 1990s, EIS evolved into a critically important backbone of software systems in large organizations. Late in the 1990s, the benefits of opening EISs became apparent, leading to a new generation (in a very compressed time-table) of EIS products. Open architecture is necessary for the addition of valuable bolt-ons to EISs. Bolt-ons provide EIS-serviced organizations the means to do many specialized tasks provided by bolt-on vendors. Another source of value comes from accessing data-oriented products, especially for data entry using modern technology. Middleware supports EIS access of external applications. Portals are specific forms of middleware, focusing especially on Internet connections to data and applications. Portals allow access to vendor enhancements, as well as individualized access to important information, no matter where that information is located.

This openness makes security an important issue. However, tools to obtain security are available. This makes it possible for all EIS vendors to deliver Web-based EISs.

In some implementations, core EIS functionality (HR, Finance, and Operations) is supplementeded with what are frequently called "bolt-ons". These are supplementary third-party or EIS vendor-supplied COTS software products that make accessible specialized functionality greater than that of the EIS itself (under license agreements with the original vendor)t. These bolt-ons, must be licensed and continued just like the core ERP software. Through the use of bolt-ons, EIS adopters may accomplish superior feature-function fit with subordinate configuration, without losing the advantages of continuing vendor upgrades.

☆ KEYWORDS

- ☆ **Application Programming Interface (API):** Software providing access to external applications to EISs.
- ☆ **Bolt-On:** Artificially intelligent execution system to add specific functionality to an EIS system.
- ☆ **Challengers:** Challengers execute well today and may dominate large segments, but are not "in synch" with the market's direction.

☆ **Leaders:** Leaders execute well today and are positioned well for tomorrow.

☆ **Middleware:** Software tying applications together.

☆ **Open Architecture:** Computer system environment where there are not excessive barriers to linking to other systems.

☆ **Optimization System:** Algorithmic software such as mathematical programming, capable of identifying the best solution to a given model.

☆ **Portal:** Software providing linkages from an EIS.

☆ **Security:** Need and strategies for security in standalone and networked systems, concept of access control list and capabilities, password and encryption schemes.

☆ **Visionaries:** Visionaries understand where the market is going or have a vision of changing market rules, but do not yet execute well.

☆ TERMINOLOGY REVIEW

1. Are you familiar with the many emerging technologies? Explain
2. Are you fully aware of the potential emerging technologies with relevance to EIS? Explain with the help of an illustration.
3. Describe the term "bolt-on".
4. What does an open architecture have to do with bolt-ons?
5. Search the library and/or the Internet for EIS bolt-ons.
6. What is middleware and what does it have to do with EIS?
7. Search the library and/or the Internet for applications of middleware.
8. Search the library and/or the Internet for applications of portals.
9. Portals have been defined by vendors in different ways. Describe some of these different definitions.
10. Discuss the relative trade-off in security and open access in EIS.
11. Compare physical, social, and network security.

☆ COMPETENCY REVIEW

1. Pragmatic Questions

a) How do you develop the data security policy using data security standards, guidelines, and requirements that include privacy, access, incident management, disaster recovery, and configuration?

b) Identify and document the appropriate level of protection for the data.

c) Specify information classification, sensitivity, and need-to-know requirements by data or data type.

d) Create data-user authentication and authorization system data access levels and privileges.

e) Develop acceptable procedures in support of the data security policy.

f) Develop sensitive data collection and management procedures in accordance with standards, procedures, directives, policies, regulations, and laws.

g) Identify an appropriate set of information security controls based on perceived risk of compromise to the data.

☆ SUGGESTED READING

Books

Bass, L., Clements, P. and Kazman, R. (2003). *Software Architecture in Practice*, 2nd Ed., Addison Wesley Professional.

Deloitte Touche Tohmatsu Research Team (2006). *Security, Audit and Control Features SAP R/3: A Technical and Risk Management Reference Guide*, 2nd Ed., Rolling Meadows, IL: ISACA. http://www.isaca.org/bookstore

Linkies, M. (2006). *SAP Security and Authorizations: Risk Management and Compliance with Legal Regulations in the SAP Environment*, MD: SAP PRESS America. http://www.sap-press.com

White Papers

Ashley, P., Powers, C. and Schunter, M. (2002). From Privacy Promises to Privacy Management: A New Approach for Enforcing Privacy Throughout an Enterprise. In *Proceedings of the 2002 Workshop on New Security Paradigms*, 43–50. ACM Press.

Impact of SAS 94 on Computer Audit Techniques (2003). *Information Systems Control Journal*, 1.

In *The Power of One — Leverage Value from Personalizaton Technologies*. Rangaswamy, A. and Pal, N. (ed.), eBRC Press.

Knorr, E. (2004). ERP Springs Eternal. *InfoWorld Magazine*.

Koch, C. (2002). The ABCs of ERP. *CIO Magazine Research Center*.

Montgomery, A. L. and Srinivasan, K. (2002). Learning About Customers Without Asking.

CHAPTER 13

FUTURE AND CONTEMPORARY TRENDS IN EIS

Quotation

An effective IT infrastructure can support a business vision and strategy; a poor, decentralized one can break a enterprise.

Holland and Light

Structure

- ♣ *Quick look at chapter themes*
- ♣ *Learning objectives*
- ♣ *Case study:* Analyzing Microsoft EIS/ERP's success in American Bible Society
- ♣ *Sketch of EIS initiation*
- ♣ Introduction
  - 13.1 Futuristic Trends In EIS
    - 13.1.1 Requirement-Oriented Applications (Tailored)
    - 13.1.2 Expenditure Trends
    - 13.1.3 Reduction In Implementation Time
  - 13.2 Next Generation of Enterprise Software
  - 13.3 Money Resource Planning [MRP-III]
    - 13.3.1 Prospective View of an Enterprise System
  - 13.4 Conclusion
- ☆ Keywords
- ☆ Terminology Review
- ☆ Competency Review
- ☆ Suggested Reading

♣ QUICK LOOK AT CHAPTER THEMES

Organizations today are swamped with a great deal of data. What is needed from information systems is easy access for business users to find the key information that they need. Lee Geishecker[1] advises CIOs that in order to do e-business, a good ERP system is required. "And because of this, the whole definition of ERP is being expanded," *he said. "Make sure you implement something that can be extended functionally." To accomplish this, we focus on electronic tools such as the World Wide Web, management sciences or quantitative techniques, and artificial intelligence. It is a 24/7 world. If you can understand the needs of the customer, which is the heart of the business's purpose, you see that the customer is one who operates in a global economy and is operating their business on a 24/7 basis. The futuristic enterprise information system should be customer-oriented. The major attribute the Internet brings in business is the spotlight on community. This creates groups working collectively.*

♣ LEARNING OBJECTIVES

Today, business solutions are expected to adapt — and to deal with fluctuating budgets and schedules. In this chapter we consider the current and future Enterprise Resource Planning (ERP) market, with a focus on the global market. After reading this chapter you will understand:

♣ The linking of people, processes and information to achieve business objectives.
♣ How companies can leverage information for competitive gain.
♣ The future scope of EIS and corporate motivation for implementing EIS.

---

[1] Lee Geishecker, Former Research VP, Gartner.

- ♣ The challenges associated with implementing such large-scale systems and the dramatic impact these systems have on future key business processes.
- ♣ How to develop future work plans for an extended EIS implementation.
- ♣ How to gain an understanding of next generation process integration inherent in EIS.
- ♣ How EIS will accelerate change, revamp businesses and force integration leading to end-to-end customer service.

♣ CASE STUDY

Analyzing Microsoft EIS/ERP's success in American Bible Society

EIS/ERP success does not happen all of a sudden in an organization. They can occur only if things are executed in a systematic manner as planned. Even if things don't go as planned, contingencies must be met efficiently and effectively. Such crisis management is a prerequisite in EIS/ERP projects because organizations should not stagger when things are not in tune with the expectations.

American Bible Society
The American Bible Society is a non-profit organization. They work towards making bibles available to every one in the language and format of their choice so that no one misses a chance of reading it. They also partner with other welfare organizations in sharing this noble pursuit. This organization is known for rendering august services to people all over the world, irrespective of caste, creed, sex, religion or any other discriminating element.

Why EIS/ERP in American Bible Society?
American Bible Society, being a welfare organization, maintains lots of data and handles queries though not for profit but for service. The stakeholders and others dealing with the organization must be assured of proper and prompt service. Just because the organization does not transact business does not absolve it of the responsibility of providing proper services. In fact a non-profit organization needs to deliver as much service as a business

478 ENTERPRISE INFORMATION SYSTEMS: CONTEMPORARY TRENDS AND ISSUES

entity. Given its nature of work, a non-profit organization may be required to deliver better service than others. More so when the organization is engaged in disseminating the message of the gospel.

American Bible Society was having several problems in handling data and managing the transactions in the organization. They were formerly using only J.D. Edward accounting system on an AS400 platform. This was undoubtedly an efficient program but could not handle the volume of operations maintained by American Bible Society.

The organization had Microsoft server as its setup. This proved to be a major hurdle because the employees could not work on one application as such. On the contrary, they had to frequently shuffle between the two for the respective functions the software programs were known to be good at. This resulted in wastage of time and added up to the confusion. Employees were even leaving tasks midway in order to use the other application for some other purpose in the same assignment. When they returned to the first application, they were not able to perform at the same speed and deliver the same results. Further the frequent changeover also put them in great discomfort. This was more so if their IT skills were limited. They would have also lost track of what and how things were going while they change the usage of applications.

These matters became worse as employees were not performing in line with the standards and targets. This brought great resentment among the customers. The organization also found it impractical to repair the existing setup because they were too costly. Meanwhile the results produced were totally unacceptable. It was at this point of time that the organization felt it imperative to go for an enterprise resource planning software. However the enterprise cannot choose a manufacturing enterprise resource planning software.

The plan of Action
They finally decided to stick to Microsoft solutions after carefully choosing from an assortment of EIS/ERP packages. One of the prime reasons for their choice was that it would coincide with the existing technology and deliver better results through the platform interface. First of all it would ensure easy working. They made EIS/ERP presentation and EIS/ERP freelance-implementation easier.

In addition they had also acquired the services of some third party solutions authorized by Microsoft to make things compact and in one unique setup. The organization implemented EIS/ERP at a stretch so that it was beneficial for all the functions. Owing to the size of the operations and the higher number of users Microsoft happened to be the organizations' favorite choice.

There was no more confusion. The workflow was smoothened. Information was properly available to the customers at the right time and in the proper manner. The departments enjoyed greater network and connectivity. Meanwhile customer queries were responded to spontaneously. All hassles faced by the organization were solved.

Other benefits
The organization also enjoyed many more benefits after the EIS/ERP software was implemented. They witnessed a huge decline in the costs incurred to procure and maintain licenses with the help of infrastructural facilities of Microsoft solutions. They were also able to reduce the amount of money spent on leasing. Due to the confusion in the organizational setup, it was very difficult to generate reports.

The reports generated were neither unambiguous nor did it serve the purpose. The increase in operational efficiency made possible by EIS/ERP helped this to happen. Above all, everything was delivered within deadline. Since the organization has already been using Microsoft, it was not difficult to install a Microsoft-based EIS/ERP application. Moreover there was no difficulty in the implementation because the organization was already familiar with its features. Change management was not necessary in this case due to the reason citied above.

Source: www.erpwire.com[2]

♣ SKETCH OF EIS INITIATION

To function in today's information market, enterprises need a vision of how they would like to exchange information with their customers and suppliers. They could work with creative vendors and consultants to create links between their EIS applications as well as new Web and E-commerce applications. Those who successfully master this new complex environment of interacting information systems will unquestionably succeed.

---

[2] www.erpwire.com is owned and managed by crewind technologies, a software development firm specializing in online marketing strategies. This website is meant to be an interactive platform for ERP users. Apart from the plethora of information we are offering, this Web portal will also serve to be a hub for enterprise resource planning.

Without sound EIS, service/manufacturing sectors cannot compete in the increasingly global manufacturing and service industry with EIS supporting e-procurement/marketing and paperless documents. Companies that install EIS applications need to be familiar with the value of integrating processes and technologies. Companies that utilize data warehouses need to be acquainted with the value of giving supplementary employees appropriate access to critical information. Companies need to amalgamate their operational and informational systems. This means creating links between packaged EIS applications and data warehouses.

♣ INTRODUCTION

Information technology is dramatically reshaping the business landscape. Technology savvy firms are exploiting powerful new technologies to attain and keep customers; handle product supply chains; authorize knowledge workers to do required work; and better support decision-making. These companies are reinventing the rules of the business game. The flourishing of a variety of EIS systems has led to substantial concentration in the past few years, but has also seen the development of many country-specific alternative EIS software products. Yet despite the many gains available from EIS, many companies have wasted many millions of dollars with little positive results to show for it.

Thus the propagation of embedded systems has resulted in enormous amounts of data. On the other hand, linking of these databases and enterprise systems in order to make their contents available as a way to support management has been a challenge.

13.1 FUTURISTIC TRENDS IN EIS

You can gain a sense of the growing enthusiasm from a business that effortlessly and professionally implemented an EIS to gain advantage. Managers and other business users can access their control panels of their EIS to quickly see what is going on in their areas of responsibility. This can enable businesses to better attain their profit goals.

At a time when "the hottest new thing" often turns out to be yesterday's news or goes up in a puff of smoke, enterprise systems have a real future as a key component of EIS software. EIS calls for stable modifications and upgrades. EIS developers are facing many new opportunities from vendors and new requirements from regulators and from top management. We need to consider EIS's trends. The future of EIS software is very bright, with many improvements on the horizon both from vendors as well as from user's.

13.1.1 Requirement-Oriented Applications (Tailored)

Organizations have implemented EIS adopting partial functionality. This has sometimes been a major stumbling block in that they may not gain full advantage from their EIS. Other firms have had to purchase bundled functionality from vendors that provided functions they did not need.

Newer EIS software products can allow greater tailoring to organizational needs. Figure 13.1 graphically depicts requirement-oriented

Requirement-oriented applications [Tailor-Made]

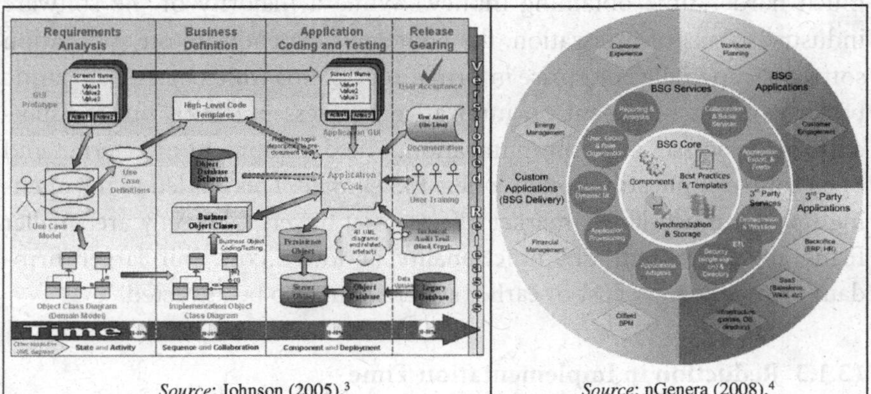

Source: Johnson (2005).[3]   Source: nGenera (2008).[4]

Figure 13.1:   Systems Development of Tailored Processes.

---

[3] Johnson, D. (2005). Association Implementation. *Journal of Object Technology*, 4(2), 81–108. Journal of Object Technology (JOT) is an on-line peer-reviewed publication, published six times per year by the ETH Swiss Federal Institute of Technology, aimed at intermediate to advanced practitioners, educators and researchers in the field of object technology. http://www.jot.fm/issues/issue_2005_03/article1

[4] nGenera helps its customers become Next Generation Enterprises, On Demand.

applications resulting from a careful systems analysis process. Firms can purchase and install EIS specifically tailored to their needs. This enables firms to gain the support they need without paying for unnecessary software components.

Batuhan Yukselen[5] has stated on a blog that "SAP will struggle in the SME market because SAP implementation projects are over-budget and over time; there is a common public perception that SAP meets only the needs of large customers; Microsoft is doing extremely well in SME market. Actually, what raises a flag of concern is that SAP pushed back Business by Design for 18 months in a fast-paced, rapidly-evolving software business."

13.1.2 Expenditure Trends

According to Michael H. Goldhaber,[6] "One of the first such standardized manufactured goods was money itself (in the form of coins). Now, increasingly, money tracks attention. Those with a great deal of attention can easily obtain money, should they want it. Those with little attention will have a much harder time obtaining money." While a majority of the software industry speaks of innovation, the enormous expenditure on application software (especially enterprise information systems which come in gigantic packages). It is not spent on innovative business practices, but for standardized processes and communication. The development of Internet and open source applications offers a new EIS climate. This has led to the opening up of a much larger market of potential buyers. Not only are smaller firms able to obtain EIS functionality at lower cost, but larger firms daunted by the high cost of earlier systems can also be attracted.

13.1.3 Reduction in Implementation Time

EIS was unattractive to many companies because they took such a long time to be installed. Current EIS applications are simpler to implement,

---

[5] BS/MS student at Drexel University majoring in computer/software engineering, http://knowledge.wharton.upenn.edu, 2008

[6] Michael, D. Goldhaber is the Senior International Correspondent for The American Lawyer magazine and the ALM chain of publications. www.goldhaber.org

and require less training of users. This has reduced the amount of time required to implement an EIS. Figure 13.2 shows how new technologies are available to broaden the use of EIS.

Figure 13.2 shows three important elements that have rejuvenated the functioning of EIS. Open Source ERP has done away with the hassles of paying license fees not only all through installation but also each time you want to modify the system.

Web-enabled EIS helps in bringing the enterprise operations online. Any stakeholder or third party can enter required information very easily from any place in the world. This can be of great help especially during emergencies.

Wireless EIS has helped organizations make use of communication channels effectively and efficiently. It has made it possible for many elements to operate in EIS which were otherwise not possible. Wireless EIS is nothing but sharing enterprise information through devices like the Internet and other devices, making it possible for outsiders to access the system.

13.2 NEXT GENERATION OF ENTERPRISE SOFTWARE

Current business circumstances demand innovative forms of enterprises. The next generation enterprise system will be a powerful two-way, real-time system applying current technology to systematically deal with innovative changes in strategy and execution at high-speed without error, persistently focused on customer needs. Next generation enterprise systems will operate on demand. By on demand, we mean a cooperative response to an enterprise's customers and in jointly assembling and deploying its resources.

Figure 13.3 lays out how organizations can obtain new functionality in new generations of EIS.

Figure 13.4 graphically displays how a core organization's EIS can be linked to external data sources.

Some of the next generation enterprise system features are as follows:

♦ The ability to modify the present system in response to dynamic organizational business needs.

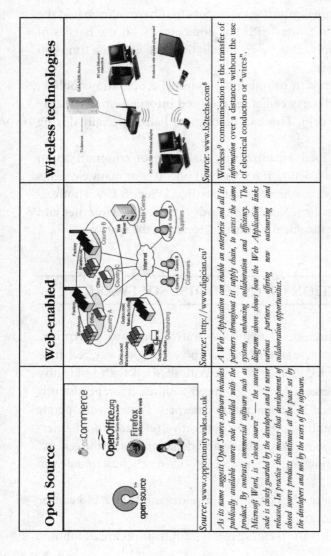

Open Source	Web-enabled	Wireless technologies
Source: www.opportunitywales.co.uk	*Source:* http://www.digcian.eu[7]	*Source:* www.b2techs.com[8]
As its name suggests Open Source software includes publically available source code bundled with the product. By contrast, commercial software such as Microsoft Word, is "closed source" — the source code is closely guarded by the developers and is never released. In practice this means that development of closed source products continues at the pace set by the developers and not by the users of the software.	*A Web Application can enable an enterprise and all its partners throughout its supply chain, to access the same system, enhancing collaboration and efficiency. The diagram above shows how the Web Application links various partners, offering new outsourcing and collaboration opportunities.*	*Wireless[9] communication is the transfer of information over a distance without the use of electrical conductors or "wires".*

Figure 13.2:   New Technologies Enhancing EIS Implementation.

---

[7] Digital + Technician = Digician. Digician specializes in the development of Enterprise Level Web Applications to replace traditional enterprise software. Their Web Applications cover a broad range of industries: logistics, warehousing, retailing, claims management, repairs insurance and mobile devices. Digician's Applications are written in-house by a team of developers who have also worked in operational roles within non-I.T. companies and understand their real world requirements.

[8] B² Technology Consultant, LLC based in the greater Kansas City metro area, is a full-service information technology consulting enterprise, servicing micro, small and medium businesses. They have eight years of extensive IT experience in providing technology solutions. B² places significant value in the relationships it develops, with the businesses it serves, and support the efforts and the roles each and everyone play in society.

[9] "Wireless Communication." sintef.no. Retrieved on 01-Oct-2008.

Generation	About	USP	Diagrammatic View
First Generation known as ERP	First generation ERP software is characterized by a profusion of procedural-type legacy code, a bloated support infrastructure, and pervasive armies of consultants draining the profit from many organizations. As overworked as the term "paradigm shift" may be, even to the point of being a cliché, the emergence of object-oriented architecture, and associated design and development tools (including visual design methodologies such as UML), have together created a total paradigm-shift — a revolution, really, in computer program design and development.	Integration of the distinguished module as the previous versions was restricted to particular department.	 *Source*: www.acsonnet.com[10]
Next Generation Known as EIS	*In a next generation Enterprise system application, the understanding of the system is enhanced by the use of context-relevant pop-up and pull-down menus — productivity demonstrated by the aptitude to carry out a task, is enhanced, while errors and frustration are abridged. By the way, training time is also engraved spectacularly.*	• Enterprise system is Web-Enabled for E-business. Incorporates the four new e-business applications that Enterprise system vendors provide to facilitate the E-business strategy. • Server-side database integration. • Shore up state-ful persistent client sessions. • Standards-based (XML, J2EE). • Supply chain management (SCM), E-commerce, CRM, BI, etc. • Support for automatic server push to the client. • Support standard security approaches (data encryption, digital certificates, client sandbox). • Sustain off-line operations on the client. • Tolerate a less complex development model. • Widen server objects to the GUI.	 *Source*: Classic System Solutions (2008).[11]
© David L Olson and Subodh Kesharwani.			

Figure 13.3: Paradigm Shifts across EIS Generations.

---

[10] Accurate Info Solution, founded in 1995, partners with various companies to plan, build, and manage application software to enable their business strategies. This is accomplished through its Business Consulting, Application Development and Integration (ADI), and Application Development and Management (ADM).

[11] Classic System Solutions, Inc. is internationally recognized for its expertise in the field of GUI design and client/server architecture. It has led numerous design efforts for large-scale, high-volume transactional systems. Its consultants are frequently quoted in major publications and speak at many industry conferences.

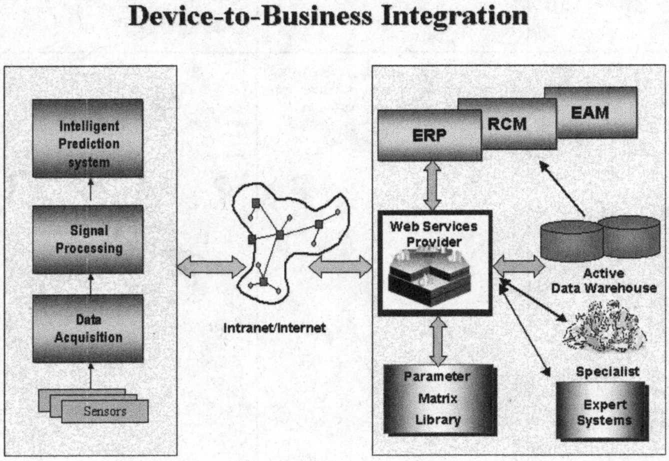

Device-to-Business Integration

Figure 13.4: Linkage of EIS with External Systems.

Source: www.acrc.unisa.edu.au.[12]

- ◆ BAAN started Intelligence Resource Planning and MRP-III to meet changing needs. New generation ERP systems include component architecture that is very much modular in character.
- ◆ Future trends include looking-backward compatibility, generalized solutions, friendlier interfaces, object orientation, and Web-enablement.
- ◆ User preferences like cost understanding, specificity and faster solutions are provided.
- ◆ Extension to SCM, E-commerce, Intelligent Applications and Customization are prime focuses in the future.

The Internet represents the foremost new technology-enabler, enabling speedy supply chain management between multiple operations and

---

[12] Adapted from Prof. Andy Koronios' research in which he had emphasized that the data collected from different types of operational systems will be integrated via a data warehouse concept. Reporting tools can then use this data to generate straightforward analyzes, such as trends, exceptions, and correlations. Further the data collected from technical systems can then be integrated with data from business systems such as ERP (Enterprise Resource Planning).

trading partners. Most EIS/ERP systems are enhancing their products to become "Internet-Enabled" so that customers worldwide can have direct access to the supplier's enterprise system. Enterprise systems are building in workflow management functionality which provides a means to deal with and control the flow of work by monitoring logistic aspects like workload, and processing times of various supply chain members. Recognizing the need to go beyond the MRP-II and EIS/ERP capabilities, vendors are adding to their product assortment. BAAN has introduced concepts like IRP (Intelligence Resource Planning), MRP-III (Money Resources Planning) and strategic technologies like Visual Product configuration, Product Data Management and Finite Scheduling.

13.3 MONEY RESOURCE PLANNING [MRP-III]

The rationale of doing business is, without hesitation, to make money. The logistical and financial concept of MRP-III (Money Resource Planning) furnishes methods for conducting simulations. MRP-III will integrate information concerning both money and material flows following the theory propounded by Schollaert.[13] What MRP-III implies is that managers should take a fundamental look at their company's objectives. Marketing, logistics and financial accounting exist for only one thing — to make money for the company. In this context, concepts such as "technology push" are no longer valid. The driver is rather "market pull", where the customer dictates what the enterprise does. When the challenges faced by the enterprise become more complex, managers who are extremely specialized lose control. Integration then becomes the primary goal in yielding tangible results. As each specialist manages only a part of the enterprise, the information flow is divided into different "sub flows." Specialized information is too diverse and even redundant, as demonstrated in Figure 13.5.

What happens if the information needs to be consolidated at the corporate level? Then things go wrong. Here, MRP-III tries to bring all

---

[13] Francis Schollaert is a professor in the Saint Aloysius School of Economics, Brussels.

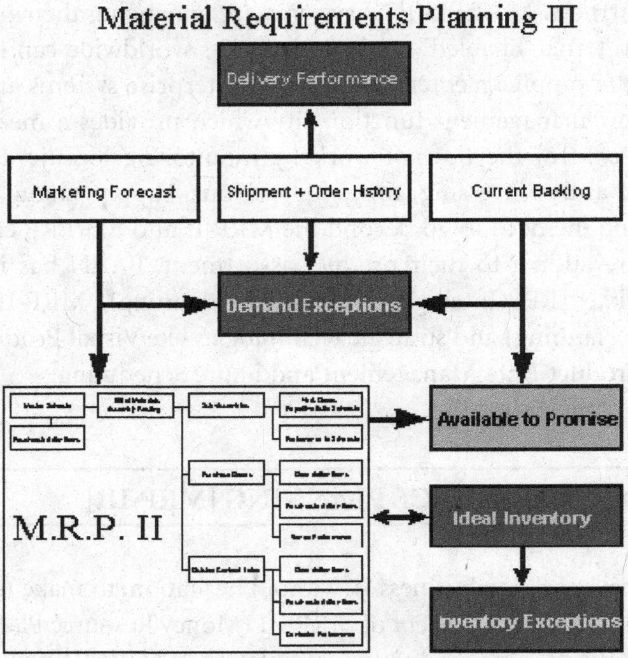

Material Requirements Planning III

Figure 13.5: Faulty Information Flow.

Source: www.mrp3.com[14]

information into line. Each manager should be able to manage the whole enterprise. This is especially true for companies that have longer lead times, such as machine factories.

The shape of the next generation of ERP software is sketched in Table 13.1.

13.3.1 Prospective View of an Enterprise System

ERP has been a tour de force for many large organizations. As other segments of the enterprise application market fight for the spotlight, the role of ERP in an enterprise's application strategy is changing. While the days

---

[14] Stewart-Frazier Tools Inc. 1996.

Table 13.1: Features of the Next Generation of EIS Software.

Step	Features	
I.	EXISTING EIS SOFTWARE	Existing EIS software should be flexible and multifaceted so that at the preliminary stage it can address the essential requirements of its users.
		♦ Composite to implement.
		♦ Extremely huge software.
		♦ Multifaceted to recognize.
		♦ Resource greedy.
II.	PROGRESSION	The software has been enhanced in such a way that users can have control over their operating environment. It must have the following features:
		♦ Trait totaling.
		♦ Backward compatibility.
		♦ Generic explanation.
		♦ Deal with wide diversity of state of affairs.
III.	TECHNOLOGY SHIFTS	The EIS software should have several features USP (Unique Selling Point) that enable users to easily switch over from their manual environment to using its software. It will allow users to incorporate individual work profiles and process flows. It will also have the following features:
		♦ Object technology.
		♦ Module technology.
		♦ Software "plug and play".
		♦ Dispersed over the net.
		♦ Web-enabled.
IV.	PREDILECTION CLIENT	The software package must be easy to understand and easy to use. It should provide features such as menu wizard, Help-file, Search Engine, etc. the layman user. It should also include for the following:
		♦ Co-work with others without difficulty.
		♦ Explicit solution.
		♦ Fewer expensive.
		♦ Quick implementation.

(Continued)

Table 13.1: (*Continued*)

Step		Features
V.	MARKET SERVICES	The vendor should have a well-organized and well-trained team to provide better on-site customer support. The training and education would be systematic and must have following features: ◆ Module-based licensing. ◆ Larger consultant base. ◆ Pick and choose across vendors. ◆ Shrink wrapped software. ◆ Purchase off the shift.
VI.	FOREMOST INCLINATION	EIS software must have a feature to integrate with the different application modules such as CRM, SCM, MRP, ERP-II, E-Commerce, etc., so that users can configure it according to their requirements. ◆ Application objects with lot of intelligence. ◆ Extension to supply chain. ◆ Repository for E-Commerce. ◆ Swift customization.
VII.	WRAPPING UP	Vendors have to be very broadminded and energetic during the process of selling as well as on delivering training so that the layman user can understand its benefits. As far as EIS users are concerned they should be austere that they are not merely upgrading their technical expertise but also develop the ability to streamline their workflow and processes: ◆ Be more outstrand focussed. ◆ Be more receptive to new business practices.

of huge budgets and massive schedules may have passed, ERP (even on the downside of a wave) has continued to thrive, according to analysts. "ERP is very much alive," said Judy Hodges, an analyst with International Data Corporation in Framingham, MA. "It has become especially strategic in e-commerce where transactions tend to be more complex, smaller, and geographically diverse." "We will be using ERP/MRP systems internally and other system externally to satisfy our customer needs. I don't like the use of 'ERPII.' It still has the flavor of ERP, and we need to think of the complete process up and down the chain. I don't suggest 'supply chain management' is the new buzzword either — we need to bring together all the terms, SCM, MRP, ERP, CRM, EDI, WMS, APS, etc, and processes. What that new buzzword is and what it represents, only time will indicate." **Thomas A. Bihun**

13.4 CONCLUSION

The fact that there is still such a strong market proves that ERP is far from over. While this market involves much change, and therefore confusion, it also offers many improvements. Most organizations look at up-front cost of the ERP software, but ignore the "hidden costs." It is generally true that ERP implementations costs are roughly five times the cost of ERP software. In a sense, one should look at Total Cost of Ownership (TCO) over a five-year period. Other issues that must be considered include Euro compliance (practically everyone is addressing this), skill availability (from vendors, implementation partners, training institutes etc.) and past performance in terms of timely implementation, avoidance of cost overruns, project management capability etc.

For most of the last decade, companies have exhausted millions of dollars deploying EIS applications and data warehouses. They have deployed EIS to computerize operational processes; they've constructed data warehouses to augment decision-making and planning. At the moment companies are increasing the use of EIS applications. Creating a bi-directional flood of data between operational and analytical systems will help companies to respond speedily and effectively to new prospects and problems.

Thus ERP trends reflect positive signals for ERP vendors and companies wanting their service. It is important to remember that both the vendor and the enterprise will be able to make use of any advantage (including the modern facilities) only through proper coordination, team-work and nurturing a cordial atmosphere. But this is not enough. Thus in considering these key elements of EIS, two things are prominent. First, from an IT perspective there are no technological impediments preventing information systems in an organization from reaching its potential. Second, if there are any obstacles, they will come from the IT industry's failure to provide products that satisfy user needs. The industry has made significant progress in applying open standards to other IT applications. There is no doubt that we can work together to build our future enterprise systems.

☆ KEYWORDS

☆ **Distribution:** Should be able to make available or access services in a distributed and multi-provider environment both for network services and application services, so that the EIS cannot be a central node that provides connectivity and services to the partners.

☆ **Extensibility:** Should be able to update formats for data interchange and the protocols for software interoperability with speedy and low cost upgrades, even in the presence of radical innovations in the application domains and in the technological scenarios.

☆ **Interoperability:** The capability for people with different systems to communicate with one another independently of the base, middleware and application software adopted.

☆ **Next Generation Networking:** As per the Wikipedia, Next Generation Networking (NGN) is a broad term to describe some key architectural evolutions in telecommunication core and access networks that will be deployed over the next 5–10 years. The general idea behind NGN is that one network transports all information and services (voice, data, and all sorts of media such as video) by encapsulating these into packets, like it is on the Internet.

☆ **Openness:** Should be able to easily interact with systems external to the Business Community.

☆ **Pervasiveness:** Should be able to use the EIS independently of the characteristics of their infrastructures (e.g., network numbering, firewalling policies, etc.).

☆ **Security:** Should be able to exchange message or do transactions with guarantees of authenticity, integrity and secrecy.

☆ TERMINOLOGY REVIEW

---

a) What is the future of ERP, i.e. the so called next wave?
b) What are the future directives in ERP?
c) What is the next generation of ERP Software?
d) What do you mean by MRP-III?
e) What do you mean by "user preference" in respect to ERP Software?
f) Explain the salient features of ERP-Software.
g) ERP is a buzzword and seems to be a hot cake in future.
h) EIS develops both a platform and specific vertical applications that are delivered on demand and meet the needs of next generation enterprises in many industries. Explain with the help of an illustration.
i) Could your business benefit from free quality software? Of course it could. But, what's the catch? As long as you're reasonably PC-literate (or know a Web developer) there isn't one. Here's how you can cut costs by tapping into a growing movement called "Open Source" software.

☆ COMPETENCY REVIEW

---

1. **Pragmatic Questions**

   a) Can the future of information management be defined? Is it possible for any of us to say where information technology will be heading in the next 10 years?

b) Has the heyday of the EIS already come and gone? Have you had success with your EIS?

c) What are your thoughts on enterprise software — where is it headed, where are the trends, where are you positioned in all that?

d) The key to success for this development process lies in the first step, "develop an Implementation Object Class Model", because the way in which object class associations are implemented can significantly affect the performance of applications that depend upon them. Conversely, any time and effort spent producing a good business class design can be completely negated in terms of object access performance due to poor association implementation. Explain.

e) People make any business by undertaking or controlling their daily tasks. Explain.

f) Companies will not be as quick to jump to the "next new thing" as they were in the past as there is no big forcing factor (true or false) like Y2K.

g) One of the alternatives to pure-build or buy has been a "blended" approach, depending upon whom you converse with, using services, components, tasks, business processes, etc. Explain.

2. **Fill in the Blanks**

   1. USP is _____.
   2. EIS should be _____ in nature.
   3. Plug and play is _____.

3. **True & False**

   a) The fact is that the software industry, indeed the entire tech industry is still 'neo-natal'.

4. **Multiple Type Question**

   1. IRP Stands for

      (i) Intelligence Resource Planning.
      (ii) Internet Resource Planning.
      (iii) Internal Resource Planning.
      (iv) Intelligence Resource Procedure.

2. MRP stands for

    (i)   Money Resource Planning.
    (ii)   Money Resource Procedure.
    (iii) Measurement Resource Planning.
    (iv)   Money Reallocate Planning.

5. **Briefly Comment on the following statements:**

    a) EIS isn't going to take over the world, because it already has.

    ....

    ....

    b) "EIS" is very much alive.

    ....

    ....

    c) It has become especially strategic in e-commerce where transactions tend to be more complex, smaller, and geographically diverse.

    ....

    ....

    d) Internet speed also makes EIS more critical than ever.

    ....

    ....

    e) "The way this market is changing is that, it used to be about 'What is the product capability you have today?' and now it's more about 'What is the product capability that you're promising to have in a few years?'"

    ....

    ....

☆ SUGGESTED READING

Books

Adam, F. and Sammon, D. (2004). *The Enterprise Resource Planning Decade: Lessons Learned and Issues for the Future*. Hershey, USA: Idea Group Publishing.

Butterworth-Heinemann (2004). *The past and future of information systems*. Oxford: Elsevier.

Hohpe, W. (2004). Enterprise Integration Patterns, Addison-Wesley.

Light, B. (2000). Enterprise Resource Planning Systems: Impacts and Future Directions. In *Systems Engineering for Business Process Change: Collected Papers from the EPSRC Research Programme*, Henderson, P. (ed.), 117–126. London: Springer.

Journal Articles

Jacobs, R. and Whybark, C. (2000). Why ERP a Primer on SAP. *Managing Automation*, 9.

Scott, J. E. and Vessey, I. (2000). Implementing Enterprise Resource Planning Systems: The Role of Learning from Failure. *Information Systems Frontiers*; special issue on The Future of Enterprise Resource Planning Systems, 2(2), 213–232.

White Paper

Robinson, P. (2000). ERP (Enterprise Resource Planning) Survival Guide. http://www.bpic.co.uk/erp.htm (accessed on 16 May 2001).

CHAPTER 14

VENDOR PROFILES: MARKET SHARE AND PRODUCT VARIATION

Quotation

EIS software vendors are innumerable in terms of service and efficiency. Choosing the right EIS vendor for the company is not an easy decision. The company has to choose a person who fits well in all the parameters. All the criteria from service to cost have to be satisfied.

www.erpwire.com, 2008

Structure

- ♣ *Quick look at chapter themes*
- ♣ *Learning objectives*
- ♣ *Case study:* Oracle to MS SQL Server Migration
- ♣ *Sketch of EIS vendors*
- ♣ Introduction
  - 14.1 Market Stake of Vendors
    - 14.1.1 Market Share of Leading Vendors Over Time
    - 14.1.2 Overview of ERP Vendors
  - 14.2 Service-Oriented Architectures (SOA)
    - 14.2.1 SOA Relevance to EIS Vendors
  - 14.3 SAP (System Application and Products)
    - 14.3.1 SAP's Products
    - 14.3.2 SAP's Market Share
  - 14.4 ORACLE
    - 14.4.1 Oracle Control Features
  - 14.5 PEOPLESOFT

♣ QUICK LOOK AT CHAPTER THEMES

With the increasing functionality and development of enterprise information systems, choosing the right software collaborator is no longer a challenge, but it requires a strategic team effort. The challenge is choosing the best implementation collaborator who can bring the installation project to successful completion. Experience, together with culture and methodologies, facilitate accomplishment of the project objectives. To understand EIS/ERP vendors' sales, one must think about the economics that constrain many of these companies. Gigantic players such as Oracle, SAP, Microsoft Dynamics, and many other new vendors have invested hundreds of millions of dollars to build up their EIS/ERP applications.

♣ LEARNING OBJECTIVES

Effective forecasting, planning, and scheduling are fundamental to productivity — and an enterprise information system is a fundamental means to accomplish it. Properly implementing EIS/ERP will furnish a competitive advantage and facilitate running the business more effectively, efficiently, and responsively. After reading this chapter one will gain insight into:

- ♣ End-user spending and attitudes.
- ♣ Vendors of EIS and their sales tactics.
- ♣ Elaborative details about SAP, Oracle, Microsoft, etc.
- ♣ How the big players sell EIS to potential customers.
- ♣ How businesses characteristically select a particular vendor.
- ♣ How EIS vendors break up their functional business areas into modules.
- ♣ How SOA (Service Oriented Architecture) is critical to the strategies of several EIS providers.
- ♣ Managing vendor relationships while assessing their com.
- ♣ Monitoring the overall vendor management with relevance to EIS.

♣ CASE STUDY

Oracle to MS SQL Server Migration

ABOUT THE CASE STUDY

The subject of the case study is a global provider of personalized enterprise solutions with a turnover close to USD 300 million. It employs over 7000 people and has over 1,000 customers across 30 countries. The ERP vendor wanted to migrate 2.5 million lines of code in ERP Aviation module from Oracle to Microsoft SQL Server. The ERP vendor looked out for an automated, reliable, and affordable stored procedure migration solution. (The name of the ERP vendor has not been revealed on request, considering the competitive environment prevailing in that segment).

ABOUT SWISS SQL SOLUTIONS

SwisSQL offered automated database migration up to 90 percent, saving costs by 80 percent. It offered productive, predictable and controlled migration environment at an affordable price. The benefits of a **Swiss SQL include**

♣ Simple and reliable migration ensuring application and data integrity.
♣ Drastic cost and time reduction, automating up to 90 percent of manual tasks.
♣ Rapid deployment.

ABOUT ADVENTNET

Enabling Management Your Way™. AdventNet provides affordable software for database migration, management and provisioning of complex networks, systems, and IT applications. AdventNet is headquartered in Pleasanton, CA with offices in NJ, MA, India, UK, China, and Japan and has a well-trained partner base around the globe. It has over 400 employees and more than 1000 customers.

OVERVIEW OF CASE STUDY

SwisSQL Helps Major ERP Vendor in Database Migration from Oracle to MS SQL Server. A Major ERP Vendor saved an estimated $200K and 52-person months using SwisSQL to migrate 2.5 million lines of mission critical module from Oracle to Microsoft SQL Server.

A. BUSINESS CHALLENGE

The ERP vendor, a global provider of customized enterprise solutions developed Aircraft maintenance solutions. Its Enterprise Asset Management for aviation, consists of modules covering all areas of enterprise management for the fixed wing aircraft and helicopter maintenance industry. The solution is implemented on client server and web transactions platform with e-business and mobile computing capabilities. Most of the

ERP vendor's applications were based on MS SQL Server, a few modules were built on Oracle. The Aircraft Maintenance solution had a critical module with close to 2.5 million lines of Oracle PL/SQL code and their business logic was implemented in Oracle PL/SQL. The ERP vendor wanted to migrate the entire application and business logic to MS SQL Server Transact-SQL. It was important that ERP application also utilizes MS SQL Server, in order to leverage its performance, scalability and cost advantage.

B. EARLIER LESSONS

The ERP vendor had an earlier experience of migrating one of the Aviation modules from Oracle to MS SQL Server manually with a 10-member team. The manual migration project did not materialize due to:

* **High Time and Resource Expenditures:** Manual migration required DB experts/Developers to analyze and understand the overall design and to manually re-structure all stored procedures. This method was tedious and proved error-prone.
* **Extensive Unpredictable Bugs:** Migrated procedures required compilation and validation before deploying them to MS SQL Server. With developers' individual programming logic, mistakes and bugs were prevalent, with unpredictable error patterns.
* **Lack of Automated Migration Tool:** The unpredictable bugs, issues, and high cost made the ERP vendor realize the need for a fast, dependable and cost-effective automated migration solution.

SWISSQL SOLUTION

SwisSQL offered the ERP vendor a quick turnaround solution to migrate and adapt to MS SQL Server and leverage its advantages instantly. Using SwisSQL–Oracle to SQL Server Database Migration Solution, the automated migration was quickly done.

A. *Project Execution:* SwisSQL's standards-based efficient database migration reduced the ERP vendors validation and integration efforts through well-designed and automated tools. With SwisSQL's purposeful design, the ERP vendor was able to execute an efficient and successful database migration project well ahead of deadline by the following steps:

a. **No pre-conditioning:** SwisSQL assisted the ERP vendor load stored procedures from local files or fetch from a live Oracle database and migrate it to MS SQL Server directly. Once the migration was complete, review and validation of the code was conducted for accuracy. This step required a small team and no heavy-handed DB expertise.

b. **Deployment and Validation:** The ERP vendor utilized SwisSQL to compile the migrated Transact SQL procedures in MS SQL Server. The compiled procedures were first unit-tested and validated from within the business application environment. This process ensured accuracy and savings of time and resources.

c. **Reduced Integration Effort:** Integration of the migrated code with live business environment is a critical component of Database migration. SwisSQL's effective and standards-based migration reduced validation and integration efforts by more than 50 percent.

B. **Technical Benefits:** The ERP vendor leveraged SwisSQL's automated migration solution, which offered simple and reliable stored procedure migration, doing away with 90 percent of manual tasks that provided some obvious benefits including:

a. **Productivity Gains:** SwisSQL's automated migration tool helped the ERP vendor's migration team to focus just on analysis, review, corrections and performance-tweaking of converted code offering efficient and productive migration.

b. **Controlled Validation and Deployment:** Enterprises understand that validation, testing, and integration phases are critical components of a database migration project. The ERP vendor saved close to 50 percent of cost and time in validation due to SwisSQL standards based migration, with minimal conversion errors, which were much easy to solve due to the predictable pattern of bugs and issues.

c. **Complete Solution:** The ERP vendor was ahead of schedule, as they leveraged SwisSQL's complete solution, in migrating, testing, validating, and integrating. SwisSQL's direct support from technical developers helped the ERP vendor resolve the issues instantly.

C. *Business Benefits*: Although the business justification to migrate to MS SQL Server existed, past experience however did not converge into real benefits. With SwisSQL, the ERP vendor recognized the impacts on business immediately. Some of the benefits to highlight are:

a. **Complete Ownership Control:** SwisSQL automated 90 percent of the code produced, thereby saving 80 percent of the investment that was spent on manual intervention. This gave the ERP Vendor complete control over the migration.

b. **Faster Time to market:** Significant amount of time was lost during manual migration exercise and the ERP vendor was sensitive to the time factor. SwisSQL assisted the ERP vendor to rapidly reach its goals through its automated and reliable migration. This short migration cycle enabled the ERP vendor to capitalize on market opportunities faster.

c. **Immediate Time and Cost Savings:** Utilizing SwisSQL, the ERP vendor saved about $200K and 52-person months of investment and ensured faster time to production. The savings are from conversion and basic testing, and does not include the savings on validation and deployment.

Source: www.adventnet.com

♣ SKETCH OF EIS VENDORS

Selecting the accurate EIS vendor is an overwhelming task for most organizations. Vendors provide a great deal of marketing information in promoting their products. For organizations that can afford the expense of any EIS solution, the superseding factors in the decision are software quality and benefits to the organization of adopting the system. Other organizations are by and large forced to settle for the functionality that they can pay for. Over the past decade, many groups have made noteworthy changes in their central enterprise system applications through enterprise information systems, enterprise application integration, enterprise resource planning, or other terms for EIS. These integrated enterprise applications have moved from a federated workstation platform en route to a disseminated client-server architecture, from very large made-to-order software systems to **commercial off-the-shelf (COTS[1])** software components with graphical expansion tools and expanded from local area networks to an environment using the World Wide Web. The EIS/ERP marketplace keeps on growing as the various EIS/ERP vendors such as Oracle, Microsoft Dynamics and SAP enlarge their footprint. Some characteristics of current and past vendors include:

SAP:	Still King of the Hill
Oracle:	Lacking in collection and variation?
People soft:	Product Cycle Makes a Difference
JD Edwards:	Still Relevant After All These Years
BaaN:	Comprehensive Portfolio of best in Class
QaD:	Specialized in manufacturing-oriented module
Microsoft Dynamics:	Showcased Software as a Service (SaaS) CRM application

From the above, it is clear that all vendors specialize in a particular area and have different USPs. In realty they operate similarly in moving towards **Integration** (presented in Figure 14.1) which is a EIS buzzword.

♣ INTRODUCTION

Unfortunately, real-world choices for EIS solutions often are based on subjective factors. Some companies may have a preference for a particular EIS vendor because it governs the EIS Bazaar in its area of operations. That shouldn't be the primary factor of choice. Some of the key points

---

[1] Commercial, off-the-shelf (COTS) is an expression for software or hardware, normally technology or computer products, that are ready-to-wear and obtainable for sale, lease, or license to the general public. They are frequently used as substitutes for in-house developments or one-off government-funded developments. The use of COTS is being directive transversely many government and business programs, as they may recommend noteworthy savings in procurement and safeguarding.

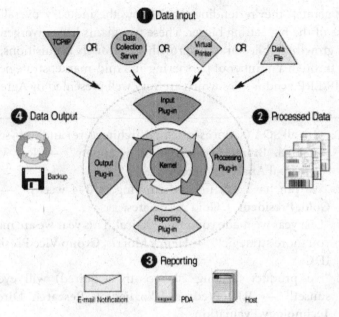

Figure 14.1: System Integration.

Source: www.pls-ltd.co.uk[2]

IT managers should consider during the evaluation process are indicated as follows. Maguire (2006)[3] noted that "The EIS/ ERP market is dominated by two 500-pound gorillas, SAP and Oracle, or rather, Oracle is a 500-pound gorilla, and SAP is the veritable King Kong of the ERP market. Of the top 10 ERP vendors by total 2005 revenues, SAP hauled in a massive $10.5 billion, to Oracle's $4.6 billion. In contrast, the other ERP vendors are mere also-rans: Infor, $1.6 billion; Sage Group, $1.4 billion; Microsoft, $855 million; and Lawson, $747 million". Not only are Oracle and SAP the

---

[2] GSM Printer & Label Systems Ltd., based in Houghton Regis, UK, is the premier provider of labels, label printers, maintenance, service and support, label printing software, barcode scanners and portable data capture systems for a wide variety of industries. Since its foundation in 1994 the company has amassed considerable experience in supplying barcode, tracking and auto ID solutions to the automotive and aerospace industries as well as retail supply chain, warehousing, distribution, logistics and healthcare.

[3] Maguire, J. (2006). The Future of ERP. www.itmanagement.earthweb.com/article.php/3643966?

industry giants, "they're tending to outgrow the industry overall."[4] It's a clear case of the big getting bigger. These two giants have divergent strategies for growth. While Oracles' growth is through acquisitions, SAP is growing through a number of partnering and mid-market strategies. There are 10 EIS/ERP vendor's lies which are very well presented by Agresso.[5]

Lie 10: "It's all SOA (services-oriented architecture) and web-service enabled. Brand new code, no wrappers!" — **Ray Wang, Principal Analyst, Forrester.**

Lie 9: "We can have you up and running in 3–4 weeks!" — **Jack Gold, President, J. Gold Associates.**

Lie 8: "Last year we made you more tactical. This year we are making you more strategic!" — **Henry Morris, Group Vice President, IDC.**

Lie 7: "No product (among 20 recently acquired) will ever be sunset!" — **P.J. (Predrag Jakovljevic), Research Director, Technology Evaluation.**

Lie 6: "Our product has EVERYTHING you need to run your business!" — **John Van Decker, Senior Vice President, Robert Frances Group.**

Lie 5: "Why would anyone want to store data in a data warehouse?" — **Henry Morris, Group Vice President, IDC.**

---

[4] Hamerman, P. D., Leaver, S. and Donnelly, D. (2008). *ERP Applications: The Battle Goes Vertical, ERP Vendors Refocus on Industry And Midmarket Strategie.* http://www.forrester.com/Research/Document/Excerpt/0,7211,44001,00.html.

[5] Agresso is the ERP Market's Definition of Agility and the leader in a new multi-billion dollar cross-vertical niche emerging worldwide that it calls "BLINC" — Businesses Living IN Change. These post millennium businesses, largely in Agresso's "sweet spot" services segment, are characterized by almost frenetic levels of dynamic business change — requiring post-implementation agility that cannot be accommodated by the perennial ERP solution giants. Today, Agresso's unique underpinning architecture is being enjoyed by thousands of BLINC organizations, with over 1,100,000 worldwide users. The company is focused on correcting the CxO's longstanding and expensive re-architect-or-die assumptions promoted by the ERP leaders. Their lack of post-implementation agility is cutting deep into corporate margins. Agresso is ERP … with NO Expiration Date™. www.agility.agresso.com

> **Lie 4:** "We're best of breed, best practice, one package fits all!" — **Cal Braunstein, President, Robert Frances Group.**
>
> **Lie 3:** "You won't need ANY more staff to run this than you have right now!" — **Jack Gold, President, J. Gold Associates.**
>
> **Lie 2:** "Buying a packaged application with pre-built processes will let you re-engineer you business faster!" — **Henry Morris, Group Vice President, IDC.**
>
> **Lie 1:** "Replacing an ERP system is like brain surgery — it should only be performed if the patient is in a coma or dying!" — **P.J., Research Director, Technology Evaluation.**
>
> *Source*: www.agility.agresso.com

14.1 MARKET STAKE OF VENDORS

If we go into its real meaning, a vendor (pronounced VEHN-duhr, from French *vendre*, meaning to sell) is any person or company that sells goods or services to someone else in the economic production chain. Parts manufacturers are vendors to other manufacturers that assemble the parts into something sold to wholesalers or retailers (whatis.techtarget.com,[6] 2008). Figure 14.2 gives different perspectives of the word vendor.

As far as ERP/EIS vendors are concerned it is dominated by SAP, Oracle and Microsoft Dynamics. Figure 14.3 shows that Microsoft is flourishing along with the big vendors in the field of EIS/ERP. Vendors with relevance to EIS and ERP are the vendors who developed the EIS/ERP packages. They are the group who has spent massive amounts of time and effort in research to generate packaged solutions. The history

---

[6] WhatIs.com® is a knowledge exploration and self-education tool about information technology, especially about the Internet and computers. It contains over 4,500 individual encyclopedic definition/topics, a number of "Fast Reference" pages and learning tools. The topics contain about 12,000 hyperlinked cross-references between definition-topics and to other sites for further information.

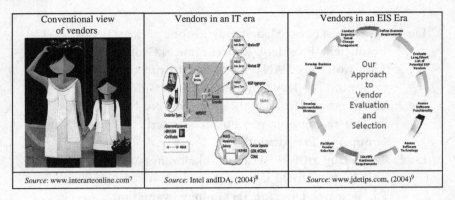

Conventional view of vendors	Vendors in an IT era	Vendors in an EIS Era
Source: www.interarteonline.com[7]	*Source*: Intel andIDA, (2004)[8]	*Source*: www.jdetips.com, (2004)[9]

Figure 14.2: Different Vendor Perspectives.

of the EIS/ERP package development makes it evident that every EIS/ERP package involved an assembly of people, working in a specific business, who created systems that could impact business. Today with the EIS/ERP market place jam-packed with many players entering the market resulting in a highly competitive environment, today's EIS/ERP packages have features and functionality catering to the needs of businesses in almost any organizational sector. EIS/ERP vendors spend billions of rupees to come up with innovations that make packages better organized, scalable, and easier to implement and use. With the

---

[7] © Carmen Sasieta, an American artist born in Peru. Since an early age, she distinguished herself for having great artistic skills, obtaining many prizes and awards in this area. But for diverse personal and professional reasons, she delayed the development of her abilities, which is why her participation in expositions is only recent.

[8] The strategic goal of the Infocomm Development Authority of Singapore (IDA) is to cultivate a vibrant and competitive infocomm industry in Singapore — one that attracts foreign investment and sustains long-term GDP growth through innovative infocomm technology development, deployment and usage in Singapore — in order to enhance the global economic competitiveness of Singapore. IDA seeks to achieve this objective in its roles as the infocomm industry champion, the national infocomm master-planner and developer, and the Government CIO.

[9] JDEtips goal has always been to publish information on JD Edwards that helps clients achieve more with the software they already own. It consistently looks for opportunities to be on the cutting edge in offering the best in previously undocumented tips and best practices when it comes to JD Edwards. Its journal continues to be considered the best of the pack.

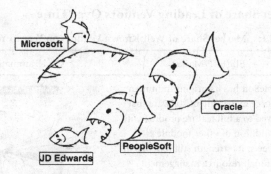

Figure 14.3:   Relative Vendor Magnitudes.

Source: www.dpu.se[10]

evolution of new technologies, the vendors have to continuously improve their product.

Thus Hamerman stated in a Forrester Research[11] publication that these giants control more than half the market, but other vendors — including Agresso, Epicor Software, Infor, Lawson Software, Microsoft, and The Sage Group — are performing well using a variety of approaches to achieve differentiation. The EIS/ ERP applications market, currently about $38 billion in total revenue, is growing at an annual rate of 6.9 percent and will reach $50 billion by 2012. What he meant to say was that business process and applications professionals should utilize EIS/ERP as the transactional system of record, supplemented with best-of-breed process solutions and industry-specific applications where appropriate.

---

[10] Data Research DPU has a mission to support companies and organisations in acquisitions and evaluations of computer software and hardware. Data Research DPU has published check-lists with standardised requirement specifications, established a public data base and a method for evaluations. The method matches custom-made needs according to the check-list and the product ratings in the data base.

[11] Forrester Research, Inc. (Nasdaq: FORR) is an independent research company that provides pragmatic and forward-thinking advice to global leaders in business and technology. Forrester works with professionals in 19 key roles at major companies providing proprietary research, consumer insight, consulting, events, and peer-to-peer executive programs. For more than 25 years, Forrester has been making IT, marketing, and technology industry leaders successful every day. For more information, visit www.forrester.com.

14.1.1 Market Share of Leading Vendors Over Time

Table 14.1: Market Share of Well-Known Vendors on Year to Year Basis.

Year	EIS/ERP Market	Diagrammatical View
1997	— PeopleSoft has its origins in human resource management software that evolved to a full feature product with the addition of other modules. However, its strength still remains in its human resource management systems. PeopleSoft has a major presence in the US federal government. — Baan has developed a number of componentized products. In recent times, it has struggled financially because of questionable financial reporting practices and changes in leadership. It is at a standstill dominant a relatively player in the ERP market. — JD Edwards has a product called One World with origins in the AS/400 environment. Its target customers are first and foremost smaller organizations with less than 2,000 users. SAP has approximately 29 percent of the world market. The strengths of its R/3 product include support for multi-country, multi-currency environments and wide scalability. The company spends a large percentage of its revenues in research and development. — Oracle is the second-largest software company in the world. Its ERP product, Oracle Applications, includes the popular Oracle Financials module. It has the reputation for developing a product that can be interfaced with others to create a best-of-breed ERP package. It should be pointed out that Oracle Applications should be distinguished from the Oracle relational database management system, which often is part of other ERP products such as PeopleSoft and SAP.	

(Continued)

Table 14.1: (*Continued*)

Year	EIS/ERP Market	Diagrammatical View
2000	According to AMR research, the ERP market in 2000 grew four percent, from $17.9B to $18.6B. The real story lies beneath the surface. While the traditional ERP market, which includes standalone financials and human resources grew at only three percent, licenses for strategic extensions like CRM, SCM, procurement, and B2B commerce platforms, grew 61 percent. This trend will continue through 2005, at which point the strategic extensions will overtake core ERP itself, creating a total market of $35.7B.	**TOP 5 ERP Vendors** **Total Revenue, 2000** Others 36%, SAP 32%, Geac Computers 3%, J.D.Edwards 5%, PeopleSoft 9%, Oracle 15% Legend: SAP, Oracle, PeopleSoft, J.D.Edwards, Geac Computers, Others
2003 & 2006	According to the Cnet, SAP is again No. 1 in the EIS/ERP business industry. **Selling business applications** Top 10 vendors of enterprise software by 2003 market share Geac 2%, Lawson 2%, Intentia 2%, IFS 2%, Microsoft 3%, SSA Global Technologies 3%, Sage 4%, Oracle 12%, PeopleSoft 13%, SAP 39%, Others 18% SOURCE: AMR RESEARCH, 2004	**Market Share before Oracle's Acquisition** (bar chart, Market Share axis 0%–25%) SAP ~20%, PeopleSoft ~7%, Oracle ~6%, Microsoft ~3%, Sage Group ~2% ERP vendors

Sources: www.isaca.org[12]; AMR; news.cnet.com[13]; After 18 months battle, Oracle finally wins over PeopleSoft. *The Wall Street Journal online*, 14 December 2004.

---

[12] ISACA was started in 1967 by a small group of individuals with similar jobs — auditing controls in the computer systems that were becoming increasingly critical to the operations of their organizations. Today, ISACA's membership — more than 75,000 strong worldwide — is characterized by its diversity. Members live and work in more than 160 countries and cover a variety of professional IT-related positions — to name just a few, IS auditor, consultant, educator, IS security professional, regulator, chief information officer and internal auditor.

[13] CNET.com shows the exciting possibilities of how technology can enhance and enrich one's life. It provides the information, tools, and advice that help customers decide what to buy and how to get the most out of technology.

Table 14.2: ERP Vendors Ranked by 2004 ERP Revenued (incl. est. '05 Growth).

2004 Revenue Bank	Company Name	Revenue 2003 (SM)	Revenue 2004 (SM)	Revenue Forecast 2005 (SM)	Revenue Share, 2003 (%)	Revenue Share, 2004 (%)	Revenue Share Forecast, 2005 (%)	Growth Rate 2003–2004 (%)	Growth Rate Forecast, 2004–2005 (%)
1	SAP	7794	9372	10403	39	40	43	17	11
2	PeopleSoft	7682	2880	0	13	12	0	7	−100
3	Oracle*	2470	2465	4534	12	10	19	0	84
4	Sage Group	900	1243	1375	4	5	6	38	11
5	Microsoft Business Solution	683	775	891	3	3	4	14	15
6	SSA Global	471	700	700	2	3	3	49	0
7	Geac	431	445	445	2	2	2	3	0
8	Intenna	361	388	40%	2	2	2	8	5
9	Infor Global Solutions	123	375	395	1	2	2	205	5
10	Lawson	341	357	358	2	2	2	5	0
Total (Including other ERP vendors)		20711	23649	24268	100	100	100	14	3

Source: AMR Research (2005).
*Oracle acquired PeopleSoft on 28 December 2004.

14.1.2 Overview of ERP Vendors

The AMR[14] report identified trends in the ERP market in 2004, together with the following conclusions:

♦ The ERP market is entering another major technology transition phase. Service Oriented Architecture (SOA) may have the same disruptive effect that other technologies have had on the market, such as the emergence of client-server systems in the 1990's.
♦ The pace of acquisitions shows no sign of slowing down. Oracle's purchase of Retek and vendors like Sage Group, SSA Global, Infor

---

[14] AMR Research provides world-class research and actionable advice for executives tasked with delivering enhanced business process performance and cost savings with the aid of technology. Five thousand leaders in the Global 1000 put their trust in AMR Research's integrity, depth of industry expertise, and passion for customer service to support their most critical business initiatives, including supply chain transformation, new product introduction, customer profitability, compliance and governance, and IT benefit realization. More information is available at www.amrresearch.com.

Global Solutions, and Epicor have all been very active in the M&A space and have grown more rapidly than the overall ERP market.

♦ The midrange ($50M–$1B in annual revenue) and SMB (less than $50M in annual revenue) markets continue to be a major focus area for many of the ERP vendors. Mid-range solutions and channels are critically important for penetrating China, India, Eastern Europe, and Latin America.

♦ ERP buyers have moved away from large, upfront purchases. Now most tend to license user seats and functional ERP modules incrementally as they deploy a product. Along with widespread discounting, this has led to smaller average deal sizes.

In their assessment of vendors and enterprises, the Gartner Group identified an influence curve that depicts vendor/enterprise relationships leading towards a win-win situation. In Figure 14.4, Gartner's "Vendor Influence Curve" shows a trade-off between a vendor's understanding of an enterprise's requirements and the value to the enterprise.

14.2 SERVICE-ORIENTED ARCHITECTURE (SOA)

With the introduction of Web Services over the last year or so, there has been a renewed interest in service-oriented architecture (SOA). A SOA is made up of components and interconnections that stress interoperability and location transparency (Michael Stevens and www.developer.com, 2008). Service-oriented architecture (SOA) is a progression of distributed computing based on the demand/respond design paradigm for synchronous and asynchronous applications. Service-oriented architecture (SOA) has emerged as the most significant shift in how business applications are designed, developed and implemented in the last 10 years, eclipsing the shift to client-server. In fact, Gartner, Inc. predicts that by 2008, "SOA will provide the basis for 80 percent of new development projects."[15] Figure 14.5 displays the benefit levels offered by SOA.

---

[15] Hayward, S. (2005). *Positions 2005: Service-Oriented Architecture Adds Flexibility to Business Processes*. Gartner, Inc.

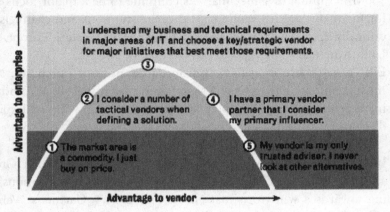

Figure 14.4: Vendor Influence Curve.

Source: Dave Roberts[16] & Vyatta,[17] 2008.

According to the Paul Hamerman report published in 2008 by Forrester Research, "The biggest factors driving market change in ERP are service-oriented architecture (SOA) and software-as-a-service (SaaS). The SaaS hosted-subscription model is gaining traction rapidly in certain application segments, including HR and CRM and it is only a matter of time before complete ERP solutions will be available via this delivery model. To a large extent, SaaS is dependent upon SOA to provide solution functionality that is rapidly configurable without source code customization." So now the million-dollar question is why there is a need of SOA? The answer is that, in a real sense, in enterprises comprises IT infrastructure assorted operating systems, applications, system software, and

---

[16] Presently a Director, IT with EMEA & CIS. www.xing.com

[17] The Vyatta Community Edition (VC) is an award-winning, Linux-based, open source software providing routing, firewalling, VPN, intrusion prevention, anti-virus, and WAN load balancing services, among others, for networks. Vyatta runs on a standard ×86 hardware system and creates a powerful network appliance that can run circles around proprietary systems. Vyatta also runs virtualized in VMware, Xen, Hyper-V, and other hypervisors, providing networking and security services to virtual machines.

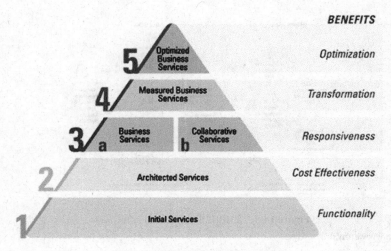

Figure 14.5:   SOA Benefits by Level.

Source: Sonic (2008).[18]

application infrastructure. Some existing applications are utilized to execute current business processes. Enterprises should respond to changes with nimbleness and influence existing investments in applications and application infrastructure to deal with newer business requirements; maintain new channels of interactions with customers, partners, and suppliers. SOA can provide existing services in a granular manner to deal with new business necessities, providing services through diverse channels, and rendering existing enterprise and legacy applications as services, thus safeguarding obtainable IT infrastructure investments.

14.2.1 SOA Relevance to EIS Vendors

SOA will have a noteworthy impact on how the business user of that technology fabricates and sets out processes and applications. Its worth is clear: For the first time, EIS vendors have the occasion to weave people,

---

[18] Business applications are the most visible part of an enterprise, but without the right data and SOA infrastructure, their full potential may not be realized. Build a service-oriented architecture (SOA) with Progress Sonic ESB and applications can share services and seamlessly interoperate. www.sonicsoftware.com

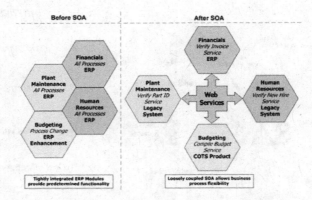

Figure 14.6: ERP/EIS Before and After SOA.

Source: www.army.mil

applications, and data to accomplish specific processes, allowing you and your business partners to meet the challenges and opportunities in comprehensive, multi-channel surroundings. Figure 14.6 shows how this is done.

Service-Oriented Architecture (SOA) is a software design movement in which client application requirements provide functionality for one or more services. This blueprint prototype allocates internal and external business processes to be combined and reprocessed, providing key functions at less cost. The SOA model provides a more flexible application architecture. EIS software users need to be concerned with developments in SOA because it enables an organization to meet business goals.

When designing business software like EIS and ERP, we should remember that the purpose is to bring agile systems into the business. To a certain extent, SOA is the loom by which we can facilitate business and technology nimbleness; it is not an end in itself. Accomplishing the flexibility that so frequently accompanies Web services is not just a consequence of adopting EIS protocols in the exploitation of systems, but also of following first-rate blueprint principles. When two companies become partners, their enterprise architecture become partners as well. In customer-supplier relationships especially, partner relationships involving conventional enterprise architecture have been problematic. EIS and their interfaces cannot keep up with the changes in these relationships.

SOA with the help of Web services can facilitate these systems in responding to new arrangements much faster.

14.3 SAP (SYSTEM APPLICATION AND PRODUCTS)

SAP stands for "Systems, Applications, and Products in Data Processing." Founded in 1972 by 5 IBM engineers in Germany, SAP is today the recognized leader among the E-business solutions firms. With nearly a third of the market, it is the first ERP editor in the world and the 4th software publisher with manpower of 22,300 people in more than 50 countries. Among the 10 largest American companies, eight use SAP software package. Of the 10 American companies achieving the highest benefit, eight also chose SAP. SAP is on the stock market of Frankfurt and New York. Presently Europe's biggest software group, SAP AG of Germany, which is also the world's largest maker of business-management software, reported today that first-quarter profit rose 9.9 percent on increased license fees and a growth in US sales. Figure 14.7 gives some historical data about SAP.

SAP is a creative organization envisioning the appearance of EIS/ERP 20 years ahead of time. Its former flagship product R/3 was based on the client-server technology of the late 80's, which was the accurate time to influence client-server technology for mission critical applications. SAP has a overwhelming early-bird benefit. The mainstream of the "top 10" companies (off the record based on measures such as yearly turnover, productivity or market capitalization) in the world are with SAP. Numerous leading companies such as Intel in microprocessor, IBM, HP, Compaq & Digital (today only Compaq) in the computer industry are with SAP. Figure 14.8 shows some of their products.

14.3.1 SAP's Products

A. SAP R/3
SAP is used by more than 60 percent of the major firms. In 1995 SAP generated 90 percent of their revenues from global companies. Now there is a trend toward automating SMEs and mid-sized companies. The R/3 system

◆ Founded in 1972, by five former IBM employees in Germany.
◆ 1973: SAP R/1 solutions launched.
◆ 1977: First International customers.
◆ 1979: SAP R/2 solutions launched.
◆ 1988: Company goes public (Frankfurt).
◆ 1992: SAP R/3 solutions launched.
◆ 1996: SAP R/3 Release 3.1 is Internet-enabled.
◆ 1996: Company launches new solutions for CRM & SCM.
◆ 1998: Company is listed on the New York Stock Exchange.
◆ Acquired Kiefer & Veittinger, a leading German CRM vendor in 1998.
◆ Suitable for wide range of industries and organizations.
◆ Particularly strong in automotive, banking, consumer products industries.
◆ 1999: SAP delivers mySAP.com.
◆ 2000: SAP forms SAP Hosting, an Internet application service.
◆ 2000: SAP forms, globally interconnected 13213 on-the Internet.
◆ 2001: SAP acquires Top Tier and forms SAP Portals.
◆ Recognized as the leader of ERP market in the world.
◆ 7.4B € in FY02 Revenues.
◆ 56% from Maintenance and Services.
◆ FY03 Expectation: Flat Revenue, Improved Profits.
◆ 19,300 Customers.
◆ 50,000 + Installations in 120 + Countries.
◆ 23 Industry Solutions.
◆ Net income rose to €310 million ($422 million), or 26 cents a share, from €282, or 23 cents, a year earlier, SAP said in a statement today. Software and related service revenue rose 9.4 percent to €1.52 billion. Software and service sales, excluding currency moves, rose 15 percent, ahead of a 2007 target for at least 12 percent growth.

SAP headquarters, Walldorf, Germany

Figure 14.7: SAP Corporate Data.

is composed of functional modules corresponding to the company's activities. We can distinguish the following functional modules families. SAP R/3 architecture is composed of 3 levels. SAP system is made up of multiple servers assigned to only one database as shown in Figure 14.9.

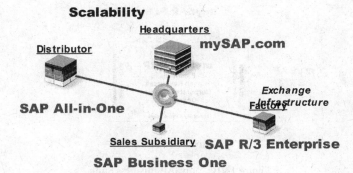

Figure 14.8:   SAP Systems.

Source: SAP AG.

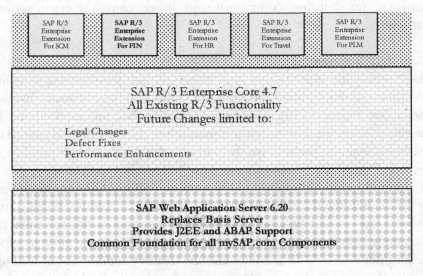

Figure 14.9:   SAP R/3.

SAP R/3 addresses the enterprise needs of typical large-scale manufacturing and trading organizations. SAP R/3 is ideally suited for large corporations that have multiple products, manufactured out of multiple plants, often distributed across multiple continents and countries. R/3 can handle multiple currencies, multiple language scripts and multiple accounting systems, multiple valuation schemes and multiple depreciation schemes exceptionally well. SAP R/3 also has outstanding consolidation

Figure 14.10: mySAP Business Suite.

Source: SAP AG.

schemes for holding companies and other complex organization structures.

B. mySAP Business Suite

SAP recently introduced a new application specifically designed to simplify electronic communications between companies and their financial institutions (see Figure 14.10). The new application has not received much attention by the press or analyst community, but it should have! If anyone is well positioned to break down the barriers of straight through processing between corporate and their financial institutions, it is SAP. In nearly every multi-national account visited by the authors, SAP is already established or will soon become the financial platform of choice for multi-national companies. SAP should be able to leverage its position as the epicenter of corporate cash management to provide simplified, straight through processing between its ERP modules and the treasury applications of leading banks. Figure 14.11 displays SAP support offered to the banking industry.

14.3.2 SAP's Market Share

Now the important question is: What makes SAP different? Traditional computer information systems used by many businesses today have been developed to accomplish some specific tasks and provide reports and analysis of events that have already taken place. Examples are accounting general ledger systems. Occasionally, some systems operate in a "real-time" mode that is, have up-to-date information and can be used to actually

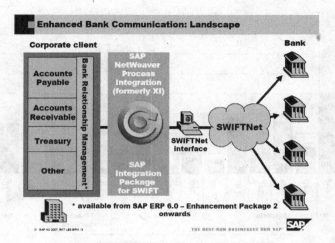

Figure 14.11:   SAP Banking Support.

Source: blogs.gxs.com (2008).[19]

control events. A typical company has many separate systems to manage different processes like production, sales and accounting. Each of these systems has its own databases and seldom passes information to other systems in a timely manner. SAP takes a different approach. There is only one information system in an enterprise, SAP. All applications access common data. Real events in the business initiate transactions. Accounting is done automatically by events in sales and production. Sales can see when products can be delivered. Production schedules are driven by sales. The whole system is designed to be real time and not historical. SAP structure embodies what are considered the "best business practices". A company implementing SAP adapts it operations to it to achieve its efficiencies and power. The process of adapting procedures to the SAP model involves "Business Process Re-engineering" which is a logical analysis of the events and relationships that exist in an enterprise's operations.

SAP is the world's leading provider of business software (see Figure 14.12). Today, more than 43,400 customers in more than 120 countries run SAP® applications — from distinct solutions addressing the

---

[19] GXS industry and technology experts are thought leaders in their fields. They conduct research, determine best practices and share their expertise. GXS maintains INSIGHTS as a service to customers and prospective customers to provide insight on critical business issues and technology.

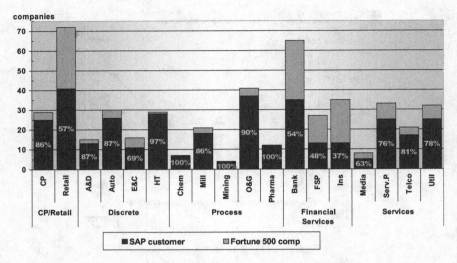

Figure 14.12:   SAP Coverage of Fortune 500 Companies.

Source: Fortune 500 2002; SAP Analysis.

needs of small businesses and midsize companies to suite offerings for global organizations. Powered by the SAP NetWeaver® technology platform to drive innovation and enable business change, SAP software helps enterprises of all sizes around the world improve customer relationships, enhance partner collaboration and create efficiencies across their supply chains and business operations. SAP solution portfolios support the unique business processes of more than 25 industries, including high-tech, retail, financial services, healthcare and the public sector.

14.4 ORACLE ORACLE

Founded in 1977 and based in Redwood Shores in California, Oracle Corporation is the first software provider in the world for information management, and the number two for software in general. Oracle offers its databases, tools and software package, as well as the services associated with consulting, formation and support, in more than 145 countries throughout the world. Oracle E-Business Suite includes more than

50 functional modules dedicated to the internal management of the company. The covered fields are Finance, Human Resources, Projects, Production, Logistics and the Warehouses.

- Country of origin: USA.
- Name of product: Applications 11i.
- Market Share: Eight percent (2001).
- Typical client: Fortune 1000.
- 2nd largest software supplier in the world with revenues of $6.7 billion.
- Revenues over $8 billion in 1998.
- 41,000 employees worldwide, 16,000 U.S.
- More than 6,000 customers in 76 countries.
- 1997 ERP market share was 8.3 percent of total ERP license revenue.

  ➢ 50 percent of applications revenue comes from services.

- Has over 33,000 employees and is located in 145 countries around the world.
- Oracle's applications license revenue is growing at 18 percent a year; significantly less than its rivals.
- Particularly strong in service-intensive environments like finance and banking industries.
- Strong in Financials and Supply Chain Management Modules.
- Leader in adding E-commerce capabilities such as CRM features (built own CRM).

14.4.1 Oracle Control Features

Oracle standard delivered automated application enablers:

- Oracle standard delivered configurable enablers.
- Oracle "Work Flow" configurable enablers.
- Oracle "Alert" configurable enablers.
- Application Security.
- Reports.

  — standard delivered.
  — newly developed.

Table 14.3: Some Oracle Features.

Financials	Supply Chain
— Planning (G/L, Analyzer) — Analysis — Consolidation — Expenditure Management — Billing and Cash Collection — Cash Management — Asset Management	Strategic Procurement — Non-production Procurement — Strategic Souring — Catalogue Management
Projects	**Manufacturing**

Costing
— Billing
— Time and Expense
— Activity Management
Gateway
   Human Resources
   Materials Management
— Inventory
— Purchasing
	Factory & Item Definition
	— Planning & Simulation
	— Materials Production
	— Cost Management
	— Integrated Technologies
	   Management

The company recently announced the release of the latest version — Oracle applications 11 I — of its ERP software that is being claimed as the industry's first 100 percent Internet-architecture global enterprise applications suite. The suite comprise both CRM and ERP applications and runs from a single code base, eliminating integration issues regardless of locale, currency, language or version. The company is now also well known for aggressively pushing its CRM business as a critical component of e-business transformation for effective customer relationship. CRM is the hottest dominating technology of today's enterprise market. Oracle has introduced many strategic initiatives in the CRM arena during this last year.

14.5 PEOPLESOFT

PeopleSoft was created in 1987 in California, USA. Present in the majority of the large cities of the world, particularly in Europe and Asia, PeopleSoft is also in the trade market. Today, the company counts more than 8000 employees and more than 4600 customers in the world. Up to now, more than 4700 companies, distributed in 107 countries, use the PeopleSoft E-Business applications. It is now part of Oracle.

- Market Share: Eight percent (2001).
- 7,000 employees worldwide.
- 2,900 clients worldwide.
- Growing over 60 percent a year.
- Target the service sector with products designed to help companies handle their intangible costs.
- Has a powerful HR module, with additional packages of varying quality.
- Strong in Service-intensive environments.
- Well suited for government, municipalities, and professional services.
- Offers variety of ERP modules like:
  (a) People soft 7.5, (b) People soft MM, (c) People soft Mfg., (d) People soft Distribution, (e) People soft Financials, (f) People soft HRMS, (g) People soft SCM and, (h) People soft Tools.
- Now it has come up with its 8.0 upgrades.

Table 14.4 shows PeopleSoft products as of 2005. These products are still supported at least in part by the new owner, Oracle.

These products were claimed to have the following features:

Implement or upgrade up to 35 percent faster than an all on-site engagement.
Reduce costs by up to 50 percent.
Fixed scope, fixed fee, condensed timeline.
End-to-end services.
High-value, fixed low-cost solutions with rapid, predictable results.
Customer project team able to focus on more strategic or customer-specific tasks.

Figure 14.13 displays some services provided by PeopleSoft products.

Since 1 June 2005, PeopleSoft has been integrated Oracle into and PeopleSoft.com content is now on Oracle.com.

Table 14.4: PeopleSoft's Product Lines Prior to Acquisition.

Product	Description
PeopleSoft Enterprise	A family of applications based on pure Internet architecture designed for flexible configuration, and open multi-vendor integration. Ideally suited for financial, government, education, health care and other services.
PeopleSoft Enterprise One	A complete suite of modular, pre-integrated industry-specific business applications designed for rapid deployment and ease of administration on a pure Internet architecture. Suitable for organizations that manufactures, constructs, distributes, services, manages product or physical assets.
PeopleSoft Word	An application suite for IBM iSeries platform. Applications are tightly integrated and pre-bundled on a single database, with a web-enabled architecture.

Source: Chaturvedi (2005).[20]

14.6 J.D. EDWARDS

J.D. Edwards is a company which has more than 6000 customers. Founded in 1977 in Denver (Colorado, the United States), it supplies an integrated solution of Business to Business management that cover the fields of CRM, Supply Chain, the Business Intelligence, and ERP. The J.D. Edwards integrated solution consists of a perfectly homogeneous set of application modules, supplemented by specialized modules intended for the trades of chemistry and oil, BTP or engineering. J.D. Edwards covers all the functional and operational fields in a company: countable and financial management, commercial and logistic management, production control, maintenance management. J.D. Edwards was acquired by PeopleSoft, which, in turn, was acquired by Oracle. There are still J.D. Edwards software products in use.

---

[20] Chaturvedi, R.N. (2005). Oracle's Acquisition of PeopleSoft. *ICFAI Center for Management Research.* European Case Clearing House.

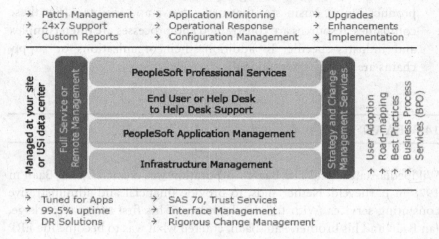

USi's PORTFOLIO OF PEOPLESOFT SERVICES

→ Patch Management → Application Monitoring → Upgrades
→ 24x7 Support → Operational Response → Enhancements
→ Custom Reports → Configuration Management → Implementation

Managed at your site or USi data center

Full Service or Remote Management

PeopleSoft Professional Services

End User or Help Desk to Help Desk Support

PeopleSoft Application Management

Infrastructure Management

Strategy and Change Management Services

User Adoption
Road-mapping
Best Practices
Business Process
Services (BPO)

→ Tuned for Apps → SAS 70, Trust Services
→ 99.5% uptime → Interface Management
→ DR Solutions → Rigorous Change Management

Figure 14.13: PeopleSoft Services.

Source: www.usi.com[21]

14.7 LAWSON LAWSON

Lawson solution is based on industry best practices and processes. With Lawson you get enterprise resource planning (ERP) software solutions that focuses deliver on your industry to the anticipated competitive advantage and suppleness in best-practice business process automation. You also take delivery of something you may not expect. With Lawson, you get the lowest total cost of ERP software ownership on the market these days.

♦ **Lawson S3 Enterprise Management System:** Business applications designed to enhance the performance of industries that focus on the areas of sourcing, staffing and service.

---

[21] Founded in 1998, USinternetworking, Inc. (USi), an AT&T company, is the most experienced Application Service Provider (ASP). The USis use a highly automated, efficient, systematic approach to deliver managed hosting, application management, remote management, professional services, SaaS enablement, and eBusiness development and hosting to more than 150 enterprise-level organizations in over 30 countries.

- **Lawson M3 Enterprise Management System:** Designed specifically for product-centric businesses that make, move and maintain. For these companies, resources are constrained and processes are often complex and industry-specific. In addition, their organizations or supply chains are usually international.

14.8 BAAN Baan

Wikipedia states that "The BaaN Corporation was created by Jan Baan in 1978 in Barneveld, Netherlands, to provide financial and administrative consulting services. With the development of his first software package, Jan Baan and his brother, Paul Baan, entered what was to become the ERP industry. The BaaN Company focused on the creation of enterprise resource planning (ERP) software."

Facts About BaaN[22]:

- Founded by Jan Baan in 1978 in the Netherlands.
- Has dual headquarters in Putten, The Netherlands and Reston VA, USA.
- FMBB (Financial Management Begeleidingsbureau Baan) was the company name under which Jan Baan started out alone.
- BMCS (Baan Manufacturing Control System) was the first package developed by BaaN for MRP I, CRP and MRP-II.
- Has a product BaaN IV that is highly ranked among the ERP solutions available.
- More than 4,000 companies use Baan in 5,000 sites worldwide.
- Products are fully Year 2000 (Y2K) compliant and based on a flexible, multi-tier client/server architecture, which can scale to meet the needs of small, medium and large enterprises.
- Revenues rose 79 percent to $388 million in 1996 while net profit more than doubled to $36.3 million. Total Revenue for 1997 is US$684 million.

---

[22] "BaaN develops software solutions and services which help companies do business in the 'networked economy' — where information, integration and Internet collaboration are ever more important." (BaaN)

♦ Since its initial public offering in May 1995, the value of the shares has risen some nine or 10 times after taking into account a share split in May 1996.

The BaaN company has become one of the world's biggest software groups and expects to remain on a fast growth track for the foreseeable future.

14.9 SAGE sage

"Business Objects is a long-standing partner of Sage Software," said Nina L. Smith, President, Sage[23] Software Business Management Division. "We applaud SAP's commitment to keep Business Objects an independent business unit, and we look forward to expanding our relationship. Together, Sage Software and Business Objects will continue to deliver tangible value to our mutual customers." Sage X3 Enterprise combines all the advantages of ERP performance, while maintaining simplicity and flexibility, principles on which the success of Sage business management solutions for medium-sized and large companies is founded. Figure 14.14 shows some Sage documentation.

Sage products are:

♦ Simple, fast to integrate irrespective of the configuration of your organization and your existing information system. Its user-friendly ergonomics ensure fast start-up for all users.
♦ Extremely simple to adapt and personalize in line with the processes specific to your organization and business activity.
♦ Flexible and able to evolve in step with the growth and the new requirements of your company.

---

[23] Sage is a leading supplier of accounting and business management software to small and medium-sized businesses (SMEs) The Sage Group plc comprises market-leading businesses throughout Europe, North America, South Africa, Asia and Australia supplying business management software and related products and services to the small and medium-sized business community.

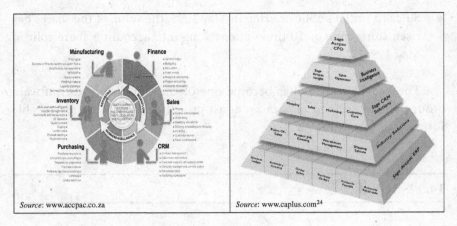

Source: www.accpac.co.za   *Source*: www.caplus.com[24]

Figure 14.14: Sage Modules.

♦ Lightweight with an easy-to-administer IT infrastructure.
♦ Used by over 1,900 companies — with 20 to more than.
♦ Relied on by 1,000 users worldwide who use Sage ERP X3 for their daily operations.

Control, speed and flexibility are the major advantages from using Sage X3 Enterprise. To fully benefit from your resources and develop your growth potential in your domestic and international markets, you can count on the reliability, responsiveness and open approach of Sage X3 Enterprise in both the shorter and longer terms.

---

[24] Established in 1993, CA-Plus Inc. has grown to become the leader in implementing Business Systems in the Mid-Market. CA-Plus offers total systems solutions to meet your accounting, manufacturing, communications, warehousing, inventory management, and CRM (Customer Relations Management) and HR requirements. A CA-Plus "Total Solution" includes complete pre-sales services for the industry-leading Sage Accpac ERP Accounting and Business Management software (formerly Accpac Advantage Series), MISys Manufacturing MRP software, Electronic Data Interchange (EDI) software and Sage Abra HR software solutions. Your confidence is assured with the knowledge that CA-Plus has delivered over 1000 completed solutions (and counting).

USP of SAGE

♦ **Process integration:**
  ➢ Common reference system for the whole company.
  ➢ Horizontal approach to management flows.
♦ **Data integration:**
  ➢ Simple analysis.
  ➢ Efficient coordination tool.
  ➢ Seamless management of Microsoft.
  ➢ Office documents within the ERP system database.
♦ **Technology integration:**
  ➢ Coherent system for implementation of all management functions.
  ➢ Rapid learning curve.

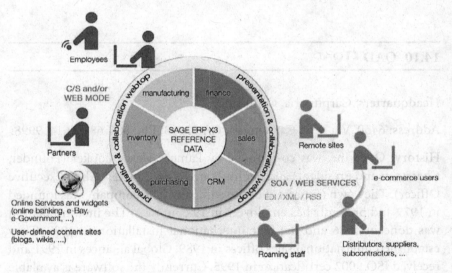

Figure 14.15: Sage Architecture.

Source: Softline Accpac.[25]

---

[25] Softline Accpac is a fully-owned subsidiary of The Sage Group, plc., a leading supplier of business management software and services to 5.5 million customers worldwide. The company is the North American arm of Sage ERP X3 operations, an international ERP solution for mid-sized companies. (Sage.)

♦ **Integrated e-business:**
> ➢ Effective communication with all company partners.
> ➢ Flexible and reactive operation.

About Sage Accpac[26]

An Enterprise Resource Planning (ERP) system doesn't have to be costly to be effective or user-friendly. **SAP Business One** and **Sage Accpac ERP** systems have been specifically designed for SMEs to do just that: provide powerful competitive advantages which are inexpensive to implement, yet remain easy to use and simple to maintain.

As two of the most popular ERP systems among SMEs in Asia-Pacific, **SAP Business One** and **Sage Accpac ERP** are definitely worth considering for any SME-owner seeking to invest in a reliable, integrated and affordable business management solution.

14.10 QAD ⋒ QAD

Headquarters: Carpinteria, California.

Address: 6450, Via Real, Carpinteria, CA 93013, Ph.: 805-684-6614, 9998.

History: QAD Inc. was co-founded by Pamela Meyer Lopker (Founder, Chairman and President) and her husband Karl F. Lopker (Chief Executive Officer). They own 67 percent of the company. The company was founded in 1979 and presently has employees in 19 countries. The first installation was done in 1986 and the first International installation in 1987. They established international sales offices in 1989, Global alliances in 1991 and received ISO 9002 certification in 1995. Currently the software is available in 26 languages:

Users: More than 3600 installations in 82 countries.

Sales: 1998 $172.2 million, 36.2 percent rise over the previous year.

Products: MFG/PRO, MFG/PRO on the Internet, On/Q, Service/Support Management, Decision Support, Enterprise Data Warehouse, Q-wizard, etc.

Partnerships: Channel Alliances for Distributors, Service alliances for Service Providers and System Integrators, Technology Alliances with World-class computer hardware, Database, OS and Tool suppliers, Whole Product Alliances with companies.

Customers: More than 2000 including Avon, Black & Decker, Borden, Caterpillar, Colgate-Palmolive, Daewoo, Ford Motor, Gillette, GM, Heinz, J & J, Kraft International, Lucent, Nestle, Pepsi, Philips, Quaker Oats, Unilever etc.

14.11 MICROSOFT DYNAMICS

Microsoft Dynamics[27] (formerly Microsoft Business Solutions) can help fuel productivity and empower businesses to succeed. Use these resources to help you deliver comprehensive business management solutions that bring benefits to your customers faster than ever before.

As described by Wikipedia, "Microsoft Dynamics is a line of business software owned and developed by Microsoft, though the individual products were originally created by other companies and known by various other names. Dynamics was previously known by the codename "Project Green". It replaced Microsoft Business Solutions, the company's previous business software family."

Variation in Microsoft:

a. As a CRM

Microsoft has emphasized Software as a Service (SaaS) CRM application. Microsoft is trying to copy Salesforce's business model with AppExchange allowing customers and partners to create their own unique software.

---

[27] © Microsoft Corporation, 2008.

Table 14.5: Types of Microsoft Dynamics Products.

♦ **Dynamics AX:** Microsoft Dynamics AX is a multiple-language, multiple-currency enterprise resource planning (ERP) solution. Its core strengths are for manufacturing and e-business and it has strong functionality for the wholesale and services industries.

♦ **Dynamics CRM:** Across industries, organizations need an easy, effective way to manage customers and constituents from first contact through to purchase and support. As a result, there's a significant opportunity for ISVs, value-added resellers and system integrators who provide customer relationship management (CRM) solutions.

♦ **Dynamics GP:** Microsoft Dynamics GP provides a solid foundation for unifying business processes. Its financial tools enhance the visibility and control of your customers' business health, resulting in more confident and smarter decisions. It is cost-effective and reliable, and backed by extensive service and support.

♦ **Dynamics NAV:** Microsoft Dynamics NAV is a cost-effective, customizable business management solution designed to meet the needs of small and medium-sized companies. It includes integrated functionality for financial and supply-chain management, customer relationship management and e-commerce.

♦ **Dynamics RMS:** Microsoft Retail Management System is an electronic point-of-sale (EPOS) software solution for retailers. Your customers can use it to process transactions and to manage stock, ordering, pricing, promotions, and customer and supplier relationships, whatever the size of their retail outlet. It combines rich functionality for retailers and an easy-to-use Windows environment in a proven EPOS package.

Source: www.partner.microsoft.com[28]

b. In a SME sector
    Small and mid-sized firms are target markets for Microsoft products, which are priced a degree lower than the industry giants such as SAP and Oracle.

28

14.12 RUMORS ABOUT EIS/ERP BIDDING

Microsoft to Buy SAP Again?

> Here we go again, financial traders are talking up SAP stock saying that Microsoft is keen to acquire SAP. This is not the first time this rumor has come out. Back in 2004 there had been talks but it was decided that the two companies would struggle to integrate. SAP has a market capitalization of $65 billion and the largest purchase Microsoft has done so far is $1.5 billion so this would be a hefty purchase. Furthermore, the combined entity would have to be approved by the Anti-Trust authorities. Another hurdle is the huge cultural differences between the two companies — all of which are likely its reduce the rumor to just talk.
>
> *Source*: www.erpsoftware-news.com

14.13 SUGGESTIONS TO AN ERP VENDOR

Deciding on the vendor to supply the ERP software is probably the most complex decision in the whole ERP project. The following factors need to be kept in mind because ERP software is so expensive, one cannot to pay for afford to correct mistakes it only later. The suggestion to ERP vendors is that they could make their product more price-competitive rather than focusing on selling because sales would come to them once the product was developed with sufficient quality. Key suggestions are:

- **Try to sell products in modules and according to need:** Specifically. If the organization is marketing-oriented, then sell the marketing module of ERP first, if production-oriented then the inventory nodule, and so forth.
- **Try to reduce the existing price:** The intention is for vendors to sell more licenses and thereby increase their market share.

♦ **Install the most required portion of a module:** Generally full fledged installation requires years to complete so it is advisable both to vendor and user to install that portion of the module which is required most.
♦ **Proper implementation of an ERP project:** Implementation of an ERP project is the most crucial activity in the life cycle of an enterprise. This requires careful planning and teamwork.

Figure 14.16 gives a clear idea of user satisfaction with the services of well-known ERP vendors.

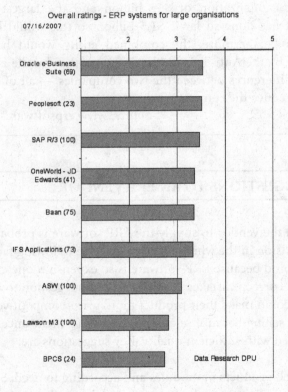

Figure 14.16:   Customer Satisfaction with Vendors.

Source: www.dpu.se (2007).[29]

---

[29] ERP systems included in the rankings are Oracle Applications, Movex, SAP R/3, Oracle e-Business Suite, Peoplesoft, ASW, OneWorld–JD Edwards, IFS Applications, Lawson M3, Baan, BPCS.

14.14 A BROADER DEFINITION OF EIS VENDORS

In a broader sense, a separate but converging set of integrated applications share many of the characteristics of ERP's, with a different application focus. Front office systems, such as Sales Force Automation (SFA), are provided by industry leaders Aurum, Clarify, Remedy, Scopus, Siebel, Trilogy and Vantive. In a more marketing-oriented locution, these applications may be referred to as Customer Resource Management (CRM). Supply-Chain Resource Management (SRM), once known as merely Logistics, provides an integrated supply-chain capability with live links to suppliers and, less frequently, customers, and is particularly useful for the planning and optimization of the flow of raw materials to finished goods. Representative companies providing packages in this rapidly growing sector include Manugistics, i2, IMI, Red Pepper and Numetrix. Table 14.6 shows some of the different levels of EIS systems.

So ERP vendor choice in the future would also look beyond ERP. In tomorrow's world when ERP would be a commodity, provision for Supply Chain Management, Electronic Commerce, Advanced Planning Systems etc would be the true differentiation as the enterprises look beyond the narrow confines of the individual enterprises. Cost is very different in the ERP context. Most organizations look at up-front cost of the ERP software but ignore the 'hidden costs.' It is generally true that ERP implementation costs roughly five times the cost of ERP software. This includes high performance servers & high-speed networking to support ERP software and the cost of expensive consultants. Support for the IT infrastructure and

Table 14.6: Levels of EIS Systems.

	Definition	Vendors
ERP	Enterprise Resource Management	SAP, PeopleSoft, Oracle, Baan, JD Edwards
CRM	Customer Relationship Management	Aurum, Clarify, Remedy, Scopus, Siebel, Trilogy, Vantive
SCM	Supply Chain Management	Manugistics, i2, IMI, Red Pepper, Numetrix

applications must also be taken into account. In a sense, one should look at Total Cost of Ownership (TCO) over a five-year period. Other issues that must be considered should include:

♦ Euro compliance (practically everyone is addressing this).
  Skill availability (both from vendors, implementation partners, training institutes etc.,).
♦ Past performance in terms of timely implementation.
♦ No cost over-run, project management capability etc.

14.14.1 Second-Tier Vendors

Second-tier ERP vendors, such as Lawson Software and J.D. Edwards Enterprise Software have built their customer bases in the mid-market, unlike industry giants like Oracle and SAP. Hodges predicted that J.D. Edwards would fare well in the mid-market.

However, they will also have to work harder to stay competitive, said Michael Herzog, managing director of KPMG Consulting, LLC.

"The major ERP vendors are continuing to globalize their products, adding support for foreign languages and currencies," Herzog said. "This is the kind of thing that presents a special challenge to the smaller vendors."

Greenbaum also expects some consolidation among ERP vendors. "I think some of the second-tier players that already have a good track record in the mid-market will survive," he said. "But there are still more vendors than the market can support."

14.14.2 EIS Vendors in American and Indian Perspectives

How are they positioned in India? All the key players in the ERP global market are practically present in India. This includes SAP with their flag-ship product R/3, BaaN Company with their BaaN IV product, Oracle with their Oracle Applications and the world-class ERP product Marshall from the rising Indian star Ramco Systems. The other major player in the global ERP Market, namely, PeopleSoft has entered the Indian market only very recently. Yet another leading product MFG/PRO from QAD has been present for a while (the two customers Hindustan Lever & Godrej have been using it for over two years). SAP has been exceptionally successful in India with nearly two-thirds of the Indian market share. The major industrial houses Tata, Reliance, Essar, Mahindra & Kirloskar have embraced SAP. BaaN has been very successful in major manufacturing companies such as TVS. Oracle has been playing a dominant role in the telecom center with a stronghold among all cellular phone companies. Ramco Marshall has a good client base among the process industry in the south and a few public sector undertakings.

14.15 CONCLUSION

Just as in the insurance sector in India, we talk about LIC (Life Insurance Corporation) when we talk about insurance, similarly in the ERP industry when we talk about ERP it leads us to SAP or vice versa. SAP stands for Systems, Applications and Products in Data Processing. SAP is a worldwide vendor of standard business application software and pioneer in ERP software. There are other ERP vendors such as Oracle, JDEdward, People soft, BaaN and a few Indian players such as Patni, Hcl, Infosys, Wipro, TCS, etc.

ERP systems are the future of the information system technology, hence it must evolve concurrently with the needs of the company, much like now e-commerce has evolved. To arrive at such a result, it would be worthwhile for ERP software providers to design their products so that they can be very easily updated, and this update should not be an investment so significant that small businesses cannot afford it. If the ERP developers don't want to kill their own business, it will be necessary that they conceive their systems in a little less commercial manner and that they aim more at effectiveness than profit.

ERP vendors make outrageous claims about the superiority of their products. Some software vendors offer million-dollar money-back guarantees if their software fails to perform at least twice as fast as the competition, while other vendors tout their products' robust functionality and ease of use. One new factor in the ERP vendor decision-making process centers on the arrival of agile ERP solutions. Agile systems are solutions that can be rapidly reconfigured to a large degree. Most ERP systems say they are configurable and often offer some small configuration capabilities like ad-hoc report writer or user defined fields. Agile solutions go far beyond this capability. They generally are configured for a given customer over several weeks and include mission-specific functionality including specialized reports, entry screens and reports that are specific to the industry of the customer.

☆ KEYWORDS

- ☆ **Organization:** Any entity with a defined organization form is called "Organization". An organization have "Classifications" according to its type and use. There can be more than one classification assigned to the organization depending upon their type and their use in the enterprise. Classification assigned can be 'Operating unit' or 'Legal entity' etc.
- ☆ **Responsibility:** It is concerned with categorizing the responsibilities under different heads. Set of books, Operating units, Inventory form the core part of the responsibility and profiles can be set according to these responsibilities.
- ☆ **Security rules:** In order to restrict the values for a specific field/s security rules are used. These rules determine the values that can be seen by the user from the database. Security rules are used to place users under different groups and allow only authorized users to gain access. For e.g., only account users can use the information about the accounting database in the company and no one else.
- ☆ **Service Oriented Architecture (SOA):** SOA is a business-centric IT architectural approach that supports integrating your business as linked, repeatable business tasks, or services. With the Smart SOA approach, you can find value at every stage of the SOA continuum, from departmental projects to enterprise-wide initiatives.

☆ **Solution Planning:** Identifying/optimizing appropriate business processes and technology. Setting relevant project, business and IT goals, and metrics planning for organisational change.

☆ **System Implementation:** Ensuring projects are goal-oriented, business-driven, sufficiently controlled and efficiently run. Tracking baseline project, business and IT goals and metrics. Ensuring change is implemented.

☆ TERMINOLOGY REVIEW

1. What do you mean by Implementation tools for the proper implementation of oracle application. Explain each of the tools.
2. What do you mean by the setup process which will be planned for installing the multi-tier organization?
3. Explain the terminology used for oracle format to case study.
4. What are the steps for formulation of multi-business enterprise unit? Explain briefly.
5. What do you mean by document definition for numbering in assigned sequences?
6. What do you mean by profile updating for operating units?
7. What do you mean by sequencing and assignment?
8. What do you mean by conversion to multi-organization?
9. What do you mean by seed replication?
10. Explain the company profile of BaaN in the ERP Market?
11. In which area is SAP relatively weak compared to BaaN? What do you mean by BaaN's ERP Tools?
12. Explain BaaN's ERP Modules.
13. What is J.D. Edward's company profile?
14. What are the difference's between J.D. Edward's Market and BaaN's Market?
15. What is J.D. Edward's Product Portfolio?
16. What are the reasons that prompted J.D. Edwards to open an office in India? Explain the company profile of SAP.

17. What is technology used by SAP and what is its product?

18. In which industrial sector is SAP present?

19. Today SAP is Global Market Leader. What are the reasons behind this? What are the nine steps to mastering SAP R/3?

20. Explain the company profile of RAMCO.

21. What are RAMCO's Products and Services?

22. What do you mean by RAMCO E-Applications?

23. Explain how QAD is useful in the Indian Context.

24. Describe the company profile of ORACLE.

25. Explain the facts about Peoples soft.

26. Explain about BOI.

27. SAP AG produced a complex, modular ERP program called R/3. The software could integrate a company's entire business by using a common database that linked all operations, allowing real-time data sharing and streamlined operations.

28. SAP R/3 is modular software offering modules for Sales and Distribution, Materials Management, Production Planning, Quality Management, and other areas.

29. An ERP system such as SAP R/3 sees a sale as a sequence of related functions, including taking orders, setting prices, checking product availability, checking the customer's credit line, arranging for delivery, billing the customer, and collecting payment. In SAP R/3 all these transactions, or documents, are electronically linked, so tracking an order's status (partial shipments, returns, partial payments, and so forth) is easily accomplished. Justify your answer with the help of an illustration.

30. SAP's System Landscape was introduced to show how changes to the ERP system during implementation (and beyond) are managed.

31. Who are the key ERP Software vendors in the world? How are they positioned in India?

32. What is the secret of SAP's success?

33. What are the special features of SAP R/3?

34. What are the special features of Oracle Applications?

35. What are the special features of BaaN?

36. What are the special features of Ramco Marshall?

37. Is there a specific place for IBM?
38. Who is the market leader in ERP?
39. Is there a segmentation of the ERP market?
40. Is there a rating agency that constantly rates ERP software?
41. Where do you get ERP software market information?
42. What R & D do ERP vendors attempt?
43. Is there a benchmarking tool to fine-tune ERP performance?
44. What do you mean by implementation tools with respect to Oracle application? Explain. Explain the terminology used for Oracle Format to case study?
45. What could be the shape of SAP R/3 system architecture?
46. What do you mean by SAP terminology & logical design?

☆ COMPETENCY REVIEW

1. Pragmatic Questions

   (a) Does your organization enjoy a dynamic change in the information system with the implementation of EIS software? Are you a mid-market company within the public sector or professional services sector?

   (b) Define the business value. Identify what benefits the organization needs to get out of an EIS/ERP, and focus on these benefits throughout the implementation to ensure that they are achieved.

   (c) Set up regular review measures. Establish metrics to measure how well the objectives of the EIS/ERP effort are being met.

   (d) Make sure that every vendor involved in the EIS project has "skin in the game" — every vendor should share in the risk of the venture; consider using the "fix time, fix price" type of contract to ensure the effort is completed on time and within budget.

   (e) Assign a high-level business manager to the project, adding credibility to the effort and forcing upper management to take ownership of the EIS project.

(f)   Engage the users throughout the process — make sure that they are aware of the progress of the implementation and upcoming changes.

(g)   Avoid customization as it is very costly both as a one-time expense and whenever there are upgrades to the vendor EIS software. However, there are times when customization is required because the software does not address some aspect of the EIS user requirements.

(h)   Make certain that the infrastructure can support the EIS/ERP, for example, the network should be built to support the web-access capabilities of EIS/ERPs.

(i)   How Outsourcing will target situations when the organization does not have a sufficient skill pool to support an EIS/ERP implementation.

(j)   Using a vendor that may not be around in a few years is risky.

(k)   One can perform pilot implementations. This helps minimize risks associated with large implementations.

(l)   Be prepared for turmoil during the transition phase. The transition period can produce a stressful environment for managers and employees.

(m) How to provide staff training and orientation. This training should not be the one-size-fits-all type; it must be customized for the particular environment. Trainers need to be familiar with the processes associated with the legacy system and understand how these processes map against the processes associated with the new EIS/ERP system.

(n)   Customizing your EIS/ERP software can maximize its benefits to you but, sometimes, at the cost of locking you into EIS software and vendor relationships that don't meet your long-term needs. So, how can you get a solution that can deliver superb value and is flexible enough to grow with you over time?

2.   Briefly comment on the following:

(a) Today SAP is a Global Market Leader. Significant shifts are taking place in how ERP vendors generate revenues. Echoing changes taking place throughout the software industry, the transition is toward recurring and variable revenue models — with maintenance charges driving industry growth.

(b) System forms for invoices, pick lists and packing slips don't match you company or customer needs.

(c) Data-entry screens don't correspond to your shipping methods, product categories, and currency codes.

(d) A technology partner who understands your industry, company, and local business requirements can be invaluable in helping you select and tailor an ERP solution to fit your specific needs.

(e) When evaluating your current software or a prospective solution, make sure it's easy to make minor modifications to match the way your employees work.

(f) Business applications also have changed to support the globalization of their organization with the addition of multi-site and multi-currency functionalities.

(g) As the economy recovers, demand for Enterprise Resource Planning (ERP) software will grow among mid-market manufacturers.

3. Multiple Choice Questions

1. BaaN is founded in:
   (i) 1970   (ii) 1978   (iii) 1979   (iv) 1980.

2. BaaN case study is related with:
   (i) Electronics manufacturing   (ii) Point manufacturing
   (iii) Automobile section   (iv) Pencil company

3. RAMCO case study relates with:
   (i) Cement industry   (ii) Electronic industry
   (iii) Textile industry   (iv) Paint industry

4. QAD was founded in
   (i) 1980   (ii) 1981   (iii) 1979   (iv) 1989

5. '3113' identifies
   (i) Low seed data   (ii) column seed data
   (iii) vertical data   (iv) horizontal data

6. OTA stands for
   (i) oracle training administrations
   (ii) oracle time administrations
   (iii) obstacle training administrative
   (iv) optimum times column factor

4. Fill in the Blanks
   (i) BaaN is founded by _____ in 1978 in the Netherlands.
   (ii) The main product of J.D. Edwards is _____.
   (iii) SAP is founded in _____.
   (iv) SAP R/3 solution is launched in _____.
   (v) The product of Ramco is _____.
   (vi) Ramco system software development practices ISO 9001 certified by_____.
   (vii) QAD Inc. is co-founded by _____ and _____.
   (viii) The Product of QAD is _____.
   (ix) ORACLE is founded by _____.
   (x) The first product of PeopleSoft is _____.
   (xi) BOI stands for _____.

Answers

(i)	Jan Baan	(ii)	One world Xc
(iii)	1972	(iv)	1992
(v)	Enterprise Application	(vi)	KPMG
(vii)	Pamela Meyer Lopker and Karl F. Lopker	(viii)	MFG/PRO
(ix)	Lawrence J. Ellison	(x)	HRMS
(xi)	Banker Orient India		

☆ SUGGESTED READING

Books

Jacobs, F. R. and Whybark, D. C. (2003). *Why ERP? A Primer on SAP Implementation*. New York: McGraw Hill.

O'Leary, D. E. (2000). *Enterprise Resource Planning Systems: Systems, Life Cycle, Electronic Commerce, and Risk*. Cambridge: Cambridge University Press.

Journal Articles

Cata, T, Faja, S. and Nah, F. F. H. (2001). Characteristics of ERP Software Maintenance: Multiple Case Study. *Journal of Software Maintenance and Evolution: Research and Practice*, 13(6), 399–414.

Davenport, T. H. (1998). Putting the Enterprise into Enterprise Systems. *Harvard Business Review*, 121–131.

White Papers

Cowley, S. (2004). Oracle faces daunting challenges integrating PeopoeSoft. *IDG news*.

Guglielmo, C. (2004). Oracle wins PeopleSoft's shareholders support for Bid. www.quote.bloomberg.com.

Hirt, S. G. and Swanson, B. E. (2001). Emergent maintenance of ERP: New roles and relationships. *Journal of Software Maintenance and Evolution: Research and Practice*, 13(6), 373–397.

James and Wolf (2000). A second wind for ERP. *The McKinsey Quarterly*, No. 2. *ERP Executive Summary, CIO Magazine*.

Keerthy, B. (2005). Oracle's Bid for PeopleSoft: PeopleSoft's Combat strategies. ICFAI business School Case Development Center. European Case Clearing House.

Mabert, V. A., Soni, A. and Venkataramanan, M. A. (2001). Enterprise Resource Planning: Common Myths vs. Evolving Reality. *Business Horizons*, 69–76.

Online Resources

Gartner Group (2000). The Next Evolution of ERP. Stamford, CT.

Koch, C. *et al.*, The ABCs of ERP. *CIO Magazine*. www.cio.com/forums/erp/edit/122299_erp.html

Songini, M. L. (2004). Oracle buyout gets mixed reviews from PeopleSoft customers. www.computerworld.com.

Stooker, R. (2000). SAP: A Hot Skill — The Current #1 Resource Planning Software Package. Inforing Press (online).

US Joint Financial Management Improvement Program. www.jfmip.gov/jfmip/default.asp

United States General Accounting Office (2000). Selected Agencies' Use of Commercial off-the-Shelf Software for Human Resources Functions (GAO/AIMD-00-270), Washington, DC.

APPENDIX A

CAREERS IN EIS

Quotation

The EIS management system model has been proposed to achieve better process integration and data integrity through the entire product development lifecycle in an enterprise.

Whether or not an EIS career is for you depends on what you want to accomplish in your life, your background, your skills and the environment in which you want to work. If you have communication skills, domain knowledge in key organizational functions (sales, manufacturing, materials, distribution, accounting, finance, HR etc.) or in areas such as project management or accounting, and software skills with one of the leading EIS/ERP softwares, you can have a promising career with attractive assignments that will compensate you very well. This assumes that you are willing to work hard and keep on top of technological developments. If you have knowledge in any of the input industry segments such as oil, finance, telecommunications, distribution, retailing, banking, medical care, etc, you will have exceptional opportunities.

Enterprise Information system solutions are software applications that deal with real-time information across the organization. EIS solutions include packaged software such as SAP, Oracle, PeopleSoft, Microsoft Dynamics and Siebel. These require joint efforts with solutions engineering professionals to develop the technical architecture. Systems need to be selected, sometimes customized, and tested. This Appendix presents how one can build a career in EIS, like:

- Job options with EIS/ERP are easily available as recruiters are very interested in such skills.
- Network linkage management can be an important aspect of your career in EIS/ERP.
- Specific application areas like SCM, CRM, BPR or E-commerce that require implementation.
- Job opportunities like:

  ➢ Planner/Analyst, Inventory specialist, Material planner, Transportation co-ordinator, Production Co-ordinator and others are available as EIS/ERP career specialties.

- Training support with certification and documentation are points to be considered in choosing a career in EIS/ERP.

CAREERS IN EIS/ERP — PREREQUISITES

A few years of knowledge and experience in software development or in functional areas such as Finance/Costing, Materials Management, Production Planning, Sales & Distribution, Development and implementation of any application Packages are useful. A Business Perspective is critical. EIS/ERP careers exist distinctly in two areas:

A. Implementation: This includes Financials (Financial Accounting & costing), Logistics (Sales & Distribution, Production and Materials), Human Resources and some industry-specific applications. One should have a strong functional background in any of the above areas to become a consultant.
B. Development. Programming experience is very helpful for a career in this area.

EIS/ERP CAREER ADVICE

Whether you're just starting out as an EIS/ERP Consultant or a fresh job-seeker, EIS/ERP recruiters can help with your EIS/ERP job search.

Fundamentally, networking with EIS/ERP recruiters, firms, and professionals gives you exposure and presents your EIS/ERP skills to companies that can advance your interests. Documenting and distributing your EIS/ERP resume to those who can employ you (or refer you to somebody who can) is important. Your objective is to gain as much exposure as possible in the EIS/ERP job market as rapidly as you can. Internet recruiting sites such as ERPCareer.com have made networking easier and much more well-organized than ever! The following information can help you promote your EIS/ERP skills and resume.

IDENTIFY AND LEVERAGE YOUR EIS/ERP PROFESSIONAL NETWORK

Who is incorporated in your EIS/ERP network? EIS/ERP recruiters, EIS/ERP co-workers, EIS/ERP suppliers, EIS/ERP vendors, EIS/ERP customers, contacts in industry associations, people you met at seminars, training sessions, trade shows, headhunters and recruiters you've worked with in the past. Get in touch with all of these people and let them recognize that you are available for a new EIS/ERP job. Call everybody you know and ask them if they've heard about any EIS/ERP positions that may match your experience. Don't be frightened to ask them if they will "continue to keep an ear out" for you, as they may need you to do the same for them in the future. Of course, you should post an EIS/ERP profile on any career-related site.

High-Quality Trainers

A perfect resume for EIS/ERP Consultants would be many years of domain knowledge (HR, Finance, Material etc) followed by widespread software training and implementation experience in real-world implementations. Technical knowledge by way of deep IT training helps but is not mandatory. Knowledge of business procedures gained from formal business school education, is helpful, but not obligatory. On the other hand business knowledge by the way of experience and consulting is a must.

EIS CONSULTING FROM THE VENDOR'S PERSPECTIVES

Accenture[1] helps large, diverse organizations aggressively manage and enhance their operational performance by overcoming their most complex integration challenges. As integration solutions enable organizations to derive greater value from their enterprises and speed return on technology investments. As approach to integration takes advantage of the full spectrum of integration technologies, including Web services. Within Enterprise Integration Consulting, you can help clients better access, manage and act upon the growing volume of data across multiple systems to achieve high performance. With nearly 500 active Enterprise Integration projects across all industries, Accenture employs more than 20,000 people trained in integrated systems design and development using the Microsoft .NET and J2EE platforms and nearly 6,000 with core Enterprise Integration skills. You will join a recognized leader in applying enterprise application integration (eAI) technologies and Web services standards and technologies to help businesses gain more value from their systems and processes.

About ERP.com.au[2]

ERP.com.au has been developed to provide a single, convenient, and effective way for Australian EIS/ERP Professionals and Employers to meet. You can give it all the fancy words you like but at the end of the day EIS/ERP.com.au is a meeting place for talented EIS/ERP professionals and the companies that hire them.

---

[1] Accenture is a company with multiple workforces. Each workforce contributes to its business in a different but complementary way. Accenture's business strategy depends on these different workforces blending together as an integrated whole, to help the company and its clients achieve higher levels of performance. Find out more about the nature of each workforce, the kind of work you could do, the roles and responsibilities, what training you can expect and how your career might develop. www.accenture.com

[2] ERP.com.au has been developed to provide a single, convenient, and effective way for Australian ERP professionals and employers to meet. You can give it all the fancy words you like but at the end of the day ERP.com.au is a meeting place for talented ERP professionals and the companies that hire them. www.erp.com.au

BENEFITS TO EMPLOYER AND JOB-SEEKERS

Some Benefits for Employers

- ◆ Informed: Know exactly what skills are available and when.
- ◆ Cost-efficient: A remarkably cost efficient way to recruit hard to find software development resources.
- ◆ Opportune: Have new resumes automatically emailed to you or RSS'd immediately to your desktop.
- ◆ Convenient: You choose the process. Search in your own way, in your own time.
- ◆ Facilitative: Helps you plan your recruitment processes own.
- ◆ Flexible: Post Job vacancies online and search the resume database anytime.

Some Benefits for Job Seekers

- ◆ Control: You are always in control of your personal details. No-one ever gets your details without your permission.
- ◆ Targeted: Your resume is being seen by exactly the right companies.
- ◆ Convenient: Why seek when you can be sought? Post your resume online and let the best jobs come to you!
- ◆ Specialized: Specialists require specialist career sites.
- ◆ Inclusive: Good jobs are not necessarily advertised. You need to look further than just at general job ads and newspapers.

WHAT EIS/ERP RECRUITERS AND HEAD HUNTERS SHOULD BE ACQUAINTED WITH?

Send an updated copy of your resume to ERP Recruiters with whom you've interacted with previously and let them know that you're in the market for a new EIS/ERP career. Keep in mind that the standard recruiter handles many search assignments at a time and more often than not does not "market" candidates. So, the more recruiters who see your resume, the better coverage you get.

The quickest and best way to get your EIS/ERP resume to recruiters is to:

◆ Post an EIS/ERP profile on ERP-related career website.
◆ Send recruiters your EIS/ERP portfolio.

This will save you invaluable time and speed up your EIS/ERP job search.

EIS CAREER JARGON

◆ Transportation arranger and Traffic forecaster: Evaluates, selects, and deals with transportation carriers for inbound goods. Manages relationships with carriers and internal customers to ensure timely delivery.
◆ Bargain hunter: Works with internal customers (marketing, production, operations, etc.) and external suppliers to efficiently and effectively manage the purchasing process for goods and services needed by the company. Responsible for identifying sources of supply, evaluating and selecting suppliers, negotiating contracts, and managing relationships with suppliers.
◆ Planner and Analyst of materials: Manages raw materials and/or components needed for manufacturing. Accountable for inbound inventory levels. Coordinates with purchasing, manufacturing and supply to ensure dependable, cost-efficient delivery of the raw materials to the production line. May be accountable for receiving, warehousing, scheduling, and inbound transportation.
◆ Production Coordinator, Scheduler, Operations Planner/ Analyst: Uses scheduling and forecasting techniques, statistical control tools and interpersonal skills. Accountable for coordinating day by day production schedules and forecasting potential production needs.
◆ Record consultant: Develops and implements plans to optimize inventory cost and customer service goals. Responsible for inventory quality

and accuracy, coordinates physical inventory process and cycle counts, monitors inventory flow through the system, and works on stock site and order picking strategies to optimize work stream, space utilization, and labor efficiency in distribution facilities.

♦ Schemer or forecaster: Uses diagnostic and quantitative methods to comprehend, envisage, and steamline chain processes. Responsible for assembling data, analyzing performance, identifying problems, and developing recommendations that support the management of a supply chain.

ABILITY & ASSESSMENT

It is necessary to assess your capabilities. As you can infer by now, people hope to get into an EIS/ERP career from different routes. Your particular approach will depend on the kinds of skills and experience you bring to the table. The new college graduate with a BTech (CS & IT), MBA IT, MCA and MTech will advertise him/herself differently from an IT professional with two or three years of excellent technical experience. Correspondingly, a financial manager with years of experience in business and consulting would present an entirely different scenario and approach accordingly.

BE CAREFUL IN SELECTING YOUR EMPLOYER

Once you have evaluated your skills & appraised your experience and career goals, you will be in a position to decide whether you want to enter the EIS/ERP market. Remember, sticking to your area of expertise, and building on it, gives consistency and depth to your resume. The best way to diminish the risk of unemployment is to search for opportunities with your present corporation (i.e. if you are employed and your corporation is implementing or has implemented a package). Countless companies are in the process of, or are about to start, an implementation. Your first assignment consequently, is to find out as much as you can about your company's EIS/ERP plans. That way you'll see if, and how, you can be included and find out the best way to take advantage of your existing skills. Most companies have some sort of methodology for implementation which defines the form the changeover will take. Your chances of getting hands-on implementation experience probably depend on the plan your company intends to follow.

E. Construct Your Personal "Tactical Entrance Diagram"

We have so far discussed various strategies for entering the EIS/ERP market. "Exhausting the internal possibilities" is how we describe these "first steps" to help you maximize your reach for the kind of' hands-on EIS/ERP work you're looking for.

F. Training

We have looked at some tactics you might use to enter the EIS/ERP field: assessing your core skills; displaying your track record; seeking creative ways to enter the field on the functional or technical side of the implementation cycle. We call this procedure "killing your internal possibilities" and some of you might respond by saying, "That is all extremely helpful and high-quality, but I don't believe I have any interior potentials. What now? Should I go for one of the training courses I see on the Web? Should I quit my job to train? Are the courses worth my time and money?" These are good questions and valid concerns. So, we will now talk about the pros and cons of training and certification, starting with some small working definitions, which we will use throughout this section.

G. Certification & Documentation

Certification come from finishing a set of training courses authorized by the software vendor, and is conditional upon passing an exam. Training typically involves formal courses, which are indistinguishable from those offered by the software vendor, or are similar in format and content, but do not require sitting for an exam. As a general rule, only consulting firms that are associated with the EIS/ERP vendor have access to these agendas and exams. E.g., a number of consulting firms insist that all their consultants be certified by a particular vendor. In some cases, the certification endorses existing skills and experience and the consultant does not need any formal training but simply takes the exam. However, if training is required, the consultant typically has access to the standardized training courses, which are designed specifically to cover the material required for certification. There is no question that certification has market value in that it carries more weight than training with no certification, but it doesn't assure you an entry into the EIS/ERP market. The reality is that those of you who have certification almost certainly have access to the EIS/ERP market anyway. A good number of people who have contacted us with questions about the requirements or advantages of training/certification are not consultants, but end users that characteristically don't have the alternative of certification, and are trying to acquire several options to enter EIS/ERP.

EIS/ERP SYSTEMS: THE CURRICULUM OUTLINE

1. **System Trends**

   This assesses the best in integrated systems for manufacturing organizations. What will an EIS/ERP system do for your organization? Few people in the U.S. had ever heard of SAP before 1992. PeopleSoft was a start-up human resource vendor in 1988. Now these two plus BaaN and Oracle are EIS/ERP systems "Top 4" vendors. These vendors rode on system trends to dominate the Fortune 1000 EIS/ERP system market. Now they have their sights set on the mid-size business. How are system trends used to identify EIS/ERP system vendors that can compete with the Top 4?

2. **Assessing Legacy Systems**

   How to complete the legacy (current) system assessment in one day? Understanding root causes of legacy system problems. How to save time and effort in defining your requirements by extracting them from legacy systems? Are any of our legacy systems worth saving?

3. **Identifying Improvement Opportunities**

   Benchmarking your firm against leading edge improvements enabled by EIS/ERP systems. How are others using EIS/ERP systems to manage the supply chain, implement plant scheduling, improve customer service, get real-time decision support information, achieve zero-close times, and route business transactions through an end-to-end workflow?

4. **Selecting EIS/ERP System Short List Criteria**

   How to define your EIS/ERP system short list criteria? Obtaining clear information on vendors and the latest EIS/ERP systems releases. How to organize information comparisons and identify your EIS/ERP system short list? Non-biased insights on the Top 4 vendors and their challengers. How to conduct a scripted system evaluation of EIS/ERP systems on your short list? Negotiating techniques to reduce EIS/ERP system cost.

5. **Aligning Client/Server Infrastructure**

   Why EIS/ERP systems are also client/server systems — some are second-tier, some are third-tier, some are nth-tier and all are true client/server? Why some EIS/ERP systems are objects and some are object-oriented. Client/server platforms — NT, UNIX, and AS/400. How to avoid the failure of poor response time due to inadequate client/server infrastructure? For mission critical applications — such as customer order processing or multi-site supply chain planning — acceptable response time is essential. Get the information and insight into the right alignment between the EIS/ERP systems and the client/server infrastructure.

6. **Selecting Implementation Services**

   EIS/ERP systems aren't the only thing selling like hot cakes — the demand for EIS/ERP system implementation services has also sky-rocketed. Sure, EIS/ERP system vendors offer implementation services, but so do Big 4 firms, system integrators, certified implementation services firms, value-added resellers, and independents. Understanding that contracting for implementation services is the biggest cost of implementation. How to reduce implementation costs by selecting the right implementation services.

7. **Planning Migration from Legacy Systems**

   How to assess the impact of the EIS/ERP system on your business: (a) business improvement projects, (b) EIS/ERP system implementation projects, (c) skill development projects, and (d) client/server infrastructure implementation projects? The pros and cons of big bang implementation versus phased implementation. Examples of migration plans for multi-division enterprises and single company enterprises.

8. **Organizing & Staffing Project Teams**

   The dilemma facing every enterprise starting an EIS/ERP system project — the best people to staff project teams are the ones that already have full-time jobs running the business. Successful techniques used by others to get the right people on the project teams. How to build a senior management coalition to manage selection and implementation? How to organize and staff the teams for a successful implementation?

9. **Making the Business Case**

   Valuing business improvements enabled by an EIS/ERP system. Order of magnitude estimates of an EIS/ERP system's license fee, implementation costs and total ownership costs. Improvements used by other businesses to justify an EIS/ERP system. Receive a proven checklist for determining the probability of a successful EIS/ERP system implementation.

QUESTION & ANSWER

1. What General Studies and elective courses should I take?

   When choosing General Studies and elective courses, think about the skills that recruiters are looking for and how the course will round out your education in your chosen area of study. For example, if you are interested in living and working in another country, focus on courses that relate to the language, history, culture, art, and politics of that country or region.

2. Does it help to get the Certificate in Quality Analysis?

   Yes, companies are very interested in quality and analytical skills.

3. What kinds of jobs (and salaries) are available for SCM Majors?

   SCM majors are prepared for entry-level positions in purchasing or logistics such as buyer, purchasing analyst, inventory control or traffic analyst with a career track to the vice president of procurement, operations, or logistics. Firms from around the country and in all sectors of the economy — public and private, manufacturing, service, health care, retail, etc. — recruit SCM graduates. Frequent recruiters include Motorola, Intel, Honeywell, Hewlett-Packard, Boeing, Tektronix, Applied Materials, Dillard's, and General Mills. Starting salaries range from $23,500–$58,500, with an average of about $39,500. Check with Career Services for more information.

4. I would like to know how an EIS/ERP related package would suit my career as a chartered accountant. Is it necessary to join an EIS/ERP related course to get EIS/ERP knowledge or would reading related journals & magazines suffice?

   You can never "know too much". If you meet clients in a manufacturing or retail environment, they certainly will have (a kind of) EIS/ERP software. Many will have stored most of the information that you rely on in this system. It is always helpful to know your away around in EIS/ERP.

5. What is the passing rate for the EIS/ERP certification exam?

   The EIS/ERP certification exam is considered to be a difficult exam. Despite its difficulty, the exam has a pass rate of over 83 percent. The certification organization works closely with those preparing for the EIS/ERP certification exam. Unlike many other professional certifications, the questions for the EIS/ERP certification exam come in directly from the specified study materials. Those that study and prepare carefully almost always pass. Those that concentrate on EIS/ERP certification preparation seminars and study ahead of time show even higher success rates.

6. I was pursuing another professional certification and I was informed that my test results were lost. I had to pay again to retake the exam. Will this happen in the case of EIS/ERP?

   While we cannot guarantee that some tests will never be lost we are proud to say that we have never lost a single exam or an individual's test results. All exams are permanently stored using quite a few different methods. In addition, we track the attendance of all examinations. If you took the exam and your test was lost, you would not have to pay again to retake the exam.

7. Will I be recognized for my accomplishment?

   Yes. You will be recognized by any organization that understands the value of the EIS/ERP certification. In addition the certified organization will make available opportunities for you to be recognized as a leader in the EIS/ERP field. Individuals may be listed on the respective EIS/ERP certification sites as a professional who has earned the EIS/ERP certification. In addition, the certified individual will receive a booklet with helpful ideas and techniques to spread the word about your new certification for maximum networking.

8. What types of people become EIS/ERP certified?

   A wide range of people choose to follow the EIS/ERP certification for a variety of different reasons. In short, almost anybody who works in or around the EIS/ERP industry may choose to become EIS/ERP certified. Some common types of people that choose to become EIS/ERP certified include:

   ➢ Authors and Journalists
   ➢ CEOs
   ➢ College Teachers
   ➢ Consultants
   ➢ End Users
   ➢ EIS/ERP Sales Personnel
   ➢ EIS/ERP Team Members
   ➢ EIS/ERP Trainers
   ➢ Functional Managers
   ➢ Help Desk Support Staff

➢ Implementers
➢ Programmers
➢ Project Managers
➢ Senior Management
➢ Students

10. How many exams are there and how long does it last?

The EIS/ERP certification in general consists of one exam lasting four hours. The exam is comprehensive in nature covering a variety of key strategic areas for the successful implementation and use of EIS/ERP systems.

11. If I do not pass the exam, do I have to wait to retake it again?

There is no waiting period for exam retakes. An individual may retake the exam at the next certification testing opportunity.

12. I have a lot of experience with EIS/ERP systems, could I pass without studying for the exam?

Actual experience provides a good foundation for building conceptual knowledge of EIS/ERP systems. Because of the enormous array of different EIS/ERP systems that exist on the market, tremendous differences in terminology can be found. The EIS/ERP certification programs create a common standard for all EIS/ERP systems in their characteristics and terminology. Professionals working with EIS/ERP systems, with one or a few, may find that the terminology used on the EIS/ERP certification exam to be significantly different from their own experience. For these reasons, it is recommended that the EIS/ERP professional review the study materials to prepare for the examination.

13. I am a student planning to graduate with a IT major. I don't have any hand-on experience with EIS/ERP systems. Can someone like me pass the certification exam?

While real experience with EIS/ERP systems is beneficial, it is by no means required. All of the EIS/ERP certification preparation materials have been written for the entry-level student. We have seen many individuals succeed without prior experience in EIS/ERP systems.

The most excellent results generally come from those that prepare carefully with the educational materials.

14. What are the educational materials available to help prepare for the EIS/ERP certification exam?

A variety of educational materials exist in preparation for the EIS/ERP examination. These materials include:

➢ EIS/ERP: A-Z Implementers Guide For Success (Textbook).
➢ EIS/ERP Sample Exam.
➢ EIS/ERP Preparation Workbook.
➢ EIS/ERP Journal.
➢ Different URL's.

All these materials are obtainable directly through the CIBRES organization or through other educational and retail outlets. Check www.cibres.com for pricing and availability. In addition, other sources such as websites, books and magazine articles are also important sources of reference and study. The EIS/ERP certification symbolizes the general body of knowledge as it relates to EIS/ERP systems.

SUMMARY

The tip to bear in mind is that unlike extra conventional IS/IT projects, EIS/ERP is a corporate-wide, mission-critical implementation motivated by business goals. As such, successful EIS/ERP implementation draws from both sides of the functional/technical divide. Look at your skills holistically — get a sense of the 'big picture'. Once you've established the gist of your career path, you can efficiently capitalize on your experience and skills, and find the right niche in the vast EIS/ERP market. One word of caution; if your skill set is not appropriate for an EIS/ERP career, then don't try to make it using the "brute force" method. Because, even though EIS/ERP is a flourishing area now, any sensible person will know that it is not likely to last forever. The EIS/ERP package you first identified may merge or be absorbed by a different corporation. So don't throw away all that hard-earned knowledge and experience. Be discriminating in your choice of package: decide clearly what fits well with your skills, experience and education. That way, you'll be better prepared to go along with the tide and flow of the EIS/ERP job market.

REFRESHER QUESTIONS

---

1. What is an EIS/ERP Recruiter?
2. What is certification and documentation? Explain.
3. What is a buyer and an inventory specialist?
4. What is a transportation co-ordinator and a traffic analyst.

APPENDIX B

FREQUENTLY ASKED QUESTIONS[1]

> **Quotation**
>
> It is better to know some of the questions than all of the answers.
>
> *James Thurber (1894–1961)*

Q-1. What is EIS/ERP? Is it a package of software? Is it a methodology of system improvement?

A. EIS/ERP is a software package intended to integrate all of an organization's computing. Of course, in reality, complete integration never happens. SAP based their software on their research of best practices, which becomes something like a methodology of system improvement.

Q-2. With which organizational function is EIS/ERP most connected?

A. EIS/ERP is usually sold in modules. Vendors would prefer to sell the entire system, but the cost is too high for most organizations, so they sell modules. The most popular module is accounting-related. For organizations with large EIS/ERP systems, management information systems often become part of accounting.

---

[1] Authors are deeply indebted to Khodadad Moradi for allowing us to adapt some Frequently Asked Questions from his research work which is available at the URl ait.unl.edu/dolson/Khodadad%20Moradi%20questions.doc

Q-3. What is the connection between EIS/ERP with MRP and MRP-II?

A. Production people often view EIS/ERP as an extension of MRP, probably because materials management modules are almost as popular as accounting and financial modules. But SAP began with accounting software (in the 1970s). Most EIS/ERP vendors offer materials management software that will do MRP, and even some planning aspects done by MRP-II.

Q-4. What is the connection between EIS/ERP with the other existing information system in an organization such as financial, commercial, manufactory, engineering, and etc.?

A. The intent of EIS/ERP is to consolidate all of these diverse systems into one integrated system, gaining efficiency through data sharing and by reducing information system staff.

Q-5. What is the connection between EIS/ERP with business process reengineering (BPR)?

A. SAP incorporated many best practices into their software, which were obtained by applying business process reengineering in general. It is advisable to use BPR in applying EIS/ERP to an organization to ensure that things are done in an integrated fashion. This is a massive undertaking, which is why EIS/ERP installations are so expensive and time-consuming.

Q-6. Is EIS/ERP software a totally complete and integrated package?

A. It is intended as a total integrated software package, but vendors will sell whatever modules their salespeople can sell to an organization.

Q-7. What is the difference between the existing information integrated systems in organizations and the existing market?

A. If an organization integrates all of their systems, they have a valid argument that they have an EIS/ERP. However, most people think of an EIS/ERP software vendor when they think of EIS/ERP.

Q-8. What cost does the EIS/ERP implementation impose on the organization? What will be the benefits in the short- and long-term for the organization?

A. EIS/ERP implementation is extremely expensive. Many organizations have been financially crippled by adopting an EIS/ERP in an incorrect fashion. Not every organization should adopt an EIS/ERP, and those that should need to be careful to design the best system for them. The first year of implementing an EIS/ERP is usually very painful in making everyone's job harder. The payback needs to be quick for financial survival, but this can be a problem. However, vendors recognize the problem and have made efforts to make installation less painful.

Q-9. What units and processes in an organization can be covered by EIS/ERP?

A. In principle, just about every aspect of organizational computing could be covered (at least those involving financial records in any way). Universities use them to include student records (not only payment, but classes and grades). As stated above, it may not be best for every organization to apply EIS/ERP to every aspect of what they use information systems for.

Q-10. What effect does EIS/ERP have on the work force?

A. EIS/ERP has a major impact on how people do their work, if it involves any aspect of information systems. The way EIS/ERP systems save money is through more efficient operations, which usually translates to reduced information system staff. (Have computers do more work, humans less.)

Q-11. What impact does EIS/ERP have on employment (managers, staff, labor)?

A. EIS/ERP can also reduce middle management staff. Mostly it impacts information system staff. It can affect everyone in the organization that enters data or queries the system for data. Also, BPR can reduce the number of people needed for some tasks, which could include manual workers.

Q-12. For which organizations is EIS/ERP logically suitable? With what sizes, services and products?

A. EIS/ERP vendors try to modify their software for just about everyone (I imagine even religious organizations). In the 1990s, only large manufacturers were clients, and prices for software started at about $5 million. Since 2000, this market has been saturated, and vendors have tried to upgrade software to sell to old clients, develop new software to sell to smaller businesses (less expensive), and moved to rapidly developing areas of the world such as India and China in efforts to retain their sales revenue. Many smaller vendors have appeared that make it possible to serve small business better as well (including Microsoft).

Q-13. Why do organizations adopt EIS/ERP?

A. Many studies have been done on this. Mostly they claim they want more efficient systems, to be more competitive. Cost reduction is also cited as a reason systems were adopted (this did not necessarily happen). Sometimes EIS/ERP is adopted to develop a competitive advantage, but organizations need to be careful that the EIS/ERP doesn't mess up the things the organization did to be profitable in the first place, because EIS/ERP can be very bureaucratic and rigid.

Q-14. What conditions are needed in the organization for effective EIS/ERP implementation? Is the subject of organization readiness meaningful in EIS/ERP?

A. Again, there is a great deal of research out there on this topic. Practically, you need to hire consultants to help, and get vendor help to install the system, and to train a core group of users who are then used to train the rest of the organization in using the system. You cannot expect to build a good EIS/ERP yourself — the main idea is to replace your existing information system staff with a system that runs automatically. There is a massive need for training organizational staff to use the system, which can also be quite expensive.

Q-15. What should be done before purchasing EIS/ERP software?

A. A good business case and analysis of whether EIS/ERP (and what type) is appropriate for a particular organization needs to be done. There is not much convincing research on this important aspect, because it involves a high degree of proprietarial information. An alternative is to rent an EIS/ERP from an application service provider (ASP), but that involves risk of the ASP failing.

Q-16. What are the stages in EIS/ERP implementation?

A. Like any IT project, there is the business case (whether to adopt EIS/ERP, what form, what vendor), system design in the sense of selecting the modules and specific features (including use of BPR), system installation, testing, and training (most organizations underestimate the effort required and the impact). Then there is maintenance, in the form of upgrades provided by the vendor, and fixes to problems that are encountered.

Q-17. Are there any differences between implementation of EIS/ERP and other information systems? Is there any special method for EIS/ERP implementation?

A. As noted in question 16, there are differences, as EIS/ERP is a massive intrusive system. Each vendor (and many consultants) have developed expertise in installing EIS/ERP software (which they charge a great deal for).

Q-18. What companies are EIS/ERP suppliers around the world? What are the characteristics of these suppliers and their products?

A. SAP is the largest, with Oracle also very large (Oracle swallowed up PeopleSoft and J.D. Edwards). Someone bought BAAN, which is still on the market. Microsoft has Microsoft Dynamics, marketing software they acquired from maybe 20 small EIS/ERP vendors. There are many smaller and mid-sized vendors, many specializing in specific countries (especially Taiwan, or China). SAP and Oracle specialize in extremely expensive systems, but are seeking to get into smaller markets too.

There are also application service providers (mentioned above) that purchase an EIS/ERP software and operate it, selling their service to clients (usually smaller organizations, but also many large ones that get tired of spending too much on SAP or Oracle).

Q-19. Can any company pretend to having an EIS/ERP package?

A. I think this is probably true. And in fact both using organizations may claim that their existing system integrates their computing when it may not, and small software vendors may overstate the capabilities of their software. Such is marketing.

Q-20. What are the roles of consultants in EIS/ERP implementation?

A. As stated above, in practice, large organizations need consultant help to select and implement an EIS/ERP system, because consultants have developed expertise that the purchasing organization cannot hope to have. Whether consultants earn their excessive rates is a good question.

Q-21. Can any organization develop their own EIS/ERP?

A. Yes they could, but it would be impractical — you have to hire and develop very expensive IT staff to reinvent the wheel. In the 1990s, this was often done, but in those days large organizations had massive IT staff. One of the benefits of EIS/ERP is to replace those IT staff with software.

Q-22. Are there any standard EIS/ERP? And are various EIS/ERP suppliers different from each other?

A. EIS/ERP vendor software's are all proprietary and thus different.

Q-23. Can organizations purchase EIS/ERP according to their specific needs?

A. Customization of vendor software is often done, and is the subject of a great deal of research. The value of customization is to retain specific operational characteristics developed by the organization to make themselves competitive. If everyone used SAP, then they would have no competitive advantage. But there aren't that many such core competencies based on software. Customizing EIS/ERP software is very expensive, and makes implementation very difficult and more time-consuming. Also, EIS/ERP vendors outdate their software through upgrades (to "provide better service") and if the software had been customized, all of that customization would probably have to be done over. The trend is to less customization.

Q-24. What is ERP-II?

A. As far as I am concerned, this is a marketing buzzword. Generally, they refer to the new generation of EIS/ERP software emphasizing user Web portals (including SAP's mySAP).

Q-25. What is the connection between EIS/ERP and subjects such as supply chain management (SCM), customer relationship management (CRM) or commercial and or e-commerce?

A. SCM, CRM and other add-ons used to be provided by external software firms, whose products were linked to EIS/ERP core systems through middleware. Since this decade EIS/ERP vendors have added new modules with SCM, CRM, and other functionality (Oracle may have started this by purchasing Siebel Systems, who had the leading CRM software product). This is part of the current evolution of the EIS/ERP market.

Q-26. Which organization or sites have useful topics about EIS/ERP?

A. I don't really know. Each vendor has their own site, aimed at marketing to paying customers. I don't consider them reliable sources.

INDEX